An Environmental History of India

India, Pakistan, and Bangladesh contain one-fifth of humanity, are home to many biodiversity hot spots, and are among the nations most subject to climatic stresses. By surveying their environmental history, we can gain major insights into the causes and implications of the Indian subcontinent's current conditions. This accessible new survey begins roughly 100 million years ago, when continental drift moved India from the South Pole and across the Indian Ocean, forming the Himalayan Mountains and creating monsoons. Coverage continues into the twenty-first century, taking readers beyond independence from colonial rule. The new nations of India, Pakistan, and Bangladesh have produced rising populations and have stretched natural resources, even as they have become increasingly engaged with climate change. To understand the region's current and future pressing issues, Michael H. Fisher argues that we must engage with the long and complex history of interactions among its people, land, climate, flora, and fauna.

Michael H. Fisher is Danforth Professor of History, Emeritus, at Oberlin College in Ohio. He is the author of numerous books, including *Migration: A World History* (2013) and *A Short History of the Mughal Empire* (2015).

New Approaches to Asian History

This dynamic new series publishes books on the milestones in Asian history, those that have come to define particular periods or to mark turning points in the political, cultural, and social evolution of the region. The books in this series are intended as introductions for students to be used in the classroom. They are written by scholars whose credentials are well established in their particular fields and who have, in many cases, taught the subject across a number of years.

Books in the series

An Environmental History of India

From Earliest Times to the Twenty-First Century

Michael H. Fisher

Oberlin College

CAMBRIDGE
UNIVERSITY PRESS

CAMBRIDGE
UNIVERSITY PRESS

University Printing House, Cambridge CB2 8BS, United Kingdom

One Liberty Plaza, 20th Floor, New York, NY 10006, USA

477 Williamstown Road, Port Melbourne, VIC 3207, Australia

314–321, 3rd Floor, Plot 3, Splendor Forum, Jasola District Centre, New Delhi – 110025, India

79 Anson Road, #06–04/06, Singapore 079906

Cambridge University Press is part of the University of Cambridge.

It furthers the University's mission by disseminating knowledge in the pursuit of education, learning, and research at the highest international levels of excellence.

www.cambridge.org
Information on this title: www.cambridge.org/9781107111622
DOI: 10.1017/9781316276044

First published 2018

Printed in the United Kingdom by TJ International Ltd. Padstow, Cornwall

A catalogue record for this publication is available from the British Library.

Library of Congress Cataloging-in-Publication Data
Names: Fisher, Michael Herbert, 1950– author.
Title: An environmental history of India : from earliest times to the twenty-first century / Michael H. Fisher.
Description: Cambridge, United Kingdom ; New York, NY : Cambridge University Press, 2018. | Series: New approaches to Asian history ; 18 | Includes bibliographical references and index.
Identifiers: LCCN 2018021693| ISBN 9781107111622 (Hardback) | ISBN 9781107529106 (Paperback)
Subjects: LCSH: India – Environmental conditions. | Human ecology – India – History. | Nature – Effect of human beings on – India – History.
Classification: LCC GE160.I4 F59 2018 | DDC 304.20954–dc23
LC record available at https://lccn.loc.gov/2018021693

ISBN 978-1-107-11162-2 Hardback
ISBN 978-1-107-52910-6 Paperback

Contents

Figures

Maps

Preface and Acknowledgments

The subcontinent of India has historically played a vital role in the world and will increasingly do so in the future. Its population of 1.6 billion people, one-fifth of humanity, totals more than Africa or than Europe and North America combined. It contains major fauna and flora biodiversity "hot spots," but also regions among the world's most polluted and vulnerable to climate change. We gain major insights about the causes and implications of the Indian subcontinent's current conditions by surveying its extended environmental history, especially the complex interactions among its people, other living beings, and the material world.

Environmental history cannot be studied in isolation, encompassing as it does history of the earth and everything on it. Thus, thoughtful choices must be made about the limits of any study. This book defines its focus as the Indian subcontinent (i.e. South Asia currently covered by the relatively young nations of India, Pakistan, and Bangladesh) – already a vast topic. This choice necessarily leaves out adjacent Afghanistan, Bhutan, Burma/Myanmar, Nepal, and Sri Lanka, and beyond them China, Iran, Tibet, and the rest of Eurasia – although arguments could be made for including any or all these, and they are each worthy of their own books. Simultaneously, this book considers the Indian subcontinent's environmental history within larger arenas as appropriate, including at the global and solar system scales.

Further, this book selects a long chronological scope (but does not go as far back as cosmic creation or even the origin of our earth). We begin when the core of the Indian subcontinent was at the South Pole, when monsoons and the Himalayan Mountains did not yet exist, and when *Homo sapiens* had not yet evolved. Tracing illustrative environmental changes, including the rise of major world religions, kingdoms and empires, and major ecological shifts, the book concludes in the second decade of the twenty-first century. This subcontinental scope and extended timescale make visible long-term patterns of change and continuity that present-centered or nationally limited accounts cannot.

Intended for general readers, this book builds on the growing body of sophisticated and insightful works of scholarship about key aspects of India's environmental history. Specialists will recognize how much their research has contributed to key arguments and evidence in this book. For the sake of clarity, however, references to these are largely concentrated in the Bibliographical Essay.

This book arose from decades of teaching "Environmental Histories of South Asia" with undergraduates at Oberlin College. Generations of students and distinguished guest faculty, including Ramachandra Guha, taught me how vital the study of South Asia's environmental history is for all our lives. Over the years, I have also learned much from my interactions with pathbreaking scholars in this field, including Paul Greenough, Sumit Guha, Mahesh Rangarajan, K. Sivaramakrishnan, John Richards, Thomas Trautmann, and Richard Tucker. I also thank Vinita Damodaran. I am grateful to Dawn Wade for her excellent copyediting and to Sunantha Ramamoorthy for her splendid project management. My Cambridge University Press editor, Lucy Rhymer, encouraged and guided me from the inception of this project through to publication.

1 Introduction

The relatively young but rapidly expanding field of formal environmental history informs us ever more about vital patterns of interactions among humans, other living beings, and the material world. Climate change, species extinction, unequally distributed and overstrained essential resources (including clean air, energy, food, land, and water), and other of today's pressing issues can only be understood and mitigated by understanding the many centuries of dynamic changes that caused them. The Indian subcontinent[1] has a distinctively complex environmental history that makes it particularly vulnerable to current environmental stresses.

This book offers an introductory survey of the constantly changing interactions that define India's environmental history, one especially rich in primary sources and secondary scholarship. Starting with the geological and climatic origins of the subcontinent itself and ending at the present, this book's vast chronological scale means it must be thoughtfully selective. Further, each of India's many diverse regions has its own distinctive environmental history, so this study's massive geographic scope means its examples must be illustrative. Yet, these broad historical patterns collectively define a distinctive part of the world. Throughout this long history, we particularly focus on how various cultures (including religions) and states altered, perceived, and adapted to the nonhuman world and tried to control it through their available technologies and ideologies.

Environmental history raises questions for us all to consider. For instance, many people today might identify groundwater in an aquifer as "natural." But what about that same water, unchanged chemically, pumped out and commercially packaged in plastic bottles with a printed label asserting it is "natural"? After being consumed and voided as liquid waste into a river, for instance the Ganges? Many in India today identify

---

[1] As the context indicates, this book uses "India" for the South Asian subcontinent until 1947 and, post-1947, "India" for the Republic of India alone.

the Ganges from a Hindu religious perspective as eternally pure, while many "natural scientists" (including devout Hindu ones) using a chemical and biological perspective would label it as unnaturally polluted. Nor are rivers "naturally" stable, for example, they meander over time, frequently shifting their channels and beds even without (or despite) human intervention. Such different perspectives hold significant implications for implementation of government programs (e.g. the Indian government's massive, ongoing Ganges Action Plan to clean up that river). Thus, with reservations, this book uses the term "natural" in contrast to "anthropogenic" (meaning human formed or transformed) and shows how diverse people at different times applied their distinctive cultural values to the living and nonliving environment.

Other examples of conflicting perspectives arise, for instance, from recent big dams and reservoir projects (like the controversial Sardar Sarovar Dam on India's Narmada River and the Diamer-Bhasha and Dasu Dams on Pakistan's Indus). Their supporters present these projects as triumphs of human engineering, harnessing nature to channel vital irrigation water to arid lands, prevent devastating floods, and produce pollution-free hydroelectric power essential for national development and poverty reduction. Simultaneously, critics condemn these same dam projects as causing the unjust displacement of local human populations, submergence of rare flora and fauna habitats, drowning of sacred sites, distortion of siltation and fish migration patterns, land degradation from salinization and waterlogging with waterborne disease proliferation, and, overall, long-term irreversible ecological damage.

Indeed, humans have always made efforts to value, understand, and interact with the environment. Over millennia, competing communities and states have developed technologies and bodies of knowledge ("sciences") for transforming "useful" or "dangerous" animals, plants, and other parts of the world around them. Each society conceives of and values specific species and geographical features in its own ways. Over time, these models for India's environment have often been articulated through religions and enforced by rulers (two of this book's continuing themes).

People in India have long devoted much thought to the environment around them, both what we might consider the sacred and also the material worlds. Indeed, people recorded their observations of India's environment in its earliest surviving sacred texts: the Sanskrit-language Vedas (Chapter 3). Later Indian authors, often patronized by rulers or religious leaders or communities, studied and described selected aspects of the environment (preserved in Sanskrit Shastras and popular-language Hindu, Jain, Buddhist, and Dravidian texts; see Chapter 4). New immigrants and cultures (including Islam and Christianity) added to people's perspectives and knowledge about India's environment, and new genres of writing about it often produced thoughtful and detailed descriptions and analyses of the climate, specific species, and human interactions with these (Chapters 5–7). During the British colonial period, European and Indian officials (often using European-style scientific training) began to compile ever more extensive records and to formulate policies of regulation about what they considered key aspects of India's material environment, including weather and disease patterns, reductions in valued hardwood species, and pollution of air and water supplies (Chapters 7–8). The level of recordkeeping and regulations about the environment increased even further in the independent nations of India, Pakistan, and Bangladesh (Chapters 9–12). But the formal discipline(s) of environmental history largely emerged during the late twentieth century as various scholars created and advanced models and methodologies.

Humanities- or social science–oriented environmental historians use sources, methodologies, and approaches featured in their specific discipline. Some individuals, approaches, or schools of thought tend to concentrate on cultural or intellectual issues, while others concentrate on material, technological, or economic ones; still others focus on political policies, laws, or judicial interpretations of these. Often scholars specialize in analytic methods, examining the source material of a particular type about a specific topic (e.g. forests, water, cities, railways, agriculture, or one animal species), in a particular language, and from a particular region and period. Historians of religion and literary scholars, for instance, often use specific bodies of written or oral sources that reveal how those communities valued the living and nonliving world around them. Some commentators argue that today's movements or public policies that incorporate reverence for sacred rivers or sacred groves, or understand their own religion as inherently environmentalist, will prove more effective than mere secular ones. Sociologists often work on contemporary resource allocation at the level of social classes or cities, while anthropologists focus at the village or family level (e.g. how women of particular communities engage with resource collection). Political scientists tend to focus on the recent formation and application of state policies about the environment through contentious interaction among various competing interests either within society or internationally (e.g. where human or national development seems to clash with conservation of endangered wild animals and habitats or forest-dwelling communities). Many environmental historians studying the postindependence period have accepted national boundaries, considering only India, Pakistan (often omitting East Pakistan), or Bangladesh (often omitting its period as East Pakistan). Nonetheless, many environmental forces and ecosystems cross those political borders, even though these new nations have significant similarities and differences in their environmental histories.

A heuristic model to describe patterns in environmental history about the Indian subcontinent is through three "waves."[2] Like ocean waves, there is much overlap and recycling of material, but each has its own energy and alignment. The first wave of formal environmental historians (broadly defined, starting in the 1970s) noticed and celebrated local movements that resisted exploitation of natural resources by government-backed commercial interests. For instance, a range of commentators have lauded the Chipko ("tree-hugger") movement in the Republic of India's western Himalayan foothills (see Chapter 10). However, these writers have attributed the prime motivation for Chipko using a range of analytic ideologies, including (among others) Marxism, feminism, or Gandhianism (e.g. Ramachandra Guha 1995; Shiva and Bandyopadhyay 1986; Weber 1989). Often such studies of contemporary popular environmental movements seek to inspire and mobilize urban elites into political and conservation engagement.

A second wave developed as scholars (within South Asia and internationally, using an array of methodologies and emphases) added historical depth to the study of the subcontinent's environment and diverse people's knowledge and interactions with it. Some scholars analyzed the historical development of ecological awareness, scientific and technological means of assessing and controlling natural resources and their degradation, and governmental policy formation (e.g. Gadgil and Guha 1992, 1995; Ramachandra Guha 2000b; Sumit Guha 1999). Much of this kind of environmental history writing concentrates on the British Raj period (1858–1947) since the volume of written records and the level of exploitation of India's resources by the government and for-profit companies both dramatically increased (e.g. Grove 1995; Richards et al. 1985; Saravanan 2016; Tucker 2012). Some writers have contrasted this colonial period with a precolonial era of alleged balance between humans and nature, when even Indian rulers (like Buddhist Emperor Ashoka, third century BCE; Chapter 4) famously revered and protected fauna and flora. Some historians writing about earlier periods have also identified the same pattern of local resistance against the state and other outside exploiters (like the Hindu devotional Bishnoi community who have historically defended trees with their lives; Chapter 7) as in today's community-based environmental movements. However, critics such as Greenough have

---

[2] Agrawal and Sivaramakrishnan (2000:8–12) write of three "generations," but the discipline is so young that many of the first "generation" are still active.

characterized this image of an earlier golden age as using the "Standard Ecological Narrative" or the "declensionist" model of constant ecological decline due to outsiders or the capitalist world system that exhausted natural resources (Greenough 2001). Further, while providing deeper historical contexts, this approach (and policies based on its assumptions, like Joint Resource Management, Chapter 10) has been critiqued for simplifying complexities into binary oppositions (e.g. animal versus human, colonial versus pre- or postcolonial, colonizer versus colonized, culture versus nature, female versus male, indigenous versus state-imposed, traditional versus modern).

Third-wave environmental historians challenge and deconstruct all such categories, often analyzing the discourse of powerful people who created them to control non-elites culturally. Some scholars reveal internal divisions, for instance power inequalities based on gender, class, or caste within communities of "villagers" or "tribals," or else ideological conflicts among "colonizers" or other elites (e.g. Agrawal 2005; Arnold 2016; Gilmartin 2015; Sivaramakrishnan 1999). Approaches considering comprehensive ecological webs or interspecies relations question human–animal binaries, for instance, showing how forest-dwellers incorporate special fauna or flora as ancestors or members of their communities (e.g. Govindrajan 2018). Yet other scholars show how people move among social and economic categories, like settled farmers moving into forests to escape famines or state-control and taxation, or forest-dwellers migrating to cities (permanently or just during one life-stage); activists argue that, to move forward environmentally, cross-cutting alliances and appreciation of multiple and shifting identities must be formed (e.g. Baviskar 1995). Such dynamic complexity, however, should not deter informed policy-formation or commitment to action concerning urgent environmental issues.

Simultaneously, "hard" or "natural" science–oriented historians have used different academic disciplines to study the origins and development of the physical world and its biota, either prior or subsequent to effects by *Homo sapiens*. For instance, geologists study earth processes in various eras, while biologists analyze how particular species of humans, fauna, and flora have spread, migrated, adapted, declined, or even become extinct. Some environmental scientists analyze the effects of chemical or biological pollution on the earth, atmosphere, water, or living things. Others concentrate on creating policies or projects to protect endangered species from extinction, especially by preserving (or recreating) their natural habitats. For scientists, there are "natural laws" about how the chemicals that comprise water, air, land, biota, and combustion, for instance, always act. Some historians, however, have shown how the civil engineers and scientists have acted as the products of their time, class, culture, and gender rather than as practitioners and discoverers of universal principles or truths. This book incorporates the fruits of diverse methodologies and disciplines to provide an overview of the subcontinent's environmental history, from the earliest times into the twenty-first century.

The Shape of This Book

This volume is organized chronologically, with each successive chapter addressing a more concentrated period in India's environmental history. The chapters highlight broad patterns, particularly featuring religions and governments since they have the coercive ideological power and larger-scale organizational authority to affect most extensively the relationships among various people and diverse parts of the material world. However, states were not hegemonic and were often multilayered, with much internal diversity. To be effective, public policy must reflect the consensus of people with power and those without; to be equitable, it should reflect the values and needs of the people most affected.

Readers wishing to delve deeper into the issues in each chapter should consult the Bibliographical Essay. Additionally, the List of References indicates the most important primary and secondary source material available. The illustrative maps and graphics are necessarily monochromatic, two-dimensional, and static, but the actual environment is polychromatic, three-dimensional, multileveled, and dynamic (on various timescales).

The second chapter outlines the context and early history of India's physical environment from continental drift (roughly 100 million years ago) to the arrival of the earliest people (defined as *Homo sapiens*) sometime between 75,000 and 35,000 years ago. Over these many centuries, the distinctive geology, topography, and climate of India all gradually developed from the terrestrial, atmospheric, and solar forces acting on them. Indeed, the earth is not a closed ecosystem, since it is affected by solar radiation, the sun's and moon's gravities, and the impact of asteroids, among other cosmic forces. Over time, species of plants and animals immigrated into the Indian subcontinent and adapted, as did bands of humans. Keeping in mind that one must avoid suggesting anachronistic biological continuities, this chapter also considers the culture and lives of forest-dwelling communities until the present.

Chapter 3 concentrates the two most prominent early cultures and societies in India for which there is surviving evidence. One centered on settled agriculturalists and built cities along the Indus River (2700–1900 BCE). The other, originally nomadic herders who immigrated (starting c. 1700 BCE), mixed with the other cultures already present, and settled mainly as agriculturalists (from c. 600 BCE). As the environment shifted, each of these groups interacted with each other and the flora, fauna, atmosphere, land, and waters around them in distinctive ways.

During this process and subsequently, each politically separate region developed its own distinct natural and sociocultural ecology, which has largely persisted until today (Chapter 4). Local, regional, and forest-based cultures and communities continued to develop. Further, by about the third century BCE, several related but distinct religions had emerged, including Jainism, Buddhism, and Hinduism; each developed a model of and for the universe and the human and natural environments around them. Simultaneously, communities, cultures, and states emerged and interacted in North India, the Deccan, and the peninsular south, using developing technologies that enabled a series of states and even fragile transregional empires. Most prominently, the Mauryan Empire (c. 320–187 BCE) drew upon the especially extensive natural resources of its home region and the mobilizing principles of Jainism and then Buddhism to expand its resource control over much of India. However, this first Indian empire's technology of rule could not reach deep enough into conquered regions or Hindu society to resist regional reassertions.

India never existed in isolation. Increasingly from the eighth century CE, overland and overseas immigrants mixed with local societies and cultures (Chapter 5). These Christians, Jews, and Muslims brought their own attitudes toward the nonhuman world and their own technologies for controlling it. Yet, as these immigrants settled, they adopted and adapted many Indian social and environmental practices. Some Central Asian Muslims established sultanates, the most prominent based in Delhi, which tried to extend their power over the subcontinent, its people, and its other resources. Meanwhile, other regional states, most prominently Vijayanagara in the Deccan, built their own economic and political systems.

The Mughal Empire (1526–1858) proved to be the largest and most powerful state to that point in Indian history (Chapter 6). Particularly under the innovative and dynamic Emperor Akbar (r. 1556–1605), the imperial administration developed unprecedented means of measuring, assessing, and using India's resources. Following Akbar, three successive emperors elaborated on his foundation, not always effectively. Portuguese armed merchants had already reached India in 1498, and they began to link it with the burgeoning Eurocentric world system, including by importing plant and animal species from the Americas.

Over the eighteenth century, as the Mughal imperial system fragmented, diverse competing regional rulers sought control over India's resources (Chapter 7). These rulers used various models for their relationships with human and natural resources under their power. Ultimately most successful of these rivals was the English East India Company (established 1600), which gradually intensified globalization through more rapid and extensive movement of people, flora, fauna, minerals, and technologies to try to master the Indian environment. Especially from the late eighteenth century onward, some Indian and European scientists began systematically recording and correlating detailed evidence about rainfall, temperature, deforestation, and diseases, and then used a variety of approaches, methodologies, and sources to advance diverse arguments into what would later be called environmental studies.

More than any previous state to that point, the British Raj (1858–1947) imposed its authority over all of India, using sciences and ideas that exploited, divided, but also unified the subcontinent (Chapter 8). Key markers of colonialism include rapid, state-sponsored expansion of land under cultivation, water control, timber harvesting with consequent deforestation, and extermination of particular species of wildlife (deemed either vermin or trophy game). By building railways and canals, and through "scientific forestry," the British Raj altered diverse aspects of the environment to unprecedented extents. Many contemporary supporters of the British Raj lauded it for harnessing or conquering nature and advancing India into modernity. Concurrently, however, a variety of South Asians developed alternative political, social, and environmental models, the most prominent of these being Mahatma Gandhi.

Chapters 9–11 address the subcontinent's environmental history over the past seventy years, concentrating especially on the relationships between the newly independent states of India, Pakistan, and (from 1971) Bangladesh and the material world they governed. From relatively impoverished British colonies, these newly independent nations have used their human and natural resources to make themselves major participants in the world economy, with India especially as a rising global economic powerhouse. Most environmental histories of Pakistan largely delete not only regions that became part of the Republic of India but also its own eastern wing, for instance, with statistics only counting Western Pakistan as if it were the whole country. Environmental histories of Bangladesh usually pass quickly over the "Pakistan period" and begin with their Liberation War. Most environmental historians of India stop considering those regions that became Pakistan. However, by presenting these three national environmental histories in parallel, comparisons and contrasts (and the reasons for each) become evident.

The late twentieth and early twenty-first centuries saw vastly increasing human impacts on the land, water, and air, which many scholars identify as causing the start of the Anthropocene. The governments of India, Pakistan, and Bangladesh have each attempted to establish laws, regulations, and policies to control their citizens' use of national resources (young Bangladesh, for instance, already has more than 200 laws and bylaws that attempt to regulate aspects of the environment). These governments, plus corporations and individuals, have deeply redirected the subcontinent's surface-water and groundwater flows through massive and small dams, extensive perennial canals, and vast numbers of power-driven tube-wells. They seek to generate hydropower, supply major industries, provide people's drinking water and waste disposal, and support agriculture's new high-yielding crops. In addition to extensively expanded irrigation, much farming has been transformed by mechanization and hybrid (and, more recently, genetically modified) crops, enabled by access to financial credits and extensive use of subsidized water, chemical fertilizers, and pesticides. Today, anthropogenic floods, droughts, and salinization cause increasing economic and environmental costs, while relatively little freshwater remains unused and unpolluted, so water scarcity is getting worse. Rising air contamination, continuing deforestation, and accelerating species extinctions remain problems across South Asia. Simultaneously, popular movements, civil-society organizations, and central and provincial legislatures, administrations, and judiciaries in India, Pakistan, and Bangladesh have made extensive efforts to conserve natural resources and yet also use them for much-needed poverty alleviation and economic development.

The three governments have assiduously participated in the growing numbers of international treaties, conventions, and protocols relating to the environment. Rich nations, international NGOs, and other organizations (like the United Nations) have given advice and financial aid and exerted diplomatic pressure to shape the policies and programs of these three governments. Yet, implementation of these international, national, and provincial laws and policies remains difficult. Violent and nonviolent social and economic tensions are interconnected and arise from unequal access to ecosystem resources and participation in democratic processes in all three nations (although to different levels at different times). As the global, national, regional, and local range of environmental options expand in some key ways and contract in others, South Asia will remain a vital arena. An emerging twenty-first-century goal for many (but not all) governments and organizations is sustainable and equitable human development that will conserve the natural world as much as possible.

The conclusion (Chapter 12) briefly considers three current environmental issues for the nations of South Asia, individually and collectively. To focus on the distinctive and the similar conditions within India, Pakistan, and Bangladesh, this chapter first looks at urban conditions and challenges. Next, the ship-breaking or ship-recycling industry in each of these nations provides an example of their competing roles within the global environmental system. To encapsulate the distinctive international approach of each government and nation, this chapter compares and contrasts their respective promised Nationally Determined Contributions to the mitigation of global climate change and its effects within the United Nations Framework Convention on Climate Change.

2 Locating and Shaping India's Physical Environment and Living Populations

The changing geomorphology of the Indian subcontinent, whose distinctive features have substantially resulted from plate tectonics, has created many of its major current physical features (see Map 2.1). Currently, the subcontinent extends 4,000 km (2,500 mi) from north to south, almost 30 degrees of latitude (8°4' to 37°6' north) – parallel in the north with Portugal, Ohio in the United States, and Japan, and in the south with Nigeria, Venezuela, and Malaysia. Over geological time, as the subcontinent migrated across the globe into the northern hemisphere and smashed into Asia, the Himalayan and other major mountain ranges were thrust upward. These and complex atmospheric forces created the dominant monsoon winds and predominant rainfall patterns plus the course of most rivers.

These geological and climatic factors have produced South Asia's four current major macroregions, each subdivided into and surrounded by many smaller ecological niches (see Map 2.2). Each macroregion has always had a distinct but shifting combination of rock and soil types, quantity of water from seasonal rainfall and river flows, and, eventually, specific (but not fixed) distribution of flora, fauna, and human populations.

One macroregion consists of the level plain extending across the north of the subcontinent, centered on the Ganges and Brahmaputra river systems. The magnitude of rainfall in the east (today's Bangladesh and India's Bengal and seven northeast provinces) declines moving west up the Ganges. A second macroregion is the vast Indus River basin, running from the Himalayan Mountains southward to the Indian Ocean, watering an otherwise dry plain. The Indus watershed covers about 1 million km^2 (386,000 mi^2), today including almost all of Pakistan and northwestern India plus Afghanistan up to Kabul and touching on Tibet and China. Third is a central, upland Deccan semiarid plateau rising from the southeast to the northeast, from an elevation of roughly 300 to 1,000 m (990 to 3,300 ft) above sea level, all within today's India. Finally, the peninsular southeastern plain is wet and fertile (also within today's India). Much like

Map 2.1 Geography of the Indian subcontinent

comparably sized Western Europe, most of South Asia's long history has seen many different ecological and human cultural identities in each macroregion.

Within each macroregion are many distinctive regions, most the size of a large nation in today's Europe. Each has had its own independent, yet interrelating, cultural, economic, and cultural history. For instance, the proportion of prevailing crops (e.g. dry wheat or wet rice) has historically shaped each regional culture, including its cuisine.

This chapter begins with the long timeframe perspective using geology to lay out the changing physical and atmospheric environment that gradually produced these distinctive macroregions. Various species gradually immigrated and populated each region, including tigers (*Panthera tigris*), leopards (*Panthera pardus*), Indian rhinoceroses (*Rhinoceros unicornis*), Asian elephants (*Elephas maximus*), and humans. Much current scientific

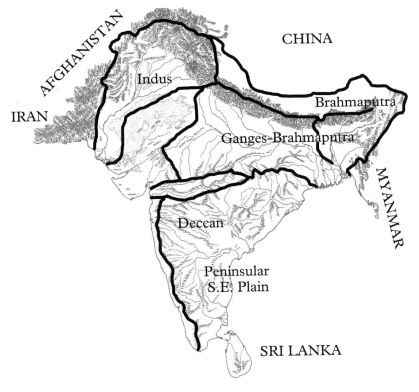

Map 2.2 Major watersheds and macroregions

work in genetic diffusion, paleobotany, and archaeology provides exciting new evidence about early animal, plant, and human migration patterns. This chapter concludes with a survey of human forest-dwellers and their changing and complex relationships to their environment, each other, and the other human communities that eventually developed around them.

The Land

While the Indian subcontinent today sits in the northern hemisphere as a tropical, southern part of Eurasia, this has not always been the case. About 150 million years ago, what we now call South Asia was located near the earth's South Pole, attached to Antarctica, Africa, and Australia – all part of a vast supercontinent which geologists named

"Gondwana" (after the central Indian Gond forest-dwelling community). Hence, the subcontinent's continually changing environment and diverse ecosystems were then far different from today's.

Plate tectonics ("continental drift") has incessantly been reshaping the surface of the earth, resulting from geological forces far beyond human agency but with profound effects on all living things. The huge tectonic plates that would become the earth's current continents are composed of a crust of solidified stone, some 100 km (62 mi) thick, floating on hot molten rock. Impelled by uprising magma, one massive plate gradually broke away from Gondwana, rotated slowly counterclockwise, split off Africa, and shed Madagascar and then the Seychelles islands, becoming the Indian subcontinent.

Over tens of million years, this Indian plate migrated more than 10,000 km (6,250 mi) northward across what is today the Indian Ocean, to just north of the Equator. The plate moved at speeds varying from about 7–20 cm/year (2.8–7.9 in/year): slowly in human time but rapidly in geological time. Sporadically, magma burst through the plate's surface, producing massive volcanoes, which added a thick layer of basalt (creating the current distinctive "Deccan traps" rock) and wiped out various Gondwana species, including some dinosaurs.

Between 40 and 65 million years ago, the northern edge of the Indian plate crashed into the larger Eurasian plate, forcing itself down and under (subduction), twisting and deforming in the process. One major consequence has been the creation of India's defining mountain ranges. Periodic earthquakes, often of great magnitude, have resulted from the continued grinding of the Indian and Eurasian tectonic plates and the vast weight of the mountains thereby produced. The nations of India and Pakistan have both suffered severely devastating earthquakes already this century.

Most prominently, the Himalayas (Sanskrit: "Abode of Snow") are the vast series of roughly parallel, connected mountain ranges in a 2,400 km (1,500 mi) arc along the subcontinent's north. These are the southern edge of Eurasia, which continues to rise as the Indian tectonic plate still slides beneath it. Today, the Himalayas are the youngest and highest mountain range in the world, dwarfing Europe's Alps and North America's Rocky Mountains (see Figure 2.1). The Himalayas contain nine of the world's ten tallest peaks, including, at 8,850 m (29,200 ft), the mountain variously called Sagarmatha (Sanskrit: "Head of the Sky"), Chomolungma (Tibetan: "Divine Mother of Mountains"), and Mt. Everest (English: named in 1865 after British colonial Surveyor-General Sir George Everest [1790–1866]).

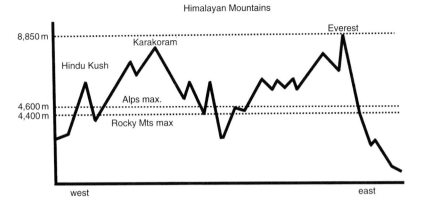

Figure 2.1 The Himalayas, Alps, and Rocky Mountains

Indeed, the Himalayas form the southern flank of the Tibet plateau, "the Roof of the World," which has ecosystem and later cultural connections with both India to the south and China to the north. But these glacier-covered mountains are so difficult to cross that historically there have been relatively limited direct exchanges between India and China, even though these two major world cultures evolved on either side of this same mountain range. From about 9000 BCE onward (early in the warming Holocene era), however, small bands of nomadic humans may have brought some plants (possibly including domesticated barley and rice), animals (including cattle, sheep, and goats), and goods (gold, salt, and wool) through summer-thawed passes into India. Most rivers in the Indus, Ganges, and Brahmaputra systems arise from melting Himalayan glaciers; their volume is maximum in the hot summer months, which overlaps with the southwest monsoon (thus intensifying flooding). The future flow of these perennial rivers is threatened as many of these glaciers shrink due to global warming.

The eastern end of the arc of South Asia's impact zone with Eurasia created a rugged knot of hills and mountain ranges (today dividing Myanmar/Burma from India and Bangladesh). Because of the angle of tectonic impact, these mountains are not as high or steep as the Himalayas. Hence, over time, plants, animals, and people have moved more extensively through them. Many communities living in northeastern India speak a Tibeto-Burman-family language, suggesting just one aspect of the mixing of cultures there. Further, the Brahmaputra River, flowing off the northern and eastern sides of the Tibetan plateau, has cut through these mountains, contributing to the wide alluvial Bengal delta.

There, the Brahmaputra (called the Jamuna River in Bengal) joins the Ganges (called the Padma River in Bengal) and the Meghna (flowing from the mountains of the northeast), all issuing into the Bay of Bengal. This combined system has the third-largest water volume in the world (after the Amazon and the Congo).

On the northwest end of the mountainous arc of tectonic impact are another complex of very rugged ranges, including the Karakoram and Hindu Kush in the northwest and the Suleiman to the west (today respectively separating western China, Afghanistan, the rest of Central Asia, and Iran from Pakistan and India). Most mountain passes in the Hindu Kush are obstructed by snow and ice all winter, but are traversable (yet still dangerous) during summer. Indeed, the name Hindu Kush, may derive from "Death for Hindus," since so many Indian merchants and other travelers died there. Only in 1979 did the first paved road, the 1,300 km (800 mi)-long Karakoram Highway, link Pakistan and China. It took nearly twenty years and the lives of over 1,000 Pakistani and Chinese workers to carve through the high glacial passes, reaching an elevation of 4,700 m (15,400 ft). However, the 2010 earthquake blocked this lone highway with rubble and an unstable high-elevation lake. Only in 2015 were these barriers bypassed and the highway reopened (except in winter) as part of the Chinese-funded "China-Pakistan Economic Corridor" project (see Map 11.1).

Over the centuries, many rivers have carved passes through the Suleiman and other western ranges to join the Indus. The Khyber Pass (from Kabul into Pakistan) has historically been the most traveled, but others include the Bolan Pass (in today's Balochistan province of Pakistan). These passes are narrow and twisting, but many people and animals have long traversed them between India and Central Asia, to China and Europe beyond.

The subduction of the Indian plate's leading edge produced a broad subsidence plain, what is now the upper Indus system in the west and the Ganges system in the center and east. This plain did not stabilize geologically until the Late Quaternary (lasting from 1 to 0.5 million years ago). Massive volumes of soil and minerals (eroded from the Himalayas by glacial runoff and seasonal rains) have accumulated on top of older rock formations. Sediment now lies up to 3,000 m (9,900 ft) thick on the Indus floodplain and up to 6,700 m (22,110 ft) deep on the Ganges plain. Today, the rivers of Bengal alone carry about a quarter of the world's total river sediment load. Parts of this eroded Himalayan rock contain arsenic, which would later dissolve and enter the drinking and irrigation water through today's tube-wells in Bangladesh and eastern India.

The Indian plate also tilted as it collided with Eurasia: the western edge rising, the eastern one sinking. Hence, most major Indian rivers run west to east. Further, a long mountain range called the Western Ghats (Hindi: "steep stairs") runs along the western coast, separating the narrow coastal plain from India's interior Deccan plateau. The lower Eastern Ghats are less imposing, but they mark off the eastern and southeastern coastal plains. Between the Western and Eastern Ghats is the semiarid central Deccan upland which contains some of the planet's oldest continental crust rocks, vestiges of Gondwana, in places overlaid by basalt. Soils produced from these two rock types differ markedly in chemical and water-retention properties, often with sharp visual and agricultural boundaries between them.

In addition to being twisted and tilted, the Indian plate also crumpled from the continued tectonic impact, thus creating smaller internal mountain ranges, most running roughly west to east. The Vindhya and Satpura ranges in the Deccan's north are split by the Narmada River (one of India's relatively few major east-to-west flowing rivers). The Nilgiris and other low ranges cross India's southern tip. However, internal dynamics also created some mountain ranges curving northward, like the Aravallis, which separate the Indus and Ganges watersheds. Over thousands of centuries, most Deccan mountains have eroded into rugged, rocky hills, cut by riverine valleys running eastward off the plateau to the coast.

These geomorphic processes eventually redirected the prevailing atmospheric wind patterns and therefore climate. By about 8 million years ago, the Himalayas had attained roughly their present heights and begun to dam the southward flow of frigid winter air from Central Asia. However, while glaciers ebbed and flowed onto the high Himalayas during various periods, they did not expand south into the adjacent Indus and Gangetic plains. Especially between 1.7 million years ago and 1.5 million years ago, then again around 800,000 to 700,000 years ago, the Himalayan region experienced revivals of tectonic uplift, producing increased glaciation there. Subsequently, there have been four glaciation–interglacial cycles in the last 500,000 years, with most recent global glacial maximum period peaking c. 24000 BCE. Global glaciations also affected India by freezing much of the earth's water, creating periods of aridity as well as lowering the sea level up to 130 m (430 ft), thus extending its coastlines considerably. Further, the volume of glacial-melt runoff has varied greatly over geological time as India's climate has periodically warmed and cooled. More runoff has meant more rocks and sediment on the Indus, Ganges, and Brahmaputra floodplains. Each geomorphic change has thus altered India's environment significantly, most distinctively by interacting with solar radiation to help create its current dominant annual monsoon wind and rain patterns.

The Annual Monsoons

Powerful energy radiates from the sun onto the earth, forcing seasonal changes. The amount of energy received and retained overall, and in any one region, has always varied in the long and short terms, depending on the energy level of the sun's rays, the distance they must travel, the angle of their impact, and the conditions of the earth's electromagnetic field, atmosphere, and surface. Some of these powerful, complex, and interacting forces that are constantly reshaping the earth's climate are beyond the power of humans to affect or even fully understand yet. Yet others are calculable, and humans affect some of them, inadvertently or (increasingly) intentionally (e.g. through altering the carbon dioxide [CO_2] levels that affect the heat-retention quality of the atmosphere).

Various scientific studies have attempted to correlate global climate changes with one or more of these phenomena. For instance, sunspots evidently indicate changes in the sun's thermal activity, hence the amount of energy it radiates, which seems associated with rainfall patterns (i.e. reduced solar activity may reduce precipitation). More clearly understood are the levels of energy due to changing distances from the sun to the earth and due to the earth's axial orientation. The earth's solar orbit has always been interactionally affected by the gravity of other planets (especially massive Saturn and Jupiter) and our own nearby moon. Further, continental drift and the variable weight of glacial-ocean transfers of mass have changed the earth's gravitational fields and thus its response to these celestial forces.

Some of the predicable consequences of these major ongoing cosmic forces are termed the semiperiodic "Milankovitch cycles." The path of the earth's orbit varies between more elliptical or more circular on roughly 100,000-year cycles, bringing it closer or further away from the sun. The oscillation of the tilt of the earth's axis relative to the plane of that orbit varies on about 41,000-year cycles, changing the angle of solar energy incidence. The axial precession (slow wobble) of the earth as it spins varies on about 23,000-year cycles, thereby also varying the solar energy received by any specific region. The interactions of these various cycles, as they reinforce or cancel out each other's effects, combine in forcing earth's seasonal changes.

Sunrays arriving at the top of the earth's atmosphere also interact in complex ways with atmospheric, terrestrial, and oceanic features, determining the amount of energy reflected or retained overall and at any point on the surface. Many of these atmospheric factors are unpredictable and uncontrollable by humans. The earth's magnetic field deflects the solar wind's charged particles, but this field waxes, wanes, and shifts relative to the earth's axis, and even reverses periodically (most recently c. 780,000 years ago). Occasional meteor strikes and volcanic activity inject reflective aerosols into the atmosphere, dramatically affecting the climate for years (especially in the hemisphere of the event, but sometimes globally).

Major changes in land cover (and hence solar reflectivity in that region) result from nonhuman causes, but also human ones. Significantly, people have increasingly created climate-changing factors over recent centuries. These include altering the atmosphere's chemical composition with emissions of airborne particles and carbon dioxide, methane (CH_4), and other greenhouse gases; changing the reflectivity of the earth's surface (from deforestation and inadvertent glacier reduction and desertification); and perhaps even restructuring the earth's gravity fields (through creating massive dam-water reservoirs, reducing groundwater aquifers, and unintentionally causing glacial retreat and regional desiccation). Many commentators argue that the current scale of unprecedented human actions (including long-lasting radiation from nuclear bombs and power plants) has brought on the Anthropocene epoch. The result of these nonhuman and human forces are complex climate changes with internal feedbacks and long- and short-term variations and trends in atmospheric and surface temperatures, both overall on the globe and in each place on it, including each region of South Asia. Humans, having created some of these climate-changing forces, are starting to work collectively to try to moderate or reverse those most destructive to a human-congenial environment.

Due to continental drift, the Indian subcontinent now sits with the Tropic of Cancer running across its middle. So, compared to north or south of the tropics, the sun radiates more directly and powerfully onto India and its surrounding ocean. The land and sea each retain heat at different rates, causing wind-flow patterns between them: whichever is relatively hotter tends to have rising air, lower barometric pressure, and thus inflowing winds. This thermal contrast became especially marked in the Asian tropics during the Holocene. Further, as the Himalayas, other northern mountains, and the Western Ghats all pushed up into the atmosphere, they reshaped these annual atmospheric flow patterns into India. Combined with the earth's rotation, all these factors created India's (and much of Asia's and eastern Africa's) current dominant monsoon wind pattern.

Concurring mineral, pollen, fossil, and other ancient evidence suggests the monsoon pattern first developed about 8.2 million years ago and stabilized around 2.8 million years ago, with notable long-term trends (including weakening during glacial periods). Periodic atmospheric and oceanic temperature shifts enhanced or weakened a particular year's monsoon in one or more regions of India. Interacting forces include the Walker Circulation of Pacific winds causing or diminishing an El Niño Southern Oscillation (warm water pooling on the South American coast, which shifts rainfall east, away from India), fluctuations in snow volume in Central Asia, and other meteorological factors that are not yet fully understood. Nevertheless, while the volume and exact timing of each monsoon in each of India's regions results from highly complex and coupled meteorological factors, the broad pattern has persisted since its inception.

The term "monsoon" comes from the Arabic word for "season" since twice each year for three to four months continuously, winds largely blow in the same direction. Starting during the northern hemisphere's spring, as the sun beats more directly down, the Indian landmass heats up, drawing in southwest winds. Annually, these winds begin blowing steadily in June, and this southwest monsoon continues all summer. These winds are heavily laden with moisture from the Indian Ocean, so when they hit the Western Ghats, they rise, cool, and drop intense rains upon the coastal plain on the western sides of the mountains (totaling some 4.5 m [14.9 ft] annually in places). These heavy monsoon rains make some Western Ghat valleys into biodiversity hot spots with high concentrations of unique species. But often this voluminous rainfall also causes eroding floods.

Spreading east beyond the Western Ghats, the southwest monsoon has already dropped most of its moisture. Hence, the interior Deccan highland, even if not far from the coast, is in the much dryer rain shadow (averaging 50–60 cm annually) and consequently is less densely populated overall. Even forested areas are mainly drought-tolerant ecosystems. The eastward-flowing Deccan rivers are channels of fertility but, with no glacial sources, tend to be highly seasonal.

Continuing across and up the Bay of Bengal, the southwest monsoon again absorbs moisture. Drawn northward by low pressure over Bengal and north India, this monsoon often produces cyclones (called "hurricanes" in the Atlantic and "typhoons" in the Pacific). These rains drench Bengal (now divided between India and Bangladesh) which averages 2 m (6.6 ft), more along its coast. Much human and animal life on this alluvial delta benefits from this heavy rainfall, making it a major global biodiversity hot spot and the subcontinent's other most densely human-populated region. But the coastline of Bangladesh has a wide continental shelf, so wind-driven waves upsurge, producing flooding disasters. A 1876 cyclone had a reported 13.6 m (45 ft) surge height.

As the southwest monsoon rises and cools over the hills north of Bengal, even more rain falls. Places in northeast India frequently receive over 14 m (46 ft) of rain in a single three-month monsoon season. But even there, water storage over the nine months between monsoons remains a problem (especially with recent deforestation).

The southwest monsoon then continues up the Ganges plain, diverted by the now looming Himalayan Mountains. There is a decreasing gradient from east to west of rainfall and consequently of biotic density. Parts of the upper Indus plain are quite arid, and the Thar Desert (in today's Rajasthan state of India) averages 100 mm (4 in) annual rainfall in places.

By autumn, the sun's impact on the Indian landmass has lessened, so it cools and the southwest monsoon pattern dissipates. Oceans hold heat longer, so they are now relatively warmer with lower atmospheric pressure, thus the northeast monsoon begins. Cool air flows from West and Central Asia, only partially blocked by the glacial Himalayan Mountains, bringing brief frosts to the upper Gangetic plain but limited rainfall. In some years, Mediterranean storms drift eastward, adding rainfall to the upper Indus watershed. Glacial runoff and rainfall means that the Indus annually conveys, for example, double the Nile's water volume.

As the northeast monsoon passes over the Bay of Bengal, it picks up moisture. So, India's peninsular southeast receives the most rain during the winter. Seasonal rivers running off the Deccan bring water to these coastal alluvial plains, making them particularly fertile.

This annual monsoon cycle of extreme seasonality, with three to four months of heavy rain but then little during the rest of the year, has had profound cultural, economic, and environmental effects across India: much human, plant, and animal life has necessarily revolved around the annual monsoon cycles. Further, geomorphic and climatic changes have caused shifts in the flora and fauna mix in each region, with some locally evolved or long-established species losing out and some new species successfully spreading in from adjacent Asian lands. Among these were immigrating humans.

Species, including *Homo sapiens*, Populating the Subcontinent

Fossils and DNA discovered so far indicate that a few species of dinosaurs, plants, insects, and animals (including frogs and a few small mammals) from Gondwana survived on the Indian tectonic plate (the "Indian Ark") during the roughly 30 million years that it moved in relative isolation north across the Indian Ocean. However, scholars currently debate the level of immigration by other species during this period. Some saltwater fish species spread out along India's coast as conditions favorable to them developed. Other species that had evolved in Africa, Madagascar, the Seychelles, or mainland Asia crossed airborne or over the sometimes-narrow maritime gaps, which were occasionally punctuated by islands. Certainly, after the Indian landmass collided with Eurasia, these continents more rapidly exchanged animal and plant species overland. Some species entering India – including the rhinoceros, horse, and camel – were American-evolved, having crossed Beringia (the temporary land-bridge during the period of sea-level fall caused by the last major ice age). As India's land and climate shifted into new configurations, some indigenous species adapted and thrived, while others died out or were outcompeted by newcomers (which themselves became indigenous).

Scattered archaeological evidence suggests the gradual expansion into India of evolving hominins. From roughly 1.9 million years ago (early Pleistocene), small bands of hominins immigrated into India's hilly northwest, as evidenced by rock cores and flakes. From as early as 700,000 and up to 400,000 years ago, a few sites in the Siwalik Hills (Rajasthan) have early hominin-made simple stone tools and evidence of fire use. Then, from about 140,000 to 130,000 years ago, various locations hold more sophisticated (symmetrically bifacially worked) Acheulean-type oval and pear-shaped hand axes, large cutting tools, knives, choppers, and other artifacts associated with *Homo erectus*. But, such early hominins remained thinly scattered and nomadic in India.

In many Indian regions, archaeologists have encountered difficulties in studying prehistoric flora, fauna, and hominin life. Heat and monsoon rains quickly decay and leach away organic material. Further, on the north Indian plains, any early archaeological evidence was buried deep by alluvial soil, and stone-tool dependent hominins may not have found the upper Indus and Ganges floodplains habitable since these regions lacked workable stone until rivers began conveying rock conglomerates from the Himalayas. Additionally, these floodplains were evidently savannas, congenial habitats for large carnivorous predators. So, early hominins may have been unable to compete or, lacking sheltering forests, to protect themselves there, preferring instead forested and hilly uplands.

Among hominin species, *Homo sapiens* evidently evolved distinctive physical features in Africa only c. 200,000 years ago; our earliest modern human social and cultural behavioral repertoire developed only c. 100,000 years ago. This modern human package included producing more specialized tools in repeated patterns by reducing raw stock (stones, bones, and antlers) through chipping, scraping, or burning away unwanted parts. They thus created crude tools for hunting and further processing of plants, animals, and minerals. Later, some groups combined multiple microliths into tools with more complex cutting faces, enabling greater efficiencies in hunting, fishing, and collecting and reducing raw materials. Sparking and harnessing fire enabled cooking for better nutrition and allowed brush and tree clearance that reshaped the local environment. People also started to use found objects and dyes to decorate themselves and to represent animals, including by painting their images on rocks. Language development empowered social coordination. Some bands buried their dead with grave goods and in ritualized postures and orientations. These techniques showed how *Homo sapiens* were reshaping, repurposing, and representing natural forces, objects, and other living beings into culturally imagined forms.

Scholars estimate that the first successful expansion of the *Homo sapiens* range beyond Africa and across the Arabian Peninsula occurred from as early as 80,000 years ago to as late as 40,000 years ago, although there may have been prior unsuccessful emigrations. Some of their descendants extended the human range ever further in each generation, spreading into each habitable land they encountered. One human channel was along the warm and productive coastal lands of the Persian Gulf and northern Indian Ocean. Eventually, various bands entered India between 75,000 years ago and 35,000 years ago, using Middle Paleolithic technologies. One difficulty in dating the arrival of *Homo sapiens* is their overlap with other hominins, since many human species used similar stone tools and fire. Eventually, not just in India but around the world, all hominin species except *Homo sapiens* died off (but the exact timing in each region is still debated).

The lives of all plants, animals, and perhaps humans in India were powerfully affected by forces far beyond their control. Just one salient example of a sudden and altering event was the Toba volcanic supereruption in northern Sumatra c. 72000 BCE. This largest of several Toba eruptions deposited a blanket of ash (terrestrial tephra) over lands from Southeast Asia to Arabia, up to 6 m (20 ft) thick in many places in India. Ash and sulfuric acid (H_2SO_4) in the atmosphere created a volcanic winter that lasted years in the northern hemisphere, causing rapid temperature drop, reduced rainfall, water poisoned by fluoride, and various particles dangerous to inhale. While the extent and effects of this eruption in each region of India remain uncertain, it may have wiped out many (or all) early hominins there.

Recently collected genetic evidence from current populations indicates how bands of *Homo sapiens* continued to migrate into and around in India, spreading out and adapting to its range of regional ecosystems. Some of their descendants expanded into Southeast Asia, China, and as far as Australia. New bands of humans entered India, both from the northwest and the northeast, leading to diverse and intermixed genetic lines and human cultures. While evidence is so far only fragmentary, archaeologists have found identifiably *Homo sapiens* skeletons on Sri Lanka from 32000–26000 BCE and on mainland India from 28000–25500 BCE. Humans inhabited many parts of Ganges plain at least from about 13000 BCE, constructing cemeteries, particularly adjacent to oxbow lakes created as rivers meandered.

Small communities of *Homo sapiens* scattered among all of India's congenial ecological niches, each containing a distinctive range of workable minerals and edible and otherwise useful plants and animals. Although similar in their broad patterns, each of these earliest Indian communities developed locally specific hunting, fishing, and gathering economies. Local dyes enabled particular colors for clothing. Shelter designs reflected local conditions, including how heavily the monsoon rains poured down and the types of local flora available.

Rarely were bands totally isolated or self-sufficient. Throughout human history, most forest-dwelling communities could not produce everything they needed or wanted, so exchanges among them (and later with nearby settled and pastoralist communities) took place, including foods and other raw materials, artisanal products, and intermarriages. Especially valued raw materials or artifacts, like soft copper forged into ritual forms, could be passed on through an extended chain. Even the people of the c. 550 (not all inhabited) Andaman Islands, who appear today as a notable example of economic and cultural isolation, have historically not been as autonomous and self-contained as many ethnographers and politicians have presupposed.

In many regions from c. 7000 to 6000 BCE, hunting, gathering, and fishing were slowly supplemented (or even largely replaced) by the cultivation of selected wild plants for food and the domestication of some wild animals for food or labor. The cumulative effects of human actions could gradually accumulate to reshape a local landscape, changing the mix of plant and animal species, preventing the growth of forests, or turning them into grassland. For instance, the Ganges plain was evidently never densely forested but rather was largely savanna. Archaeobotanists have found "cultural pollens" of weedy plants associated with human planting or burning from early in the Holocene (however, pollen preservation is not necessarily representative since plant species producing airborne pollen are disproportionately represented compared to those reproducing through rhizomes or insect-spread pollen). The lands that burning cleared and domesticated animals grazed befitted certain wild plant and animal species, and were also more exposed to erosion. The popular image of a pristine, prehuman India covered by climax forest thus needs reconsideration.

Forest-Dwellers in South Asian Environmental History

The limited available archaeological evidence about early *Homo sapiens* living in South Asia's forests can be cautiously supplemented by historical and ethnographic accounts from later periods about forest-dwelling communities in India and elsewhere. In so doing, however, one must not presuppose unchanging or continuous forest-dwelling communities over the many centuries to the present. The earliest humans in India may have been forest-dwellers, but not all their descendants remained so. Instead, over the Indian subcontinent's long history, diverse people have moved fully or partly into forests and adapted to life there. Periodic droughts or other environmental stresses, as well as the depredations of bandits, armies, or tax collectors, have occasionally forced settled farmers to resort to forests as a reserve where uncultivated forest food sources were available for foraging. Pastoralists may spend part of their annual cycle grazing their animals in forests. Conversely, as settled agricultural villages and then towns and cities arose, they attracted some forest-dwellers who sought better opportunities for themselves – particularly young men and women who left for employment or, more recently, education or political advancement. Hence, many people currently living outside of forests have some biological heritage from ancient forest-dwellers. So, while throughout human history in India there have always been some communities living in forests, they have not always been of the same lineages, as recent DNA testing has demonstrated.

South Asian and foreign scientific teams are increasingly analyzing saliva and blood samples given by many different people, including forest-dwellers. Historical genetics often uses mitochondrial DNA (passed from mother to children) and the Y-chromosome (passed from father to son) to trace ancestry. Since biologists have calculated the likely rate of genetic mutations, they can also reconstruct roughly when and in what order different branches of human beings diverged and intermarried. All this enables reconstruction of ancient migration patterns, including into and out of India's forests.

Linguists are analyzing the vocabulary and grammar of many distinct forest-dwellers' languages. However, only about 100 of these languages survive today, many others having died out as their speakers adopted the dominant cultures around them. Within specific regions, such as central

India or the northeast, many forest-dwellers' languages are related, forming broad linguistic families like Gondi, Munda, or Tibeto-Burman. Such linguistic evidence suggests how various bands migrated into India, settled in specific regions and developed their distinct cultures there, but also interacted with others.

Consequently, most scholars agree that the term "forest-dweller" most accurately describes a set of current economic and cultural relationships with a forest ecology. Pathbreaking environmental historians Gadgil and Ramachandra Guha (1992) use the term "ecosystem people" to discuss people who, by their lifestyle, are highly and immediately dependent on the natural world around them for their daily sustenance. Thus, being classed a forest-dweller comes from current practices, not necessarily biological descent from India's original inhabitants.

Nonetheless, some current forest-dwelling communities today believe themselves (and are regarded by some outsiders) to be indigenous, always present right there since the beginning of time. Indeed, often elders still proudly teach their sacred oral traditions to their children and recount to guests how god created their own ancestors and all plants and animals at that sacred site. These revered accounts also highlight the kinship that members of their community share with one another and with distinctive plants and animals around them, reflecting their sense of themselves as part of the forest world, albeit a special part of it.

Each forest-dwelling community has one or more sacred histories. In some accounts, the forest and its fauna and flora were divine gifts to the community for approved uses, gifts withdrawn by the divine for improper human actions. However, such oral traditions were first recorded in writing by outsiders, and long post-dated extensive contact with outside cultures (from Vedic through Islamic and Christian), so we should expect exogenous as well as indigenous themes in them.

Box 2.1

Oral history of the Kharia community of central India:

"God Ponomosor created the earth ... first filled with plants and trees. Then the god fashioned two clay images, one each of man and woman, and placed both inside a hollow banyan tree. As the milky sap of the tree dropped into their mouths, the images became animated. When they grew up and came out of the tree, they began to dwell in the caves of the hills. They knew of no clothing and lived on wild fruits and roots ...

Box 2.1 Cont

In course of time, the race of man multiplied so much that there ensued a great scarcity of food.

Men prayed to the god to provide them with some other kind of food. So he sent a violent storm, which blew the leaves of trees high up in the air which were then transformed into different kinds of birds, according to the various sizes of the leaves. Men began to kill the smaller birds for food.

[Again] Ponomosor was displeased . . . So he sent torrents of rain to destroy man through floods. Many men died by drowning. But a few clever persons covered themselves up with gungu leaves and fled to the hilltops and survived . . . Now Ponomosor sent a rain of fire . . . All men died except a brother and a sister [from them are descended today's Kharia people]."

–Transcribed and translated in Roy and Roy 1937.

Some commentators have extended these indigenous ideas to romanticize forest-dwellers: living from the earliest times to the present as "primitive ecologists" in natural harmony with their environment. Certainly, some of their customary practices are sustainable, given a large enough resource-extraction area. But that does not mean that they were consciously conserving biodiversity. Indeed, these sacred accounts often include a series of tense, conflicting relationships with forest animals or gods. Repeated ecological destructions and recoveries may reflect the collective memory of dynamic but recurring cycles including devastating monsoon floods or forest fires. These oral histories may also reflect the periodic nature of their distinctive agriculture.

Various forest-dwelling communities have used (and today continue to use) fire for clearing brushwood and undergrowth, thereby creating temporary fields. They use the ash to fertilize the soil for their crops until its productivity is exhausted. Then, they migrate to a different area, again cutting and burning the undergrowth and cropping there for a time. Anglophone outsiders call this "swidden agriculture," "shifting agriculture," or (more negatively) "slash-and-burn agriculture." It is *jhum, bewar, kumri,* or other local names for many of the diverse communities currently practicing it (each with its own particularities of timing, location, cropping, and gendered types of participation). Eventually, when the first area has recovered fertility, they can circle back to it. If population density remains low enough for the area of forestland available, these cycles can be sufficiently extended so that swidden agriculture is sustainable. Often, twenty years or more (about a generation) pass before a community returns to a prior site. Perhaps only elders would remember the location of sacred sites and the best places to hunt, fish, or gather valued plants.

From c. 7000 BCE, in the hills west of the lower Indus River (and perhaps elsewhere yet undiscovered), some communities developed a more intensive, settled, agriculture-based economy. The next chapter considers that environmental history. Here, however, we concentrate on those communities who are currently largely living in India's forests.

Collectively, these forest-dwelling communities have rich knowledge of their surrounding forest and its wild products such as game, medicinal plants, and foodstuffs. But because swidden farming, hunting-gathering, and fishing are not productive enough to generate permanent surpluses and because they move often, most bands cannot accumulate much material wealth. So, most such groups are largely egalitarian – not stratified except by age and gender. Typically, elders hold great respect. Men and women customarily specialize in different, complementary productive activities. Men often go on extended hunting or raiding expeditions, including taking cattle from the surrounding communities. Some oral traditions celebrate wildness, especially with respect to men, as constituting their collective identity (Skaria 1999). Women often do more domestic labor like weaving, cooking, and gathering forest products, especially fuel, food, and water. Hence, ecological damage usually affects women more immediately by reducing the amount and quality available.

The relationship between gender and environmental practices has been much debated. Some ecofeminist commentators argue that women, either due to culture or biology, have stronger and more sympathetic relationships with forests, and with nature generally (Shiva 1988). However, anthropologists have shown that some women of forest communities cause much of the local environmental damage (Jewitt 2000). Many such communities customarily take their brides from families living in other parts of the forest. This means these wives may not initially know much about local conditions in which they forage. Further, given the heavy workload often demanded from young brides, typically by their mothers-in-law, they may not have time to follow the best practices to conserve the sources of wood, water, or food around them. Such ecological damage by forest-dwellers, however, is far exceeded in scale by commercial timber and mining operations sanctioned formally or informally by the government.

Other major debates have been about state policy concerning human communities and animals in forests. On the one hand, the British colonial government tried to protect allegedly innocent "tribals" and their endangered cultures against Indian exploiters, especially outsider moneylenders and land purchasers. Notably, the 1874 Scheduled Districts Act created a separate legal category for lands largely inhabited by forest-dwellers. British officials also sought to block largely urban and middle-class Indian nationalists from agitating among supposedly vulnerable tribals.

Simultaneously, many British colonial officials and South Asian and international conservationists regarded forest-dwellers and their swidden agriculture and animal grazing as destructive of the commercial value of forests and of trophy or endangered animal species. Hence, they thought authorities should exclude forest-dwellers from those forests designated as worthy of government protection, and wild animals should be protected from these allegedly wild "tribes." Many of the Forest Acts (from 1865 onward) have asserted the government's right to exclude local people from hunting, timbering, or practicing swidden agriculture in official forests.

Yet, from the early twentieth century onward, some colonial and post-independence government programs have sought to improve the lives of tribals by recognizing their economic "backwardness" and asserting policies intended to improve their lives by developing their economy and health through integrating them into mainstream society. The official British colonial 1931 census created the legal category "Scheduled Tribe" (ST): forest-dwelling communities whose names (often in arbitrarily transliterated forms) were included on an officially compiled list (or "schedule") based on their alleged tribal "primitive" lifestyle and relative isolation from the surrounding majority society. Inclusion on this list conferred special access to opportunities in education and government employment intended to end their impoverished and isolated condition, eventually making them "modern."

Following independence in 1947, these debates have continued. The official Indian government definition of ST in part continues the colonial geographic and sociological approach, by identifying these communities as "suffering from extreme social, educational and economic backwardness ... on account of their primitive agricultural practices ... geographical isolation [and] shyness of contact with the community at large" (India 2013:1). There is also a special subgroup of "Particularly Vulnerable Tribal Groups" characterized by "pre-agricultural level of technology, stagnant or declining population, extremely low literacy, and subsistence level of economy." Some policy-makers sought to protect the tribals by isolating them. One of Prime Minister Jawaharlal Nehru's close advisors, anthropologist Verrier Elwin (1902–64; English-born but an Indian citizen), largely advocated this position (see Chapter 9). But later, the Government of India largely sought to conserve forests and endangered animal species by removing communities from forest reserves and designated wildlife sanctuaries and finding alternative sources of income for them. Additionally, the government has promised to improve the lives of ST by integrating them into developing society.

Further, the Indian government, like its British colonial precursor, also presupposes a biological definition by legally including all their descendants as ST, regardless of their actual current location or occupation. In India today, 8.6 percent of the total population is legally recognized as ST. Consequently, even more extensively than under the British Raj, they are entitled to receive affirmative action ("compensatory discrimination") rights, with a fixed quota or "Reservation" of a negotiated 7.5 percent of all vacancies and promotions in government employment, to reserved seats in Parliament and the state legislatures, to reserved places in state-run educational institutions with scholarships, and to preferential loans to start businesses.

Hence, admission onto this ST list (or not) has always been highly politicized and based on administrative and political decisions that are not always fully informed. The names of included (and excluded) tribes are often inconsistent; the same community sometimes appears on one provincial list but not on another, or on the central government list under one spelling but not under another. Further, given the advantages of inclusion, the number of people legally classed as ST has more than tripled over the last half century. In just the decade between the last two censuses, their number has risen by a quarter, from 84 million to 104 million. This exceeds what simple population growth could generate. Rather, entire (or parts of) various communities have been newly added to the schedule, often for political reasons, thus gaining access to these Reservations. Further, the benefits of Reservations have tended to be concentrated within ST elites (the "Creamy Layer").

On their part, during the 1930s, forest-dweller and outside activists coined the Sanskrit (not forest-dweller's) neologism *Adivasi* ("original inhabitants," "aboriginals") which asserts their biological continuity with India's earliest humans. They did this to build transregional ethnic solidarity, and also to claim that these forest communities were entitled to moral, legal, and financial compensation for all the lands that they once "owned" but had been taken from them by later immigrants, government dams and other projects, or commercial corporations. This concept combines a wide range of cultures and communities with different historical pasts into the single politically powerful category of "indigenous people." India is the nation with the largest number of indigenous people in the world (by most criteria). Even if some activists recognize the historical fiction of the unity of all Adivasis as India's indigenous people, they also recognize the mobilizing and rhetorical force of the concept. The United Nations and other international bodies sponsor declarations and conventions advocating "indigenous people's rights."

Further, in various other nations, legally indigenous people have successfully made claims to land or compensation for what later immigrants took from them. Therefore, the Indian government officially rejects the term Adivasi, and denies that these ST are descendants of India's original inhabitants. Accepting this would run against what it seeks to protect: national integration in the face of perceived regional secession. Similarly, Hindu nationalists, many of whom claim Hindus as India's original inhabitants, prefer to call non-Hindu forest-dwellers by the Sanskrit terms *vanavasi* ("forest-dweller") or *vanjati* ("forest-born"), terms which lack any indigenous implications.

In post-1947 India, Adivasi activists were successful in some of their demands for separate provincial governments. In India's northeast, there are now seven provinces, divided along cultural ("tribal") identities; additionally, armed movements by as yet unrecognized groups demand their own provincial autonomy. In 2000, two new provinces (Jharkhand and Chhattisgarh) were carved out of existing larger ones in central India so Adivasis could elect people who claim to look after their special interests. Nevertheless, Alpa Shah (2010) writes of the "eco-incarceration" of forest-dwellers when (largely outside) activists assert that out-migration to towns and cities by Adivasis is a betrayal of their alleged essential or "authentic" identity. Further, imposing on these people life among protected but dangerous wild animals has often led to the deaths of people and these animals, like elephants and tigers, when they clash over who gets to eat the crops and cattle in or adjacent to Protected Forests.

From their first arrival in India, most forest-dwelling bands interacted extensively with each other and, later, with outside communities. Thus, there has neither been unilineal evolution from tribal/hunter-gatherer to settled farmer, nor have pockets of India's earliest people have simply survived to the present as distinct from the surrounding society, nor are they all part of a single biological or even cultural community. Rather, such communities have always comprised parts of India's diverse human population. As the environments changed in various regions, a combination of local developments with outside influences gradually produced a new, urban-based civilization on the Indus plain.

3   Indus and Vedic Relationships with Indian
      Environments (c. 3500 BCE – c. 600 BCE)

The ecology of each region of the vast and diverse Indian subcontinent continued gradually to transform over the long period from 3500 to 600 BCE, as did the many diverse human communities in (and entering) prehistoric India. At different points, two cultural groups distinguished themselves for the distinctive ways each conceptualized and interacted with their respective physical environments and various fauna and flora species. These two followed very different lifestyles. They also endowed today's historians with quite different types of this early period's richest source materials.

The first set of communities settled on the broad Indus River plain. There they collectively intensified and unified their innovating culture and technologies, transforming for their own uses the minerals, plants, and animals around them. All this enabled them to produce an urban-centered and pastoral-, agricultural-, and trade-supported, literate "civilization" that flourished from c. 2700 BCE until c. 1900 BCE.[1] Hence the retrospective names "Indus civilization" (from its location) or, alternatively, "Harappa civilization" (after one of its largest and most extensively studied cities).

Eventually, the changing regional ecology could no longer support this civilization's economy. The cultural coherence among its cities dissipated, and many of its people dispersed or returned to more localized lifeways. Surviving evidence about the Indus civilization is largely archaeological, including city sites, artifacts, and human, animal, and plant remains, with only indirect evidence about its cultural attitudes toward the environment.

As India's physical environment continued to shift, from c. 1700 BCE onward, small nomadic bands of pastoralists migrated into India from the northwest, spread out, began to settle, adopted agricultural methods of

[1] The concept of "civilization" has a long and contentious history but is appropriate here since the Indus civilization was literate and urban-centered, two of the consensus features of a civilization.

existing cultures there, and mixed socially and culturally. Unlike the Indus urban communities, they left few material artifacts. But they preserved their sacred oral tradition, which they called *Veda*, by ritual recitation and dedicated memorization. Vedic hymns contain much about this culture's attitude toward and interactions with the land, plants, and animals around them.

The cultural and biological descendants of these two groups interacted in diverse ways with each of India's still changing regional ecologies, with each other, and with local forest-dwelling communities. From c. 600 BCE onward, they formed what would become the dominant culture, society, and economy in most of India's regions thereafter.

The Indus Civilization Emerges

The earliest discovered instance in India of well-established, settled agricultural society is at Mehrgarh in the hills between the Bolan Pass and the Indus plain (today in Pakistan) (see Map 3.1). From as early as 7000 BCE, communities there started investing increased labor in preparing the land and selecting, planting, tending, and harvesting particular grain-producing plants. They also domesticated animals, including sheep, goats, pigs, and oxen (both humped zebu [*Bos indicus*] and unhumped [*Bos taurus*]). Castrating oxen, for instance, turned them from mainly meat sources into domesticated draft-animals as well. These people caught and consumed fish, grew cotton for woven cloth and other uses, and produced wine and beer from grapes and barley. They also adopted a species of wheat indigenous to the eastern Mediterranean or southern Turkey, perhaps one of several types of plants and animals brought by immigrants or traders. They may also have benefited from influxes of flora and fauna species, people, and ideas from the Deccan and north India, regions which also began to show agricultural development during this broad period.

Such an "agricultural revolution" enabled food surpluses that supported growing populations. Their largely cereal diet did not necessarily make people healthier, however, since conditions like caries and protein deficiencies can increase. Further, infectious diseases spread faster with denser living conditions of both humans and domesticated animals (which can spread measles, influenza, and other diseases to humans).

Nonetheless, increased agricultural production enabled more diversification of labor. Mehrgarh communities had long collected copper from available surface ore eroded out of the hills and transformed it into tools and ornaments. Some groups discovered how to mine deeper deposits, increasing the supply. Artisans innovated technologies for processing

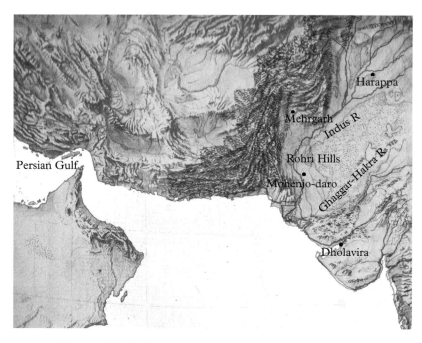

Map 3.1 The Indus civilization

minerals, plants, and animals into finished products. For instance, some people devoted some or most of their time to developing pottery for cooking and storing surpluses. They produced distinctively styled wheel-thrown "Painted Gray Ware" pottery by firing in high heat (but with limited oxygen) and decorating it with complex red or black designs. Traders transported and exchanged these artifacts and raw materials, facilitated by the invention of wheeled carts pulled by domesticated animals. Gradually, specialists in governance, art, and religion also emerged.

Increasingly from around 3800–3500 BCE, some communities moved or expanded down from Mehrgarh's hilly uplands onto the alluvial Indus plain, developing new relationships with and transforming that ecology. Evidence from pollen and mineral deposits suggests that this shift occurred early in a long-term warmer and dryer climate phase of weaker southwest monsoons due to the interconnected factors of reduced solar radiation and uneven increases in El Niño events. Further, the Indus River and the roughly parallel Ghaggar-Hakra system had recently entrenched themselves in more stabilized beds. Biannual seasonal inundations from these rivers both irrigated fields and fertilized them with silt, supporting rather than threatening fixed settlements and agriculture along their banks. So, just when rain-dependent agriculture in the hills may have become more stressed and less productive, the perennial river-banks became more nurturing. These developments seem to have produced localized economic and cultural systems, so the period is often termed the "Regionalization Era."

Collectively over the next millennium, these Indus settlements not only benefited from these more productive environmental conditions, they also developed a package of cultural and technological innovations in their relationships with the regional ecology. Collectively, the people of these Indus cities created and shared innovative pyrotechnical, chemical, hydraulic, and other methodologies that transformed raw materials at vastly more rapid rates than nonhuman processes would have done. Some were unique at that time anywhere in the world.

By c. 2700 BCE (the start of the Integration Era), various communities on the broad Indus plain had come together into a sophisticated urban-based, literate, and innovative civilization with expanding effects on the physical environment around them. Numerous Indus cities grew until the largest each contained between 30,000 and 50,000 people, all sharing this same cultural and technological package, although each city produced or interpreted it in locally distinctive ways. Some cities, like Harappa, developed out of existing settlements; other large cities (including Mohenjo-daro and Dholavira) were evidently more rapidly built, integrating this Indus package into their infrastructure from their foundation.

This was the same broad period that saw the rise of the civilizations of Mesopotamia (between the Tigris and Euphrates Rivers), Egypt (along the Nile), and northeast China (in the Yellow River basin). At its peak, the Indus was the most extensive of these ancient civilizations, extending 1,500 km (930 mi) up the Indus plain, with a core area of 30,000–100,000 km^2 (11,600–38,600 mi^2) and with more ecologically diverse peripheral spheres of economic and cultural influence extending out to ten times that area. The cultural and technological uniformity of the Indus cities is especially striking in light of the relatively great distances among them, with separations of about 280 km (175 mi) whereas the Mesopotamian cities, for example, only averaged about 20–25 km (12.5–16 mi) apart.

Further, in contrast to Egypt or China, where the term "kingdom" or "empire" is appropriate, there was evidently no unifying political center for the Indus civilization. Rather, each city was apparently the cultural and economic center for a local network of large and small surrounding villages. Further, the Indus civilization was much less militaristic than its contemporaries. Only a few cities built strongly defensive walls (most notably Dholavira on the Gujarat coast, which was especially exposed to seaborne incursions). The relatively few copper or bronze weapons that have been found lack a stiffening ridge that would have made them more lethal.

The cities of the Indus civilization imposed its conceptual order on the land, water, and material world generally. Urbanizing communities laid out streets on a grid, oriented largely north to south and east to west. Further, over hundreds of years, the walls of often two-story houses were built on the same plot, showing long-term respect for land boundaries. The skilled workmanship of bricklayers is especially remarkable. Further, all the Indus cities used fired bricks of the same 1:2:4 physical proportions (although not always the same size). They also all used small blocks of chert stone that had been mined and imported from the distant Rohri Hills, which they shaped into uniform sets of cubical weights, each in the same mathematical proportions. All this uniform ordering of space and weight was sustained for seven centuries.

Further, these cities shared a deep and unprecedented concern for domestic water control. They integrated elaborate wet-waste disposal systems that had large, watertight sewage drains from bathing and toilet rooms inside each substantial house, connecting into collective channels with soak pits beneath the streets. This kept wastewater separate from the drinking water that was drawn from brick-lined wells. At least one large building in many cities seems to have been a public bathhouse with a sizable pool, whose brick walls were waterproofed with pitch and with a water well to fill it. Surrounding the pool were smaller rooms, perhaps dressing rooms or places for massage or washing. Since the culture devoted such attention to sanitation and bathing, it suggests how concerned people were with personal and public health and hygiene, to a degree that distinguished them from all other cultures of their age, and for many centuries afterward.

Most of the Indus region does not show extensive irrigation damming or canals, although there were a few small check-dams in valleys. However, Dholavira built a large and complex freshwater-control system, with permanent dams diverting the seasonal rainfall into large reservoirs surrounding the city. These reservoirs provided drinking, sanitation, and irrigation water, as well as defensive protection to this coastal city, which also had an unusually prominent citadel.

The Indus concept that raw materials could be transformed led to improving metallurgy. The ore of copper, tin, silver, gold, and other minerals were not just melted but smelted into purer forms or more useful alloys like bronze. Much once-used metal seems to have been recycled. Jewelers crafted metals, shells, ivory, amber, and agate into impressive jewelry by careful heating, carving, drilling, polishing, and mounting. Unfinished and scrap residue shows that individual workshops often specialized in only one stage in the production process, with semi-finished items then traded on to the next workshop. Clearly, there was enough wealth present to commission or purchase such works of ornament and art.

Indus artisans in many distantly located workshops also made pottery and high-fired stoneware for implements and ornaments with similar production methods and standardized figurative and abstract patterns. They used the transformative power of pyrotechnical expertise, including grinding stone to produce malleable pastes and enhancing color by the measured application of heat to bring out latent mineral colors. For pottery decoration, they used a characteristic red slip with black painted designs; some inscribed lettering on pots, bowls, and plates. Some artisans also made clay masks with stylized faces, possibly for rituals or dramatic performances. Technologically cruder terra-cotta pottery and human and animal figurines were evidently widely used, based on their frequency and distribution. But close study also reveals local variation, for example in the proportion of each specific animal or abstract motif on its pottery, seals, and other artifacts.

Significantly, Indus people created a unique writing system that represented key aspects of the world around them, including distinctive animals. Using hot-fired (and thus whitened) engraved steatite (soapstone), they created square seals (more than 4,000 have been found so far). When pressed into soft clay that then dried hard, the seals probably identified ownership. Some clay shows indentation patterns from woven cloth on the back, suggesting that the seals were on bundles of goods. These seals also customarily had a loop on the obverse, probably for grasping or a suspending string for the neck or a wall peg. Many seals not only had concave inscriptions, usually around five characters each, but also stylized images of select animals, some in static poses and others in apparent narrative motifs (see Figures 3.1a and 3.1b). City-gateway signboards and tablets show writing as well

Frustratingly, the Indus writing system has yet to be decoded. Despite approximately 400 individual characters, most writing appears to be names and so lacks the grammar that would enable decipherment. Nor has there been found a Rosetta-stone equivalent, with the same words in the Indus characters and in a known script. Scholars have tried in vain to find similarities or common origins between the Indus writing system and that of the nearest other contemporary civilization, in Mesopotamia. Further, instead of the flat-faced Indus seals, the Mesopotamian culture used tubular seals that were rolled to produce repeated patterns. Nor have

(a)   (b)

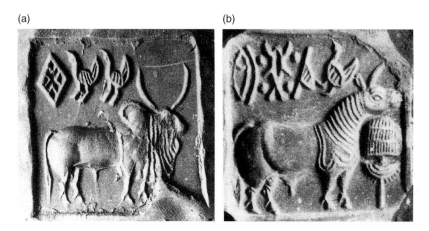

Figure 3.1a and 3.1b Clay impressions from Indus seals

archaeologists agreed about the cultural meanings of the many Indus terra-cotta figurines, and few stone or metal statues that have survived. So, the Indus civilization's understanding of its environment remains unknown.

Nonetheless, careful analysis of representations of animals on seals and as figurines – combined with pollen, sediment, and deep-sea coring analysis and radiocarbon dating – reveals that the regional environment was much wetter than at present. Some images are direct, anatomically correct depictions of actual creatures (including livestock). In contrast, bones in waste pits and figurines show they also kept dogs and pigs, but these were not depicted on seals. Some animals on seals, like the rhinoceros, crocodile (*Gavialis gangeticus*), and antelope, seem to have been common locally, while others, like the elephant, seem to have been culturally significant but rare (since no bones have been found there). Other seal and figurine images are unrealistic combinations of several animals (e.g. tiger stripes on an animal with a bull's horns). Additionally, some images depict animals in a cultural setting. For example, one recurrent image has a humped bull or bull-like unicorn standing in front of an elaborate object (which different scholars have variously identified as a manger from which the creature is eating, a lamp, a brazier, or a sacrificial altar for ritual slaughter). The civilization also occasionally made images of trees, which some commentators interpret as evidence of worshiping a sacred grove, or nature generally. Clearly, the Indus people were not just copying animals and plants; they were creatively transforming faunal and floral forms for their own cultural purposes.

The Indus economy also moved natural materials in both semi-processed and processed forms beyond its region, including overseas through trade. Adjacent to but outside the Indus core area were marginal villages that evidently served as cultural and economic gateways. They differed from the cities of the heartland not only in their ecologies but also somewhat in cultural practices. There, Indus traders interacted with local hunter-gatherers, exchanging ceramics, metal artifacts, and domesticated animals and grains for valuable local raw materials (such as semiprecious stones for making beads and seals).

Further, port cities on the Arabian and Mesopotamian shores of the Persian Gulf clearly received minerals, grains, and artisanal goods from Indus cities, probably traded for dates and other locally extracted raw materials. Burial mounds in today's Bahrain contain lapis lazuli and other stone artifacts that can be traced chemically to quarries in the mountains surrounding the Indus. Possible examples of the Mesopotamian seals have been found in Indus sites, and what may be adaptations or copies of some Indus seals have been excavated in Mesopotamian sites. Mesopotamian records indicate that the level of trade reached many tons of copper annually. These texts seem to call the Indus region Meluhha and laud its etched carnelian beads, shell and steatite ornaments, wheel-thrown ceramics, ivory, copper, cotton, wool, silk, jute, cloth, barley, and oil. Metal and stone products like agate beads, evidently sourced in the Indus region, have been found in Central Asia and Turkey.

Identifying the biological origins of the Indus people is difficult. But their extensive trading networks and some limited physical evidence suggests some immigration and ethnic diversity. The vast majority of the Indus people processed their dead through cremation not burial, so the few cemeteries that have been excavated would not seem to be representative of the main population. So far, no usable DNA from these skeletons has been found. But the specific ecology in which a person (or animal) grows leaves permanent chemical traces. Thus, minerals in the early-forming teeth and bones show that many came to the Indus region after childhood. So, perhaps these skeletons were immigrants, or sojourner traders or transporters, who were interred in wooden or stone coffins, often with food and some other simple grave goods, according to their own exogenous traditions. Little valuable jewelry or metal ornaments, however, was put into most graves, so it appears that these individuals either did not possess much or else it was given or taxed away.

The contributing causes of the decentralization and decline of the Indus civilization after 700 years are also complex and not yet fully understood. A range of independent sources (using paleobotany, paleozoology, and geology) combine to show the Indus region became more arid from c. 2000 BCE onward, with a possible sudden reduction in total rainfall (especially the southwest monsoon) and decrease in the Indus River's flow volume. For instance, pollen residues show both an increasing proportion of millet and other drought-resistant crops and also shifts in the wildflower mix. Skeletons of Central Asian two-humped camels (*Camelus bactrianus*), horses, and donkeys began to appear, also suggesting a long-term drying climate. But such agricultural coping and adaptation had limits. One theory is that the Indus people used so much timber for building and fuel that they deforested the region, contributing to dehydration and fertile topsoil erosion. Additionally, geological evidence indicates uplift along the coast, part of the continuing smashing of the Indian tectonic plate into Asia. This would have shifted, reduced, or terminated the flow of key rivers into the Persian Gulf, causing the hydroclimatic stresses of swamping or desiccation upstream. Tributaries of the Ghaggar-Hakra were apparently captured by other river systems, including the Ganges system to the northeast (today the Ghaggar-Hakra can be traced only in subsurface remnants). All this would also have inhibited riverine trade as well as agriculture. Cultural factors, like the exhaustion of innovative energies or disillusionment with the Indus package that bound together its many cities, may have also occurred.

As a consequence of these multiple forces (and perhaps others not yet discovered), the main Indus cities began to be abandoned after c. 1900 BCE (the beginning of the Localization Era). Urban order and infrastructure clearly declined. For instance, after centuries of fixed plots, some houses encroached into the streets. The upper levels of brick walls lacked the long-sustained high quality of materials and workmanship. No new seals or pots with Indus character inscriptions or cubical chert weights were created. Bioarchaeological evidence in the few cemeteries show increasing patterns of infectious diseases (including lesions consistent with leprosy and tuberculosis) and also higher levels of interpersonal violence (Robbins Schug et al. 2013). Overseas commerce evidently declined since fewer Indus trade goods and references appear in the Arabian Peninsula or Mesopotamia. While many smaller towns and villages persisted in the Indus region, they participated much less in intraregional and transregional commerce as their economy and society reverted to local levels. Some shifted away from settled agriculture to depend more on pastoralism. Clearly, the complex relationships among the people of the Indus cities and the changing environment around them altered significantly.

But, while the Indus civilization dispersed, its people did not die out, and much of their culture probably also survived in India (although there is not yet definitive genetic evidence linking the Indus with today's south or north Indians). However, the Dravidian language family of the southern Deccan and peninsular South India may have derived from the language of the Indus civilization. Strikingly, the Brahui community still living in the hills northwest of the Indus plain (in today's Balochistan region) also speak a Dravidian language; they may either be a vestige of the Indus culture that continued there or else a later immigration from South India. Additionally, Indus-style Painted Gray Ware pottery was made in the Gangetic basin from c. 1200 to 700 BCE. As the next chapter shows, dating roughly from 600 BCE, there was a second rise of Indian urbanization supported by intensifying agriculture and trade that was centered in the Gangetic plain. The technology of fired-brick making and the geometry of their placement in rituals and urban construction there may have its roots in the Indus civilization. Thus, the biological and cultural influences of the Indus civilization evidently continued to be vital components of India's environmental history down to the present.

The People of the Vedas

When any species enters a new ecosystem, it brings specific behavioral and genetic characteristics but also may have to adapt (to lesser or greater degrees) in order to thrive. For humans, culture can be acclimatized more quickly than through the multigenerational genetic "natural selection" process of adaptation. Communities carry their own knowledge and values, but they also learn from each other and compete. Further, humans are all the same species, so interacting communities inevitably mix genetically, making phenotype differences unstable.

Around 1500 BCE, bands of pastoralists from west-central Asia, speaking Vedic-Sanskrit (an Indo-European family language), began moving through the Khyber and other passes into the upper Indus and then Gangetic plains. The period of drying climate that evidently overstressed the Indus cities' economy made the north Indian plains especially suited to pastoralists. Until the mid-twentieth century, some historians thought that the Indus cities had been conquered by invading Vedic people, since their oral tradition mentions destroying cities. But that theory has now been largely discredited since there is no convincing archaeological evidence. Further, the Vedic bands seem to have migrated into India through an incremental process, not as an invading wave and not until centuries after the Indus civilization had already localized into scattered towns and villages.

As long as the Vedic-Sanskrit speaking bands remained nomadic pastoralists, they did not leave archaeological evidence like buildings or artifacts. They evidently cremated their dead, so there are no graves containing skeletons (although today's genetic testing can help reconstruct migration and intermarriage histories). But some among these incoming pastoralist bands created sacred hymns, which collectively comprise a body of oral texts they named collectively the *Veda* (body of "sacred knowledge").

For almost 4,000 years down to the present, dedicated people, mostly Brahmin men, have devoted themselves to memorizing Vedas. Many have internalized every sound perfectly, with every syllable precisely intact, and are able to start at any single point in a text and then recite it forwards and backwards. Major parts of what is known today as Hinduism are largely based on this Vedic foundation; some Vedic hymns are still chanted as vital components of Brahminic Hindu rituals, including weddings and funerals. Hence, the Vedas comprise the longest continuously used body of sacred texts in human history and are an unmatched source for this early period's environmental history. Each hymn can tell historians much about how its author and community conceptualized and valued various natural forces, lands, plants, animals, as well as other human communities during that prehistoric time.

The *Rig Veda* contains 1,028 poetic hymns totaling some 10,600 verses.[2] They are arranged into ten books, with the middle six known as the family books, since each was preserved by a particular lineage. These six appear to be the oldest, since their language is earliest, and they describe related clans starting to migrate into northwestern India. These hymns seek to placate deities, each identified as a powerful natural force – including the sun (Surya), wind (Vayu), dawn (Ushas), the bull (Parjanya), and fire (Agni). Collectively they are the "shining ones" (*Deva*; this Indo-European term also appears as the Greek *theos* and Latin *deus*).

The invincible Deva war leader was the fierce, black-bearded Indra (god of stormy rainclouds), wielding lightning bolts in the form of a mace. In this, he appears comparable to other Indo-European warrior deities: Zeus (for ancient Greeks) and Thor (for ancient Scandinavians). The authors of some early Vedic hymns call upon Indra to guide them to victory against other clans of Arya ("the noble people," as the Vedic clans called themselves). In the oldest hymns, another group of divinities were the Asura (sometimes described as the elder brothers or father of the Deva). But later hymns portray the Asura as evil demons whom Indra

---

[2] In addition to the *Rig Veda*, there are three other collections of Vedas that highlight respectively the rituals of sacrifice to divine beings (*Yajur Veda*), provide the rhythmic models for recitation of the hymns (*Sama Veda*), and contain charms, spells, and medical guidance (*Atharva Veda*).

strips of their powers, supporters, and resources (including water, mountains, and cattle).

Significantly, this chronological shift also suggests growing human conflict between those Indo-European clans entering India and those migrating into Iran, despite the shared origin of their cosmologies. As the Zoroastrian religion developed in Iran, its divinities were Ahura and the demons were Daeva. Thus, as these communities separated and conflicted, their religious traditions did as well with the gods of each becoming the demons of the other.

Further, the Vedas reveal much about the clans' material culture and relationship to animals. They had some gold, but it was one of the few measures of wealth other than knowledge of the Vedas and their livestock. They evidently had goats, donkeys, and dogs (some trained to hunt boar). Cattle were especially highly valued. Cow's milk was savored, including in a heated drink, so the Vedic people were evidently not lactose intolerant as adults, unlike many East Asians. Indeed, *ghi* (clarified butter) was the essence of milk, worthy of offering to the gods. Cows themselves were dedicated as the very highest sacrifices.

These clans had also mastered horses (which flourish in Central Asia but find the Indian environment unhealthy). Like Indra, they used horses to pull three-wheeled chariots, especially when charging into battle. The hymns describe halters and harnesses, but not horseshoes or stirrups or saddles, so they may not customarily have ridden horseback. Charioteers and other warriors had quivers full of feathered arrows with bone or bronze metal heads, sometimes poison-covered, shot from powerful bows.

Early Vedic hymns largely describe pastoralist communities. Like tribes everywhere, they apparently did not have much internal social differentiation, except that elders were honored, and men and women tended to contribute in different ways to the community. Some men seem to have specialized as warriors in protecting the community and in capturing cattle and other resources. Some people devoted themselves to composing and reciting the Vedic hymns to obtain divine favor and gifts. Since some hymns apparently produced the desired result, the reciters preserved and passed these on to students. The Vedic deity Varuna was an early model of the moral and religious leader among the gods, and perhaps also a model for these emerging human priests with expertise in rituals as well. These priests also mastered the transforming power of fire, which can turn raw, imperfect things into cooked, finished ones, both creating food for the gods and purifying dead bodies through cremation.

Later Vedic hymns, evidently composed c. 1000 BCE, show these clans settling in Gangetic north India and trading, contending, and mixing with the other communities already living there and jointly affecting the material world around them. Warfare between their deities and the deities of other groups recurs frequently. Many poems call upon Indra to defeat the demonic Virtra ("shoulderless serpent" or "son of a spider"). When Indra defeats Virtra, Indra frees for his own people the rivers, cows, forests, and mountains that the demon has hidden away for his followers, known as the Dasa and Pani.

These superhuman conflicts probably reflect the environmental history of the Vedic clans as they migrated into India and encountered other communities. The Dasa seem to be settled farmers, probably cultural and biological descendants of the dispersed Indus civilization. Thus, to the Vedic clans, Indra was liberating the water and land from Virtra's Dasa followers who had barred their herds from them. Perhaps Dasa communities regarded the Vedic herders as encroaching on their irrigation systems and crops. Often in human world history, there are conflicts between nomadic "free range" herders and settled "sod-busting" farmers over resources, with each considering the lifeways and cultural values of the other communities as inferior. Eventually, the Vedic culture dominated. The word "Dasa" eventually comes to mean slave, but not in the sense of dehumanizing race-based chattel slavery as practiced, for example, in the post-European-conquest Americas. Rather, one can proudly be a slave or devotee of a god, as in Indradasa ("slave or devotee of Indra") a Hindu name used today.

The Pani appear in later Vedic hymns as groups that emerge from forests to raid and carry off cattle. So, this may be the Vedic name for forest-dwellers they encountered and classed among types of predatory creatures that erupted from dangerous wilderness. We do not have surviving sources showing the forest-dweller's perspective, but the long history of these communities often involved raiding and as well as trading with outsiders.

Most scholars assert that new Vedic texts continued to be composed until c. 600 BCE. Bands of Vedic-Sanskrit-speaking peoples had gradually migrated into north and central India, encountered India's diverse ecological regions, and mixed with communities already living there, including forest-dwellers. Linguists can calculate the probable overall speed with which Vedic-Sanskrit (like other languages) evolved by looking for datable patterns of shifts in vocabulary, phonemes, and grammar. These scholars have put Vedic hymns into a general chronological sequence with estimated composition dates. Further, scholars have plotted geographically the regions and animals mentioned in each Vedic hymn. So, when a hymn mentions a land of many rivers, this suggests that it was composed as (or after) this band emerged from the mountains into the many-rivered upper Indus region called Punjab (literally "the land of five rivers," today divided between India and Pakistan). When a hymn describes dolphins or 100-oared ships, the composer may have encountered the wide Indus River or else reached the shore of the Arabian Sea – both containing dolphin species and relatively large ships (if not literally 100-oared ones). Some later Vedic hymns mention Indian animals, including monkeys and hyenas, and specific freshwater fish species in lists of food. Indra rides an elephant, no longer a horse-chariot.

Later Vedic hymns also indicate that, as these clans settled and developed trade, their society became more complex as did their effects on the environment. These hymns describe peaceful villages, surrounded by fields, soothed by the lowing of well-fed domesticated cattle. Some people seem to have been drawn to specialist occupations that intensified transformation of natural resources.

Within the developing Vedic cosmology and priesthood, the sacrifice became the core transformative ritual. The Vedas often specify the blood sacrifice of a valued animal like a horse, with fire carrying the essence of that offering to the gods, as a powerful creative act. In one late hymn, the entire universe, in the form of a cosmic man, was dismembered and sacrificed to produce all the natural forces, the Vedas, and the orders of all beings, animal and human (*Rig Veda* 10.90; Jamison and Brereton 2014:1539–40). This monistic concept of everything emerging from the same oneness recurred in various Indian cultures. Yet, at the same time, orders of living beings were also hierarchically ranked. In particular, the four orders of humans (called *varnas* or "ritual colors") came respectively from the head (Brahmins), arms (Rajya or later Kshatriya), loins (Vaishya), and feet (Shudra) of this cosmic being. Today, the first three varnas contain only about 20 percent of the Hindu population, while members of the Shudra varna comprise over half. The remaining quarter of the settled population had no varna, and elites historically called them "the fifth order," "outcastes," or "untouchables." Forest-dwellers also had no varna rank. However, any essential distinctions between the divine and the human, among humans, and between humans and animals, are all negated by what became the philosophy of *advaita* ("nondualism," monism) that still lies at the core of much of Hindu thought.

Analyzing the spatial and chronological structure of an important Vedic Srauta, or "higher" sacrifice, suggests how the Vedic people represented their environment and broad historical migration patterns. In such rituals, many different priestly specialists participated, conducted by a leading priest called the Brahmin. This ritual continues to be performed today, although very rarely.

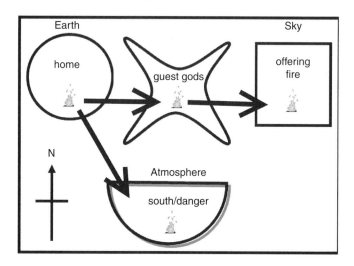

Figure 3.2 Vedic sacrificial site plan

The sacred site contains four altars made of clay (see Figure 3.2). In the west is the home altar, made circular to represent Earth. This is where the ritual specialists guide the sacrificer to kindle his household fire. Then, the fire ritually moves eastward, first to the site where the divinities are invited to be fed pure substances like ghi and *soma*. The southern semi-circular altar represents the atmosphere, which protects against danger-ous forces. Finally, the fire moves fully eastward to a square altar, representing the sky. Some scholars interpret this movement of the ritual fire as representing eastward migration into India's physical environment by the Vedic clans, with danger coming from the south.

Such later Vedic rituals required the construction of mathematically complex clay-brick foundations, typically in the form of a vast bird. This bird, able to move between earth and sky, would ritually convey the sacrifice, and the sacrificer, to heaven. However, the Vedic clans did not have their own developed tradition of geometry or expertise in building out of bricks. The Indus civilization, however, did. So, these altars and the structure of the vast bird may indicate how the Vedic tradition absorbed the knowledge and artisanal skills of the remnants of the Indus culture.

Further, today's genetic evidence indicates that there was intermar-riage among Vedic clans and local people. What emerged across north India, therefore, was a composite culture, although Sanskrit and Sanskrit-derived languages tended to dominate there. However, today people speak distinct, regionally based languages (with thousands of local dialects) and are largely biological descendants (in different proportions) of all three sources: Vedic, Indus, and forest-dweller.

In contrast, the four major (Dravidian) languages of South India are not derived from Sanskrit, and thus not part of the Indo-European language family. This suggests that the descendants of Vedic communities did not migrate as much into that region. And those who did either remained a small but distinctive minority, often preserving Sanskrit, or else merged into the local communities, which may be more heavily descended from the people who left the Indus region as that civilization's capacity to control its environment declined.

Divergent retrospective readings of the Vedas have been shaped by the beliefs of later interpreters. According to many believing Hindus today, the Vedas collectively are uncreated Truth, the entire universe in the form of sound, eternally beyond human historical time. In this model, ancient sages, known as Rishi, were so in harmony with the cosmos that they could hear this universal knowledge. These Rishis then spoke the Vedic hymns so that other humans could also hear these sounds. Therefore, the Vedas hold sacred status as *Sruti* ("knowledge from hearing"). It is the sound of the Vedas recited that holds significance and power, not necessarily the literal meaning of its words.

In fact, since all languages shift over the centuries, at present even experts in Vedic Sanskrit can only speculate about what certain words meant originally, including specific plants or animal names. For instance, the vital ritual offering of soma (a drink which inspires ecstasy in humans and gods) was pressed from a specific vine or creeper that is not currently identifiable or available in India. So, today's Vedic practitioners openly admit that they must use a substitute plant (which lacks the same ecstatic effects on humans).

Nonetheless, many Hindu nationalists believe passionately that India is their primordial and eternal homeland. They hold that Vedic hymns have preserved knowledge of an ancient, ideal Indian society with morality, technology, and other achievements that far surpass any other culture, even those of the twenty-first century. Such believers do not recognize as valid any scholarly reconstruction of chronological immigration patterns or the evolution of cultural conceptions about the local environment in sequentially produced Vedic texts.

There are many contemporary environmental implications of these divergent readings of the Vedas. For example, the Indian government led by the Hindu nationalist Bharatiya Janata Party used its Hindutva ("Hindu-ness") interpretation of the eternal Vedas to shape its official "Nationally Determined Contribution" for the 2015 United Nations Framework Convention on Climate Change Conference of the Parties in Paris (see Chapter 12). This document's epigram cites the *Veda*: "Unto Heaven be Peace, Unto the Sky and the Earth be Peace, Peace be unto the Water, Unto the Herbs and Trees be Peace." The text then asserts "India has a long history and tradition of harmonious co-existence between man and nature. Human beings here have regarded fauna and flora as part of their family." This thus locates Indians (presupposed as Hindus, the official religion of some 80 percent of the Republic of India's citizens, totaling about a billion people) as morally blameless throughout eternity for causing any damage to the environment.

But many South Asian and non-South Asian scholars have questioned this essentialist reading of the Vedas and of Hinduism's sacred harmony with nature. Conflicts between such fundamentally different ideologies, for instance, arise when sacred rivers like the Ganges are believed by many Hindus to be sacredly purifying, indeed beyond any possible pollution. In contrast, environmentalists show the Ganges and many other rivers to be dangerously polluted in scientific and public health terms.

The emerging community in each region developed its own distinct culture, including cuisine based on the local flora and fauna, and language. All this produced a range of composite cultures and genealogies, as well as some settled, urban-based states by c. 600 BCE, forming the foundation for the next phase in India's environmental history, which the next chapter considers.

4 The Environment and Forest-Dweller, Late Vedic, Hindu, Jain, Buddhist, and Dravidian Cultures, Societies, and States (c. 600 BCE – c. 800 CE)

Over the final five centuries BCE and first eight centuries CE, India's physical landscape and Holocene climate continued to shift dynamically, but not as rapidly or intensely as earlier. The monsoon pattern was well established, although its intensity varied annually due to global atmospheric forces. The massive Himalayan uplift and expansive glaciation slowed. India's major rivers had largely settled in their courses, although with short-term floods and long-term meanderings from siltation. Hence, due to the relatively moderate climate changes during the first millennium of this period, major variations in flora and fauna species became ever more subject to gradually expanding and intensifying human actions within each of India's diverse regions. Then, starting c. 500 CE, El Niño events rose in frequency, causing regional droughts and weaker monsoons overall, which contributed to economic and political contractions.

Around 600 BCE, regionally based communities, which descended from intermixing forest-dweller, Indus, and Vedic cultures, were still quite small and scattered unevenly across India. Over time, each developed its own distinctive attitudes and engagements with its local environment. Some communities mainly lived in forests, hunting, gathering, and using swidden agriculture. Pastoralists herded animals across the most productive grasslands and thinner forests, although some bands practiced seasonal agriculture as well. In fertile river plains and valleys, settled farmers gradually cleared forest or grassland for fields, and drove off what they considered predatory creatures – human, animal, and "demonic." As regional economies and states grew, some increasingly mined coal, iron, and other minerals, while artisans forged tools and weapons with more powerful effects on trees, land, animals, and other people. Traders and merchants exchanged animals, plants, minerals, and artisanal products within and among regions. These communities and their ways of life competed for resources and status, including through raiding and warfare. But they also complemented each other's economies and exchanged ideas about their environment and technologies for manipulating it. Indigenous and incoming species of plants and animals that humans favored (or inadvertently created favorable habitats for) thrived while others lost out.

In various regions, communities diversified internally, developing different degrees of social and political hierarchies, each with a distinctive relationship to the nonhuman world. Especially in regions with more mineral or bio-resources, humans concentrated in growing towns and cities. Rising social classes sought to advance themselves in status by supporting religious teachers who synthesized and articulated cosmologies that became what we call Jainism, Buddhism, and Hinduism. These (and various later) Indian religious movements taught the essential unity of the universe, including all life forms, with each "self" moving among lives as human, animal, deity, tree, or (in some traditions) rock. The specific nature of that self, the ranked hierarchy of levels of beings, and the exact mechanism for moving among or beyond them, varied according to each religion. But nonviolence toward all other living beings became an increasingly prominent value in several Indian religious traditions.

Simultaneously, ambitious rulers asserted more control and force over their region's environment. Especially in the well-located and resource-rich middle Gangetic region of Magadha, government expanded under a series of dynasties. Most prominently, the Mauryan dynasty's Emperor Ashoka (r. 268–231 BCE) developed an imperial model that exerted unprecedented power within and beyond his home region while proclaiming Buddhist nonviolence among his subjects and imperial protection of valued animals and trees. Although his dynasty did not last, he was emulated by various later rulers across India and, indeed, much of Asia.

During the following ten centuries, economic, social, and political developments at the local, regional, and transregional levels alternately intensified and declined during short- and long-term shifts in their environments. Only occasionally could a dynasty rule transregionally, precluding any single political narrative for India as a whole. Nonetheless, a range of evidence still enables reconstruction of broad phases and patterns in India's environmental history.

Scattered archeological sites provide evidence about some local, non-elite engagements with the environment. Manipulating clay, fire, and minerals for decoration, some cultures produced their distinctive style of pottery. Due to the durability of pottery shards, they preserve cultural patterns of production technique and decoration. For instance, Painted Gray Ware pottery links the Indus civilization with later expanding farming communities on the Gangetic plain. Then, from c. 700 BCE, that style gave way in north India to "Northern Black Polished Ware," which predominated for the next five centuries – a style more delicately crafted for rising social elites in expanding towns and cities.

Additionally, environmental historians can analyze the representations of the universe produced by teachers, scholars, and rulers of several religious traditions. These sources include the last of the Vedas, the massive Sanskrit epics, and the sacred teachings of non-Brahminic religious traditions, including Jainism and Buddhism (many composed in vernacular languages). None of these texts were intended to be "history" in the contemporary Chinese or later post-Enlightenment European sense of dated chronological narratives of worldly human actions or the material world. Rather, they were largely moral and exemplary accounts, teaching ethical truths, by self-identified divinely informed authors. Nonetheless, today's historians can explore these authors' attitudes toward their environment, including their conception of the environment as a whole and the degree of protection of particular parts of that environment expected for rulers and the adherents of that religious tradition. Often, mundane details reveal the types of plants and animals present and the technologies humans used on them. Some teachings were preserved orally but, from this period onward, some were written. Thus, a diversity of sources enables us to recover key aspects of India's environmental history.

Sanskritic South Asia (c. 600 BCE onward)

After Vedic Sanskrit–speaking bands migrated into north and central India, their successive sacred texts articulate a growing spatial understanding of India's geography. They also reflect a slowly settling society adapting to, and identifying with, ecologically specific regions. Several texts describe the earth as a circular disk, with sacred Mt. Meru at the center, and four continents extending out from it, each surrounded by the great ocean on three sides (see Figure 4.1). In this innovative model, where tree and animal species define Indian space, *Jambu-dvipa* ("Land of the Rose-Apple Tree [*Syzygium cumini*]") identifies the Indian subcontinent as a single, bounded geographical entity extending south from the Himalayas (similar to today's maps).

Simultaneously, however, Sanskritic culture conceptualized distinct physical environments as defining each region within Jambu-dvipa. Best was *Madhyadesh* ("Central/Middle Land") or *Aryavarta* ("Noble People's Land"), containing inhabitable areas defined as where the blackbuck (*Antilope cervicapra*) roamed: open grasslands where water is

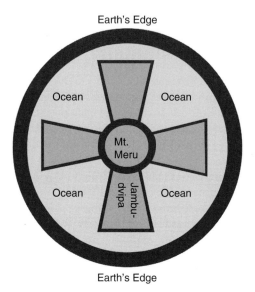

Figure 4.1 Vedic model of the cosmos

perennially available. Within Madhyadesh were internal ecological fron-tiers: *jangala* (dry scrub-forests), which could be cleared and settled; *vana* or *aranya* (forestland), which provided retreats from society for religious seekers; and *anupa* (marshes), which were to be avoided. Beyond Madhyadesh were uncongenial regions with inferior people termed *mlechha* ("uncultured," "barbarian") among other uncomplimentary names.

Late Vedic sources identify 600–700 *jana* ("people," "community," "clan"), each settled in a *jana-pada* ("people's place") in north or central India. Sanskrit texts also highlight *tirtha* (sacred "river-crossings"), sug-gesting how agricultural communities concentrated along a riverbank for drinking and irrigation water, fishing, and trade, but also the danger (and power, if mastered) of crossing over to the other shore. Gradually, each jana-pada developed its distinctive human-animal-plant ecosystem and cultural identity with a distinct Sanskrit-derived language or dialect. Dominant immigrants sometimes absorbed the preexisting population's locally powerful deities, often fierce forest goddesses or gods who both defended their devotees and punished opponents.

Expanding settled agriculture with enhanced water-control generated food surpluses. Artisans refined technologies to craft greater numbers of more sophisticated products. Trade within and among jana-padas grew, as did socioeconomic differentiation. Archaeologists are discovering

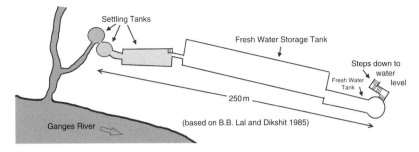

Figure 4.2 Water desiltation system (Sringaverapura, c. first century BCE)

evidence of a "second urbanization" (the Indus civilization being the first), as various jana-padas built walled cities as economic, cultural, and political centers.

Further, jana-padas varied in their political configurations. Especially on Madhyadesh's margins, an all-male council of the heads of leading families formed something like an "oligarchic republic." Only in wartime would command go to an individual "raja." However, in many other jana-padas, the raja became the hereditary king. Yet even kings depended on sponsored Brahminic sacrificial rituals that recurrently legitimated their sovereignty. The most elaborate was the *Ashvamedha* ("horse sacrifice") in which the Brahmin priest identified the king with a sacred horse. Wherever the horse roamed for a year became the king's domain. All other kings whom the horse encountered had to submit to his sovereignty (or kill the horse, discrediting the patron-king). In earthly terms, the king's army guarded (and probably guided) the horse to complete the ritual successfully. This was among an array of emerging contemporary articulations of the concept of the universal king, lord of the four quarters of the universe, to which many rajas aspired but none had yet achieved except in symbolic terms.

Archaeological evidence shows some small-scale, low-technology forms of water control for irrigation and for drinking by humans and their livestock. One of the earliest Ganges sites (see Figure 4.2) drew water out of the river into a shallow canal excavated from the soft, alluvial soil. This water was diverted into a series of three small tanks or pools where silt incrementally settled out, leaving ever-cleaner water. Similarly, communities in each region evidently created or adapted locally appropriate forms of resource harvesting (given their level of technology); people shared the maintenance and benefits, although not necessarily equally. But other, more elaborate, early dams with stone faces and sluices are of a scale suggesting at least some state sponsorship (most surviving inscriptions credit a ruler as donor).

Sanskrit-speaking religious elites sought to reconcile locally evolving cultural and social practices with the Vedas by projecting the *varnashrama* model of cosmic order. Males of the top three varnas – Brahmins, Kshatriyas, and Vaishyas – went through a ritual rebirth, becoming "twice-born." The rest of society ranked below them. Many scholars today correlate the development of the four varnas with the settlement pattern of Vedic Sanskrit-speaking clans in the Gangetic plain as Brahmins, Kshatriyas, and Vaishyas, according to their social roles. Local social groups were incorporation as Shudras. So, Brahmins, Kshatriyas, and Vaishyas form a much greater proportion of the population in north India than elsewhere. Then these twice born persuaded ambitious elites in other regions to emulate them (what Srinivas [1952] termed "Sanskritization"), spreading the varna model across much of India.

Further, the Brahminic social order identified four *ashrama* ("stages of life"). The first (mandatory for twice-born men) was as celibate student and the second (mandatory for everyone) as married householder, both within human society. Wedding rituals transformed a bride into her husband's half-body, as part of his lineage. Then, outside of settled society, religious seekers could enter the optional third state as *vana-prastha* ("retiring to a forest") or fourth as *sannyasi* ("wandering ascetic," fully removed from society and human desires).

Indeed, various texts from this period describe forests as ambiguous and liminal places, both dangerous and sacred. Forest-dwellers supplied timber and other forest products needed by the jana-pada's villages, towns, and cities. But wild predatory forest-dwellers, animals, and demons also threatened herds, crops, and the moral order of settled society. Forests could be wild, dangerous places, especially for village women as they gathered non-timber forest products (like grass and other fodder, fruits, small branches and brush for fuel). Expanding settled agriculture often meant clearing forests and driving away everything living in them, while mastering valuable forest creatures and products.

Trautmann (2015) argues that over the centuries following c. 1000 BCE, Indian rulers developed the martial institution of the war-elephant. Many ancient Indian kings built their armies around these massive and intimidating animals, which were powerful symbols of sovereignty. Some of the very earliest coins issued by Indian kings bore images of them riding royal elephants. However, creating and sustaining an elephant stable required major manpower and financial investments. Elephants do not breed well in captivity and consume massive amounts of food, even during their growing years when they are unsuitable for battle. Hence, it makes economic sense to capture and then train elephants, especially males, after physical maturity, although this is more perilous for both hunters and hunted. Consequently, rulers preserved forested wild elephant habitat and also favored forest-dwelling people skilled in capturing and taming full-grown wild elephants so as to have a continuous mature stock available. Further, kings also had to support large establishments of expert elephant attendants and drivers. Some kings patronized authors who analyzed and classified the characteristics, care, and uses in battle of elephants.

Forests were also sites of sacred power, where religious explorers in the optional third ashrama renounced society to form an *ashram* ("sylvan hermitage or retreat") and experiment with powerful but potentially dangerous ideas and practices. There, thinkers and philosophers considered the nature of *Atman* ("self"), and its relationship to *Brahman* ("the universe as an undifferentiated unity"), producing the Sanskrit *Aranyaka*s ("forest books") and *Upanishad*s ("esoteric books"). These texts (which most scholars date c. 900–500 BCE) later were labeled *Vedanta* ("the end, culmination, or goal of the Vedas").

In some Vedantic cosmographies, valued trees like the pipal (sacred fig, *Ficus religiosa*) are the dwelling place of gods, or the hairs of the cosmic being. In others, the entire universe is a tree, with its roots, trunk, and leafy crown identified as the three worlds. This *advaita* ("non-dualism," monism), which predominated in various Indian religions henceforth, contrasts with the philosophy of *dvaita* ("dualism"), the idea that the divine is separate from humans and all other parts of the manifest world.

Increasingly from c. 600 BCE onward, trade expanded within and among jana-padas, with imports of needed resources and exports of locally sourced animals, plants, raw materials, and locally produced artisanal goods. Kings authorized some artisans to create silver or copper coins with images. Such an even partially monetized economy enabled commerce to flourish. Mercantile groups and specialized artisans formed *sreni*s ("trade guilds") that collectively established codes of conduct and set prices, leading to cooperation rather than competition. To carry cash crops, hand-manufactured products, and other goods, communities of transporters and mobile traders emerged, likely from pastoralists, who linked regions economically and crossed over boundaries among forest, savanna, and agricultural areas. They loaded their cargo on the backs of bullocks and other cattle, which were not dependent on smooth roads (unlike carts or wagons) since many rulers felt no obligation to build roads or annually repair them after the torrential monsoon rains.

Yet, many people were not systematically integrated into these agriculturally based and urbanizing kingdoms. Many forest-dwellers periodically emerged to trade, as well as raid, rarely paying taxes or even tribute to outside rulers. Others migrated into the surrounding settled agricultural society, often as marginal, low-ranked groups.

Starting as early as 500 BCE, a series of mostly male Brahmin authors compiled two epic poems in literary Sanskrit: *Mahabharata* and *Ramayana*. These authors described and glorified Kshatriya martial life but also taught moral lessons about human-animal-deity interactions, thus inadvertently preserving evidence about their attitudes toward various features of their environment. The *Mahabharata* stands today at 200,000 lines, containing about 1.8 million words, the longest major poem in the world (many times the length of Homer's *Iliad* and *Odyssey* combined). As such, this complex multilayered text preserves collective memory but also reflects cultural innovations over the nine centuries of its compilation (roughly to 400 CE).

The *Mahabharata* stands as the first major work of *itihasa* ("that which happened"), a genre with many similarities to today's dominant historical genre: a sequential narration of past events mostly on earth, mostly carried out by human beings on a relatively realistic scale. However, in itihasa, no dates are given, key episodes take place in heaven, anthropomorphic Sanskrit-speaking animals are key characters, and divinities occasionally intervene, including by having offspring with human and animal partners.

"Mahabharata" literally means the great account of the ancient Bharata royal dynasty. The central narrative recounts how succession to rule over an historic northern Gangetic jana-pada was disputed between two sets of royal cousins, the Pandavas and the Kurus. The narrative ends with the mass destruction of almost the entire Bharata lineage and most of both opposing armies, marking the beginning of the Kali Yuga: the last and worst of four ages of the universe (to be followed by the end and re-beginning of time). Some historians of religion trace a shift in tone from glorifying war and conquest (in the *Mahabharata*'s chronologically oldest sections) to (in the more recent sections) violence as necessary tragedy, epitomized in the *Bhagavad Gita* section where the divine Krishna teaches Pandava Arjuna the need to perform one's own *dharma* ("code for conduct") selflessly and in personal devotion (*bhakti*) to the universal god.

One powerful early *Mahabharata* episode suggests how the dominant expanding agricultural-based society in north India treated forests and forest-dwelling beings. At this point, elder statesmen have sought to avert the looming war by dividing the disputed kingdom between the claimant cousins. The Pandavas receive as their share the wild Khandava forest. Their methods for transforming that forest into a prosperous, agriculturally rich kingdom with a glorious capital city, Indraprastha, probably reflects prevailing practice during that historical period. Agni, the Vedic (and later Hindu) god of fire, seeks to consume the entire forest as a great sacrifice, thus killing his enemy, the snake king, who is a devotee of Indra (the rival god of stormy rainclouds). But, as Agni laments: "As soon as [Indra] sees me [set this forest] ablaze, he starts raining with floods of the clouds, so that I cannot burn this wood, much as I would love to." Therefore, Agni provides invincible weapons to his devotees (Krishna and Arjuna) who incinerate the forest, causing

a vast massacre of the [forest-dwelling] creatures on every side . . . The creatures in their thousands leapt up in all ten directions, screeching their terrifying screams . . . with burning wings, eyes, and paws until they perished. As all the watery places came to a boil . . . the turtles and fish were found dead by the thousands . . . Snakes, hyenas, bears and other forest beasts, rutting elephants, tigers, full-maned lions, deer and buffalo, and hundreds of birds [died] . . . [Agni], having burned down the forest with its animals and birds for five days and one, was satiated and came to rest. (Vyasa 1973–2003, 1:415–31)

The indiscriminately slaughtered (not selectively hunted) creatures included not just animals, but also beings the *Mahabharata* calls "Nagas," meaning snakes. However, Naga was (and is still) a name for certain forest-dwelling human communities. Hence, in explicit terms, wilderness and forest beings must be subdued or destroyed by Aryas, with limitless divine power as the reward. Yet, the narrative tone suggests compassion for the suffering of forest creatures and horror at this "eco-chaos," perhaps reflecting later reforms toward nonviolence in Hinduism (Menzies 2010).

The *Mahabharata* has remained very prominent in Indian culture (and in several Southeast Asian cultures) where the general plot is widely known, and many Hindu men and women are named after leading characters. People still draw moral lessons from it. When nationalists chose the official name in Indian languages for today's independent Republic of India, they selected "Bharat." Indian economic development has historically included clearing forests for farmland, industrial raw materials, and hydroelectric reservoirs, in the process displacing forest-dwellers – human, fauna, and flora.

The somewhat shorter *Ramayana*, compiled roughly contemporaneously with the *Mahabharata*, stands as India's first major work of Sanskrit poetic literature (*kavya*). Indeed, the *Ramayana*'s first book explains how its putative author, the sage Valmiki, so identified with animal suffering that he unconsciously invented the *shloka* poetic meter (used in both epics and much later Sanskrit poetry). Seeking retreat from settled society, Valmiki had entered a forest hermitage. At a riverside, he

saw an inseparable pair of sweet-voiced *kraunca* [demoiselle cranes, *Grus virgo*] wandering about. But even as he watched, a Nishada [forest-dweller] hunter, filled with malice and intent on mischief, struck down the male of the pair. Seeing him struck down and writhing on the ground, his body covered with blood, his mate uttered a piteous cry. And the pious seer ... was filled with pity ... [and] uttered these words: "Since, Nishada, you killed one of this pair of krauncas, distracted at the height of passion, you shall not live for very long." (Valmiki 1984–2017, 1:127–28)

Valmiki then realized that his *shoka* ("grief" or "compassion") had spontaneously created the shloka meter. Brahminic lessons from this episode include: personal empathy with wild animals is virtuous; animals share human emotions; and forest-dwellers who wantonly kill animals deserve punishment.

The *Ramayana*'s central story line has Prince Rama (divine Vishnu incarnated) and his wife, Princess Sita (daughter of the Earth Mother goddess and Vishnu's wife), enduring forest exile for fourteen years. Some scholars locate their journey going south from the Gangetic plain into the Deccan, but popular understanding has these exiles travel to the peninsular tip of India. The demonic King Ravana abducts Sita from their woodland encampment. Rama recruits local forest-dwellers (described as monkeys and bears), defeats Ravana's demons, and eventually rescues Sita. Here too, the north Indian–based community describes other beings as animals (if subordinate allies) or demons (if hostile).

The authors of both epics present wilderness in polyvalent terms. One meaning is a dangerous, chaotic space. As Rama proclaims, "The name 'forest' [*kantaram*] is given only to wild regions where hardships abound" (Valmiki 1984–2017, 2:136–37). But, throughout the *Mahabharata* and *Ramayana*, settled society can turn wild forest creatures into gate-guardians, secondary wives, or devoted servants, without losing their raw power. Additionally, humans can transform the forest into supranatural, hybrid forms as a garden, that can serve as a romantic, sensuous arena for lovers:

Rama ... entered the *asoka* ["without sorrow"] grove. It was adorned on every side with sandalwood trees, aloe trees, mangos ... Some of the trees there shone like gold, some resembled flames of fire, while others were as dark as black collyrium ... Rama's grove, which he had created, was ... endowed with many seats and dwellings, and was filled with bowers of creepers. And he sat down on a beautifully formed seat, adorned with bunches of flowers .... (Valmiki 1984–2017, 7:331–32)

As cities developed over this period, gardens became places where control over tamed nature was exerted by kings and rich merchants. Indeed, Rama combines his ordering of plants with his virtuous ordering of the human world through his reign: *Ram Rajya* (still the premier Hindu vision of moral government).

Alternative Universal Models: Jainism and Buddhism (c. 600 BCE onward)

From the sixth century BCE onward, India's shifting social, cultural, political, and economic environments produced various models of and for the universe. The two most prominent new movements coalesced as Jainism and Buddhism. These new religions had roughly contemporary founders as role models: Mahavira Jain (variously dated 600/540–527/468 BCE) and Siddhartha Gautama the Buddha (c. 560 – c. 480 BCE). Both were born Kshatriya men, raised surrounded by pleasures, who abandoned family, wealth, and sensuality by withdrawal of the senses and thus attained release from the cycle of rebirth, redeath, and rebirth. Mahavira devoted himself to the path of extreme asceticism to burn off the material residue of action (*karma*). Gautama, in contrast, renounced asceticism and preached the Middle Way of selfless giving. Both men left behind monastic orders (*sangha*): men and women who sought to escape earthy existence into absolute transcendence and peace (*nirvana*).

While Jainism and Buddhism differed in their metaphysics (about the nature of the self, for instance) both regarded human and animal bodies as just varying levels of birth, ranging from imperceptible motes through animals and humans to deities. For instance, in the Buddhist *Jataka*s (accounts of the Buddha's previous lives), he was born as variously elephant, tiger, monkey, rabbit, tree god, and in a variety of human roles (but always as a male, perhaps suggesting the gender attitudes of the compilers). As the Buddha, he achieved nirvana under the *Bodhi* fig tree in Bodhgaya (Bihar); pilgrims still reverently identify this tree with his enlightenment.

These two religious movements advocated similar social structures for humans, with individual achievement of total nonviolence and compassion toward all living creatures as the basis of status. They thus critiqued Brahminic sacrifice of animals via fire to the gods and birth into a varna. Instead, highest in the Jain human social order are monks and nuns, committed totally to nonviolence. Ideally, they cover mouth and nose with a fine cloth, to avoid breathing in the smallest life form suspended in the air. Drinking water is strained to remove all living things. They eat only the most purely nonliving foods like unsprouted grain, and never in the dark when unperceived insects might be consumed inadvertently. When walking, the ground is gently swept to avoid stepping on any being. Next highest in Jain society are laypeople who practice nonviolence as best they can while living in the world, perhaps to join the sangha later in life. Lowest in society are people who do not follow the Jain teachings and practice killing or other violence, including Brahmin priests, Kshatriya warriors, Shudras, and forest-dwelling hunters.

In the Buddhist social model, people are ranked according to *dana* (from the same Indo-European root-word as "donation" in English) – that is, how much they give, in the broadest sense, including repudiating violence on anything in the environment. Monks and nuns give up everything, donating their lives to following the nonviolent path of *dhamma* (the popular Pali-language form of Sanskrit's dharma). So, they rank the highest. But laypeople can also follow the Middle Way, to the extent that they are able. Consequently, any individual who practices nonviolence and dana could rise socially and morally.

Much of the initial support for Jainism and Buddhism initially came from groups and individual men and women who found the Brahminic order unpersuasive, particularly since it ranked them low and seemed so identified with violence. This included upwardly mobile merchants who could live without themselves killing and also donate much wealth. Additionally, some Shudras and other non-Kshatriyas who had fought their way to kingship sought to harness the economic and political power of these thriving merchants. To advance their personal and imperial goals, Mauryan Emperor Chandragupta famously turned to Jainism while his grandson Emperor Ashoka turned to Buddhism.

The Mauryan Dynasty in Magadha and Beyond (320–187 BCE)

Already by c. 600 BCE, sixteen *mahajana-padas* ("great people's places") had emerged across India through conquest and consolidation of the earlier 600–700 jana-padas. Smaller jana-padas still survived in their own home regions, but as provinces within these sixteen larger states (thirteen in the extended Ganges basin, two in Afghanistan, one in the northern Deccan). Then, over the next century, five even larger maha-jana-padas arose through coalescence and conquest. One seems to have been governed by a council, the other four, including Magadha, by a hereditary raja as king. Over time, the Mauryan dynasty brought multiple ecological and cultural regions into India's first empire by mobilizing human and nonhuman resources while combining persuasive cultural

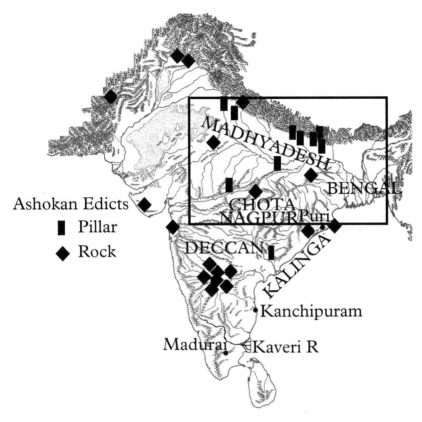

Ashokan Edicts
 ▮ Pillar
 ◆ Rock

MADHYADESH

BENGAL

CHOTA
NAGPUR Puri

DECCAN

KALINGA

•Kanchipuram

Madurai ◆Kaveri R

Map 4.1 India at the time of Ashoka Maurya (r. 268–231 BCE)

appeals with a burgeoning army and administration (see Maps 4.1 and 4.2).

The Magadha region of the middle Ganges plain (today India's Bihar province) is particularly well endowed with mineral and bio-resources. For centuries, the Ganges River and its tributaries have been eroding soil from the Himalayan mountains and the upper Gangetic plain and depositing alluvial silt in Magadha (and Bengal downstream). Himalayan glaciers keep these rivers flowing perennially, even in the driest months. Abundant groundwater lies not far below the land's surface. Additionally, the southwest monsoon's rainfall supplements these other water sources. But, Magadha has historically suffered fewer floods and less destruction from cyclones than Bengal.

So, Magadha held much economic and political potential. As people increasingly settled during this moderate climatic period,

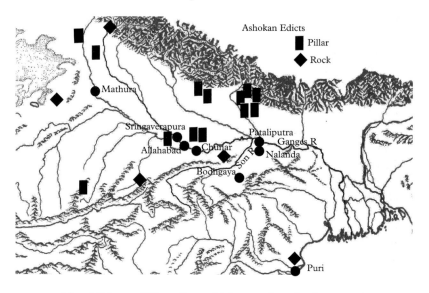

Map 4.2 Inset of Magadha and Mauryan heartland

they turned savanna and forests into fields, incorporating or pushing away pastoralists and forest-dwellers. Enterprising farmers learned how to manage the water and soil to cultivate wet rice, even mastering the multistage method and specific varieties of rice for producing two harvests annually. This requires farmers to start the second rice crop in nursery fields, even before the first has been harvested from the main fields. Then, farmers must carefully transplant seedlings right after the main fields are harvested. In addition, rice takes much nutrition from the surrounding water, so being dried out stunts the growth of, or kills, many varieties. However, too much water flow flushes away plants or drowns most varieties. So, farmers must slope each field exactly, sometimes with elaborate terracing, and must manage the water supply throughout the growing season.

All this huge investment of labor and expertise in controlling the environment results in harvests about three times larger than dry crops like wheat, millet, or barley. The surplus sustained higher population density and fostered commerce. Further, wet rice farmers often submit to higher tax rates than do farmers of dry crops that require relatively less commitment to their fields, making them more willing to flee heavy revenue demands. So, whoever ruled the Magadha region during this period had an especially concentrated and valuable agriculture, denser population, and more valuable revenue base.

Thus, Magadha's ruler could employ more men in public works and warfare, especially during seasons when crops needed less intensive labor. In addition, the king's enhanced income allowed him to hire a core of full-time professional soldiers. So, his army could extract further resources from farmers and forest-dwellers in and around Magadha and from neighboring jana-padas.

The mountainous and hilly areas nearby were natural habitat for wild elephants. Magadha's rulers obtained these elephants by taxation, trade, or raids from forest-dweller communities who had mastered the difficult and dangerous expertise of elephant catching and taming them for war or transportation. In addition to elephants, forest-dwellers enriched Magadha and its ruler by exchanging timber and other forest produce for cultivated grains, artisanal goods, and other city- or town-made products. Further, these same areas (especially the Chota Nagpur plateau) contain coal, iron ore, and other minerals. These resources enabled artisans in Magadha's growing towns and walled cities to smelt and forge high-quality iron and steel, producing tools, weapons, and other artifacts. These hand-manufactured products were used in Magadha and profitably exported to other, less well-endowed regions. This intra- and inter-regional commerce especially benefited Magadha's merchants, who generated wealth for themselves and loans and taxes for the king.

Many ambitious merchants rejected the relatively low status assigned to them in the Brahminic varna system and sought alternative religious and social models. Magadha lay beyond the Madhyadesh heartland of Brahmanism, so non-Vedic models arose more easily. Gautama the Buddha gained followers in Magadha; Mahavira personally taught and then gained nirvana there.

Chandragupta (r. 320 – c. 298 BCE) led a rebellion that seized power in Magadha and founded the Maurya Dynasty. He located his capital Pataliputra (today's Patna) at an especially strategic trading and defensive location, on the south bank of the Ganges where the Son River joined it. The actual origins of the Maurya family remain uncertain, but consensus holds that Chandragupta was low-born. One popular account asserts he was the previous king's son by a low-ranked queen or concubine and overthrew his royal half-brothers. Maurya means "peacock," and some Jain texts identify his family as low peacock herders, ranked by Brahmans as Shudra at best. Alternatively, he may have arisen from a clan having the peacock as its totem (but since his grandson regularly dined on peacocks, this is less likely).

Chandragupta also benefited from dramatic events on India's western frontier, nearly 2,000 km (1,250 mi) away. The dynamic Persian Achaemenid Empire had long extended its power up to the Indus

River. Indeed, Indian war elephants and soldiers had fought in Persian imperial armies as far west as Greece. But Alexander of Macedonia (r. 336–23 BCE) rapidly conquered the Achaemenids. By 327 BCE, he had led his army across the Indus, and subdued Punjab's rajas in bloody and exhausting campaigns. Finally, the Greek core of Alexander's army convinced him to return westward. His army's martial migrations left behind many distant colonies that amalgamated Greek and local cultures and biological descendants. These cities enhanced trade routes linking Greece, Egypt, and India, along which many subsequent people, ideas, goods, and animals would travel in both directions for centuries thereafter. Magadha lay at the eastern end of this new intercontinental trade network, so it prospered as its economy was further stimulated.

Additionally, Chandragupta expanded into the political disorder that Alexander's invasion created in India's northwest. There, Chandragupta fought for years (until 303 BCE) against Alexander's successor in Asia, Seleucus Nicator (r. 323–281 BCE). Finally, a truce treaty gained Chandragupta the daughter of Seleucus as a bride and also rule as far west as Balochistan and Kabul. In exchange, Chandragupta gave Seleucus 500 war elephants and their Indian trainers (both then highly valued by Mediterranean rulers).

Chandragupta's many military and diplomatic conquests extended his overlordship further than any previous Indian ruler: from Afghanistan to Bengal and from the Himalayas down into the northern Deccan. But his administration lacked the technology and infrastructure to penetrate very deeply into society outside of Magadha. Either as a rejection of his low varna rank in Brahminic society, or to gain the support of increasingly influential and wealthy merchants, or from personal conviction (perhaps recoiling from his many bloody wars), Chandragupta reportedly abdicated after more than two decades on the throne and became a Jain monk. Jain texts describe how he devoted himself to total nonviolence toward all living beings and fasted to death, thus burning off the bad karmic matter from his many acts of violence.

By 268 BCE, Chandragupta's grandson Ashoka seized Magadha and its subordinate provinces. Then he used force to crush people who opposed him but also developed an imperial culture that attracted their adherence to his regime. Ashoka's own inscriptions tell how, eight years into his reign, he conquered Kalinga (today India's Odisha province). Then, as now, many communities lived in its forested interior hills. As Ashoka regretfully confessed (perhaps exaggerating), his armies killed 100,000 local people, deported or enslaved 150,000, and starved even more. Consequently, he remorsefully turned to Buddhism. Ashoka also credits one of his most charitable queens, Karuvaki, for guiding him toward Buddhism.

Claiming universal empire in the Buddhist model, Ashoka imposed his moral and physical power over the human and nonhuman environment by building an innovative and effective army, administration, and imperial culture. To foster commerce, as well as the movement of his officials and armies, Ashoka built roads across his vast empire, lined with shady trees, mango groves, and water-wells. Profitable trade in animals, plants, valuable minerals, and products made from them, expanded not just interregionally within India but also overland and overseas to Europe, Central Asia, China, Southeast Asia, and east Africa. Ashoka also erected some of India's earliest state-constructed water control structures: reservoirs for irrigation and domestic uses, often at geologically appropriate sites associated with Buddhist monasteries or *stupa*s (reliquary structures, often surmounted by the umbrella of sovereignty).

To persuade (and warn) his subjects to abide by the Buddhist morality of his regime, he erected tall stone pillars in his empire's core, often transported long distances from quarries at Chunar and Mathura (respectively in eastern and western Uttar Pradesh [UP] province of India today). On these, he had inscribed his difficult personal moral progress along the Buddhist path. For instance, he admitted struggling to make his imperial household completely vegetarian: "Formerly in the [imperial] kitchens ... many hundreds of thousands of living animals were killed daily for meat. But now ... only three animals are killed, two peacocks and a deer, and the deer not invariably. Even these three animals will not be killed in future" (Romila Thapar 1997:250). To attract and admonish people on his expanding empire's external frontiers, Ashoka had the surface of prominent rocks polished and inscribed with his edicts, occasionally in the local languages. These proclaimed that Buddhist dhamma prevailed within his borders. Ashoka also sent his representatives as far west as Greece and Egypt, bearing not only the message of Buddhism but also Indian medicinal herbs, thus contributing to their spiritual and physical health. None of his surviving edicts discusses Buddhism's more abstract, theological, or cosmological concepts, like nirvana.

Instead, Ashoka in his edicts promised to protect the poor and weak among his subjects. But he also claimed control over the empire's forests, water-bodies, and valuable animals. He specifically outlawed swidden agriculture and hunting with fire; should any forest-dwellers or villagers resist his authority, they would be executed remorselessly. Following the Buddha's message, he banned Brahminic Vedic animal sacrifices in his capital (although he evidently lacked the administrative control to stop them outside of it). Overall, Ashoka's edicts proclaim his compassion for animals, perhaps motivated by an environmental ethic (in addition to his revenue or administrative goals). Consequently, today many environmentalists evoke Ashoka as an ancient Indian exemplar.

But Ashoka's heirs could not sustain his Buddhist imperial model against regionally based warlords and kings or the reforming Brahminic tradition. The Mauryan dynasty collapsed by 187 BCE. While many subsequent kingdoms rose and fell, none achieved the Mauryan Empire's territorial extent or environmental controls for a millennium. Nonetheless, imperial Buddhism continued to attract emperors and rich merchants, especially those of non-Kshatriya birth. They earned spiritual merit and social status by making massive donations to the Buddhist sangha. Some monasteries and nunneries became seats of great scholarship, ivory towers of learning. Many in north and central India also became centers of water control, through dams and reservoirs. But Buddhism gradually lost its connections with the general populace. Although Siddhartha Gautama the Buddha lived and taught in India, Buddhism gradually died out there. Nonetheless, over the centuries, Buddhism became a world religion, spreading throughout much of Asia.

The Post-Mauryan Gangetic and Indus Plains to c. 700 CE

Following end of the Mauryan Empire, each region across northern and western India developed its own distinctive environmental history, although there were commonalities among them. A few rulers mobilized sufficient resources to expand militarily beyond their home region for a generation or two, some proclaiming themselves the Buddhist universal emperor (imitating Ashoka), but none could establish an imperial culture, army, or administration powerful enough to glue multiple regions together for very long. Amid such political instability, merchants struggled. However, when successful, royalty and merchants developed sophisticated urban lifestyles, including by constructing elaborate pleasure-gardens where they could savor tamed and restructured nature.

Among the welter of kingdoms of this millennium, the Gupta dynasty stands most prominently, for both its power over humans and natural resources and the extent of the source material about it. This family arose from uncertain origins in the early fourth century CE, established its regime in still wealthy Magadha, and ruled for two centuries. Although the Guptas favored the worship of the Hindu god Vishnu, they also patronized Buddhism. Some Gupta monarchs identified themselves with Ashoka; for example, Samudragupta (r. 335–75) had a list of his claimed triumphs over forty kings inscribed on an originally Ashokan pillar in Allahabad.

In addition to developing a powerful cultural appeal, the Guptas conquered by recruiting huge armies, mostly bow-armed infantry. Magadha supplied the iron ore, abundant coal, and metallurgy technology to make steel longbows. Unlike more traditional bamboo bows, these steel ones did not warp in the humidity of the monsoons. They could also drive an arrow accurately over long distances, with great penetrating power. Further, the jungles of the lower Ganges are a prime habitat for elephants, which Gupta kings armored and rode victoriously into battle. Despite military pressures from within and without India, the Guptas eventually built an empire that, at its peak, stretched as far west as the Indus River and as far south as Kanchipuram. Even in the Gangetic plain, however, most of this vast territory was ruled by largely autonomous kings who nominally recognized or just paid tribute to the Gupta emperor.

Under direct and indirect Gupta authority, commerce and culture expanded, benefiting many. The economy continued to monetize, which enriched bankers and moneylenders. More trade came with increased production of craft goods, so artisans prospered. With the need for more administrators, scribes, and tax collectors, those classes also rose.

Sanskrit literature also reached an aesthetic peak, preserving urbane elite attitudes toward forests and forest creatures. The two great Hindu epics, *Ramayana* and *Mahabharata*, reached their final and most polished form under Gupta patronage. The playwright Kalidasa (fl. fourth to fifth century CE) wrote widely admired sophisticated Sanskrit dramas including *Shakuntala*, the love story between a king and a forest-raised, semi-divine princess. These texts customarily presented forests variously as sites for the royal pastime of hunting, as the refuge for Brahmin ascetics, as a resource to be exploited for revenue or forest-products or tamable animals and people, or as territory to be cleared for extending agriculture.

Indian sciences advanced insightful theories about the principles underlying the cosmos. The famous center of Buddhist learning at Nalanda (in Magadha) excelled in astronomy and mathematics, evidently including the concept of zero and decimals. The Indian system of *Ayurvedic* ("health knowledge") medicine developed a holistic model of the human body and its interactions with its total environment. Each person's three *guna*s (qualities) – *sattva* (air/purity), *rajas* (fire/energy), and *tamas* (earth/heaviness) – should be in appropriate proportion according to the patient's specific gender, life-stage, social status, diet, air, water, and environment.[1] Extensive *Ayurvedic* texts then classify 360 separate disorders and list the transformative power of vast numbers of individual herbs and other substances, each with heating or cooling (strengthening or weakening) effects on a guna.

Across India, Brahmans tried to consolidate their Hindu model of society and of kingship by absorbing many of the most persuasive features of Jain, Buddhist, and other rival religious traditions and movements, especially nonviolence toward other living creatures. Brahmin teachers increasingly reinterpreted the Vedas into ways that the vast majority of India's population found more compelling, including coopting popular devotional (*bhakti*) movements and Sanskritizing forest or other local gods and goddesses as objects of Brahminic *puja* (ritual worship).

Further, largely Brahmin male scholars and courtiers wrote Sanskrit *Shastras* ("teachings" or "treatises") that each analyzed one aspect of human life and prescribed rules for its practitioners, according to their social identity. These Shastras customarily aspired to the status of a Veda and often cited Vedic verses as the basis for their exposition, but they were generally recognized only as *smrti* ("remembered knowledge" or "tradition"). Complied over centuries by a series of authors, these texts responded to challenges posed by rival religions and movements, thereby addressing stresses within their own society and the environment around them. Each had the ultimate goal of *moksha* (release from the cycle of rebirth and redeath). Each took the form of lessons by divine or divinely informed teachers about key aspects of life, including *artha* (political and material power), *natya* (the dramatic arts), and *dharma* (social morality), as well as *kama* (sensuality), *shilpa* (sculpture), and *vastu* (architecture). These Shastras also made clear that the physical environment of each region shaped its human inhabitants' distinctive complexion, hair type, dialect, and sexual practices.

Among the Shastras, the one on *artha* most extensively addressed state policy toward the material world. Although scholars reshaped this text during later centuries, its putative author, Kautilya, was popularly believed to have been the political genius behind the rise of the Mauryan dynasty. In this political model, the ruler should protect all key resources, including not only domesticated animals, human-made crafts, agriculture, mining, commerce, and society generally, but also wildlife, forests, forest produce, and water (Kautilya 2013:Book 2). There are many species of "deer, game animals, birds, [and] fish that are legally protected from harm ... living in sanctuaries" (unless they

---

[1] These three gunas were similar to the four Greek humors, suggesting possible intercontinental cultural exchanges.

"become wicked [and so] should be killed"). For instance, kings "should establish an elephant forest" and his wardens "should put to death anyone who kills an elephant." Those wardens, disguised by rubbed-on elephant dung and urine and by tree branches, "should find out the size of the elephant herds by means of clues provided by where they sleep, their footprints and dung, and the damage they have done to river banks." They should keep a written census of "elephants – those moving in herds, those roaming alone, those driven from a herd, and the leaders of herds, as well as those that are vicious or in rut, the cubs, and those released from captivity." Forest-chiefs should be made to serve the king as revenue or tribute payers and as irregular military leaders, buffering the kingdom's frontiers against enemy incursions and guarding trade routes through the forest. Additionally, kings should build dams, reservoirs, and irrigation systems, subsidize subjects who do so, exclude from the benefits any who shirk their duty, punish with death any who damage them, and reserve as state property "fish, waterfowl, and commercial vegetables" grown in them.

The four-part Brahminic varna model never fully matched social practice, as these Shastras recognized. Instead, the concept of *jati* ("birth") gradually emerged, paralleling but not exactly matching the varna model and more relevant to everyday life. Jati comes from the same Indo-European root as the Latin taxonomical term "genus," but is conceptualized in the Shastras closer to Linnaean animal or plant "species": an intrabreeding set of beings hereditarily similar in form, behavior, and diet. Each animal and plant type belongs to a distinct jati. In addition, Sanskrit texts also referred to human males and females (and sometimes a third sex) as different jatis.

Based on textual evidence from this early period and on later Hindu practice, anthropologists describe a human jati as a social group having a specific dharma that included a traditional occupation (e.g. weaver, potter, herder, temple priest, or warrior) and hierarchic rank both in the local society and also within a varna. Each jati has a specific customary diet. For instance, some are traditionally vegetarian (though for some jatis that includes eating fish). Some jatis are not vegetarians but customarily eat only certain animal species. On ritual occasions such as weddings, jati members dine commensally, with the qualities of the shared food affecting them collectively. Since all physical bodies are almost entirely composed of foods consumed, eating the same food from the same cooking pots makes all members of a jati share bodily substance. Customarily, each jati was endogamous. However, the Vedas and many later Hindu texts tolerated hypergamy: women marrying into higher-ranked families within a jati, or even into a higher-ranked jati or varna. Indeed, several recent genetic analyses show evidence of hypergamy: members of many higher jatis have relatively concentrated Y-chromosomes (male lineage) but more diverse mitochondrial DNA (received from mothers), including some associated with lower-ranked jatis (Bamshad et al. 2001; Indian Genome Variation Consortium 2005). Many jatis today claim genealogies that begin with an inter-varna marriage, including a divine father and human mother.

Anthropologists and Indian government officials today identify between 10,000 and 20,000 jatis (depending on their methodology). The median jati size is 5,000–15,000, but they range from a few dozen to millions. In practice, each jati is part of a varna, so each of the four varnas contains hundreds or even thousands of jatis. However, some jatis claim to be higher ranked or even part of a higher varna than others in society recognize.

The reasons why and when jatis developed in India alone are highly disputed. The *Dharmashastra* presupposes that varnas were primal (as were the Vedas) and then devotes much attention to the permutations of inter-varna marriages that allegedly produced the array of jatis – depending on relative status and distance between the father's and mother's varna (Manu 2004). This Brahminic model parallels the pattern recognized by today's biologists for fauna and flora, where hybridized offspring have mixed genotype and phenotype, with male and female parents making different contributions.

European "discoverers" of India from the late fifteenth century imposed their own "racial" concepts, calling both varnas and jatis as *casta* ("breeds" in Portuguese). Subsequent Europeans and Anglicized Indians applied developing European racial theories to explain "castes." Many British colonizers ranked India's "races" (and themselves) using social Darwinist ideas, which Hitler's Aryan race propaganda brought to its extreme. Even some Indian nationalists, like Jawaharlal Nehru, accepted varnas as separate "races" (Nehru 1946). But many Indian nationalists also praised India for its history of more peaceful racial coexistence that produced the "caste system," particularly in contrast to European race-based enslavement or extermination in Africa and the Americas. Further, socialist-influenced Nehru also explained jatis as the product of an economic division of labor, in which families specialized in one or another occupation, which became hereditary. Yet, Nehru and M. K. Gandhi both worked to end the caste inequalities and discrimination that marked much of Indian history.

Some leading environmental historians (Gadgil and Ramachandra Guha 1992) have argued that jatis were natural adaptations to local environments. Each ecological niche provided an opportunity for a specific social group, parallel to how particular animal and plant species colonize and thrive in specific conditions. Many other historians (e.g. Bayly 1999; Sumit Guha 1999) question such assumptions of environmental and social stability, seeing jatis as more fluid cultural constructions, with their composition changing with migrations, intermarriages, and shifting socioeconomic roles, environmental conditions, and state policies.

After two centuries, the Gupta Empire finally succumbed to repeated militant immigration movements from the northwest by Central Asians. Thereafter in north India, while occasionally regional rulers managed to conquer and bind subordinate allies into transregional states, none of these persisted. Some historians identify major urban contractions as long-distance commerce declined and artisans shifted to rural areas. Overall, as El Niño events occurred significantly more frequently starting around 500 CE, India began to suffer economic and social disruption from monsoon failures and droughts. Textual sources from which environmental history can be written also grew sparser. But, as the next chapter shows, the various new cultures entering India also brought new technologies and attitudes toward the material world. We now turn to the distinctive southern regions and their human-animal-plant ecosystems during this chapter's period.

The Deccan, South India, and Dravidian Cultures, c. 600 BCE – c. 800 CE

Throughout ancient Indian history, the Deccan and South Indian macroregions each had distinctive environments and human-animal-plant interactions. Scanty southwest monsoon rains across the Deccan and on the upland south only supported pastoralism and some dry-crop agriculture, largely oriented around seasonal river valleys. In contrast, the wetter narrow southwestern and wider southeastern coastal plains became intensive rice growing regions, especially as local kings, temples, landholders, and villages constructed dams, weirs, irrigation channels, and other water-control infrastructure to manage the seasonal rivers and northeast monsoon rainfall.

While these regions differed in many ways environmentally, they were also connected. Rivers flow eastward off the Deccan to the seacoast, carrying fish, plant seeds, and rich silt. Their fertile valleys channeled plant species expansion and animal migrations, both seasonal and longerterm. Merchants conveyed grain, vegetables, raw materials, and finished products on these rivers between the interior and the coast. These ecological and commercial corridors occasionally enabled kings to control the whole river system.

Distinctive cultures emerged in each region. The northern Deccan was more influenced by north Indian Sanskrit-based cultures. But in the southern Deccan, two major Dravidian languages emerged: Kannada in the west and Telugu in the east. The peninsular South was the Dravidian language heartland with Malayalam along the southwestern coastal plain and Tamil in the highland center and lowland east.

Each language had words and concepts that associated distinctive human relationships with its regional environment, both natural and supernatural. For instance, the Tamil concept of *nadu* (region/microregion) includes a fusing of the identities of the locality's earth, atmosphere, animals, plants, and people within a specific ecological niche. Should people migrate from the nadu of their ancestors, they often were uncertain if the new locality would be congenial. Only if sanctioned by the original nadu's deity, or given precedent by an earlier emigrant from their nadu who succeeded there, would environmental compatibility be assured (Daniel 1987). However, these ecological microregions did not always coincide with the boundaries of kingdoms, since kings (and their deities) periodically led armies to seize territories from their neighbors to gain even more lands that would be donated those deities and their temple establishments.

One of the clearest cultural typologies of environments appears in Tamil poetry from the Sangam ("academy" or "fraternity") of the first three centuries CE. Famously, some 500 poets collectively and explicitly categorized five *tinai* ("landscapes" or types of ecosystems): arid; montane; riverine; littoral; and pastoral (Ramanujan 1967). Each landscape featured a stage or mood of human love, respectively: elopement and consequent painful separation from parents; clandestine lover's union; patient waiting and domestic fidelity; anxiety in love during separation; and lover's unfaithfulness. Each landscape also had a distinctive repertoire of plants, birds, beasts, seasons, type of water, human economy, musical instruments, and kinds of food. Poets then conventionally included one or more specific elements to convey subtly that landscape's love-mood. For instance, to evoke elopement, the poet might mention an evergreen tree or cactus in a wasteland, an eagle, a fatigued elephant, midday in summer, stagnant water, or bandits. Lover's union symbolically occurred in mountains, among bamboos, peacocks, or monkeys, around midnight early in the cool season, near a waterfall, as hill-people gathered honey or millet. Poets conveying lovers' patient waiting might include the jasmine in a forest, a jungle hen, a deer, the rainy season, pastoralists, or drums. Although their reasoning for thus collating specific flora, fauna, times, spaces, and human activities was not described explicitly, poets, grammarians, and their audiences of that period all concurred about these, revealing their collective ecological vision.

Throughout history, Dravidian-language-speaking communities have interacted with forests and beings living within them, as many sacred and dynastic histories reveal. Historically, forest-dwellers have had fierce and powerful deities who often manifested or incarnated in a distinctive tree or stone. Often, as a forest was cleared for agriculture, that forest deity's isolated domain became a sacred grove. Sacred groves also sprang up on previously cleared forestland or savanna, as humans planted revered trees embodying their ancestors or just allowed reforestation to occur around a shrine. Hence, sacred groves often preserve biodiversity (either from environmentalist intent, as some Hindu nationalists assert, or as an unintended consequence, as many scholars argue).

In South India, but also elsewhere, kings who conquered forests often transformed local deities under the guidance of prestigious Sanskrit-speaking Brahmins. Forest-dwellers and local villagers (especially those ranked low by Brahmins) often worshipped the forest deity as untamed, vernacular-speaking, and meat-eating, still surrounded by spiritually powerful trees. Many such deities were fierce warrior goddesses who ate the meat offered them by their non-vegetarian devotees, enhancing their *shakti* (female, martial, and cosmic "energy"). Since these goddesses were unmarried, their shakti was not controlled by a husband, which made them especially powerful but also dangerous to those who opposed or disregarded them. Typically, Brahmins Sanskritized important forest deities into their all-Indian pantheon as benevolent, Sanskrit-speaking, vegetarian, and married. The original grove was cleared to construct formal temple buildings. Especially today, some sacred groves are being sold for timber, with the proceeds funding upwardly mobile village festivals, more elaborate temple construction, and Sanskritized rituals. As an example of amalgamation of rulers, Brahmins, and forest-dwellers, under regional kings (and even today) the extremely popular Hindu temple of Jagannath in Puri (Odisha) periodically had forest-dwellers fell neem trees (*Azadirachta indica*) and carve new massive wooden images of Krishna and his siblings, which Brahmins then consecrated. So, these images were both forest and Brahminical deities.

In the Dravidian-state model (strongest in peninsular South India but also found in the southern Deccan), many kings historically identified themselves as the chief worshiper and earthly agent, or even descendant, of warrior goddesses or gods. The king could lead armies that conquered on earth due to the divinity's power, authority, and grace. A prime moral duty of the king was to donate lands and riches to that deity's temple.

Gradually, many Dravidian dynasties began patronizing Brahmins (many of whom were, or claimed to be, immigrants from the North), thus linking themselves to the prestigious Sanskrit-based culture. Brahmins received gifts of tax-free land, control over many sacred sites, temple tanks (reservoirs), and irrigation distribution systems (sometimes taken over from Buddhist monasteries). The hereditary attending Brahmin priests and temple councils mobilized local labor for infrastructure building and maintenance. They also used their income from agriculture and gifts to enhance the worldly power of the deity, the kingdom, themselves, and the temple's large staffs of cooks, dancers, sculptors, and other workers and functionaries necessary to the deity's household. Starting around the fourth century CE, temples to Brahminic deities began to be major complexes with brick or stone palace-like buildings, concentric surrounding walls, and massive gateways. These temples thus became economic as well as ritual centers for the local kingdom.

The Pandyan dynasty and the goddess Minakshi serve as excellent examples of the Dravidian model of kingship and of the Sanskritization process. The royal Pandyan dynasty is mentioned in texts dating from the fourth century BCE and the dynastic title lasted, in one form or another through a series of families, for about 1,500 years. They were based in the dry upland interior of the Tamil-speaking region. While the Pandyans did not customarily build dams, they developed a distinctive technology of two specific types of piston valves to control water flow from reservoir sluices.

In sacred histories, Minakshi first emerged in a sacred grove in the forest, from a pond full of golden lotuses. She conventionally has a green complexion and holds a parrot. All this indicates her probable origin as a local forest goddess taken over by Dravidian culture. The earliest historical accounts have her as Tamil-speaking, fierce, unmarried, and meat-eating. Her divine shakti enabled Pandyan kings to conquer and rule the region for generations, with her Madurai home as the dynasty's capital.

Over time, the Pandyan dynasty, like many other Dravidian kings, patronized Brahmins. So, Minakshi also became recognized as the all-Indian goddess Parvati, ritually wedded to the male Brahminic god, Shiva, with Vishnu as her brother who bestowed her on the groom. In this form, the goddess became vegetarian, passed her shakti over to her divine husband, became benign, and spoke in Sanskrit – at least in the eyes of Brahmins. They translated her Tamil name, Tadadakai, into Sanskrit, Minakshi; both names mean the "fish-eyed one," since her eyes had the shape of a beautiful carp.

Today, the major temple in Madurai includes Minakshi's original golden lotus pond and her special shrine. But they are now off center, with the main part of the temple now being the home of Shiva, with Parvati/Minakshi as his consort. This vast temple complex dominates the heart of the original city of Madurai. The historic palace of the kings, as chief servants of these deities, lies in the southeast part of the city, not at its center. Various individuals and groups competed for social status based the value of their donations to the divinity.

But many local people still envision Minakshi in her earlier, local identity as their own: still unmarried, meat-eating, powerful, dangerous, and a speaker of their own Dravidian language. Thus, the royal strategy of enhancing status in Brahminic terms led to many important deities in South India simultaneously having two identities: Brahminic and local. This sometimes let to tension over possession of the identity, and property, of that deity.

Not just in South India, but in other regions as well, some popular local goddesses represented major diseases, for example, smallpox. A devotee who survived that disease customarily attributed that to the grace of the goddess – smallpox scars being permanent signs of her mercy. Clearly, such a deity was an awesome guardian and a fearsome foe. (Now that smallpox has been eradicated in India, such deities now control any feverish disease; some are especially associated with power over HIV/AIDS.)

Other Dravidian dynastic histories also suggest forest origins. For example, for about six hundred years (from the fourth century CE onward), a series of Pallava dynasties dominated the agriculturally and commercially rich lands around Kanchipuram, in India's southeast coastal plain. This region receives irrigation from the Kaveri and other rivers flowing down from the Deccan and also from northeast monsoon rains.

The origins of the Pallavas are ambiguous, perhaps intentionally obscured, as different families over the centuries each tried to claim that dynastic name. Some accounts claim descent from Emperor Ashoka, evoking the Buddhist universal sovereign model. Indeed, Buddhist tradition in the region has Ashoka himself building a Buddhist stupa near Kanchipuram. Another Pallava origin account describes how a Hindu Kshatriya (or in other versions, a Brahmin) fell in love with a Naga princess (i.e. a daughter of the legendary chief of serpents in the forest/underworld). The princess became pregnant. When the prince left, he told her to tie a soft twig around their child when he was born and set him adrift down a river toward the coast. When the prince later found the baby, he recognized him from the twig. The prince gave his son part of his kingdom, the region around Kanchipuram known as Tondaimandalam – the region of Tondai, which means "twig" in the local Tamil language.

This rescued child thus founded the Pallava dynasty, with the name Pallava also meaning "young twig" in Tamil. So, forest-dweller culture, identification with a plant, the Sanskrit and Buddhist models of kingship, the name of the dynasty, and the region it governed were all linked by these traditions. Some outside scholars interpret this origin story as revealing that the family probably arose among a forest people, but, as their power grew, they claimed royal ancestry in Buddhist, Brahminic, and Dravidian terms.

Over the centuries, the Pallava state and its subjects gradually domesticated the Kaveri River delta, establishing wet rice agriculture wherever they could. They also developed their characteristic water-control technology for their large reservoirs: stone sluicegates housing distinctive piston-valves which controlled water flow into hierarchies of canals and conduits to the surrounding fields. The Pallava period also saw growth in interregional trade, by land and sea.

With this economic base, Pallava armies sporadically conquered north and south along the Tamil coast. At their peak in the late sixth century, their armies also marched westward up the rivers into the dry interior, even as far as the Western Ghats, covering about 18,000 km^2 (7,000 mi^2). The Pallavas also created a navy to impose their regime onto Sri Lanka. Eventually, Pallava kings lost power, and their empire fragmented by the late ninth century, in part due to less stable rainfall patterns and occasional El Niño-caused droughts. But South Indian kings, trade, and culture continued to extend overseas as far east as Java (today in Indonesia) where Buddhist and Hindu architecture and cultural features remain.

So, no region of India was isolated from the rest of the world. The next chapter highlights immigrations by sea along the entire western coast and overland from the northwest. These were shaped by periods of significant and relatively rapid climatic changes. The incoming communities and cultures brought new animals, plants, cultures, and technologies, strongly effecting India's subsequent environmental history.

5 Insiders, Jewish, Christian, and Muslim Immigrants, and the Environment (c. 700 – c. 1600)

Over the eighth to sixteenth centuries, India's environmental history altered considerably due to internal and global forces. In the context of relatively intense climate changes, overseas and overland human immigrants brought new animal and plant species, as well as agricultural, hydraulic, military, administrative, and other technologies, which enabled innovative rulers and their subjects increasingly to affect local ecosystems. These diverse immigrants from the west, including Jews, Christians, and especially Muslims, also brought new cultural valuations of specific fauna and flora species and of Indian people. Some already-established communities, plants, and animals adapted more successfully than others to these changes. All this gradually created societies, states, and ecosystems with composite identities in India's many varied regions and dynamically shifting environment.

Scientists are still reconciling sometimes inconsistent evidence about long-term climate change patterns – globally, subcontinentally, and regionally. For South Asia overall, much evidence shows the phasing out of an arid period (roughly the fifth to seventh centuries) that had contributed to the contraction of agriculture, commerce, cities, and towns. Instead, over the tenth to twelfth centuries in India, popularly termed the Medieval Warm Period, rainfall and temperature rose unevenly. Among the evident causes were intensified solar activity and changes in the earth's orbital parameters that resulted in more direct-sun radiation onto the northern hemisphere. The resulting stronger southwest monsoon pattern enabled more prosperous agriculture, essential to the economy. Much wildlife also flourished. Occasional drought-induced famines in specific regions, however, still occurred during El Niño events. But broadly, economic stresses evidently declined.

Then from roughly the thirteenth to the mid-nineteenth centuries, solar activity waned, orbital forcing weakened, and the earth's volcanism increased, each contributing to cooling in the northern hemisphere – popularly called the Little Ice Age. El Niño events increased so southwest monsoons weakened. For instance, the recorded number of major famines in India rose 1350–1450 (although this was also a time of better recordkeeping). However, as the climate dried, stronger states – including the Delhi and Deccani Sultanates, Vijayanagar, and various smaller regional kingdoms – extended their use of water-controlling, administrative, and military technologies, and encouraged agricultural expansion for taxation purposes. This increased production but also contributed to substantial land-cover changes, like deforestation, that affected soil moisture, erosion, and the specific mix of animal and plant species in each region. Additionally, these states relied heavily on horse-cavalry as the core of their military force, which more arid conditions favored tactically and in terms of equine health.

From the end of the fifteenth century onward, but on limited scale, Portuguese warrior-merchants arrived by sea, sailing around Africa. They began to import from the long-isolated Americas hitherto unknown plant and animal species, plus silver and gold. They also brought new ideas about the environment and Indian society. This started the transformative economic, military, and political processes collectively called European imperialism. By about 1600, India became even more integrated into global environmental history.

In addition to physical evidence that we can analyze to reconstruct the histories of the land, flora, and fauna, this period also saw new and expanding types of written source materials. Many regional languages developed increasingly extensive descriptive and analytic accounts of the events and values of their times and places. Further, cultures from various western traditions imported their own concepts of "history" writing. Sultanates and other transregional kingdoms, like Vijayanagar, expanded their administrative power, with more inclusive recordkeeping and the commissioning of works of history, literature, and representational art that contain information about the environment, and cultural attitudes toward it. In addition to written, numismatic, and architectural sources, surviving oral traditions (often religious), archaeology, and other evidence enables reconstruction of some of India's diverse regional and local environmental histories in more depth than ever before.

South Asia in the World c. 700 to c. 1200

For centuries, traders, transporters, raiders, and other immigrants of various ethnic communities from Arabia, east Africa, and West and Central Asia had been pressing into India, either across the Indian Ocean or overland across India's rugged mountainous northwestern frontier (see Map. 5.1). The rapid expansion of Islam and Muslims

Map 5.1 India c. 700 to c. 1200

(from the seventh century CE onward) created a new, widening Arabic-based cosmopolis of enhanced Asian-African-European scientific and technological exchanges, including in administration, astronomy, biology, botany, hydraulics, mathematics, medicine, metallurgy, military weaponry and tactics, navigation, philosophy, and theology. Indian sciences (e.g. in mathematics and herbal medicine) contributed to this body of knowledge but were also broadly enriched by it; traditionally Sanskritic sciences tended to be more theoretical than empirical. These immigrants interacted with already-established human, animal, and plant populations in India, reshaping local physical and sociocultural environments.

Indian Ocean trade has continued for thousands of years, ever since seamen and merchants recognized how wind-powered sailing ships could predictably ride across the Indian Ocean on the four-month-long southwest monsoon from Arabia and Africa to India and then back on the equally long northeast monsoon. Imperial Roman coins and trade goods have been found in South India, for instance. Similarly, but fewer in number, Southeast Asian and Chinese vessels rode the reverse wind flows. However, a single monsoon only carried these small wooden wind-powered ships one way. So, merchants sailing from Arabia or Africa and Southeast Asia or China customarily sold their cargoes in South Indian ports, bought new cargos, and waited months until the monsoon wind reversed for their return voyage. Thus, two interoceanic trade networks overlapped there, with largely distinct shipbuilding technologies: Arab dhows (evidently originally developed from dugout canoes) and Chinese junks (from bamboo rafts). Dhows were lateen-rigged and generally smaller, but more numerous, so their merchants preferred low-volume but high-value goods. Larger, multi-mast junks carried rectangular sails stiffened with bamboo cane, capable of transporting greater cargo volume. Indian-based shipping favored dhows but also used junks. While the scale of this transoceanic trade was relatively small, some animals, plants, and their products, plus diseases, moved along those corridors, as did certain human cultures, classes, and communities.

Some regularly visiting merchants, seamen, and holy men – especially those coming across the Indian Ocean from Arabia, Africa, Iraq, or Iran – married local Indian women, had children, and converted them (and parts of the surrounding population) into their outsider's faith. Particularly along India's Kerala coast, some Hindu jatis were matrilineal and relatively open to relationships with outside men. That is, mothers held the family property which daughters inherited, along with the family's traditional domestic culture. Hence, in such communities, a woman's children with a visiting man were strongly part of her family, although they were also identified with their father.

From the early centuries CE, this process created early Jewish and Christian communities on India's southwest coast. Then, after the Prophet Muhammad created the first Muslim community (622CE/ 1Hijri), many of the arriving Arab and east African merchants and seamen had converted to Islam, as did their local Indian families. Some Indian Muslim communities became known as Mapilla, literally "son-in-law," since they derived their identities from in-marrying men. Some Dravidian-style popular Hindu temples were converted to Christian or Muslim shrines, although earlier worship patterns often persisted – often the plants, animals, and diseases over which the local deity held power remained the same, although with a changed religious identity.

Such Abrahamic communities became substantial in some parts of Kerala, where Mapillas or Christians are a majority. Further, Cochin port had a small but thriving Jewish community. Many public aspects of these communities' practices and beliefs conformed to paternal traditions, including personal names and formal prayer rituals. But many domestic beliefs and practices including valuation of specific plants and animals largely followed maternal traditions. Therefore, such families held jati-like social ranks, each with its own separate places of worship, endogamous marriage patterns, distinctive diet of foods to savor or avoid, women's clothing styles, and inheritance customs. Their orientation across the Indian Ocean mean that such communities usually did not expand very far inland.

Their outward links, however, meant that Jewish, Christian, and Muslim communities within ports often prospered through Indian Ocean trade diaspora networks, combining privileged access both to Indian markets and products (including cloth and spices) and to African, Arabian, and European ones (including trade in horses and other animals, gold and other minerals, and human slaves) via their distant co-religionists. All these communities particularly benefited from the Baghdad-based Abbasid Caliphate (750–1258), which fostered trans–Indian Ocean trade with efficient communications systems and uniform and stable laws and currency. Jewish communities in India customarily sent their sons to Baghdad for higher education. The most prominent Christian community in Kerala recognized the authority of the Syrian Patriarch of the Nestorian Church. Indian Muslims joined pilgrims on Hajj to Mecca and sent students there and to Baghdad. These communities thereby gained commercial correspondents throughout the Indian Ocean world.

These Indian Ocean exchanges both contrasted with, and were complemented by, concurrent overland ones. Over the centuries since Alexander's invasion of the Indus plain (327–325 BCE), commerce and migration linking India with the Mediterranean and China had periodically flourished. This later became known as the Silk Road, although various high-value animals, minerals, plants, and products made from these were also carried by humans and pack-animals in both directions. Indian merchants participated both as importers, with the trade in horses particularly extensive, and as exporters, especially of finely crafted artisanal products.

The Prophet Muhammad's proclamation of Islam created powerful reform, conversion, political, and military movements within and outward from Arabia. The Abrahamic creed of strict monotheism, reinforced by the prescribed duties of prayer, fasting, pilgrimage, and alms-sharing, focused all Muslims into a single, egalitarian community (at least in theory). As in the Jewish tradition, certain animals, especially pigs, were unclean. Abraham's blood sacrifice was commemorated on Eid al-Azha by the ritual killing of animals, especially camels and sheep.

By 711, this dynamically expansive movement of Islam reached the lower Indus plain (Sindh), when an army under an Arab general, Muhammad ibn al-Qasim (695–715), extended the Caliphate there. This directly introduced into western India an originally Arabian culture that carried many new environmental concepts, including the belief that the entire material world was the creation of Allah, entrusted to select human communities and under the authority of the ruler as agent of the divine. Thus, Islam, as well as the "right of conquest," gave these Muslim rulers legal authority over the land, fauna, flora, and people of Sindh, which has remained under Muslim rulers almost ever since. But relatively few Muslims immigrated, so gradually this became more of an Indian-based sultanate, de facto politically independent of the Caliphate after 985. (Sindh now forms the second most populous province in Pakistan; Sindh's capital, Karachi, is Pakistan's largest city and economic powerhouse.)

Additionally, a series of martial-pastoralist West and Central Asian ethnic groups (including Shakas, Kushanas, Parthians, Huns, Scythians, Mongols, and Turks) had long been pressing into India. There were many ecological and political reasons for these immigrations and invasions. Central Asian grasslands flourished during warm, moist years, fostering rapid increases in horse and cattle herds. But these steppes occasionally suffered a devastating *dzud* – a snowy cold winter combined with a summer drought. This denied the more numerous animals grazing all year, forcing herders to emigrate rapidly in large numbers, seeking pasturage. They drove neighboring ethnicities out, forming a cascading wave. Furthermore, pressure from strong Chinese emperors marching into Mongolia or from more powerful communities wanting their pastureland periodically forced emigration of the local community, which then drove out neighboring ones. Occasionally charismatic leaders focused this collective martial force. Most famously, Genghis Khan (c. 1162–1227) and his Mongol successors conquered or raided China, Southeast Asia, Iran, Iraq, and Europe, as well as north India as far as Delhi (1297, 1306). Some of these communities eventually settled in India as pastoralists or farmers, often Sanskritizing into Hindu Rajput jatis.

For Central Asians, India had both environmental deficiencies and attractions. They found India's seasonally hot and humid climate uncongenial, especially since it gradually weakened their horses and delaminated their horn-composite bows. Further, overland access to India was geographically constrained. Peaceful or martial entry through the western mountains into the Indus plain was funneled by the narrow Khyber, Bolan, and other passes, which strong Indian rulers could defend. Then, physical geography channeled further overland movement into India. East of the lower Indus lay the inhospitable Rann of Kutch and Thar Desert. East of the upper Indus lay the more promising but narrow corridor between the Himalayan foothills on the north and the Thar Desert and Aravalli Mountains on the south. At the strategic choke point, just before reaching the fertile, well-watered Gangetic plain, sat Delhi. On this site, where life-giving streams running off the most northern spur of the rocky Aravalli ridge flowed into the Jumna River, and where the warhorse and war-elephant trades intersected, a series of dynasties built fortified capitals. (The British Raj built the most recent imperial capital, New Delhi, there starting in 1911.)

Nonetheless, India was far more prosperous and populous than Central Asia, with rich royal and temple hoards to seize, many people to enslave, and skilled artisans to recruit, sometimes by force. Invading Central Asian Muslims clashed militarily with Indian rulers over ninety times between 636 and 1205. Indeed, the Afghan warlord, Mahmud of Ghazni (r. 998–1030) raided India seventeen times, paying his armies with Indian loot (gold, silver, gems, human slaves, and valuable livestock). Mahmud used Islam to enthuse his warriors and justify his conquests, but his main goal was mercenary not religious – his 1008 assault, for example, was against Sindh's Muslim ruler.

Sufi holy men also immigrated overland into India. From early in Islamic history, some Muslims sought direct, personal experience of God. Some charismatic Sufis gradually formed religious orders, in which the founder inspired many devotees and passed spiritual power to chosen successors, often sons. Each Sufi order developed distinctive devotional methods, including song, dance, or ritual austerities. Some Sufi orders remained within mainstream Islam; more heterodox orders transcended Islam's conventional religious duties. Especially from the eleventh century onward, Sufis spread their spiritual message in India, extending their sacred authority and protection over the lands (and their human and nonhuman inhabitants) where they settled.

Sufi devotionalism often paralleled the Hindu bhakti movements which each regional culture had developed. Some Sufis and bhaktas amalgamated traditionally Muslim and Hindu forms of devotion, denying any distinction between Allah and Hindu deities. Many Indian communities responded by accepting Sufis' composite religious message (reflected in much of popular Islam in Pakistan, Bangladesh, and India today).

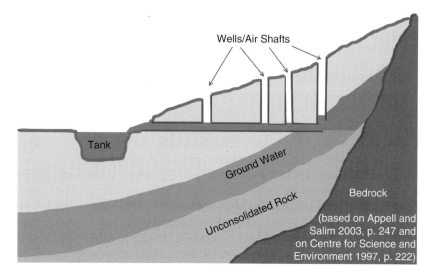

Figure 5.1 Underground water channeling, *qanat, karez*, or *surangam*

These different types of overland Muslim immigrants were often re-ciprocally supportive. Merchants imported horses and other goods valued by warriors, rulers, and in regional markets. They also bought surplus grain, which enabled farmers to purchase products and pay taxes to their Muslim rulers in a gradually monetizing economy. Pious Muslims, including mer-chants and rulers, donated land to Sufis and their hospices, often land not yet uncultivated due to aridity, heavy forests, or lack of farmers, which Sufi institutions then made productive of crops for sale to merchants.

Consequently, some Sufi hospices became economic as well as social, cultural, and religious centers. In the upper Indus region (especially western Punjab, now the dominant and most populous province in Pakistan), much land was arid, unable to support settled agriculture through rainfall alone. So many people were herders, whose grazing animals required less surface water. Arriving Sufis taught those who settled around them hydraulic technologies, developed particularly in Iran, including and the "Persian waterwheel" (whose series of buckets driven by gears and powered by draft animals could raise large volumes of river or groundwater to the surface). Iranians had long used underground canals (*qanat* or *karez*) that channeled groundwater to wells and reservoirs (see Figure 5.1).[1] According to Islamic doctrine, water was God's gift to

---

[1] Other regions with appropriate geology developed similar water-channeling structures, for instance *surangam* in the western Deccan.

living creatures, not to be squandered but also not as a commodity to be taxed (although irrigated lands could be taxed at higher rates). These pious acts of supplying water by Muslim rulers and Sufis enabled pastoralists to settle as farmers around a Sufi hospice, adopt Islam, and prosper.

Especially in eastern Bengal, much of the land was still heavily forested, so many people living there followed swidden agriculture. Sufis and their followers brought the technology of steel axes and plowshares that enabled cutting down and uprooting large trees. They guided the construction of seasonal inundation canals with earthen canal walls that could be breached as necessary, thus both controlling floods during the rains and providing irrigation during the dry season. Wet rice cultivation spread. So, former forest-dwellers prospered as settled farmers on Bengal's rich deltaic soil, clustering around Sufi hospices and converting to Islam (Eaton 1993). As in Punjab, many converts preserved parts of their pre-Islamic culture, creating eclectic amalgamations of popular Hindu and Muslim customs and beliefs. (Muslim-majority eastern Bengal became East Pakistan in 1947, then Bangladesh in 1971.)

All these economic and cultural developments both caused some environmental changes and were also affected by others outside human control. The long period of strong southwest monsoon rains that had fostered these expansions of agriculture and, hence, the entire economy and society faded over the thirteenth century. Then the climate shifted to cooler and dryer conditions, which forced other adaptations and favored particular types of plants, animals, and human communities. To different degrees, new kinds of states gained advantages over their many rivals through technologies of warfare (including horse-cavalry and early gunpowder weaponry), water control, and administration (especially in revenue collection). Most prominent among the states early in this new climatic period were the Delhi Sultanate (ruled by five successive Muslim dynasties), its offshoots of the northern Deccan sultanates, and Vijayanagar, based in the western Deccan and ruled by Hindu dynasties.

The Delhi Sultanate (1206–1526)

For more than three centuries, Delhi-based Muslim sultans intermittently conquered vast sections of South Asia, but none succeeded in creating a stable empire due in large measure to dynastic instability and infrastructural weakness. Their policies varied widely, but there were recurring patterns in the fragility of their military-fiscal state and administration, and their mixed relationships with India's living and physical environments. While all these sultans identified as Turk, Afghan, or Arab, some of their female ancestors were Indians who converted to Islam.

The first "dynasty" (1206–90) was a series of sultans, most who began as Turkish *mamluk*s (slaves, captured or purchased in youth but trained as military commanders or governors). During this period, various Islamic states relied on mamluks (including Egypt, 1250–1517), since they enabled a ruling patriarch to expand his core of army officers and administrators with slaves who, unlike biological sons, could not own property or claim the throne (at least in theory, although some did so). In 1290, the Turk-Afghan Khalji clan ended the first mamluk dynasty and then ruled in Delhi until one of their own Turkish mamluk commanders rebelled and established his own Tugluq dynasty (1320–98).

To enhance their cities' glory and comfort, sultans recruited Persian or Central Asian artisans skilled in constructing domes, arches, and reservoirs, decorated with colorful fired-tilework. To encourage long-distance commerce, sultans widened roads, punctuated with wells and *serai*s (guesthouses, often fortified). To increase agricultural revenues, some sultans sponsored technologically simple canals, reservoirs, and stepwells (in which water carriers or bathers used a series of stone stairs between the water and ground levels), useful for irrigation, drinking water, and sanitation. Firoz Shah Tugluq (r. 1351–88), for instance, is credited with constructing a 250 km (155 mi)-long canal that diverted Jumna River water to his lands in Hisar (in India's Haryana state). His court also kept a kennel of tamed Indian cheetahs (*Acinonyx jubatus venaticus*) to hunt down antelope and other game. Some sultans decreed that designated forested areas or grasslands were their own exclusive hunting reserves. Pastoralists, forest-dwellers, and villagers who had been using these areas for grazing, swidden agriculture, hunting, or gathering forest products resisted, either covertly or in what sultans regarded as banditry or rebellion.

Each Delhi sultan survived only with military backing, which he insecurely held by periodically rewarding key commanders with war spoils and *iqta* (appanage land assignments). This system required frequent conquests of enemy treasuries and territories. Additionally, sultanate armies, mostly professional cavalrymen, needed a constant supply of expensive and short-lived warhorses, necessarily obtained overland from west or Central Asia or overseas from Iran or Arabia. Horse-cavalry enabled swift movement and encircling tactics that repeatedly defeated larger, slower Indian armies of massed infantry led by kings or generals on war elephants. But sultans themselves also captured, received in tribute, or purchased elephants which they used in battle as well as in processions that displayed their prestige and legitimacy in Indic tradition.

These sultans struggled to mobilize sufficient resources through administrative and military means, so many turned to gaining support from influential Islamic leaders. Some sultans sent gifts to the Caliph in Baghdad. Some donated to prominent Sufis areas of revenue-free land (often on the agricultural frontier, requiring forest-clearance and the suppression of forest-dwellers).

All sultans incorporated large numbers of Hindus as manual laborers, infantrymen, artisans, and officials. One of the issues faced by all Muslim rulers in India was the legal status of the vast majority of their subjects who remained non-Muslim. Within Islamic doctrine, some non-Muslim communities can hold status as *zimmi* ("protected subjects") if Allah had once chosen them to receive the Quran. Indeed, the Quran itself specifically mentions earlier prophets, including Abraham, Moses, and Jesus. Women of those "chosen" communities could legally marry Muslim men, for instance. These zimmis should pay *jizya* (a wealth tax) to their Muslim ruler in exchange for being protected. However, many Muslim legal scholars and theologians claim that there is no specific Quranic evidence that Hindus were ever chosen by Allah and so could not legally be zimmi. Yet, since Hindus formed the massive majority of their subjects and taxpayers, most Muslim rulers in India allowed them zimmi status anyway. Some more strict Muslims rulers made their Hindu subjects pay jizya, but other Muslim rulers abolished jizya and largely respected the beliefs and practices of their Hindu subjects.

Conversely, many established Rajput clans recognized some Muslim martial immigrants as also following the dharma of warriors and rulers. This partly incorporated them into the Sanskritic social order. Indeed, many Rajput and other Hindu oral and written texts identified Turks as a jati, rather than classifying all Muslims collectively as a single community. Additionally, some Rajput clans, or parts of them, converted to Islam while still retaining much of their traditional dharma and social status (e.g. clan members who interacted with Muslim rulers often become Muslims, but others remained Hindu, particularly those who dealt with their Hindu tenants).

Even the most militarily powerful and innovative Delhi sultans controlled only limited administrative technology and manpower. Muhammad Shah Tugluq (r. 1325–51) seized the throne from his father and then conquered down to India's southern tip. Attempting to re-center his regime, he moved his capital 1,200 km (750 mi) south to a west Deccan city that he renamed Daulatabad. But this weakened control over his state's heartland, so he soon returned to Delhi (which soon recovered to a population of about 400,000). He also tried to expand his finances by issuing copper coins, but this also failed since forgers simply made copies and demanded their nominal value in silver from the royal treasury. He received 15 Chinese ambassadors from the Yuan imperial court, sending a return delegation with gifts, including 200 Hindu slaves, songstresses, and dancers, 15 young courtiers, 100 horses, and an array of costly textiles, dishware, and swords. A Moroccan scholar and Arabic-language poet, Ibn Battuta (1304–57, in India 1333–46), richly detailed the geography, flora, fauna, commerce, periodic draught-caused famines, society, culture, and history of Muhammad Shah's kingdom (Ibn Battuta 1976).

No Delhi sultan proved able to secure the loyalty of the bulk of the population or establish a military monopoly. Many communities, especially pastoralists, dry upland farmers, and forest-dwellers, resisted fiercely all outside rulers, whatever their origin or religion. Occasional incursions from the northwest also shattered sultanate armies. Most notably, the Turkish warlord Timur/Tamerlane (1336–1405) invaded India (1398–99), deposed the weak Tugluq sultan, sacked Delhi, and took vast wealth and many skilled artisans back to Samarkand, his capital. He installed as governor in Delhi a Sayyid (claiming Arab descent from the Prophet Muhammad) who soon broke away, starting the fourth Delhi Sultanate dynasty. But, after only thirty years, the Indianized Lodi Afghan clan seized the throne.

As gunpowder weapons, especially cannon, gradually spread into India from the Ottoman Empire (founded 1453) and from Western Europe, the cost of warfare rose, further the straining the sultanate's always-uncertain finances. Additionally, the considerable weakening of southwest monsoon rainfall during much of the fourteenth and fifteenth centuries reduced agricultural production and caused periodic famines, putting added stress on the economy, society, and government. Then, in 1526, the factionalized Lodi dynasty fell to yet another Central Asian invader, Babur, who laid the foundation for what his grandson would make the Mughal Empire (Chapter 6).

Throughout the Delhi Sultanate's three centuries, its decentralized structure meant its military-governors periodically hived off independent sultanates, most notably in Madurai (1334), Kashmir (1339), the Deccan (1347), Bengal (1345), Jaunpur (1394), and Gujarat (1407). These sultanates suffered similar internal weaknesses due to succession wars and limited administrative and military technology. Indeed, the Bahmani sultanate in the Deccan itself gradually fragmented into warring successor sultanates: Ahmadnagar, Berar, Bidar, Bijapur, and Golkonda. Economic and political links across the Indian Ocean to Iran meant perilous overseas sourcing of warhorses, and also more Persian cultural and Shi'i religious influences in the Deccan than in north India. For centuries, these competing Deccani sultanates survived multiple challenges, most notably the expansions of Vijayanagar and then the early

Portuguese Empire in Asia, before the last of them was finally terminated by the Mughal Empire in the late seventeenth century.

Vijayanagar (c. 1340 – c. 1672)

In the dry uplands of the southwestern Deccan, the overarching military-fiscal conquest state of Vijayanagar ("City of Victory") prevailed for centuries. Much of Vijayanagar's initial success came through enhanced rain-fed, reservoir-based, canal-distributed irrigation, which was especially vital during the particularly dry early fourteenth century. Then, from about 1350 onward, rainfall sporadically increased in the region, continuing the state's expansion of dry- and mixed-crop agriculture, along with livestock pasturage. The resulting revenue funded professional warriors (including mercenaries), enabling conquest from rival states of more territories, including fertile Deccan river valleys and the eastern and western coastal plains. The high degree of seasonality of agriculture meant much male labor was periodically available for mobilization as semiprofessional soldiers. Vijayanagar's capital (on the Tungabhadra River) featured royal palaces and temples which brought prestige and culturally adhered people to its regime through displays of ritual submission by surrounding rulers and merchants.

Vitally, the decentered Vijayanagar economy also fostered commerce in sandalwood, indigo, diamonds, cotton cloth, and pepper and other spices, exchanged (via diverse merchants including foreign Muslims as well as Hindus, Indian Muslims and Christians, Jains, Jews, and later Portuguese) for Persian Gulf warhorses and luxury goods from Arabia, Africa, the Mediterranean, and China. Territories subordinated to Vijayanagar eventually stretched across the entire peninsula south of the Krishna River to include major ports on both coasts, with Vijayanagar city's markets as the focus for major trade routes in a gradually monetizing economy. By the sixteenth century, Vijayanagar rulers were buying cannon and other gunpowder weapons as well as recruiting mercenaries from the newly arrived Portuguese who were dominating Indian Ocean trade.

While some older-style historians try to pose Vijayanagar as a bastion of Hinduism against Muslim sultanates, this erases their many similarities in administration, army, and culture. Like many Indian kingdoms (including the Delhi Sultanate, the Pandyans, and the Pallavas already discussed), Vijayanagar state was ruled by a sequence of dynasties. Brothers, Harihara and Bukka Yadava, established the kingdom around 1340. According to many local accounts, they were Hindus who had converted to Islam and served in sultanate armies, gaining military expertise, before striking out on their own and reconverting to Hinduism. Their followers were mostly mixed Telugu and Kannada speakers – Hindus and also some Muslims. In 1485, a Vijayanagar general seized power; in 1505, yet another general usurped the throne and founded the Tuluva dynasty. This dynasty expanded the empire to its greatest extent – some 360,000 km^2 (140,000 mi^2) under its direct and indirect rule.

Even Vijayanagar's strongest rulers effectively controlled only the dry upland core, one-fifth of this vast territory. In much of the peninsular south, the state's semi-autonomous *nayakas* (military-governors, usually immigrant Telugu-speaking chiefs) employed soldiers, Brahmins officials and temple priests, and cultivators, all personally loyal to them. These formed a new layer atop existing Tamil or Kannada speaking landholders and local society. These immigrants also expanded agriculture into hitherto less developed semiarid ecological niches, especially where they could apply their expertise in cultivation of rich black-soil tracts.

Further, Vijayanagar rulers thought deeply about their relations with forest-dwellers on their external and internal frontiers. For instance, King Krishnadevaraya Tuluva (r. 1509–29) wrote a Telugu-language poem on statecraft: *Amuktamalyada* (c. 1515–21). This text advises kings to preserve protective, impenetrable forests on all external boundaries. Within the state, deforestation for expanded settled agriculture should be constrained, thus retaining lands for "the tribal people, who roam about in the forest and hill areas" (Murali 1995:89). Since these forest-dwellers cannot be disciplined "by imposing severe punitive measures ... it is better to maintain friendship with them by a policy of truthfulness and offering gifts. By doing so the king can get their physical support during his expeditions against rival kings [by getting] his enemy's lands looted." Subordinated forest-chiefs in the Western Ghats also provided the king with war-elephants in tribute.

Eventually, the adhesive power of Vijayanagar's cultural, political, military, and economic formulation gradually dissipated. In the 1540s, the faltering Tuluva dynasty was subordinated by an ambitious Vijayanagar general who later founded his own Aravidu dynasty. Over the next century until 1672, the remaining Vijayanagar state sporadically fragmented due to repeated internal revolts, overambitious expansion northward that provoked disastrous wars against surrounding Hindu-ruled kingdoms and a coalition of Deccani sultanates (marked by the sack of Vijayanagar city in 1565), the decline in its control over resources and commercial advantage, and the rise of new forces, including the Portuguese.

The Portuguese Empire in Asia (1498 Onward)

The arrival of Vasco da Gama (1469–1524) on Kerala's coast in 1498 began the introduction into Indian environmental history of significant new technologies, as well as resource and species flows on a global scale. Blocked in the Mediterranean from the rich eastern trade by Venice and the Ottoman Empire, Portuguese kings had pushed into the southern Atlantic. Their naval architects and shipwrights had developed relatively fast-sailing, well-armed *carrack*s that could brave Atlantic storms. These innovative vessels had sturdy wooden frameworks onto which butted planks were nailed and pierced for multiple cannon ports, allowing more firepower and more stability. Over decades, Portuguese shipmasters explored the wind patterns, oceanic currents, natural and human resources, and politics ever further south down the West African coast and then, in 1498, east across the Indian Ocean. While occasional Europeans had visited India overland or through the Red Sea or Persian Gulf via local vessels, this royal Portuguese enterprise created an un-precedented direct sea route connecting Europe, Africa, the Americas, and all of coastal Asia into one increasingly integrated system. In terms of the movement of flora and fauna species, this undid the continental drift's isolation of the Americas, Eurasia, and (to an extent) Africa. Ottoman war fleets had sporadically but unsuccessfully sought to extend their imperial control over the Indian Ocean (as they had already established in the more placid eastern Mediterranean). In contrast, Portuguese royal war-ships and heavily armed merchant vessels established a naval monopoly in the Indian Ocean that land-based Indian states never successfully challenged.

The Treaties of Tordesillas (1494) and Zaragoza (1529) between the kings of Spain and Portugal (and blessed by the Catholic Pope) awarded Portugal sovereignty over all non-Christian lands from Brazil to Japan. However, limited national manpower confined the Portuguese Empire in Asia mainly to a string of fortified coastal enclaves. Their initial bases were in Kerala (especially Cochin and Cannanore) but eventually their most significant Indian colonies were up the coast: Goa (seized from the Bijapur Sultanate in 1510) and Daman and Diu (taken from Gujarat in 1531 and 1535 respectively). The Portuguese also established less-secure trading outposts in Bengal at Chittagong (1528), Satgaon (1550), and Hugli (1579), and on the southeast Coromandal coast at St. Thome (1540). Within the walls of these enclaves, the Portuguese king's law classed land, animals, and even enslaved humans as legal property. In 1560, the Portuguese established the Inquisition, in part to assert their Catholic control over South India's existing Syrian Christian community.

Since Portuguese ships could carry only limited commercial cargo, the crown profited from transoceanic trade between Asia and Europe in low-volume, high-value cargoes: purchasing plant products (particularly pepper from Kerala and other spices transshipped from Southeast Asia) with silver from the Americas and silver and copper from Japan. Rather than attempt to compete in markets with their limited royal financing, the Portuguese often used coercion against commercial rivals and suppliers. Additionally, the crown forced all Indian Ocean shipmasters to purchase a *cartaz* (license) or be subject to seizure. Using unprecedented levels of ruthless violence, especially against Muslim ships (including those filled with Hajj pilgrims), Portuguese warships repeatedly captured unlicensed vessels, slaughtering passengers and crews, seizing cargoes, and burning the hull. While the cartaz fee was modest, the document carried Christian images, which offended many Muslims. More materially, it could only be purchased in Portuguese colonial ports, which redirected trade routes there.

Most Portuguese officials and officers worked for the king. But they personally profited most by investing in Asian commerce, including trade in warhorses and advanced cannon and other weaponry. A growing number of Portuguese men and their descendants (usually from marriages with Indian women) rented their military expertise as mercenaries (especially as experts in cannon forging and aiming, and as musketeers) to the many contending sultans and rajas, greatly contributing to increased martial lethality and cost across India.

Further, although Portuguese rule did not penetrate inland, the gradual introduction of American flora, fauna, and silver nonetheless affected India widely. Though the "Columbian Exchange," chili pepper (capsicum), cashew nuts, groundnuts, guava, maize/corn, okra, papaya, pineapples, potatoes, tomatoes, and tobacco soon became significant parts of Indian agriculture and diet (Crosby 1972). Massive inflows of silver initially stimulated the economy and then contributed to inflation (by the seventeenth century). Portuguese profits also attracted the interests of northern European merchants whose joint-stock corporations (particularly the English East India Company, founded 1600) affected India's environmental history far more extensively (Chapter 7).

Over the centuries, India's environmental history had tended to be regionally based, with few transregional states. The levels of technology available to rulers and economies remained modest, heavily depending on human and animal energy sources rather than fossil fuels. Hence, their carbon footprint remained relatively small. Then, starting in 1526, India saw the rise of its most extensive and powerfully resource extraction state yet, the Mughal Empire, which is considered in the next chapter.

6   The Mughal Empire (1526–1707)

The Mughal dynasty proved the final and most successful of the many Central Asian families that over millennia had successfully conquered, adapted to, and altered India's environment. Most prominently, its third ruler, Emperor Akbar (r. 1556–1605), developed an imperial army, administration, and ideology that attached people from many regions and cultures to his state and enabled his regime to make use of India's natural and human resources to an unprecedented extent. Then, over the seventeenth century, three emperors idiosyncratically elaborated on Akbar's foundations. At its peak, the empire contained most of the subcontinent: 3.2 million km^2 (1.24 million mi^2) and 150 million people (roughly half of Western Europe in size but double its population) (see Map. 6.1). The Mughal Empire at that point stood as the world's most powerful and richest state (perhaps excepting imperial China) with at least a quarter million soldiers and nearly a quarter of global wealth. Each emperor tried in his own ways to possess parts of Indian environment through forcible seizure in war or hunt, land control, urbanization, religion, and art. Yet, after two centuries, the extent and complexity of the subcontinent's population and environmental challenges overstretched the empire's capacity to control them.

Recent scholarship has used the particularly extensive sources generated by this empire. These include massive volumes of written records about taxation (down to the level of individual fields), and about imperial officials, officers, courtiers, and holy men, as well as some enemies. Further, the court commissioned histories, especially ones using the Persianate *tarikh* genre of chronological narrative, often with moral commentary, culminating in events of the author's own lifetime. The court also commissioned works (for instance about elephants and other valuable species or curiosities) in representational art and literature or biology, in Persian but also Sanskrit and some regional languages. In addition, a diverse range of outside visitors from India, Central Asia, Iran, and Europe described the empire, its people, animals, plants, and conditions. Hence, environmental historians have many new kinds and

Map 6.1 India at the time of the Mughal Empire (sixteenth to seventeenth centuries)

volumes of source material which supplements the types available for earlier periods.

The First Two Generations: Babur and Humayun (1526–56)

The dynasty's founder, Babur (1483–1530, ruled in India 1526–30), boasted descent from "world-conquerors" Turkish Timur and Mongol Genghis Khan. After seizing Kabul at age twenty-one, Babur invaded much richer northwest India. On his first incursion (1505), he confided, "I had never seen a hot climate or any of Hindustan ['land of the Hindus,'

meaning north India] before ... a new world came into view – different
plants, different trees, different animals and birds, different tribes and
people, different manners and customs. It was astonishing, truly astonishing" (Babur 2002:186).

Not until Babur's fifth incursion (1526) did he defeat the Delhi
sultan, whose already fragile and divided regime had been disrupted
by repeated droughts (1491–1526). Babur noted, "Neither grain for
ourselves nor straw for the horses was to be found ... The people
had turned to brigandage and thievery" (Babur 2002:353–54).
At Panipat (a frequent battleground on the narrow corridor to
Delhi), Babur's Mongol horse-cavalry encircled the larger but
slower Sultanate army, whose elephants stampeded over its con-
stricted infantry. Babur then seized and distributed to his followers
the vast royal treasuries at Delhi and Agra, probably including the
famous Koh-i Nur diamond (after many owners and cuttings, its
remaining core is now possessed by the English queen [Dalrymple
and Anand 2017]).

Babur spent his last four years incompletely subduing regional and
local rulers from Balochistan to Bengal, recruiting Indian Muslim and
Hindu officials, and trying to adapt his new environment to his desires.
He understood South Asia as a geographical unit: "To the east and south,
in fact to the west too, it ends at the ocean. To the north is a mountain
range ... " (Babur 2002:270–72). Babur sought to classify this "strange
country" using the Arabic environmental model (derived from Ptolemy)
of seven climes:

Hindustan lies in the first, second, and third climes, with none of it in the fourth
clime ... Compared to ours [Afghanistan and Central Asia], it is another world.
Its mountains, rivers, forests, and wildernesses, its villages and provinces, animals
and plants, peoples and languages, even its rain and winds are altogether different.

His candid autobiography extensively details the individual qualities (and
utility to him) of its unfamiliar climate (particularly the monsoons), flora
(e.g. the mango, plantain, and jackfruit, but lacking the excellent melons
of his Central Asia), fauna (e.g. the elephant, rhinoceros, and peacock),
and economy (especially its rich treasuries and numerous, inexpensive,
skilled artisans).

Further, Babur sought to make this physical environment more congenial to himself and his core Central Asian commanders. Notably, Babur
constantly explored for promising sites to construct Central Asian-style
bath complexes and Persianate water-cooled gardens as refuges (especially from India's dusty heat and people) – a constructed environment
with intended benefits to physical and emotional health. Some scholars

identify such gardens as designed microcosms of the Islamic paradise, but Babur did not express such views in his surviving writing. Mughal gardens, however, did sometimes include experimental fruit and medicinal plants.

In contrast, Babur condemned wild forests and those who lived or took refuge in them. Forest-dwellers had tense relationships with settled agricultural society, both raiding and also trading for grain and artisanal products, but in ways that evaded taxation. Further, recalcitrant landholders, political rebels, and outlaws took refuge in thick forests, often planted for that purpose, against revenue-collectors as well as marauding warlords and recent invaders like Babur. Babur bemoaned the "forests of thorny trees in which the people ... hole up and obstinately refuse to pay tribute" (Babur 2002:334). Conversely, such forest-dwellers often felt the brunt of Mughal coercive efforts to cut military roads through forests or clear them for settled, revenue-producing farmland.

Babur died, leaving four contending sons and a shallow, fragile conquest state. His main heir, Humayun (r. 1530–40, 1555–56), failed to stabilize his reign. Instead, Humayun was forced into a fifteen-year exile by a resurgent coalition led by Sher Shah (r. 1540–45).

Sher Shah, a charismatic Indian-settled Afghan, quickly eliminated virtually all traces of Mughal rule. Knowing the north Indian environment far better, he and his key commanders and officials efficiently developed unprecedented administrative control, including assessing crops to optimize revenue demand and constructing roads for military and commercial transportation and communication. Only after his dynasty fragmented did Humayun gather sufficient resources and manpower from Afghanistan and Central Asia to reinvade north India in 1555.

Humayun died just seven months later, however, leaving two sons; Akbar, the elder, was only thirteen. In addition to the disorder and uncertainty inherent in this succession, north India was wracked by a major famine. As noted by a contemporary,

At this time there was great scarcity in the cities and villages of India, and there was a terrible famine in many parts, and especially in the province of Delhi ... they could see no trace of corn [grain]. Men took to eating one another; some would join together and carry off a solitary man, and make him their food. Though this recompense of men's acts lasted for two years, the intense distress was for one year. (Abu al-Fazl 1873–94, 2:57)

This Mughal historian concludes that this famine was miraculously ended by Akbar's accession.

North India under Emperor Akbar (r. 1556–1605)

Surviving a perilous regency and several near deaths in battle, assassination attempts, and rebellions, Emperor Akbar reigned for five decades, establishing institutions that bound expanding parts of north India's human and nonhuman environments to the Mughal regime. His empire was primarily a military-fiscal conquest state that required a vast and ever-growing army and administration in order to seize enemy treasuries and extract revenues and tribute from ever more territories. That income supported the expanding imperial household, army, and administration. So, Akbar constantly engaged in warfare on his internal and external frontiers, often having to repeat a conquest after new rebellions there. However, his long reign coincided with fewer El Niño events and better monsoons overall, and thus a period of general prosperity.

Akbar's personal curiosity and his regime's need for information both led to the substantial growth in state-sponsored Persian-language records, histories, and compilations of diverse knowledge. In particular, Akbar's closest advisor and publicist, Abu al-Fazl Allami, wrote the massive official regnal history in the tarikh genre: *Akbarnama*. To this text, he appended the vast *Ain-i Akbari*, an encyclopedic compilation of the regime's structure, personnel, finances, and knowledge. It included descriptions of the arrangement, contents, equipment, management, and staffing of the imperial fruit gardens, orchards, stables for elephants, horses, camels, cattle, and mules, kennels for hunting-dogs, cheetahs, caracals (*Caracal caracal schmitzi*), and deer, and aviaries for birds of prey and trained pigeons. For each animal, Abu al-Fazl systematically detailed the appearance, behavior, habitats, taxonomy, and (often) religious significance to Hindus and Muslims. Throughout, Abu al-Fazl credited Akbar with comprehensive guiding knowledge and insights into the universe and with empirical studies, for instance of interspecies crossbreeding and alchemy. Abu al-Fazl also included the history, ethnography, and geography of each region of India and its religious and philosophical schools of thought. Additionally, various other state-supported authors wrote more focused works. The imperial librarians collected widely, especially works of history, literature, and theology, in Arabic, Persian, and Sanskrit, as well as much representational painting of animals, architecture, people, and plants. Hence, even just highlighting the environmental aspects of Akbar's long reign must be illustrative rather than comprehensive.

Akbar's military victories and generous rewards attracted the service of Central Asian and Persian immigrants and diverse Indians. Many regional rulers and landholders whom he defeated or who submitted voluntarily were incorporated as imperial officials. Indeed, many leading Hindu Rajput regional rulers gave their daughters to Akbar as brides. Unlike previous Muslim kings, he allowed these wives to continue as Hindus, and he promoted their fathers and brothers into his army's upper ranks. The wealth and territorial acquisitions gained by some Rajput ruling clans through imperial service afforded them status, resources, and political power unavailable to their merely locally based ancestors, especially since their Rajasthan homeland was not agriculturally rich.

Akbar integrated all his high imperial officials and commanders into a single hierarchy of *mansab*s ("ranks") – their decimal rank indicating how many cavalrymen they must provide the state. By 1595, Akbar had 1,823 mansabdars, with an official collective obligation to provide 141,000 cavalrymen; he also directly commanded many troopers and artillerymen. Detailed records, using a standardized Persian-language format, unified Akbar's administrators and empowered them effectively to allocate to mansabdars land revenue assignments (*jagir*s). Innovatively, Akbar made these assignments temporary, subject to transfer at his will.

Tapping into the agricultural economy more systematically, from around 1566, Akbar's central administration used locally knowledgeable officials to produce an official record of the resources in each village, both within the empire's heartland and less extensively in newly conquered territories. They surveyed its arable, residential, forested, pasture, and uncultivated lands, and listed exactly who was responsible for paying which revenues. They calculated tax rates based on each field's average production over the past ten years. Once set, this demand largely continued, with periodic inquiries into actual production to keep rates realistic, and with remissions or reductions should the harvest fail. Imperial revenue extractions absorbed a significant share of the harvest (historians differ but reasonable estimates range from a third to half of the crop, with regional variation). Should revenue demand become too high, however, farmers could resettle on hitherto uncultivated yet arable land. Hence, land itself had limited economic value, although many farmers had invested considerable labor to bring it into cultivation.

Farmers held occupancy rights to plant and harvest (although not full property landownership). Village headmen, servants, accountants, and temples and mosques also often had customary rights to a share of the produce. Most prominently, one or more levels of *zamindar*s ("landholders") held rights to collect the revenues, retain a portion, and convey the rest to imperial officials. The amount of revenue retained by zamindars depended on whether the land was directly managed by them or not, as well as on their power relative to the cultivators and the state.

Akbar's imperial officials increasingly demanded that land revenues be paid in cash (not in kind as earlier) at fixed times with written receipts and records kept by village and provincial accountants. This further monetized the economy. Moneylenders and merchants based in *qasba*s (market-towns) made loans and purchased produce for sale in regional markets, providing money for taxes. These wholesalers transported the crop to towns and cities, imperial armies, or markets in food-deficit regions.

Even under Akbar, however, the empire never achieved hegemony. Tensions persisted between officials and settled farmers, the core of the economy. The annual rainfall cycle shaped the agricultural year, which determined seasons of peace and war. During the fallow season, many village men with varying military experience and weaponry joined mobile armies or formed their own bands, seeking plunder. The Mughal state never fully controlled this vast seasonal military labor market. Further, repeated armed rebellions by local rulers, landholders, farming communities, high mansabdars, and even by Akbar's brother and eldest son, punctuated his regime.

Forest-dwellers traded vital fodder, fuel, fruits, medicinal herbs, wood, and other forest resources to villages, towns, and cities in exchange for their crops and hand-manufactured goods. But imperial forces struggled to penetrate forestlands, collect revenues, or even locate their inhabitants. Shifting cultivation meant that surveying and assessing those crops was beyond the capacity of Mughal officials. So, forested regions remained interior frontiers for the empire, with local rajas and other forest lords sometimes being forced to submit tribute (including military service, cash, and elephants), but only after expensive military expeditions into that geographically, logistically, and politically hostile terrain.

Similarly, migratory pastoralists supplied cattle and produced meat and dairy products for local and regional markets and transported grain and other products, often over long distances, while largely evading imperial control. Nonetheless, imperial armies relied on huge caravans of bullocks (sometimes over a quarter-million strong) carrying grain on their backs. But such pastoralists and itinerant traders also proved difficult for the Mughal administration to tax.

Throughout his reign, Akbar combined his efforts to control people, land, and crops with demonstrating his mastery over wild and dangerous animals. For instance, he repeatedly risked his life taming elephants – valuable for military transport and impressive Indic symbols of sovereignty in procession and battle. He audaciously rode bull elephants in *mausth* – aggressive behavior associated with periods of testosterone surge in the elephant (and perhaps also in the rider).

Akbar initially savored the massive Mongol-style *qamargha* hunt. This required considerable organizational skill since hundreds (or even thousands) of beaters were systematically linked in a great circle, enclosing all wild animals within. Subordinate officers then maneuvered these rings of beaters simultaneously and evenly inward, concentrating the animals for Akbar and his chosen companions to slaughter with arrows, spears, swords, and matchlock guns.

In 1578, amid his final qamargha, Akbar collapsed unconscious, to the consternation of his attendants and danger to his regime. Earlier, Akbar had similar episodes, although contemporary sources are vague about their severity and duration since any disclosed weakness in the emperor would be perilous for the state. This time, after regaining consciousness, Akbar suddenly ordered the enclosed animals freed, designated the site as sacred, and had the top of his head shorn, reportedly to enable his soul to escape at death. Akbar's publicist proclaimed this a transfiguring infusion of the divine spirit into Akbar.

Akbar apparently felt empowered by this mystical experience to expand his assertions of spiritual authority over people, and the universe. He had long linked himself to influential Muslim and non-Muslim mystics. Indeed, in 1571 he had constructed an entirely new capital, Fatehpur ("City of Victory"), at the shrine of Sheikh Salim of the Chishti Sufi order. Later, Akbar began minting on his coins and using in his decrees the Arabic phrase "Allah-o-Akbar." This conventionally means "God is Great" but also, controversially, "Akbar is Allah."

Around 1583, Akbar reportedly ceased performing the five daily Islamic prayers and began worshiping the sun four times daily and divine light more generally. Akbar's new rituals may have multiple sources. Mongol tradition proclaimed divine luminescence as impregnating the Mongols' mythic mother. Some of Akbar's Rajput Hindu wives claimed descent from the sun, and performed Brahminic solar-worship in his harem. Indeed, Akbar reportedly included in his noontime ritual the recitation of the sun's 1,001 Sanskrit names. Further, Akbar invited Portuguese Jesuits to court, and questioned them about Mary's sinless impregnation by the Holy Spirit, among other topics.

From 1578 onward, Akbar also welcomed leading Jains to court. Jains (then and now) credit their leaders' personal and spiritual influence on Akbar for his empire-wide ban on animal slaughter during the annual Jain holy season. Indeed, Akbar experimented with vegetarianism, explaining:

It is not right that a man should make his stomach the grave of animals . . . Were it not for the thought of the difficulty of sustenance, I would prohibit men from eating meat. The reasons why I do not altogether abandon it myself is that many others might willingly forego it likewise and thus be cast into despondency . . . From my earliest years, whenever I ordered animal food to be cooked for me, I found it rather tasteless and cared little for it. I took this feeling to indicate a necessity for protecting animals, and I refrained from animal food. (Abu al-Fazl 1873–94, 3:394–96)

He thus explained avoiding meat in personal and ethical terms, not religious ones.

Akbar searched for a universal basis for all religions, seeking to enhance congeniality among all his subjects' religious communities. This became his policy *sulh-i kul* ("universal peace" or "tolerance for all"). He thus respected everyone who submitted to him as "the perfect man" and "universal sovereign." Since his armies continued to suppress dissidents and conquer neighbors, Akbar did not give up warfare, however. Rather, he and his core advisors creatively integrated his family's Turko-Mongol traditions with Persianate and various Indic cultures, projecting him as the millennial sovereign, the lord of the four quarters – master over people, land, plants, animals, and time itself (Moin 2012). Akbar redefined time by imposing a new solar-based calendar, *Tarikh-i Ilahi* ("Divine Era"), that began with his own accession. This calendar also had practical administrative advantages since the annual harvest and thus the revenue cycle varied within the lunar Islamic Hijri calendar. Akbar's millennialism resonated with the end of the first thousand years of Islam (corresponding to October 19, 1591 CE).

A devotional sect dedicated to Akbar developed at court, perhaps as early as 1582. This imperial cult had secret mystical practices known only to full initiates. Today generally termed *Din-i Illahi* ("Divine Religion"), it was apparently called at court *Tauhid-i Illahi* ("Divine Unity"). Initiates received from Akbar an icon of the sun, a special turban, and a small portrait of him to wear on head or heart. Further, initiates stopped using among themselves the conventional Arabic greeting *as-salam alaykum* ("peace be upon you") and response *wa alaykum al-salam* ("and unto you be peace"), instead substituting *Allah-o Akbar*, with the response *jalla jalaluhu* ("glorified be His glory"), evoking one of Akbar's titles, Jalal al-Din ("Glory of Religion"). Akbar and his initiates periodically performed sun and light worship. This imperial cult bound its members to him, overriding their other loyalties like family and community.

Further, a more diffuse devotional cult to Akbar emerged among the populace. Each morning, he displayed his radiance from a palace balcony.

Akbar's publicist described this as Akbar bestowing "the light of his countenance" by giving *darshan* (Sanskrit for the "auspicious sight" that a deity bestows on devotees) (Abu al-Fazl 1873–94, 1:165). From this balcony, Akbar also observed spectacular elephant and other animal combats.

Despite Akbar's innovations, there were limits on his power and authority, and the technologies available to his regime to control the environment. Repeated popular uprisings tested his armies and administration. Further, courtiers formed factions around each of his three sons (and even grandsons), knowing only one of them would accede to the throne. Eventually, his eldest son, Prince Salim (1569–1627), outlived his brothers, openly rebelled, established himself as a rival emperor (based in Allahabad), and only submitted to Akbar on the latter's deathbed, reigning henceforth as Emperor Jahangir.

A Century of Mughal Imperial Rule over South Asia (1605–1707)

Over most of the seventeenth century, the Mughal Empire appeared to many unassailable and able to command many of the subcontinent's human and natural resources. In retrospect, serious internal and external strains are apparent. During this period, Emperors Jahangir (r. 1605–27), Shah Jahan (r. 1628–58), and Aurangzeb 'Alamgir (r. 1658–1707) each fought his way to the throne. Then each reshaped Akbar's institutions, often overstretching the empire's technology and weakening bonds among its components. Even as imperial expenditures rose, resistance by regional rulers and local communities periodically reduced revenues. Global climate changes brought periodic El Niño events, so droughts compounded famines caused by imperial policies and regional wars. In the unsettling context of a globalizing world economy, European imports of silver from the Americas and Japan, which originally lubricated the economy, eventually created inflation that unbalanced imperial finances. All these factors altered the empire's complex relationships with India's environment. Without detailing these three regimes, select examples illustrate each individually and also overall patterns.

Each new emperor devised his own means for asserting his sovereignty over his domain, human and nonhuman. Emperor Jahangir determined to distinguish himself above all other monarchs, including Akbar, not personally in battle but through his court's glory. He bound his mansabdars to him through a refinement of Akbar's imperial cult in which even distant commanders achieved victory through Jahangir's mystical power.

Jahangir personally took to the field as an animal hunter rather than as a warrior (see Figure 6.1). He prided himself on his bow- and musket-shooting, boasting that, by age forty-seven, he had already successfully killed 17,167 animals (and another 11,365 in hunts which he supervised) (Jahangir 1914, 2:369). His skill was not in tracking animals, only shooting them from close range. Yet, he also saw hunting in moral terms. Evidently due to the teachings of leading Jain ascetics at his court, he himself vowed not to hunt on certain weekdays or for specific time periods. Further, for five years, he promised to give up personally killing any more animals to bring about the recovery of his ill grandson (although he continued to supervise hunting by his courtiers, including his favorite wife, Nur Jahan).

Jahangir avidly acquired natural rarities, having them embellished by his workshops into fine objects for his pleasure. For instance, Jahangir detailed in 1619,

... out of the veined spotted tooth [walrus tusk] ... I ordered to be cut off sufficient for two dagger-hilts [carved in] the Jahangiri fashion ... One hilt came out coloured in such a way as to create astonishment [since] the flowers looked as if a skilful painter had depicted them ... In short, it was so delicate that I never wish it to be apart from me for a moment .... (Jahangir 1914, 2:98–99)

When he acquired a rare flower, fruit, or animal (including a North American turkey and the nearly extinct dodo, both imported by Europeans), he had it documented in paintings, and sometimes physically dissected to satisfy his curiosity and enhance his knowledge of divinely guided natural principles.

Jahangir created pleasure gardens and pavilions, hunting lodges, bridges, caravanserais, and tombs. When Jahangir's favorite antelope died, he marked the grave with an impressive tower, decorated with a sculpture and an engraved prose eulogy. Jahangir's architecture displayed his aesthetics using light and airy spaces and costly white marble exteriors. He adorned the interior walls of his vast encampment tents and buildings with rich textiles, murals and portraits. Thus, Jahangir's possessions reflected his self-proclaimed mastery over the world's refinements.

Despite the vast treasury he inherited – about 150 percent of the empire's total annual income – Jahangir's expenses far exceeded his revenues. Further, his reign was punctuated by strong El Niño events and consequent severe droughts and famines (1614–16, 1623–24), plus outbreaks of bubonic plague (1619). Jahangir responded not with any systematic adaptation measures but rather by bestowing charity and some tax relief, enabling people could cope (or even just survive). He also gave

Figure 6.1 Emperor Jahangir Hunting, by Muhammad Nasir al-Munshi, 1600–04 (Allahabad period). Courtesy Los Angeles County Museum of Art (M.83.137), www.LACMA.org

vast alms to the needy and Muslim holy men at the solar and lunar calendrical commemorations of his birth and accession. Throughout his lifetime, Jahangir consumed debilitating amounts of opium and alcohol (like many men in his imperial family). Yet, he did not approve intoxication in his subordinates. For instance, he banished William Hawkins, the first English ambassador to his court, reportedly for attending while drunk.

As Jahangir aged and his health declined, he increasingly devoted himself lovingly to his final bride, famous as Nur Jahan (strikingly, she was a 35-year-old widow with a daughter when they married; she had no children with Jahangir). In his personal diary, Jahangir celebrated her accomplishments. For instance, while hunting with him, she killed four tigers; he boasted, "Until now such shooting was never seen, that from the top of an elephant and inside a howdah … " (Jahangir 1914, 1:305). As her Iranian family rose to power, she effectively ruled in Jahangir's name, including trying to orchestrate the succession. Instead, after Jahangir's death, her estranged stepson and nephew-in-law, Shah Jahan, executed the other imperial claimants and acceded in 1628.

Rather than an imperial cult (like his father and grandfather), Shah Jahan favored a stately, dignified, and conventional Sunni court culture. After reigning ten years, Shah Jahan changed from solar to lunar dating (thus conforming to the Islamic calendar but altering revenue and other official record systems). As emperor, he supervised military campaigns, for instance in the Central Indian forests and against the remaining Deccani sultanates, but did not himself fight. Further, he closely directed fixed material manifestations of his sovereign splendor, most notably the Peacock throne, Taj Mahal, and Shahjahanabad as his capital.

Soon after Shah Jahan's accession, he commissioned the uniquely brilliant golden Peacock Throne: a raised 6.3 m^2 (70 ft^2) platform under a 4.6 m (15 ft)-high canopy surmounted by ornamental peacocks, everything thickly gem-encrusted. Peacocks have long represented both integrity and beauty in Indic traditions (and are now the Republic of India's national bird). It took seven years to accumulate the vast amounts of bullion and precious stones (worth about 10 million rupees) and to craft the throne that Shah Jahan considered worthy of his reign. From when he first occupied his Peacock Throne in 1635, all who saw or heard of it were awed with Mughal magnificence (this throne remained intact until 1739 and remains legendary today).

Shah Jahan had daughters by his first and third wives, and he gave these womenfolk honored places in his imperial harem. But he remained devoted to his second wife, Mumtaz Mahal (married to him by her aunt, Nur Jahan). When he acceded as Emperor, Mumtaz Mahal had already borne him eleven children – four sons and two daughters were still living. In 1631, only three years into his reign, Mumtaz Mahal died at age thirty-eight while giving birth to her fourteenth child. She had joined him for a Deccan campaign. Shah Jahan eventually sent her body 800 km (500 mi) to Agra for burial in the Rauza-i Munauwara ("Illuminated Tomb") – a personal tribute and a stone manifestation of his imperial power. This tomb has been celebrated globally as the Taj Mahal. By the time of its completion, this tomb-garden had cost about 5 million rupees (a vast amount, but only half the Peacock Throne's cost). For nearly four centuries, the Taj Mahal has stood as an architectural masterpiece, famous worldwide for the technology of its construction, and, even more, for the quality of its workmanship and the exquisite balance and proportion of its forms.

After this tomb's construction, Shah Jahan ordered the skilled builders and workmen to migrate to Delhi in 1639, where he commissioned his imperial city, Shahjahanabad. The city's imposing red-sandstone-walled citadel, the Qila-i Mu'alla ("Exalted Fort," popularly known as the Red Fort), cost 6 million rupees. This new fortress overlooked the Jumna River, designed for defense and to enclose the imperial palace complex. Perfumed water canals extended throughout, cascading over illuminated falls. The separate structures for dwelling, administration and pleasure were mostly constructed with interior and exterior walls of white marble (or stucco burnished to appear marble), often with highly ornate, semiprecious stone inlays. Some glazed tiles even depicted European-style images of jointly Quranic-Biblical people and angels. Shah Jahan used the Bengali regional style of deeply curved sloping roofs, sometimes with gilded metal coverings. Near the Red Fort, and also of red sandstone, Shah Jahan constructed the Jami' Mosque (1650–56), the largest in India at that time, costing another million rupees. In 1653, he faced Shahjahanabad's city walls (initially brick and mud) with red sandstone.

Within the city walls, high mansabdars built mansions surrounded by their workshops and their attendants' homes, each forming a distinctive neighborhood. Courtiers and leading imperial women sponsored additional mosques and pleasure gardens within and without the city. The main market boulevard, Chandni Chawk, ran from the Red Fort west to the city's Lahore gateway, with shops lining both sides and a canal running down its center. This canal, reconstructed by 'Ali Mardan Khan from an earlier Delhi Sultanate one, diverted water from the Jumna River.

Throughout the citadel and city, imperial engineers constructed elaborate and efficient water-supply and sewage systems with complex lifting-devices and pottery piping to supply water for drinking, cooking, sanitation, bathing, and pleasure. Plentiful potable water came from wells in each neighborhood or from the Jumna, either raised by Persian water-wheels or channeled from upstream by gravity-fed canals. This system also provided for wet-carriage sewage into the Jumna downstream. Since most waste was organic, and the city's human population was only in the tens of thousands, the river could absorb it without ecological damage. Further, surrounding market gardens received human and animal dry-carriage sewage and produced vegetables for the city.

In building Shahjahanabad, Shah Jahan sought to combine a newer model of an omnipotent monarch ruling from a stable capital with the Central Asian tradition of imperial mobility (Blake 1993). Many Indic rulers based themselves in a hub capital, the center of the realm and universe. But the Timurid model favored the ruler's constant military and hunting expeditions, by which he personally imposed his authority throughout his domain. In layout, Shahjahanabad's palace complex had many freestanding buildings which resembled a military encampment. During the next nine years following the Red Fort's completion in 1648, he lived there a total of five and a half years (during six visits). In between, he traveled: supervising his domain and military campaigns and visiting Lahore and thrice Kashmir (1634, 1645, 1651).

Huge but unproductive wars intensified long-standing strains within the mansab-jagir system. These expeditions cost more than double Shah Jahan's massive building projects (which totaled 29 million rupees). Further, land revenues were strongly affected by El Niño events (1629–32), and a continuing period of droughts until 1640.

By 1647, Shah Jahan's total assessed revenue was 220 million rupees: a quarter more than Jahangir's peak and more than double Akbar's. This increase came from a combination of newly conquered territories in the Deccan and elsewhere, growth in the overall economy, but also inflation (especially from the continuing substantial influx of roughly a hundred tons of silver annually via European merchants). Shah Jahan shifted resources from mansabdars into his own treasury (nearly empty at his accession but after twenty years' worth about 37 million rupees, even after his vast expenditures). However, the gap widened between the official assessed revenue and the actual amount collected. Further, as Shah Jahan's four sons reached maturity, their factions intensified their preparations for the coming bloody accession war.

Even before Shah Jahan died, his third son, Aurangzeb, defeated and executed his brothers and imprisoned Shah Jahan (for nearly eight years, until his death). As Emperor ʿAlamgir, he ruled for five decades until his death during his ninetieth year in 1707. During that long reign, he reformed the regime according his own strong Sunni beliefs. He constantly campaigned, asserting his imperial authority over opponents across almost the entire subcontinent. While he did not spare himself, he often saw his subordinates fail to accomplish his goals. Under his direction, the empire reached its territorial limits, but vital imperial resources were overreached. In many ways, his reign marked the empire's peak but also its significant deterioration.

ʿAlamgir believed his personal piety would secure God's blessing on his empire and assure its triumphs over its enemies and those of Islam. He began to purify his court's culture and protocols of alleged unorthodox and un-Islamic practices. An early reform ended the solar *Nauroz* ("New Year") festivities – a pre-Islamic Iranian tradition celebrated since Akbar's reign, which differed from the lunar Hijri calendar. To protect the Islamic creed from possible disrespect, ʿAlamgir removed it from imperial coins. He sent a richly laden embassy to Mecca seeking validation for his reign; when this first mission failed, he sent a second, eventually gaining approval.

As a pious Muslim and emperor, ʿAlamgir renounced his own earlier personal pleasures that diverted him from sober fulfillment of his religious and imperial duties. He had frequently indulged in hunting, but he relinquished that pastime. As he advised a son, "Hunting is the business of idle persons. It is very reprehensible for one to be absorbed in worldly affairs, and to disregard religious matters" (ʿAlamgir 1908:14–19). Although ʿAlamgir had been a connoisseur of music, he came to believe music excited emotions, so he eschewed it for himself. However, he did not ban music for his courtiers and officials; indeed, significant texts on music theory emerged during his reign under such sub-imperial patronage. Similarly, he closed the imperial painting atelier and stopped much poetry recitation in court, although courtiers and women in his household patronized and savored these arts.

The succession war had devastated much of north India, compounded by El Niño events which led to droughts and then famines in much of India (1660–62). In response, ʿAlamgir officially suspended or abolished some taxes. Further, he performed his charitable obligation as sovereign by increasing food distribution from imperial alms houses. This temporarily aided his exceptionally needy subjects, but his regime did not invest in infrastructure for long-term improvements in their condition.

From his accession onward, ʿAlamgir sought to demonstrate his power by controlling the empire's long-troublesome internal and external frontiers. For instance, in 1661, he ordered Bihar's governor to end the persistent resistance in that province's heavily forested south. Simultaneously, ʿAlamgir commanded Bengal's governor to annex hilly Cooch Bihar and Kamrup. After seven years of costly campaigning,

Mughal armies forced the ruler of Assam to submit, cede his western territories, and send a daughter to wed ˈAlamgir's third son, ˈAzam. In 1663, ˈAlamgir ordered Gujarat's governor to annex Navanagar kingdom. In 1665, he directed Kashmir's governor to force Tibet's "zamindar Dalai" to submit tribute. The next year, Mughal forces seized Chittagong from Portuguese and Arakanese "pirates." Starting in 1667, some Afghan communities expelled Mughal authorities; imperial armies sent to crush them instead suffered major defeats (1674, 1675). Only after ˈAlamgir himself went to supervise were these risings suppressed by combining force and subsidy-payments (protection money), thus securing the vital route to Kabul. These hard-won successes, however, proved unexpectedly expensive in financial and human resources, with little gain in revenues. Further, almost every victory proved temporary: imperial administration soon weakened; many of these rulers regained their territory and independence.

Peasant communities in the Mughal heartland also persistently rebelled. Through the late 1660s, Hindu Jats around Mathura rallied under their popular leader, Gokula. Eventually in 1670, Mughal troops subdued this insurrection (albeit temporarily) and captured Gokula's children. ˈAlamgir renamed Mathura "Islamabad" and ordered the demolition of the major temple there (recycling its stonework into a mosque in nearby Agra). Yet, Jat uprisings reemerged in the late 1680s. In Punjab, Sikhs under their Gurus, revolted repeatedly against Mughal rule and repulsed several Mughal suppression campaigns.

The Marathas of the western Deccan were the community on the Mughal frontier most powerfully resistant to both imperial arms and enticements. Many Marathas had rallied under their charismatic leader, Shivaji (1627–80). ˈAlamgir sent some of his best commanders and troops against Shivaji, but they repeatedly failed. In a daring, lucrative, and politically significant expedition, Shivaji sacked the rich and strategic port of Surat in 1664, which Mughal authorities proved incompetent to defend. In 1666, ˈAlamgir sought to incorporate Shivaji by investing his seven-year-old son, Sambhaji, with mansab 5,000 and by summoning them both to the imperial court at Agra.

Like many outsiders at the court, Shivaji was alienated rather than assimilated. One imperial courtier reflected their condescending attitude toward Shivaji (and other newcomers) whom they regarded as bestial:

... this wild animal of the wilderness of ignorance, who knew not the etiquette of the imperial court, went into a corner and made improper expressions of dissatisfaction and complaint ... The Emperor ordered that he should return to his lodging ... in view of the fraud and satanic trickery of this arch-deceiver. (Khan 1947:36–37)

However, Shivaji dramatically escaped back to his homeland and rallied his followers there.

As various other rulers and rival factions within the Mughal administration all engaged in multisided conflicts in the Deccan, Shivaji intermittently supported or opposed each of them. In 1670, Shivaji plundered Surat again, adding to his own wealth and fame and humiliating its imperial defenders. In 1674, Shivaji further enhanced his status through an elaborate Brahminical enthronement as *Maharaja Chatrapati* (Sanskritic "Emperor of the Four Quarters"). Shivaji had made the Maratha coalition the most expansive force in the Deccan, mobilized around potent Hindu cultural symbols – like so many other rebellions against 'Alamgir's regime and policies.

'Alamgir increasingly ordered constraints on non-Muslims. He was both offended by the non-Muslim ideologies that motivated many opponents and also swayed by his own self-identification as leader of the Muslim community. Among other policies, he reinstated the pilgrim tax for non-Muslim religious festivals and tried to curtail them. While 'Alamgir gave financial support to some Hindu temples, he also canceled revenue grants and directed the destruction of others, especially those belonging to rebels. He restored the jizya that Akbar had abolished.

Despite 'Alamgir's considerable expenditures of manpower and financial resources, his reign proved disappointing to him and to many mansabdars who formed the imperial core. Many also resented the appointment to high mansabs of former enemies, particularly those considered culturally inferior. This resentment intensified since there were insufficient available jagirs and since even those jagirs usually failed to produce their nominal income. As 'Alamgir admitted, "We have a small sum of money and many have a demand for it" ('Alamgir 1908:23). All this led many inside and outside the imperial establishment to question 'Alamgir's authority and act to control resources in their own interests.

In 1679, 'Alamgir left Shahjahanabad, never to return to that city. Until then, he had traveled out relatively rarely: supervising campaigns in Afghanistan, visiting Agra and Allahabad and once (severely exhausted) resting in Kashmir. His 1679 departure initiated the pattern that would dominate his remaining four decades: 'Alamgir moving among military encampments and provisional capitals in Rajasthan and then the Deccan to deal personally with imperial crises, sometimes himself commanding battles.

Overall, the empire was losing effectiveness due to structural stresses from financial imbalances, over-expansion, natural events including droughts, and conflicting interests among ʿAlamgir, mansabdari factions, his diverse subjects, rival powers, and his own heirs. The empire had always needed perpetual conquests to capture enemy treasuries and gain productive territories. This income paid for its armies that enabled that expansion and for its administration that collected the revenues. But over ʿAlamgir's final two decades, the costs of empire came to outweigh the benefits for many mansabdars and subjects. Strong El Niño events compounded famines (1685–88) caused by the seemingly endless wars. Neither the imperial center, nor its armies, nor its administration had the policies, technology or manpower to control resources over such a vast territorial expanse and array of regionally based rulers and communities.

As ʿAlamgir passed through his seventies and eighties, he struggled to manage the empire as a whole. Imperial commanders raided kingdoms as far south as Thanjavur during the early 1690s, making those rulers nominal tributaries. But the imperial administration exerted little control there, or even over earlier captured territories. Seeing few of his goals accomplished unless he directed them personally, ʿAlamgir concentrated imperial revenues and manpower in his own hands.

Consequently, the empire began to segment as resource flows and communication links between north and south were periodically interrupted due to predations by bandits, warlords, and even intermediate imperial officials. Most mansabdars in north India faced regional uprisings without the prospect of military reinforcement or financial support from ʿAlamgir in the Deccan. Further, distant mansabdars did not bond to the emperor through recurrent direct personal exchanges as they had earlier. Conversely, most governors had little effective supervision from the imperial center and retained provincial revenues for themselves. By the time of ʿAlamgir's death, no north Indian province was sending substantial revenues to him – except for prosperous Bengal where an especially effective official, Murshid Quli Khan, managed an expanding agricultural base, developing artisanal production, and increasing exports.

During ʿAlamgir's long Deccan campaigns, many mansabdars who originated in north India – including Rajputs and many long-settled Muslims – had been serving far from home through decades of frustrating harassment by local insurgents, especially Marathas. One official lamented the frustrating and interminable Deccan campaigns: "Ever since His Majesty had ... adopted all these wars and hardships of travel, ... the inmates of his camp, sick of long separation, summoned their families ...

and ... a new generation was thus born (in the camp)" (Bhimsen 1972: 233). Imperial commanders often saw little prospect of defeating these insurgents or benefit to the empire or themselves from doing so. Instead, many imperial generals preserved their own financial and manpower resources by negotiating private settlements with those enemies, despite 'Alamgir's repeated, explicit orders forbidding this. On their part, many new Deccani mansabdars, whose submission had been thus purchased, had little loyalty to the empire. They often saw better prospects in repudiating imperial service to carve out kingdoms for themselves or to join leaders from their own community who were doing so. These included various Marathas and other regionally rooted warlords.

In both north India and the Deccan, many tributary rulers, landholders, and other subjects – including peasants, artisans, merchants, and bankers – faced revenue demands from the empire but increasingly doubted the value of paying. Imperial officials had diminished capacity to provide justice, law, and order, or to compel tax payments. In contrast, local rajas and zamindars often had bonds with the local population and retained more resources, which they used to bolster their own power. Particularly in the Deccan, much of the economy had been devastated by decades of warfare and disrupted commerce. Expanding areas were subject to annual levies by Maratha-led war bands: *chauth* (payment of a "quarter" of the assessed revenue) plus other tribute in exchange for relief from even more costly depredations. Imperial officials often acquiesced in these exactions, since they were often unable to resist them.

While European assertions in India would not appear prominently until long after 'Alamgir's death, their effects were already significant. Parts of the Indian economy were engaging more extensively in exporting cloth, saltpeter, spices, and other goods aboard European ships. Gradually, the English, Dutch, and French East India Companies were replacing the Portuguese as controllers of the Indian Ocean trade and passage to Mecca. These joint-stock corporations also established trading enclaves along India's west and east coasts and inland, seeking profits and negotiating with local officials and with 'Alamgir himself for tax concessions. When negotiations broke down, violence sometimes ensued, for example in skirmishes between imperial officials and the English at Hugli (1686–90), Bombay (1688–89), Surat (1695–99), and Madras (1702).

Further, various independent European sea-captains also preyed upon merchant shipping as pirates and privateers, which imperial officials could not prevent. 'Alamgir scolded his son, 'Azam, Gujarat's current governor:

... ships cannot sail without the permit of the *Firangi*s [Europeans]. The Muslim community has become so impuissant that even the imperial vessels are unable to cruise. For the last twenty years, the ships of the Surat merchants and those destined for the Holy Land are being plundered on the high seas. Steps taken by [mansabdars] to combat the problem have proved fruitless. Negligence, indolence, and indifference towards this matter are contrary to the Islamic sense of honour ... Concession and favour to the *Firangi*s have been shown beyond measure. Moderation will not work. Severity and harshness are required. (Farooqi 1988:198)

'Alamgir himself futilely tried to force English and Dutch ambassadors to make their Companies protect Indian shipping, or even cease seizing it. But the lack of a Mughal imperial seagoing navy and pragmatic and self-serving collaboration in port cities between imperial officials and Europeans meant continued insecurity for Indian ships, their cargoes and pilgrim passengers.

'Alamgir also feared for his dynasty, not perceiving much capacity in any of his potential heirs. His eldest surviving son, Mu'azzam, was already aged sixty-three at 'Alamgir's death. Mu'azzam and his family had for seven years been imprisoned by 'Alamgir for treachery. Even after Mu'azzam's release, he remained in disfavor, posted from 1700 onward far from court, as governor of Kabul and Lahore. However, there he gathered supporters among mansabdars for the coming succession war which he won. He ruled briefly as Emperor Bahadur Shah (r. 1707–12) but the glue that had bound most of India's regions and many of its people to the empire had largely dissolved. While the Mughal Empire fragmented over the next century and a half, the effects of Eurocentric globalization increased.

European East India Companies (c. 1600 Onward)

During the seventeenth century, northern European joint-stock corporations were gradually exerting their control over human and nonhuman Indian resources. In 1600, a group of London merchants had received a charter from Queen Elizabeth I giving them the monopoly over trade within all lands from southern Africa to the Philippines. Since the English had no presence in these lands, this was a pretentious decree (but also portentous, as subsequent events would prove). The English East India Company [EIC] was founded on capitalism, seeking commercial profit for the owners of its stock, the "proprietors" who elected its managing Court of Directors. With larger-capacity ships and more investment capital, the EIC could trade in larger volume goods than the Portuguese. European markets valued Indian exports of plant-derived products (especially cotton cloth, spices, indigo, and sugar) and minerals (including saltpeter for gunpowder). However, since England's own early exports (including woolen cloth and lead) found little demand in India, the EIC had for its first 150 years to finance much of this trade with silver and gold, largely originating in the Americas and used by the Spanish and Portuguese to purchase English products. Rival Europeans also competed for Indian resources, especially the Dutch East India Company (established 1616) and French East India Company (established 1664).

The EIC protected its investment by acquiring and fortifying warehouses ("factories"). Three became the EIC's main port-enclaves: Bombay (Portuguese Princess Catherine of Braganza's dowry to King Charles II in 1661, then rented to the EIC), Calcutta, and Madras (the latter two purchased from local rulers). Unlike many indigenous towns and cities that emerged from regional markets, these three were imposed from the outside and remained oriented toward the export of Indian plant, animal, and mineral products, only slowly creating their own catchment hinterlands.

While British EIC employees went to India as salaried merchants ("factors") and clerks, many soon engaged for their own personal profit and fame in various ways with India and Indians, including in commerce, employment, and acquiring resources. For instance, to gain favor, some high EIC officials sent rare Indian beasts, including caracals, cheetahs, and lions (along with their Indian trainers) as presents to the British king. During this period, roughly half the British EIC personnel died in India (or on the passage there or back), of disease, dissipation, or warfare. But some rich survivors illegally repatriated their wealth in diamonds, easily concealed from official EIC taxation. Retiring Britons also brought back with them to Europe a growing number of Indian wives and servants, along with a taste for Indian-style clothing, art, and cuisine.

These factories also employed ever more Indian commercial intermediaries, weavers, other artisans, subordinate officials, armed guards, seamen, teachers, and scribes. Indian servants and wives or mistresses attended in the homes of its officials and officers. During this early colonial period, some Europeans were open to learning about India's environment from Indian scholars. But increasingly, European imperialism introduced new economies, policies, attitudes, and technologies which subordinated Indians and the Indian environment, making ever more of them part of the extending and intensifying Eurocentric world system, as the next chapter considers.

7 Mughal Imperial Fragmentation, Regional State Rise, Popular Environmental Movements, and Early British Colonial Policies and Institutions (c.1700–1857)

Over the eighteenth and early nineteenth centuries, a range of interacting forces strongly affected India's environmental history and our knowledge and understanding of it. As the Mughal imperial system fragmented, competing over India's resources were imperial governors, regional rulers, warlords, uprising social and religious communities, and European joint-stock armed-mercantile corporations. Each had distinctive and divergent attitudes toward India's people, land, and fauna and flora species, and had specific technologies to control them. Devastation from this period's wars and political transitions was intensified by relatively frequent El Niño disruptions of the monsoon rains and other natural disturbances, plus human actions like altering the mix of flora and fauna species, deforestation, and pollution of air and water. The expanding English East India Company (EIC) and other contending regional rulers imposed some policies that worsened conditions (for instance, droughts that were made worse by administrative policies caused a dozen famines and four severe food scarcities in Bengal alone during this period). However, some Indians and some Europeans with scientific training were developing ways to understand the parts of the environment they valued and means to avoid damaging these.

Between 1757 and 1857, the EIC increasingly mobilized British and Indian resources more effectively than its Indian and European political and commercial rivals. Over this period, the EIC defeated ever more Indian rulers and made the Mughal emperor its palace prisoner. On average, the EIC annexed 26,000 km^2 (10,000 mi^2) annually; by 1857, it directly ruled about 2.6 million km^2 (1 million mi^2; two-thirds of India's landmass containing three-quarters of its population), forcing the rest under its indirect rule through subordinated Indian princes. Hence, the EIC dramatically expanded its technologies of commerce and rule to profit from the entire subcontinent and greatly escalated India's integration with the expanding British-centric world system.

More than any previous regime, the EIC used its technologies – including military hardware and software, water-control through perennial canals, railways, state management of forests, and communication via electric telegraph – to affect the entire subcontinent, including land, wild and domesticated animals and plants, and people. New subcontinental and world trade demanded ever more raw materials for industrializing Britain, plus wood for ships and crates and jute for sacking and ropes with which to transport them. Overall, this period saw the "Great Divergence" as industrializing Britain enriched itself as the core of its imperial world system and India became its prime periphery, supplying capital (including from seized royal treasuries and taxes), labor, artisanal goods, and raw materials, while becoming a market for finished British manufactures. Further, British (then Euro-American) industrial and other fossil fuel combustion increased CO_2 emissions that were beginning to affect the globe's climate (although humans would not become aware of this until a century later).

Our knowledge of India's environmental history for this period is greatly expanded by diverse new sources, including European-originated histories, biographies, scientific studies, and other genres preserved in archives and printed media. Exceeding the Mughal imperial bureaucracy, the EIC used systematic recordkeeping, detailed data collection, surveys, and regulations to classify all land and many other resources by ownership. The colonial government also sponsored growing numbers of studies using botanical, chemical, meteorological, zoological, and other new scientific methods. Some Euro-American and Indian scholars, from then until today, contrast India's precolonial conditions (variously characterized as "Oriental," "traditional," "medieval," or "early modern") with those following British colonialism (often termed "modern," "Westernized," "Anglicized," or "postcolonial"); some commentators presuppose or argue that these changes were progress, while others highlight their costs to many Indians and the Indian environment. Indeed, many issues concerning the environment that were developing during EIC rule still generally pertain globally today. Among them are community versus state versus private capitalist ownership of natural resources; development, preservation, or romanticizing of wilderness and particular fauna and flora species; awareness of and responsibility for anthropogenic damage to the environment; and the effects of "scientific management" of, and codified laws about, forests, waters, land, flora, and fauna.

The First Half of the Eighteenth Century

As the Mughal imperial center lost control, India's strong regional identities resurfaced, and diverse individuals, groups, communities, and

Map 7.1 India in the eighteenth and early nineteenth centuries

classes competed for resources (see Map 7.1). The most powerful imperial governors still nominally recognized the Mughal dynasty but created de facto hereditary kingdoms, including in the largest, richest provinces of Bengal, Awadh, and Hyderabad. In many regions, the dominant farming community or a religious movement arose under charismatic leaders (e.g. Marathas in the Deccan and Sikhs in Punjab). Further, the EIC (among other European trading companies) began to expand inland from coastal trading enclaves. Each of these regimes, and diverse people within them, had complex relationships with and attitudes toward the nonhuman environment.

Many scholars assert that, compared to contemporary China or Europe, early eighteenth-century Indian farmers grew an especially wide range of dry and wet crops. Sericulture was practiced in some regions. Grafting techniques also spread, for example, for some types of mango. Farmers, landholders, temples, and the state each sometimes built small reservoirs for agricultural irrigation, drinking, and fish production. Simple check-dams across watercourses, usually earthen but sometimes reinforced with stone, pooled rainfall runoff, thus allowing water to seep into shallow aquifers. More elaborate dams and weirs, some having stone or wooden outflow sluices, diverted water into channels, sometimes lined with stone or fired-brick and extending for long distances to bring water to fields. In the driest regions, households and communities developed impermeable catchment basins in fields or within courtyards for rainwater harvesting and storage in underground cisterns. Villagers also dug many wells, lined by unfired or fired bricks. Wooden scoops and leather bags, sometimes on balance arms, raised shallow water; bullocks pulled ropes drawing leather water-bags from deeper wells. Relatively costly Persian wheels with gearing-pin mechanisms were used by wealthier communities.

Further, temples, kings, and landholders mobilized labor and artisans to expand simple wells into larger stone-faced stepwells or reservoirs, often elaborately ornamented and with dated inscriptions. Some rulers reshaped rocky hilltops into forts that combined protection with water supply; excavating rock for ramparts and buildings created internal reservoirs; building fortification walls across watercourses or seepage vectors created dams that incorporated settling tanks and cisterns to produce cleaner water supplies. In the upper Gangetic and Indus plains, there were seasonal inundation or diversion canals for irrigation and perennial ones for urban sanitation.

Simultaneously, however, India had developed relatively few mechanical means or inanimate energy sources to extract or transform raw materials. Inexpensive labor meant humans and domesticated animals provided most of the applied energy, although some was multiplied by wooden cranks, levers, pulleys, and gears. Weavers did not use flying shuttles, multiple linked spinning wheels, or machine energy. Wheels were used on carts and wagons, but not customarily in wheelbarrows; pack bullock or small, wind- or oar-driven river- or shore-craft provided most bulk transport. Nor were windmills used for power. The only major internal combustion engines were gunpowder weapons. Wood and charcoal rather than coal or coke heated stoves, houses, and forges (so metals tended to be low-temperature wrought, not fully smelted for purity or casting). Often a series of artisans crafted individual artifacts. Blacksmiths handmade tools and weapons, none to uniform standards, although the best examples were of high quality. Further, an unfavorable climatic period, frequent wars, and interprovincial barriers often disrupted production and long-distance commerce.

Some cultural historians look for traditions of reverence for the environment in Indian religious movements. For instance, as their sacred foundational account, 363 Bishnoi community villagers died in 1730 while nonviolently resisted the cutting of Khejri (*Prosopis cinraria*) trees by soldiers of the Raja of Jodhpur (today in Rajasthan). The Bishnoi were followers of Jambho-ji (1451–1536), famous for preaching nonviolence toward all living things. As remembered by his Bishnoi followers, Jambho-ji was a simple cowherd who achieved sacred insights and then preached twenty-nine "commandments," including not killing any flora or fauna, not castrating bulls or goats, and no lying, addiction, or adultery. Many of these commandments paralleled vows by the much larger ongoing Jain community and some other Hindu sects, such as Vaishnavas. Bishnois, by nonviolently giving their lives to protect these trees and continuing to guard local biota (especially some endangered species like blackbuck), have inspired some of today's other "tree-hugging" and other wildlife conservation movements.

Some agricultural communities coalesced as the foundation for expansive regimes. For instance, Maratha soldiers and commanders, who had mobilized under Maharaja Shivaji, continued their expansion throughout the eighteenth century, creating a loose coalition of conquest states across much of the Deccan and large parts of north India. Within their kingdoms, some Maratha rulers imposed state controls over forest products and local ecosystems that had been based on relatively autonomous small-scale irrigation networks and cooperating farmers, herders, and forest-dwellers.

Many new or restored regional rulers built or developed their capitals, forming regional centers of elite consumption. For instance, ruling Muslim Nawabs (originally imperial governors) enhanced Murshidabad, Lucknow, and Hyderabad cities. Some Rajput rajas also developed their capitals. For example, Sawai Jai Singh (1673–1743, r. 1699–1743) planned and built Jaipur city in 1728 using a grid street pattern. He also was a skilled astronomer, erecting observatories there and where he served as imperial governor (i.e. Benares, Delhi, Mathura, and Ujjain), and calculated tables of lunar and planetary orbits with great accuracy. Jaipur and some of its surrounding villages were also famous for deep, stone-faced stepwells.

Regional rulers still needed coordinated human labor and water management to generate revenues. As sultans and Mughal emperors had long done, Muslim regional rulers continued to grant land to Sufis who would attract and anchor farming communities. For instance, in the arid Indus plain, Sufi hospices mobilized farmers for building long, gravity-fed inundation canals and annual silt clearing during the dry, winter season, in exchange for a share of the irrigation water flow. In the Godavari and Kaveri deltas, little kings, temple councils, merchants, and villagers managed the construction and maintenance of extensive hydraulic management through reservoirs, weirs, and small dams. Indeed, the Kaveri River's ancient Grand Anicut – from Tamil *anaikuttu* ("dam building") – was a weir roughly 325 m (1,000 ft) long and 12 m (40 ft) wide, constructed of interlocking rough and shaped stone embedded in sandy soil. During the often violent political transitions of the eighteenth century, however, many irrigation systems were destroyed or neglected.

Even as the established states and elites were destabilized, the reshaping economy advantaged some merchants, bankers, artisans, and soldiers who rose up. Many gained by reorienting themselves toward the new regional states or the EIC. Further, some established rulers recognized the financial advantages of monopolizing key resources. From the 1740s, for instance, the rulers of Cochin and Travancore asserted their exclusive right to sell teak (*Tectona grandis*; especially valued for shipbuilding due to its strength and durability) and other timber from the dense forests of the Western Ghats.

Over this period, European political and economic power increasingly began to affect the Indian environment, altering markets and commodity flows. European merchants and their Indian associates or agents purchased growing volumes of Indian raw materials and artisanal products for export (including saltpeter, indigo, and cloth), often paying in silver or gold. Further, the EIC's three main enclaves (Calcutta, Madras, and Bombay) acquired immediate hinterlands by conquest or purchase, extended their economic reach ever further inland, and became production centers (especially for cotton cloth weaving). These three each became a "presidency" (since its governor was president of an administering council of high EIC officials), which retained considerable independent authority; hence, in India the EIC had three separate civil and military services and laws about land, forests, water, and other resources. (Strong provincial autonomy would continue, to varying degrees, through the British Raj and in post-1947 India and Pakistan.) In addition, EIC officials and officers began to explore and assess the lands around their enclaves. By the mid-eighteenth century, EIC officers and officials began to intervene more decisively in Indian politics, with increasingly powerful effects on the environment.

The Second Half of the Eighteenth Century

Increasingly over the late eighteenth century, the EIC used its collateral (i.e. its exclusive legal right to Asian trade and its possessions in India) to borrow substantial British, continental European, and Indian capital that funded its rising war expenses and its purchase and shipping of Indian raw materials and artisanal products to European markets. To fight its battles and enforce its financial demands on Indian farmers, merchants, and princes, each presidency hired Indian mercenaries ("sepoys"), armed and uniformed them with imported, standardized British-made equipment, and trained them as a disciplined infantry. Sepoy regiments under British officers maneuvered and fought using military science as developed during centuries of war in Europe, including close coordination with British manufactured and commanded artillery. These expensive sepoy regiments anchored a military revolution, defeating larger but predominantly cavalry-based and more loosely organized armies under other regional rulers. EIC armies negotiated long supply lines with pastoralist-transporter communities using pack bullocks. The EIC also created stud farms for cavalry horses, bullocks, and camels, and used stables of elephants to drag heavy equipment (but the battle-elephant as an institution succumbed during this period to gunpowder-weapon technology). British naval power in the Indian Ocean supported the EIC, particularly during repeated English-French Wars that started in Europe but became global. The European Seven Years' War (1754–63), for instance, also raged in North America (called the "French and Indian War" by the British and the "War of Conquest" by the French) and in India (mainly between the EIC and the French East India Company). Crucially, the EIC used its military and political gains to enforce its commercial advantages, eventually outspending, isolating, and driving the French out of India (except for a few enclaves like Pondicherry) and dominating each Indian ruler it sequentially faced. Every branch of the EIC had a budget for its expenses and, wherever possible, found ways to extract revenues from India's human and natural resources.

The 1757 battle at Plassey highlights these many interlocking processes. The British factory at Calcutta had long been intervening economically and politically with the Nawab of Bengal and Bihar (de jure the imperial governor but de facto independent ruler) to gain profitable tax exemptions and trade monopolies over salt, saltpeter, and other Indian resources. When newly enthroned Nawab Siraj al-Daula (r. 1756–57) allied with the French and drove the British out, the EIC shipped 2,200 sepoys from Madras, commanded by a merchant-turned-officer Robert Clive (1725–74). Aided by the British navy, this sepoy army recaptured

Calcutta. Then, more by bribery than warfare, Clive's forces divided and defeated the Nawab's vastly larger army, installing one of his turncoat generals as his puppet successor. This suddenly extended the EIC's power over territory about three times the size of England, with a much larger population of humans, fauna, and flora.

Seeking profit from trade and land revenue, the EIC did not at first want to govern Bengal and Bihar, while it prevented the weak Nawab from doing so. Meanwhile the EIC (and Clive and other high officials personally) took loot and land revenue, and decreed commercial advantages over its rivals, especially after 1764 when the Mughal emperor appointed the EIC his provincial *diwan* (chief financial officer) over Bengal and Bihar. As diwan, the EIC asserted its right to collect (and largely keep) land revenues, sending only relatively small pensions to the Nawab and Mughal emperor, both largely palace prisoners. An early consequence of this administrative absence was the death of about 10 million people (roughly one-third of the population) during the devastating 1769–71 drought-turned-famine.

Often, EIC officials did not consider the costs on local ecologies or economies. For instance, under Governor-General Hastings (r. 1771–84), the EIC's Bengal Army violently pushed aside local forest-dwellers to cut a wide new military road between Calcutta and Benares, reducing the journey by 300 km (186 mi) but opening the forest to exploitation. Thriving shipbuilding, particularly in Bombay, denuded teak and other valuable tree species from an ever-expanding catchment area.

The EIC's cumulative martial, political, and commercial assertions created new demands for Indian manpower and other resources. Traditional Indian service elites became EIC subordinate employees. In some fields, the EIC slowly created classes of Indians who formally trained in some European-style technologies as draftsmen, illustrators, or surveyors. In 1763, Calcutta established a Western-style medical school for Indian students; other presidencies followed. Indian artisans and laborers concentrated in EIC port cities, becoming dependent on the British-centered world system; then, as Britain industrialized from the late eighteenth century onward, Indian cloth weavers and other craftsmen lost out, many returning impoverished to the countryside. Within the expanding EIC's directly ruled territories, its policies empowered some Indians as property landowners or capitalist merchants, often at the cost of tenants, artisans, pastoralists, and forest-dwellers. Since agricultural land revenue provided a major source of income for the EIC, measuring and assessing croplands became central undertakings. Further, commerce in cash crops (including opium, indigo, and cotton) received official encouragement, as did roadbuilding and riverine transportation of these to the coast for export.

Simultaneously, and especially on the EIC's unstable internal and external frontiers, diverse Indians resisted and developed their own initiatives. Uprisings by forest-dweller communities and villagers also challenged the EIC's rule, but its sepoy armies suppressed rebellions, sometimes coopting their leaders. On the EIC's borders, some Indian rulers recruited their own new model armies, often hiring European mercenary officers to train and command sepoy regiments. For instance, in Mysore, Hyder 'Ali (r. 1760–82) and his successor-son Tipu Sultan (r. 1782–99) were particularly successful in turning this new military technology against the EIC. But the cost of such armies exceeded the resource base and revenues of those princes, including Tipu Sultan, who was outspent, defeated, and killed by the EIC in 1799.

The EIC eventually forced each Indian prince under its indirect rule. The subordinated prince kept his throne but was prohibited from war except in support of the EIC, whose sepoy army he had to subsidize. But the hundreds of princes developed a range of attitudes toward the world around them. For example, in the early 1770s, the Nawab of Arcot hired as his state naturalist Johann/John Gerhard Koenig (1728–85), a German surgeon and student of Carl Linnaeus (Madras Presidency lured him into its employ in the same role in 1778).

For many princes, instead of battle, hunting became their expression of martial manhood. Some commanded vast hunting expeditions into uncultivated deep and open forest lands within their territories, similar to the Mughal-style qamargha, where hundreds or even thousands of their subjects formed a large circle and drove all animals within toward the waiting shooters, often on elephant-back. To create exclusive hunting reserves where they increased or conserved trophy or game species and sold off valuable timber, some rulers expelled local communities and outlawed tree felling, cattle grazing, fodder collecting, and undergrowth-clearing fires. The Amirs of Sindh, for example, created vast hunting reserves (when the EIC annexed Sindh in 1843, these reserves became the core of the Bombay Forest Department's holdings).

Nevertheless, in its structure and personnel, the EIC was not monolithic or consistent in its policies, including ones about resource control and extraction. In London, diverse interests competed within and among the British Parliament, its Board of Control (established 1784 to supervise the EIC), the EIC's directors, and its shareholders. Among the EIC's British employees in India there were always competing individuals, interests, and policies, which differed within and among the three presidencies over time and even among localities. Most governors-general spent most of their careers outside of India (and often expected to remain there only for one term, during which they enhanced their wealth through lavish salaries and perquisites). Hence, many arrived with little knowledge of India's environment, although they often tried to impose their abstract theories and ideologies on it. Frequently discordant with actual conditions, these policies rarely produced their expected results, and were sometimes superseded by those of successors. In contrast, the core of EIC rule consisted of career civil servants and army officers who arrived young and, if they survived, became "old India hands."

The EIC was one of the first major multinational corporations, based on the principle of capitalist private ownership over land, animals, plants, and humans (through slavery). A particularly salient example of this principle came in Bengal Presidency as the 1793 "Permanent Settlement" under Governor-General Charles, Marquis Cornwallis (1738–1805, r. 1786–93, 1805). Having been defeated at Yorktown (1781) during the American Revolution but still a rich and influential English landowner, Cornwallis arrived unfamiliar with India. But he believed in physiocratic principles: thriving agriculture under "improving landlords" was the core of any economy and the basis of public health, while cities and commerce were secondary. His Permanent Settlement recognized specific Indians as landowners with private property rights over their estates, including the land, riverfronts, enclosed bodies of water, fish, animals, plants, and minerals. Further, this settlement permanently fixed their revenue assessment, so landowners could (in theory) invest their profits in improving the land. However, there were unintended consequences, including dispossession of customary tenant rights. Additionally, the assessment was often more than many zamindars (formerly landholders, now landowners) could pay, leading to considerable seizure and auction of their estates for tax arrears. Instead, rich Indian merchants, often urban-based, invested capital in these estates, often living as absentee landlords. Their intermediary managers often extracted whatever rents they could from the now at-will tenants, with the income diverted to Calcutta (making it the "city of palaces" and funding the "Bengal Renaissance" and then early Indian nationalism). Further, the legal boundaries between estates and the termination of community land-tenure security often ended the earlier collective maintenance of long water-channeling embankments, so they silted up and deteriorated. Many later British officials considered the Permanent Settlement a failure, so it was not widely repeated elsewhere; each presidency instead subsequently tried a variety of other proprietary land settlements including peasant-tiller ownership or collective clan ownership.

Many Europeans envisioned traditional Indian rulers as "Oriental Despots," with sovereignty over everything. Hence, many British officials asserted the EIC's ownership of all resources within its territories unless they were specifically and legally (in British documentation) owned by someone else. So, when the Bengal government sought ways to increase its revenue, it enforced state ownership over all forests, grasslands, rivers, and new alluvial lands that were not specifically part of landowners' estates or permanently populated by settled farmers. This made the state the owner of large amounts of territory (a condition continued in postindependence India, Pakistan, and Bangladesh).

The EIC's legal system also sought to combine British and Indian models. On the one hand, British legal theory valued codified written law in ways not found in India previously: some British "Orientalists" worked with Indian elites in turning Sanskrit texts into the Hindu personal law and Arabic or Persian texts into separate Muslim personal law. Many scholars today see this EIC process as encoding and enforcing both the rigid Brahminic caste system and legal separation between Hindus and Muslims. (Independent India, Pakistan, and Bangladesh have continued British colonialism's separate personal law systems based on communal identity.)

Simultaneously, the British judiciary and administration often valued the precedent of established custom as common law. Various Indian communities argued to the EIC's administration that they had rights over lands, livestock, trees, fish, and water based on custom "from time immemorial." Once approved by British judges and officials, these became legal precedents. Some Britons also saw themselves as protecting Indian non-elites from despotic Indian rulers or landlords and from exploitative Indian moneylenders, merchants, and other middle classes. Other British legal theorists argued that the EIC, as the state, had the right (and obligation) to protect resources (as trustee for the common good, as the EIC defined that), particularly against "wasteful" uses by local communities. However, to manage revenue collection and public order, many British officials pragmatically negotiated compromises with local power-brokers or communities.

Increasingly from the late eighteenth century onward, various British officials with scientific training, especially Scottish-trained surgeons, began to recognize and document the increasing consequences of excessive resource exploitation for short-term gain. Their ideas drew upon a variety of European concepts, for instance, the Hippocratic or sanitarian and the physiocratic ideas that the health of a human body depended on a healthy material environment. Many scholars highlight the EIC's exploitative, pragmatic, and economic motivations for preserving forest resources. But in philosophical and scientific conservation policies that Grove (1995) calls "Green Imperialism," these EIC surgeons "helped to create a context conducive to rigorous analytic thinking about the processes of ecological change and to the formation of a conservation ideology" (Grove 1993:320). Some EIC officials linked deforestation with erosion, aridity, deserts spreading through sand drift, harbor siltation, irregular monsoon rain patterns, and human diseases. As EIC government employees, they regarded the state as the only agency with a long-term perspective and the power to check wasteful deforestation and other environmental degradations by Indian communities and British and Indian commercial contractors.

For instance, Scottish EIC surgeon William Roxburgh (1751–1815) kept detailed meteorological records in Madras Presidency from 1776–93. He systematically recorded the barometric pressure, temperature, and rainfall thrice daily, thus producing detailed multiyear tables. He then used this data to correlate monsoon failures punctuated by brief devastating downpours (1789–92) with 600,000 deaths, half the population of northern Madras Presidency.

Drawing on European science, each presidency established botanical gardens (from 1778 onward), the most prominent in Calcutta (founded 1788), which experimented methodically to improve the commercial production of apples, breadfruit, coffee, cotton, mulberry, silk, sugarcane, tea, teak, other valuable timber, and drought-resistant plants. In 1781, Roxburgh supervised the creation of Madras Presidency's botanical garden; in 1789, he became that presidency's state naturalist. Later, as director of the Calcutta Botanical Garden (1793–1813, intermittently due to illness), he continued his experimental planting projects, publishing lavishly illustrated taxonomies of Indian flora and extensively corresponding and exchanging plants with leading naturalists internationally.

The EIC's applications of various British concepts of the state and capitalist property ownership over the physical environment differed from those of previous Indian regimes and local practices, even when the EIC proclaimed it was following Indian precedent. The Mughal Empire, especially under Akbar, had surveyed much of the agricultural land under its authority (see Chapter 6). But British surveying technology and its goal of universal knowledge based on "science" created new disciplines to control information and knowledge. British surveyors, with Indian assistants, began to measure all land under EIC direct or indirect rule. For instance, Francis Buchanan (later Buchanan Hamilton, 1762–1829) mapped and collected extensive data on Bengal (1807–14); Major James Rennell (1742–1830), the first surveyor-general, made relatively detailed maps of Bengal (1764–71) and then much of the rest of

India, charting forests, mountains, rivers, roads, towns, and other features (especially ones useful for moving armies), as well as administrative boundaries and political frontiers. Indeed, the EIC sought to maintain a monopoly on data and discoveries about India's natural resources, employing and encouraging its own scientists for its own profit, while largely excluding other Europeans, even other Britons. As technology improved, so did detail and accuracy. The EIC celebrated this disciplining of the land of India and found it valuable for administration, while postcolonial critics have analyzed this creation of knowledge and its orientalist assumptions about European cultural and racial superiority (Edney 1987).

The First Half of the Nineteenth Century

Over the early nineteenth century, the EIC subordinated every remaining Indian ruler (the last big campaigns being the third Anglo-Maratha war in the western Deccan [1817–80] and the second Anglo-Sikh war in Punjab [1849]). This brought the entire subcontinent under one sovereign, exceeding even the Mauryan and Mughal Empires in extent and depth of governance. Simultaneously, each presidency tried to extend its control over its part of the subcontinent's human and natural resources. While each presidency's relative autonomy meant that there was considerable variation in the specific methods and chronology, each reflected prevailing patterns of European scientific trends and governmental technologies.

British concepts of "race" for humans were shifting into parallels with Linnaean botanical and zoological classification systems. Until the early nineteenth century, Europeans variously used behavioral and environmental explanations of racial identity: Indians (especially more malleable women) who became Christian and Anglicized could become British (or close below British). Further, Britons believed different climates shaped human bodies, so Indians were physically the product of their tropical land while European bodies there functioned (and were subject to endemic diseases) differently (Harrison 1999). Many in Europe blamed India as the source for "Oriental" diseases like cholera. Further, debate would continue among British policy-makers as to whether British scientific principles were universal or else India's tropical environment and Indian bodies were essentially different and therefore subject to separate "natural laws."

But European concepts of hereditary "blood" identities were shifting. Many British ethnographers and Europeans generally, tried to categorize Indians on racial hierarchies by their religion and caste, often associated with specific animals (e.g. pig-dreading Muslims or cow-worshiping Hindus). Many Britons stereotyped "tribals" as animists, either condemned as inherently wild and racially close to forest animals, or deserving uplift through conversion to Christianity, or else romanticized as Rousseau's "noble savage" whose wilderness should be preserved from corrupting outsiders (especially Indian exploiters). European-Indian "interracial" liaisons or marriages allegedly produced hybrids, judged physically inferior to the European (usually the father) or, in some eyes, inferior to both parents. This model paralleled some long-standing Brahminic ideas about different regions being congenial to different types of people and inter-varna marriages producing new jatis (see Chapter 4).

The EIC also increasingly tried to maximize its knowledge and use of India's natural resources. From 1802, the British began the Great Trigonometrical Survey project using theodolites to survey the entire subcontinent through triangulation from precisely calculated points. Some Indians resented the tree-cutting and platform-building necessary to create a clear line of sight. Nonetheless, this survey had covered about half the subcontinent by 1857 (and was completed by 1890). Additionally, within British India starting in 1822, British professional surveyors supervised the measuring and cadastral mapping of each village's fields for more precise revenue assessment. This unprecedented body of knowledge fostered British commercial exploitation of India's lands and forests.

Simultaneously, however, some EIC officials in all three presidencies gradually came to recognize detrimental effects of rapidly increasing and relatively unrestricted timbering by Indian communities and landowners and British plantation owners and contractors. In particular, Indian teak forests were vital for expanding shipbuilding in Bombay and other colonial-related industries but were being visibly denuded. Consequently, each presidency began to take some action, but not very effectively. In 1806, Police Captain Watson of Madras Presidency became the first "Conservator of Forests" and tried to assert government's monopoly over teak in the Western Ghats (including in Cochin and Travancore kingdoms).

Uneven and inconsistent presidency forest policies, however, created early but ongoing conflicts between government and legal private property rights as well as between the revenue department seeking profit from timbering and the nascent forest department seeking long-term preservation of forest productivity. Local communities of villagers and forest-dwellers also resisted state appropriation of forests that they had long used. In London, the EIC directors claimed sovereignty over forests, but did not enforce it (the British Raj established stronger forest departments during the later nineteenth century).

Much of the EIC's political and military establishments were based in long-standing Indian cities. Particularly for the section of those cities where British officials and officers lived, the EIC revived some infrastructure. For instance, the EIC restored (1817–20) a long-neglected drinking water canal into Shahjahanabad, but much else was ignored, for instance its gravity-fed wet-carriage waste sanitation system.

Over this period of intermittent EIC wars and territorial expansions in India, its entanglements with British and Indian politics and economics changed its nature, marked by each twenty-year renewal of its charter by Parliament. In 1833, after much debate and lobbying pressure from rival British commercial interests, the EIC's directors convinced Parliament to renew its charter, but at the cost of abolishing its monopoly over trade in Asia. This enabled other British merchants legally to increase their profitable export-import businesses there.

The EIC itself sought other income sources from India to pay dividends to its shareholders, its employees' salaries, its substantial debts, and other running expenses. Hence, it permitted or contracted out to other companies the exploitation of India's resources, including valuable timber in its forests. For instance, the smelter at Porto Novo on the coast south of Madras (from 1827, founded by a retired Madras Presidency official, Josiah Marshall Heath [d. 1851]), used 3.75 kg (8.3 lbs) of charcoal per kilogram of pig iron, eventually deforesting the surrounding region (the EIC supported this business with numerous loans, eventually took it over, and then closed it as unprofitable). Similarly, British planters bought land from the EIC at low prices to clear forests and create estates for commercial crops, including plantations for coffee in the Western Ghats and tea (*Camillia sinensis*) in India's northeast. (Tea planters used smuggled Chinese stock since they did not understand that the Chinese-pruned tea bushes were indigenous to Assam.)

Simultaneously, each governor-general tried to impose his personal policies on the EIC career civil service, and through them, on India. For instance, Governor-General William Bentinck (r. 1828–35) supported utilitarianism, Anglicization, and using British technology, science, and "rationality" to extend power over India's environment. His regime devoted state resources to improving major all-weather roads for the movement of troops, commerce, and postal communication, like the Grand Trunk from Calcutta west to the edge of British-ruled north India. British-engineered steam power appeared to be the latest technology, driving tugs in harbors, river vessels on the Ganges, and transoceanic

Figure 7.1 Image of the government opium warehouse, Patna, Bihar, from *The Graphic*, 656 (June 24, 1882), p. 640. Photograph: DEA / Biblioteca Abrosiana / Getty Images

ships. From the 1830s, a few Indian shipbuilders ventured to Britain for advanced training in naval steam-engine engineering. This made subcontinental and intercontinental commerce in high-volume, low-value resources more profitable, deeply affecting the Indian economy and environment.

The EIC also profited indirectly from expanding opium exports to China. All opium grown in British India (Bihar's environment was especially suitable) was a government monopoly, purchased from producers at prices it set (see Figures 7.1 and 7.2). Since the Chinese empire outlawed opium importation, the EIC auctioned the harvested opium to private merchants (Britons, Americans, and some Indians) who smuggled it into China. This drug trade would rapidly grow (from 250,000 kg [550,000 lb] annually in 1820 to 6 million kg [13 million lbs] in 1880), with much Indian wood also needed for ships and shipping crates. When

THE MANUFACTURE OF OPIUM IN INDIA.

Figure 7.2 The manufacture of opium in India, from Bourne and Shepherd (1899), *The Queen's Empire: A Pictorial and Descriptive Record*, vol. 2 (Cassell)

the Chinese empire forcibly resisted, the British navy won two "Opium Wars" (1839–42 [gaining Hong Kong] and 1856–58 [gaining even more access to Chinese markets]).

Especially from the 1830s onward, growing numbers of scientifically oriented officials and officers in India, Britain, and throughout the world corresponded, joined professional societies, published articles in scientific journals and books, and submitted research reports that noted how human actions were degrading the natural world. They studied deforestation, recurring famines, and epidemics from water and air pollution, made worse by inadequate EIC policies. Many called for rational solutions and more intrusive government actions to harness Indian human and nonhuman resources to what they determined to be the "public good." For instance, Scottish surgeon Alexander Gibson (1800–67) used his position from 1838 onward as superintendent of Bombay Presidency's Botanical Garden (near Poona) to study and report on the degradation of forests and other natural resources in the region, noting detrimental effects on public health and the economy. This led to

Gibson's appointment (1847–60) as the presidency's first Conservator of Forests with a small staff. Madras Presidency followed, appointing India-born but Scottish-trained surgeon and later botanist Dr. Hugh Cleghorn (1820–95) as its Conservator of Forests in 1856, with authority also over forests in the adjacent princely state of Mysore, currently under EIC regency. Determined to maximize wood production for use by the expanding railways and other government purposes, Cleghorn prohibited swidden agriculture in forests under his control. (In 1861, the Punjab provincial government had Cleghorn create its Forest Department; in 1864 and 1866–67, the central government appointed him officiating inspector-general of its Indian Forest Department.)

Indeed, reflecting the EIC's self-image as patron of the "public," Governor-General Dalhousie (r. 1848–56) established central Public Works Department (PWD) in 1855, as did the presidencies of Bombay and Madras, and other EIC provincial bodies (created from 1833 onward). Other "modernizations" during Dalhousie's regime included starting the electric telegraph network that revolutionized communications, initially in Bengal (1851) but soon spreading across British-ruled India (and later linking to Britain-based lines).

Dalhousie also supported the emerging technology of railways, something his regime should support as "national works," controlled by government and supervised by its own consulting engineers even if funded privately by for-profit companies. In 1849, two British joint-stock companies, the Great Indian Peninsula and the East Indian Railway companies, secured long-term government contracts with free land and guaranteed interest on the investment to construct railways, the former from Calcutta, the latter from Bombay, opening in 1853 and 1854 respectively. The Madras Railway Company followed, its initial line opening in 1856. Royal Engineers and civil engineers from Britain designed most routes. British Indian Army engineers were largely untrained technically to undertake this (unlike contemporary canal building discussed below), but they did supervise as consultants; railways were initially under the Military Board (before being transferred to the PWD). The bid-winning major contractors (mostly but not entirely British) imported the engines, tracks, and most heavy equipment while subcontractors (mostly Indian) hired many thousands of Indian laborers. Over decades, railways would rapidly spread, transforming the movement of freight, passengers, troops, and mail. Compared to roads, the railways moved cargoes much cheaper and faster, although both were subject to destructive floods.

When the EIC wanted to transform India's hydraulic landscapes, it often used its military engineers to provide the needed technical expertise, as the careers of Arthur Cotton (1803–99) and Richard Strachey (1817–1908) illustrate. Both officers trained at the EIC's Military Seminary at Addiscombe (established 1809, just south of London) and then at the Royal School of Military Engineering at Chatham (established 1812). Cotton reached India at age eighteen with a commission in the Madras Engineers; Strachey arrived at age twenty-one with a commission in the Bombay Engineers and then transferred to the Bengal Engineers. One of Cotton's early assignments was surveying the Pamban Strait between mainland India and Sri Lanka; he recommended dredging it for deep-draft vessels. Then, he learned from pre-British dams, especially the Kaveri River's ancient Grand Anicut, about building on sandy riverbeds. His two large dams on the Kaveri (1835–36) revived widespread, but neglected, water distribution channels, generating for the EIC calculated profits of 70 percent and 100 percent annually. (Madras Presidency recognized that many of these distribution canals had been privately built, so it generally did not charge for irrigation directly but rather profited from higher taxation rates on irrigated land.) Cotton also constructed major dams on the Godavari and Krishna Rivers (1847–62). After retirement, he was hired as a consulting engineer by the for-profit East India Irrigation Company (see Chapter 8).

Strachey started his career in 1839 by training at the EIC's first major perennial canal irrigation project in north India (begun in 1823). This was an expansion of the Delhi Sultanate-era Doab inundation canal stemming from the Jumna River. After just two years, and still only a lieutenant, Strachey became executive engineer of the much larger Ganges Canal project, including building its headworks at Hardwar (opened 1854 but expensively reengineered after critical investigation by Cotton in 1863). (After extensions, this canal system today has 960 km [600 mi] of main lines, 5,600 km [3,480 mi] of distributary channels, and irrigates 9,000 km^2 [3,475 mi^2].) In 1855, Strachey directed the Bundelkhund irrigation project. Later, he headed the PWD (intermittently 1862–71), was the first Inspector-General of Irrigation (1867–71), helped create Bengal's Forest Department, and supervised railways (including as chairman [1889–1906] of the private, for-profit East Indian Railway and the Assam Railway companies). Both Cotton and Strachey periodically joined their armies in wars, were ultimately knighted, and retired as generals. Other officers who had also graduated from Addiscombe trained under both men, continuing their infrastructure projects. But their growing staffs of Indian subordinates also needed technical training. So, in 1848 at the Ganges canal headworks in Roorkee (near Hardwar), the EIC set up the College of Civil Engineering (renamed Thomason College in 1854).

The EIC's forest departments, however, required expertise less transferrable from military engineering, although they eventually developed a similar bureaucratic structure of British elites and Indian subordinate officers and workers. Dalhousie's Memorandum (August 3, 1855, sometimes called the "Charter of Indian Forestry") asserted the EIC's right, even duty, to take over all forests (unless privately or communally owned) and manage them through emerging European "scientific forestry," since deforestation was creating harm to human health and land fertility. In 1856, Dalhousie appointed Dr. Dietrich Brandis (1824–1907) to secure for the EIC the teak and other valuable forest products in Pegu (western Burma) and then in all British-ruled Burma. Brandis was German by birth and training, with a doctorate in botany from Bonn. His wife was related by marriage to one of Dalhousie's confidants, but he also brought with him the prestige of German scientific forestry. As the next chapter discusses, Dalhousie's successors would reward Brandis by empowering him (and Cleghorn) to establish the British Raj's Indian Forest Service using continental European-style scientific forestry.

Dalhousie also used force and coercive diplomacy to annex any allegedly defectively ruled Indian kingdom. He devised the "Doctrine of Lapse" (i.e. the EIC inherited from any ruler who died without an heir whom the British approved), for instance with Satara (1848) and Jhansi (1853). He defeated the Sikh kingdom of Punjab (1849), annexing it. He took over Oudh/Awadh from its allegedly misruling king (1856).

These diverse and accumulating British interventions into the lives of Indians built up growing hostility to EIC rule, especially in north India. In 1856, a major rising of Santal forest-dwellers in Bihar challenged EIC rule. Then, in the torrid summer of 1857, a range of north and central Indian deposed princes, disgruntled sepoys, alienated merchants, farmers, pastoralists, and forest-dwellers arose, largely in the name of the last Mughal emperor, Bahadur Shah II (r. 1737–58). They recaptured cities, towns, villages, lands, forests, and other resources, destroyed material embodiments of British rule (including treasuries, armories, post offices, and telegraph lines), and killed or expelled British officials, officers, their families, and Indian supporters. The British soon reconquered with even bloodier reprisals, followed by intensified controls over India's resources, using technologies and methods derived from across the British Empire and continental Europe. This massive loss of life and destruction on all sides led Parliament finally to abolish the EIC, creating the British Raj and reformulating many government policies, as the next chapter explores.

8   The British Raj, "Mahatma" Gandhi, and Other Anti-Colonial Movements (1857–1947)

During the late nineteenth and early twentieth centuries, the scale and pace of change in South Asia's environmental history rapidly accelerated as many diverse Britons and Indians used new technologies to try to control key aspects of the India's biota and material world for their respective purposes. The British crown, to preclude a repetition of bloody 1857 revolt and to make India a more valuable imperial colony, in 1858 completed its decades-long process of taking over the EIC and thus officially established the British Raj, headed by the viceroy and dominated by British officials and officers with commissions from the British monarch. This regime sought to measure, appraise, and assert its rule over India's people, fauna, flora, land, minerals, waters, and other resources for its gain and that of the British Empire, combining political and military goals with commercial resource extraction. The systemic scope and level of technology of state intervention into the environment and into the lives of local people, was unprecedented in Indian history. Forests had been cleared and animal species hunted to extinction before, but not on this scale and these had not hitherto drawn the attention of the state. However, contradictions and miscalculations within British policies and programs, India's specific environmental conditions, and rising elite and popular Indian resistance all interacted to produce complex outcomes.

As part of the larger British-centric globalization process, technology enabled the British imperial government to bind ever closer the Indian colonial administration and economy. Faster communications (especially direct Britain-India electric telegraphy starting in 1865) shifted much key decision-making to London. Consequently, viceroys had to consult regularly about major policies with the prime minister and the secretary of state for India. British parliamentary committees and the India Office compiled detailed surveys and reports about the budgets and results of every department and aspect of the Raj. The expansion of steam-driven steel ships and the opening of the Suez Canal in 1869 meant far more rapid and voluminous shipment of information as well as Indian raw

135

materials to Britain and British manufactures to India. Increasingly, British industrialists pressured Parliament to strengthen mercantilist policies toward India.

Further, Europeans and Indians traveled and communicated more rapidly and frequently between India and Britain. This reduced significantly the social autonomy of British officials through more frequent "home leaves" and the longer-term presence in India of their British wives and families. This also meant that ever more elite Indians (including most prominent nationalist leaders) lived and studied in Britain, learning about and experiencing their legal rights within the empire and gaining global perspectives on colonialism. Such Anglicized Indians served the government but also increasingly advanced their own models for their nation, variously imagined. Additionally, South Asians emigrated in large numbers as free or indentured (contracted) workers, bringing their labor, skills, and ideas, which altered environments throughout the British Empire.

The Raj simultaneously revised and extended several of the EIC's key policies, including its multifaceted "divide and rule" strategy. Official ethnographies, district-by-district gazetteers, censuses (every decade starting in 1871), and legal and policy distinctions divided and codified all Indians into competing interests by "race" (including as Hindu, Muslim, Sikh, "Anglo-Indian," "untouchable," or "tribal," with each of these subdivided by "caste"). The British also developed other "racial" distinctions, especially by reclassifying Bengalis (who had comprised the core of the Bengal Army that had conquered north India for the EIC) as "effeminate," in contrast to "martial races" like Punjabi Sikhs (who largely supported the British in 1857 and who henceforth became the core of the Raj's Indian army). The Raj then devoted much infrastructure investment to making Punjab a loyal bastion: canals and railways made it a major source for cash-crop agriculture and military manpower. Intending to protect "simple peasants" from extortion by moneylenders, merchants, and other Indian elites, some provinces also prohibited land acquisition by "nonagricultural castes" (e.g. Punjab's Land Alienation Act of 1900, strengthened 1907).

The Raj also reinforced India's political divisions. Instead of deposing Indian rulers and annexing their territories, the Raj kept a quarter of India's population and a third of its territory under Indian princely rule, relatively isolated from direct British political, economic, or environmental interventions.[1] The Raj then tried to indirectly rule these princes through British political residents and agents, creating a feudal order

---

[1] Further, the British Raj extended its political control beyond India (as this book defines it): over Bhutan (from 1866), parts of Burma (through wars 1824–26, 1852, 1885, but detached from India in 1937), and Afghanistan (1880–1919).

bonded to Queen Victoria (promoted by Parliament to "Empress of India" in 1877). Princes judged incompetent by the British due to youth or misbehavior sometimes had their kingdoms or estates temporarily taken under British regency or a "court of wards," thus preserving the dynasty if not necessarily the incumbent. Within their states, some Indian rulers marked out animal and forest reserves for their exclusive use. Thus, until 1947, hundreds of princely states (the largest as big as France, the smallest only a few villages) politically fragmented the subcontinent, although regional and subcontinental ecosystems, and human effects on these, crossed such political boundaries. Some Raj canals, for instance, required the cooperation of princes to build and operate. While the Raj had more difficulty extracting resources from these "native states," it also expended less manpower and money in controlling them than British directly ruled territories.

Within "British India," the premier (all male) Indian Civil Service (ICS) headed the administration. Young ICS men dominated at the district level, supervising land revenue collection, having judicial authority, and commanding all other officials (including government foresters and irrigation engineers). During a successful career, an ICS man rose to provincial or central government appointments, often moving among different departments. The ICS remained exclusively British until a few Anglicized Indians began to enter during the late nineteenth century; then as the world wars drew off (and killed) Britons, the proportion of Indians grew to almost half by the end of the Raj.

Working under the ICS, separate professionally trained civil services each managed and manipulated one of India's key resources. The 1865 and 1878 Forest Acts and the 1873 Canal Act (and comparable provincial Acts during these same decades) were landmark assertions of state power and ownership, implemented through scientifically trained "experts." The Raj funded the Royal Indian Engineering College at Coopers Hill, Surrey, England (1870–1905), where British canal engineers and (from 1885) foresters combined training in imperial service and science. The irrigation and forest departments each had largely racially segregated, hierarchically ranked parallel structures: expatriate European elites above less securely employed Indian subordinate officers, staff, and daily waged workers. For decades, private British joint-stock companies contracted to build canals, railways, and other infrastructure for the state and for their own profit. While nominally working in accord with official policies, all these individuals and groups had their own personal interests and loyalties.

The Raj also increasingly categorized India's nonhuman world, even as its policies and economic effects changed ecologies. Britons (and fewer Indians) trained in Western-style science, for instance, collecting and naming distinctive Indian flora and fauna species using the Latinate Linnaean system. The Raj officially declared certain species under its special authority as "protected," especially if they were potentially profitable. Some animals and plants (including cattle and cash crops) thrived in these conditions, but others (including elephants, lions, cheetahs, tigers, teak, cedars, and other valuable hard and soft woods) declined with retreating habitats and increased killing.

Much of India's environment (and many of its people) remained beyond British technology to control. Official forest conservation and irrigation projects clearly had only mixed results. Occasional cyclones, weak monsoons, regional and multiregional famines, and epidemics (like the 1918–19 Spanish influenza) highlighted the limitations and often detrimental effects of the Raj. Indian forest-, village-, town-, and city-dwellers and pastoralists also engaged with the environment and the state according to their own needs and interests, often resisting government controls. However, by the early nineteenth century, the amount of thinly populated, noncultivated but arable land decreased. Along with British landownership laws and commodification of land and its produce, this reduced agricultural mobility and altered markets, weakening the status of the landless (including almost all women).

Many of the Raj's efforts to master the Indian environment, and its policies, had consequences unintended or opposite to its claims. Railway, forest, and irrigation departments transformed the economy, but often benefited Britain while causing major ecological damage and distorting the Indian economy and society. British laissez faire famine policies led to millions of deaths (Davis 2002). Indians, and some Britons and Europeans (including Karl Marx) criticized the evident discrepancy between the government's often incompetent and brutal behavior versus its claims of conquest over nature and protection of public interests through British-driven "modernization."

Box 8.1

Karl Marx predicted for his American newspaper readers the inevitable effects of British exploitation of India:

> "The [English] millocracy have discovered that the transformation of India into a reproductive country has become of vital importance to them, and that, to that end, it is necessary, above all, to gift her with means of irrigation and of internal communication. They intend now drawing a net of railroads over India...with the exclusive view of extracting at diminished expenses the cotton and other raw materials for their manufactures. [T]he railway-system will...become, in India, truly the forerunner of modern industry (Marx 1853).

Increasingly over this period, Indian alternative models for governance and the relationships between humans and the material world emerged. In addition to popular movements and a burgeoning vernacular press, various elite Indian political movements arose using British-style political models and English-language speeches and publications. Most prominent was the Indian National Congress (INC) – established as a lobbying group in 1885 but with escalating demands for self-rule and then independence, particularly after 1915 under the guidance of Mohandas "Mahatma" Gandhi (1869–1948).

The Raj only grudgingly expanded participation in decision-making by loyal princes and Anglicized or wealthy Indian elites, although popular collaboration and resistance nonetheless shaped policies and their outcomes. World War I (1914–18) and World War II (1939–45) marked significant transitions, as did the rise of various types of popular movements and elite-led Indian and Pakistani nationalism. In 1947, the new nations of Pakistan and India replaced the battered Raj, thereafter perpetuating many of its environmental policies and patterns while disrupting others.

The sources available to environmental historians for this ninety-year period also expanded exponentially as significant consequences of the vastly more extensive recordkeeping and scientific work of the Raj and the prolific letter, memoir, and history writing of British and Indian officials and officers and their families. Many accounts were published using the expanding print media of newspapers and books; others are preserved in manuscript archives in Britain, India, Pakistan, or Bangladesh. Further, historians have in recent decades been trying to recover otherwise silenced subaltern voices by reading colonial-era sources "against the grain" and evoking popular oral traditions (Ranajit Guha et al. 1982–2012). Thus, especially compared to earlier eras, there is a rich and rapidly expanding body of scholarship on the British Raj period of Indian environmental history (see Map 8.1).

The End of the Nineteenth Century (1858 to the 1890s)

British equipment and manpower losses during the 1857 fighting in north India and the northern Deccan added pressure on all government departments to increase revenues without provoking renewed resistance by increasing land-tax rates or annexing new territories. Railways and telegraphs had shown their military value to the British during the fighting, adding to ongoing British faith in science and technology-driven progress, while also making profits. Hence, the Raj expected its railway, forestry,

Map 8.1 India at the time of the British Raj (1858–1947)

irrigation and other departments to increase the productivity of current British-held territories through "scientific" infrastructure improvements while generating budget surpluses. The Raj therefore initially continued the EIC's practice of issuing contracts (often with guaranteed return on investment) to British companies which used British financing to build and operate rail, canal, and other infrastructure; as the Raj took over construction, it also sold bonds in British financial markets.

These private and government projects served several of the Raj's integrated purposes. For instance, canals in the peninsular southeast largely enhanced the productivity of existing farmlands while canals in the upper Indus basins largely transformed vast new tracts of arid lands from pasturage to agriculture. These newly watered lands generated tax revenues from irrigation charges and increased agricultural productivity, especially from cash crops including wheat, rice, and cotton. New railway lines then enabled merchants profitably to purchase these crops, transport them to the ports of Madras, Bombay, Calcutta, and (later) Karachi for export to Britain and the rest of the world. Some canals and railways also justified their investment by promising to save the Raj the economic costs of moving troops and famine relief (and the moral cost of famine deaths). But railways consumed vast volumes of wood, most of which government foresters had to provide. Overall, the Raj deepened its effects on India's natural and human resources, expanding railways, forests, and canals simultaneously, with parallels and differences among its administrative models.

Looking first at railways, the Raj over time varied its policies about private versus state construction and operation of specific routes. Particularly following 1857, when government finances were strained and much infrastructure in north India and the northern Deccan had been destroyed, the Raj continued to negotiate contracts whereby British for-profit companies raised funds through stock offerings in British markets to construct railways. Some Viceroys and British politicians also philosophically or politically favored private enterprise over state investment. But the Raj always specified the routes, supplied the land, and supervised construction. When the Raj particularly wanted a route built (especially when it was economically risky or for military or famine-relief reasons), some contracts guaranteed a profit on the investment (generally 5 percent with net revenue-sharing above that). By 1870, the government shifted from reliance on private companies to having PWDs build rail projects; after 1877, the government occasionally bought out existing private companies, however sometimes that company contracted to continue that route's operation. The total track length rose from 1,350 km (840 mi) in 1860 to 28,100 km (17,460 mi) in 1892 (see Figure 8.1): a quarter state-owned and operated, almost half government-owned but privately operated, about 15 percent privately owned and operated, with much of the rest in princely states (MacGeorge 1894:8). By 1891, total capital investment in railways exceeded £225 million (two-thirds directly by government) with about 5.6 percent overall net return. The Raj intended specific railway lines to serve in different proportions the goals of production (profit, revenue, and commercial enhancement) and protection (military and famine-relief).

While much of India was level plains and thus was relatively inexpensive for track laying, the rest of India's varied terrain presented British railway engineers with challenges, often quite different from those they had mastered in Britain. The Western Ghats, lower Himalayas, Vindhyas, and mountainous northwest, the seasonally variable rivers

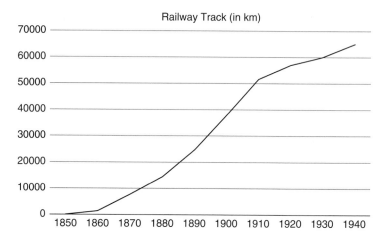

Figure 8.1 Growth of railway track under the British Raj

and flooding, and the damaging climate, insects, and human diseases all required special skills and experience, mostly learned on the job. Railway engineers carved extensive tunnels (sometimes blasting and drilling through dense quartz) and extended massive iron or steel bridges across rivers, technologies hitherto unknown in India. Further, Indian manual labor was relatively inexpensive, so humans often laid track, moved earth, cut tunnels, and lifted materials, which steam-driven machines did in Britain. Railways employed an estimated 10 million Indian workers during the late nineteenth century, most of them daily-waged manual laborers.

As with the Raj's other services, among salaried employees of the railways, Britons held the highest positions and Indians served as subordinate officers or workers. But men of mixed Indian and European descent (called variously "Eurasians," "half-castes," or "Anglo-Indians") gained more positions in the railways than in many other services. Indeed, a man's proportion of European "blood" shaped his status (e.g. mostly Indian-descended stoker below engine-driver below mostly British-descended station manager). By 1891, of the more than 260,000 regular employees of the railways, over 95 percent were classed as "natives," with "Eurasians" slightly outnumbering "Europeans" among the rest; by 1905 the railways had 437,535 permanent employees and many more on daily wages (Kerr 2007:65). The 1890 Indian Railway Act consolidated on an all-India basis the rules that had accumulated in various provinces over the previous decades.

Railways did much to transform India's environment, moving goods and people, altering culture and rural–urban relations, and accelerating integration into global trade networks. Railway embankments often crossed (and thus blocked) ground- and surface-water flows, producing waterlogging and disease-breeding grounds on the upstream side. By 1871, railways annually transported some 3.6 million metric tonnes (4 million US tons) of freight and 19 million passenger trips among 2,427 stations; by 1901, it was 43.5 million tonnes and 183 million passenger trips; by 1929, 116 million tonnes and 630 million passengers. Since trains required precise schedules, the system enforced a single, standardized clock-time across India; their speed also in effect compressed distances, bringing all of India closer together. But the railways also prescribed race and class segregation, with ranked classes of tickets, separate waiting rooms, and often special stations for British parts of cities or military cantonments. The ports of Bombay, Calcutta, Karachi, and Madras all expanded in large measure due to their railway linkages, as did some interior junction towns (e.g. Nagpur; see Map 8.2). Further, railways extracted grain, cotton, and other cash crops for export, raising government revenues and land and food prices that benefited rich Indian farmers, moneylenders, grain merchants, while often depriving the poor of sustenance.

The railways also consumed vast volumes of metal, wood, and coal and Indian capital. Engines, other machinery, rails, rolling stock, iron and steel bridges, and metal sleepers (ties) came almost exclusively from Britain as did much of the coal and wooden sleepers chemically treated to reduce decay. The Indian economy had to pay for all these expensive imports. Railroads also rapidly used up stocks of Indian hardwood trees, especially teak, sal (*Shorea robusta*), and deodar (*Cedrus deodara*) for sleepers – each kilometer of track initially used about 1,000 sleepers, about 200 large trees, with periodic replacement as they decayed. Many hardwood forests have never recovered. Sleepers from softer woods such as chir (*Pinus roxburghii*) and blue pine (*Pinus wallichiana*) rotted more rapidly (only after 1912 were commercially viable chemical treatments established in India). Much of the more than a million tons of railway fuel burned annually was extracted from Indian forests, either as firewood or from forest-located coal mines (beginning in the 1880s). All this caused major deforestation, in addition to expanding commercial timbering made profitable by railway transportation.

The Raj established the Imperial Forest Service in large measure to provide wood for railways and other parts of India's and the empire's expanding economies. In 1863, the government officially declared that "the proper growth and preservation of the Forests is as important to

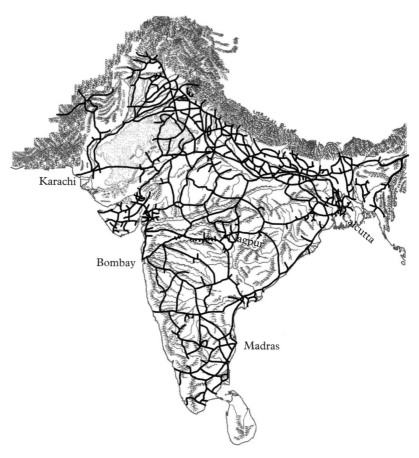

Map 8.2 Railway lines by 1930

Government as the cultivation of any other crop which the soil produces, and in some instances more important, since the destruction of
the Forests would affect most injuriously the climate, and perhaps the
fertility of the soil" (Stebbing 1926, 1:350). Most prominently,
Cleghorn and Brandis (see Chapter 7) intensified their efforts to
create a corps of professional European experts, with a substantial
number of trained Indian subordinate officers and guards, empowered
to manage India's vast forests. Brandis was the first Inspector-General
of Indian Forests (1864–83) while Madras, Bombay, and other
provinces already had (or would soon create) their own provincial
Forest Departments.

The 1865 Forest Act and the expanded 1878 Forest Act asserted government authority over forests. But British officials disagreed about how encompassing its control should be. Some, particularly in Bombay Presidency, argued that Indian rulers historically had ultimate ownership over all forests not under continuous cultivation or permanent settlement, so the Raj should as well. Others, particularly in Madras Presidency, recognized that local communities had preexisting customary rights in some forests (this paralleled Madras' recognition of private, customary irrigation distribution channels). Brandis both had faith in the overarching expertise of trained European government foresters to manage valuable forests most effectively but also recognized some traditional rights, for instance through the religious tradition of sacred groves. Hence, the Raj instituted a broad tripartite categorization: Reserved Forests (fully government-owned and Forest Department–controlled, intended for commercial production with profits to the government); Protected Forests (managed by the Forest or Revenue Departments but with local communities having some or as yet unsettled rights, potentially subject to later transfer into the reserved category); and forests under village or private control or unclassified (over which Forest Departments had varying levels of authority). Not until 1890 did all the provinces finally pass their own Acts to accord with the central 1878 Act.

Brandis also determined to professionalize the Imperial Forest Service, but in ways different from other Raj departments like railways or canals. From 1866 onward, Britons who transferred into this service were sent to train in the French National School of Forestry at Nancy. This school had been established in 1824 by the French government to teach scientific methods developed in the southern German states that stressed state control over monocultural plantations of economically valuable species. The school's early French directors themselves trained in Germany. They then taught the science of calculating cubic useful wood in standing forests; how to draw up 100- or 150-year "working plans" of balance sheets for clear-cutting "coupes" in rotation to maximize economically sustained-yield production; ways to limit erosion and floods; and the need to exclude non-expert government officials, commercial exploiters, and local users from interfering in "their" forests. In 1878, Brandis also founded the Dehra Dun forestry school (becoming from 1906 the Imperial Forest Research Institute, where subordinate Indian forestry officers trained after 1938). Following Sir Dietrich Brandis's retirement to Bonn, two more Germans whom he had recruited served as sequential inspectors-general, continuing the Imperial Forest Service's Franco-German principles: Sir Wilhelm/William Schlich (inspector-general, 1883–85) and Sir Berthold Ribbentrop (inspector-general 1885–1900).

While practical training continued in continental Europe, the Raj established another forestry school for British officials in 1885 as a department in the Royal Indian Engineering College at Coopers Hill (in 1905 this branch was transferred to Oxford University). British officers of the Imperial Forest Service were posted to run provincial Forest Departments. By 1885, there were about 100 British foresters and thousands of Indian forest guards; by 1899 this had grown to about 2,000 conservators, rangers, and foresters, and 8,500 guards (Ribbentrop 1900:81, 93).

Forest Departments did not have large initial investments (unlike railways or canals) but too rapid tree-felling diminished its "capital." Foresters were professionally committed to preserving sustainable forest production, but also had to produce budget surpluses, their main revenue source being timber sales (sometimes by auction to a contractor but also carried out by Forest Department employees). Further, the Forest Department remained in tension with other branches of the Raj, particularly the Revenue and Agriculture Departments (periodically within which the Forest Department was administratively located). Rival departments regarded foresters as preventing immediate income from rapid timber sales, hobbling wood supplies for construction and commerce, and preventing agricultural expansion.

In lands officially declared to be forest, local communities of forest-dwellers, villagers, and pastoralists often resisted foresters in order to hunt; gather fruits, medical herbs, fuelwood, other useful timber; and to graze their livestock. For instance, some communities had long used fire to clear undergrowth, removing dried grasses and shrubs to make room for new growth more palatable to their grazing livestock. As Ribbentrop wrote, "a Forest Officer's heart may bleed that he cannot bring all his forests to that state of perfection, nor effect their regeneration as rapidly, satisfactorily, and completely as might be achieved if grazing were entirely excluded" (1900:134). Forest Department officers on inspection tours compelled local people to provide *begar* (unpaid labor, especially carrying baggage). Further, the commercially valuable species on efficiently harvested plantations preferred by foresters often had little utility for local communities, so protesters occasionally burned them. The Forest Department's 1891 Regulation and 1894 Forest Policy for the whole of British India reclassified customary forest-access rights into government-granted "privilege," for which foresters charged fees and could unilaterally deny.

In addition to trees, provincial Forest Departments also increasingly asserted their control over wildlife, although this long remained unevenly implemented due to pressures from British, princely, and local hunters.

The 1878 Forest Act expanded the 1865 Act's definition of "forest produce" to include valued animals and their parts (including skins, horns, and tusks). Both the central government and many provinces passed acts claiming authority over wildlife generally (e.g. the 1887 Preservation of Wild Birds and Game Act and the 1897 Indian Fisheries Act) or specific species like elephants (e.g. protection acts by Madras in 1873 and the central government and Assam in 1879). Following the earlier model of government botanical gardens, the Calcutta Zoological Garden (established 1875) collected and analyzed valued fauna species.

During this period, some Indian elites also imposed their agendas onto Indian wildlife. Some princes decreed their own game reserve and hunting laws. For instance, from 1879 onward, rulers of Janagarh on the Gujarat coast asserted control over Asiatic lions (*Panthera leo persica*) in their Gir forest (consequently, this is the last area where this species survives in the wild) (Rangarajan 2013). Similarly, the Rajas of Bharatpur over the late nineteenth century dammed streams near their capital to create a wetland for bird-shooting (in 1971 this became a reserve and in 1982 became the 29 km^2 [11 mi^2] Keoladeo Ghana National Park, a World Heritage Site and a Ramsar Convention wetland). Additionally, in 1883, Anglicized Indians joined Britons in starting the Bombay Natural History Society to study, publish articles, and lobby the Raj about a range of issues concerning flora, fauna, and other environmental issues. Ornithologist Salim Ali (1896–1987) and a growing number of other Indian naturalists published catalogues of India's birds, plants, and animals.

Another major Indian resource that the Raj determined to control was fresh water, vital for irrigation of crops, drinking, and sewage (especially in cities), but also central (by absence) to droughts and (by excess) to floods. The EIC had initiated some water-control projects, particularly reconstructing and expanding existing but neglected pre-British inundation canals in the Godavari and upper Ganges basins for irrigation and for some urban water supplies. But under the Raj, dam and perennial canal projects had scale jumps in scope and technology, with the government asserting its right to control irrigation and its stated duty to mitigate droughts and floods (see Map 8.3). As under the EIC, most of the canal engineers were initially military officers, including Cotton and Strachey (see Chapter 7) and those they trained.

Early in the Raj, the Madras and Bengal Presidencies "privatized" some canal building (as they were doing with railways) by contracting for their construction and management with joint-stock British companies that raised funds in British financial markets. The Madras Irrigation

Map 8.3 Major canals by 1930

Company (established 1857) contracted to build the Kurnool-Cuddapah weir and irrigation canals on the Tungabhadra River in 1860, with the Raj guaranteeing at least 5 percent profit on its £1 million capital. The East India Irrigation and Canal Company (established 1860) contracted to build canals for irrigation, flood control, and navigation in Orissa (on the Mahanadi and Brahmani deltas), Bengal (in Midnapur), and Bihar (on the Son). This for-profit company also purchased and expanded the existing Ganges Canal in 1863.

Many of these hydraulic projects were based on proposals by government military engineers who then sometimes (on leave or post-retirement) worked on them as well-paid consultants or even chief engineers. But many companies overspent their budgets, often producing inadequate and delayed results despite emergency government loans. Consequently, provincial governments ended up purchasing these companies. For instance, the Bengal government bought out the East India Irrigation and Canal Company in 1869 and the Madras government bought out the Madras Irrigation Company. Many of these companies' British engineers were absorbed into the PWD staff. Under General Sir Richard Strachey, the first Inspector-General of Irrigation (1867–71), and his successors, provincial governments completed these canals (often using loans raised from British financial markets) and operated them (usually with modest profits). But irrigation departments competed with railways for government funds, receiving more through the 1860s but only about half as much from 1872 onward as the government bought out guaranteed railway companies and built its own lines.

In the 1873 Northern India Canal and Drainage Act, the NWP government declared its authority to "use and control for public purposes the water of all rivers and streams flowing in natural channels, and of all lakes and other natural collections of still water." Other provinces followed with comparable laws. "Public purposes" meant maximizing the state's revenue and spreading irrigation water as extensively as practicable (in the jargon of the engineers, the amount of land that a canal "commanded"). Rates charged for "flush irrigation" that flooded whole fields at once were less than rates for targeted or lift irrigation that were administratively harder to manage. All this, however, did not necessarily optimize the entire system's irrigation productivity by concentrating water in the most fertile lands at the ideal times. While practices varied, generally water was not sold by volume. Rather the outflow gate size and open time were regulated, with rates calculated by the type of crop irrigated. Since the volume and timing of irrigation were often not ideal, upstream (head-end) users often took more than they needed because it was their right, sometimes producing inefficient use and waterlogging while leaving downstream (tail-end) users short. Further, wherever landownership predated the canals, Irrigation Departments had to negotiate customary and other legal rights.

While provinces varied, the Raj had three main categories of water canal projects (in parallel with railways and forests). The largest in number and scale were "productive" canal works which were projected to generate sufficient profits from charges to Indian users for irrigation water (and miscellaneous income like fines and navigation fees) to pay off within a decade the bonds taken for their construction. The government also gained considerably in increased revenues from both improved existing fields and new lands brought under agriculture (the former usually credited to Canal Departments, the latter to Revenue Departments). By 1890, canals overall earned an average 5.8 percent net return on investment of £25.5 million (MacGeorge 1894:213–14).

Major perennial irrigation canal building accelerated from the 1880s onward in the Indus basin, turning what government considered "wastelands" into productive resources for market-oriented farmers and its own revenues. This network of dams and canals was innovatively conceptualized as an integrated surface water system. For example, the Punjab Irrigation Department transformed and greatly extended the Chenab inundation canal into a perennial system that eventually commanded 9,100 km^2 (3,515 mi^2). This canal system proved particularly profitable with a calculated 40 percent financial return to the government by 1892.

Government canal engineers also transformed the local society. They systematically laid out new "canal colonies" (especially in Punjab) for farmers to settle using water-intensive cash-crop agriculture. But all this came at the cost of disrupting existing pastoralist and seasonal crop economies. Since many cash crops (e.g. cotton, indigo, opium, rice, sugarcane, and wheat) respond well to heavy irrigation – but many crops grown for local consumption (e.g. millet and pulses) do not – ecological, economic, and social changes benefited wealthier exporting farmers.

There were also uncalculated environmental costs. The unlined canals produced much seepage, raising water tables and often causing salinization (as the evaporating water brought crop-killing salts to the surface) or waterlogging (that reduced productivity, collapsed existing wells, and increased mosquito and waterborne diseases). Canal foundations often disrupted groundwater flows. Uncovered, the canals also lost much water to evaporation.

Further, there were ideological and economic stresses between PWD irrigation engineers and the revenue-, agriculture-, and security-oriented ICS, as well as within the PDW itself. Some engineers were committed to self-proclaimed abstract, rational, objective, universal or "imperial science" independent of local natural conditions (Gilmartin 1994; Lewis 2007). But other officials recognized the need to incorporate local knowledge from Indian farmers and the pragmatic need to mobilize labor for canal construction and maintenance – the science of effectively implementing imperial rule.

The Raj's second category was "protective" canals, designed to prevent floods and famines. These were usually funded out of land revenues, often only earning the government little net profit. But British advocates asserted that these canals saved the government the costs of famines: relief projects, reduced land revenues, and human and domestic animal deaths.

The third category, "minor" works, included: a range of preexisting small dams and canals taken over by government; off-budget, small-scale government-funded projects; and community and private irrigation systems. Additionally, some provinces, especially deltaic Bengal, also had the categories major and minor navigation canals. Overall in India, by the end of the nineteenth century, there were more than 22,400 km (14,000 mi) of main and branch canals (of which one-third were navigable) "commanding" 52,000 km^2 (20,000 mi^2).

The 1882 Indian Easements Act established the distinction between state-controlled surface water and privately owned groundwater. Every landowner had "the right . . . to collect and dispose within his own limits of all water under the land which does not pass in a defined channel." Hence, some landowners, for their own use or sale to others, legally pumped from aquifers that extended far beyond their land's surface boundaries. (This has led in recent times to extensive commercialized extraction and aquifer depletion.)

Drinking water and sanitation are, of course, also vital for towns and cities, although the policies and economic, social, and political dynamics of water supply and control varied from those in the countryside. Most major pre-Mughal and Mughal cities were inland, with much of those period's inundation canal- and reservoir-building intended to support them. Some early EIC hydraulic projects restored a few of those long-neglected canals. The EIC also began to design and construct water systems for the British-centered cities of Bombay, Calcutta, and Madras. The 1860 Indian Penal Code (still largely in place today) outlawed some kinds of water and air pollution, but enforcement remained highly limited since the prosecution had to prove specific harm.

In the imperial capital of Calcutta, some British doctors observed that mostly British-owned workshops and poor sanitation clearly polluted the drinking water supplies and air (the effects on European inhabitants were the Raj's special concern). They pushed the government into early efforts at official monitoring and mitigation of discharges (e.g. the Calcutta Smoke Abatement Act, 1863), often blaming Indian workmen rather than British or Indian factory owners.

Under the Raj, municipalities gained a degree of self-government, starting with the 1872 Bombay Council Act. Municipal councils were usually elected by ratepayers and became one of the first arenas where Indian politicians gained experience in governing. Simultaneously, some Indian civil society groups starting to demand better water supply and sanitation (e.g. the Bombay Association and the People's Association of Poona from 1870 and the Kashi Ganga Prasadini Sabha of Banares from 1886). These councils and NGOs arose during a period of increased urbanization, including the influx of workers into crowded slums, the rise of some industries (e.g. mechanized textile mills in Bombay and Ahmedabad), and the physical transformation of urban space (e.g. the expansion of Bombay's landmass by a quarter through physically extending shorelines, termed "reclamation" from the sea).

Municipal authorities, however, often had limited effectiveness in supplying water, sanitation, and other public services, while the interests of Britons and Indians (customarily living in segregated and unequally served parts of the city) often diverged. Most cities had no building codes, so construction varied considerably in terms of safety and health. Municipal revenue sources were constrained, and their budgets relied on often inadequate funding from the central and provincial governments (which had other priorities). This meant that the technology used by municipalities was often inadequate in quality and scale, leading to further public frustration and health problems. In some ways, India became a laboratory for British sanitary science. For instance, in a drinking water tank in Calcutta in 1884, Robert Koch (1843–1910) discovered the cholera bacterium. But he long struggled to convince government medical officials who clung to the miasma theory of contagion. By the 1890s, many municipal governments were constructing water supply systems with loans from the central government, although sewage disposal lagged (and remains a major issue in South Asia today). British urban planners, trained in "imperial science," often blamed the failures of sanitation technology on allegedly anomalous unsanitary Indian customs or India's tropical climate.

During the late nineteenth century, the Raj's policies and its railways, forestry, and irrigation projects had interacted in various combinations to cause widespread effects, often damaging to the environment and to many Indian people and flora and fauna species. This period also saw frequent El Niño-related droughts in one or more regions (1860–61, 1864–9, 1873–81, 1896–97, 1899–1902, 1907–08), which, intensified by government policies, resulted in massive famines. While some railway projects claimed to be designed to relieve famine, they often instead extracted grain from drought-stricken, impoverished regions for shipment to wealthier cities or international markets. Further, viceroys and the British government were committed to other budgetary priorities and to ideologies of nonintervention and reliance on free market-supply. Government "test works," were designed to discourage alleged malingerers and the ordinary, chronically impoverished: they doled out inadequate or minimal nutrition, but only for those famine victims who would (or could) travel often long distances to do hard manual labor in PWD projects. But some British officials advocated "gratuitous relief," which rose to between a third and a half of government famine expenditure by the end of the nineteenth century, but also remained nutritionally inadequate. A series of government Famine Commissions gathered evidence and made modest ameliorating recommendations like allowing the starving to collect food from forests, ordinarily barred to them by government foresters. Some provinces created famine codes (e.g. Bengal in 1896) to guide official policies and implementation. Various British, Indian, and international critics at that time (as well as many later historians) tried to document and calculate the many millions of additional human and livestock deaths from starvation or disease and the long-term economic and environmental effects of such government actions and policies. Among the most prominent and effective in challenging the entire British imperial project was Mohandas Gandhi.

The Gandhian Alternative to the British Raj

Many recent environmentalists, both international and South Asian, cite Mohandas "Mahatma" Gandhi as their inspiring model for nonviolent resistance to ecological exploitation and for a range of "back to the land" movements. Yet, he was not a systematic philosopher nor wrote or spoke specifically about the environment or wilderness preservation. Nonetheless, he selectively synthesized a range of multicultural concepts, derived from his personal experiences and his reading, into distinctive practices that later environmentalists (and other social activists) have used effectively. Gandhi invented the method for public protest that he named *satyagraha* ("truth grasping," nonviolent noncooperation with evil), using the tactics of "passive resistance," the public fast, peaceful marches and sit-ins against injustice, and effective publicity generation.

Gandhi used the term "nature" in the sense of *dharma*, the ultimate Truth of how the universe and everything that composed it should function. He titled his autobiography *The Story of My Experiments with Truth*, presenting a series of episodes through which he "discovered" whether his actions accorded with Truth or not, largely by observing the results as positive or negative. For instance, in a youthful effort to make his body as strong as the carnivorous Muslims and Christians who had successively conquered and long ruled over Hindus, he ate goat meat for about a year (lying to his parents about it). But he eventually repented, returned to a vegetarian diet, and taught about its health benefits.

Some central and pervasive strands in Gandhi's culminating model of satyagraha stemmed from his upbringing in a mercantile Vaishnava Hindu community in coastal Gujarat. The name Gandhi means "grocer," used by his jati (in the Vaishya varna). Among Hindus, Gujarati

Vaishnavas particularly shared the strict nonviolent traditions of Jainism, long present in that region. As we have seen (Chapter 4), Jains (like Buddhists) regarded all acts of violence (including thought, action, and nonvegetarian consumption) as degrading. Indeed, Gandhi's mother, Putlibai, explicitly showed self-suffering rather than breaking her own vow (for instance, fasting despite her children's pleas to relent). While some critics characterize this as moral blackmail, many who opposed Gandhi respected his sincerity in self-sacrificing, some converting to his perspective (or at least being willing to find a common ground).

During Gandhi's youth, he also Anglicized, starting in an English-medium school in Gujarat and then in London (1888–91) where he qualified as a British barrister. The contrast between British imperialism and racism practiced in colonial India and the democracy and humanism celebrated in Britain impressed Gandhi, as it did many other Indians who likewise made this journey. While Gandhi's career as a barrister in India was relatively brief, his understanding of the British judicial system enabled him to use it on his own terms.

Gandhi developed satyagraha during his decades (1893–1915) living largely in British-ruled Natal, South Africa, during a period when legal racial apartheid was beginning. There, he learned to use British law, and disobedience of it, for the preservation and recovery of the rights of the substantial Indian community (c. 40,000 in Natal, about the same as the number of white Britons and Afrikaners, but a tenth the number of black Africans). For instance, he pleaded guilty of breaking laws he opposed as immoral, calling for punishment or else revocation of them. He also served the Indian community as a social worker, organizing them to unite in nonviolent protests and to keep sanitary their designated ghettos.

In 1908, Gandhi wrote and published his most powerful manifesto, *Hind Swaraj*. In this pamphlet, he created a fictional dialogue between the Editor (himself) and a Reader (a composite of Indians advocating violent revolution against the British, some of whom he had recently met while visiting London). He advocated his vision of Indian civilization and critiqued Western immorality, citing Tolstoy, Thoreau, and Ruskin. Further, in Gandhi's celebration of agriculture and devaluation of urban industry, his ideals had parallels with those of European sanitarians and physiocrats, including the dependence of human health on a healthy rural environment. Overall, he created an indigenous Indian alternative to the culturally dominant concept (which many Britons and Indians found convincing) that Western science and capitalism should conquer Indian "nature," thus justifying British-model "progress."

After Gandhi's return to India in 1915, he practiced satyagraha to try to end both British oppression and Indian social inequalities. By advocating self-sufficient, organic village communities, he sought to restore Indian self-esteem and nonviolently withdraw from cooperation with British colonial rule and the capitalist world system (e.g. by hand-spinning cotton thread for one's handwoven cloth, *khadi*, rather than purchasing British factory-made fabric). He made himself and his communes models for nonwasteful "economy" (from the same word root as "ecology"). They reused or repurposed every resource, for instance turning human "waste" into compost, and using the minimum necessary water, food, and mechanical energy. All animals, plants, and inanimate objects deserved loving respect, although he considered them in relation to human needs.

A prolific journalist, he also skillfully publicized his fasts and protests. Most famously, he notified the government and world press that he would defy the regressive British salt monopoly and tax with a widely reported three-week, 390 km (245 mi) procession by men and women to the seashore at Dandi where he picked up natural salt crystals. The salt tax brought about 8 percent of the Raj's revenue. But it was also a highly regressive tax, easily affordable by the rich but a considerable financial burden on the poor whose sweating labor required more salt consumption. Further, Gandhi highlighted the absurdity of a tax on a substance freely available on India's extensive coastline and customarily mined inland as well. This nonviolent campaign mobilized many Indians to collect beach salt and nonviolently march into official salt flats. The frustrated government's mass arrests and then imprisonment of Gandhi failed to suppress this movement (although the salt tax was largely maintained until 1947).

Several of Gandhi's direct and indirect disciples later used his methods in specifically environmental causes (for instance Chipko and anti-dam movements, see Chapter 10). Further, people around the world have been inspired by their appreciation of him and his ideals. In addition to anti-dictatorship movements, these causes include animal rights, deep ecology, pacifism, anti-capitalism, and anti-development based on technology like major dams and industrialization.

Gandhi was not, of course, alone among Indian nationalists advancing models for human relationships with the environment during the decades leading up to 1947 and thereafter. Even the leading elite political movement of the INC, which most respected Gandhi, contained a range of other agendas. The most prominent leaders of the next generation supported variations of many of the Western models that Gandhi rejected: Jawaharlal Nehru (1889–1964), Subhas Chandra Bose (1897–1945), and B. R. Ambedkar (1891–1956) all advocated India's industrialization while M. A. Jinnah (1876–1948) did much the same for Pakistan. (As the next chapter shows, the independent governments of India and Pakistan largely followed combinations of those leaders' models while Gandhi's ideas continued to be powerful among popular and some elite environmentalists.)

The First Half of the Twentieth Century

Many of the Raj's projects of environmental control intensified during its last half-century. But so did challenges to British rule at all levels, from various classes of Indians. Despite shaky official efforts to subdue them, a range of elite, Anglicized Indian and Pakistani nationalists requested and then demanded more political power while popular movements asserted their rights to India's resources. Particularly during the two world wars, the British Empire struggled, relying heavily on Indian finances, manpower, raw materials, and manufactures. Finally, in August 1947, the Raj partitioned South Asia and its environment into the independent new nations of India and Pakistan.

At the start of the twentieth century, many of the Raj's "public works" were expanding and incorporating technological advances. Railways reached 51,600 km (32,000 mi) of track by 1910 (and 65,600 km [40,800 mi] by 1947) and used electric engines from 1925 onward. Further, in 1921, the government adopted a gradual policy to not renew the remaining contracts with private railway companies (making the system almost entirely state owned and operated by 1944).

Irrigation departments, particularly in the Indus basin, extended their reengineering of India's hydraulic systems. For instance, the Triple Canal project (1905–17) redirected water from the Jhelum and Chenab in western Punjab into the Ravi in its east, to command huge government "wasteland" in Lower Bari Doab, doubling the province's irrigated area. Later, demands by farmers in Sindh (part of Bombay Presidency) that Punjab was taking a disproportionate share of Indus waters encouraged the Sukkur barrage scheme (1923–32), which greatly expanded perennial irrigation in Sindh. By 1947, 120,000 km (75,000 mi) of canals irrigated a quarter of India's entire cropped area.

Nonetheless, the Raj had difficulty controlling the social and environmental consequences of these ambitious public works projects. Many Indians living in Punjab's canal colonies protested the 1906 Colonization Bill that increased government intervention and water rates. Meanwhile, proliferating canals produced unexpected salinization, waterlogging, and increased disease, even as Indian farmers developed their own ways to mitigate some of these effects (Stone 1984; Whitcombe 1972).

Forest Departments also extended their authority, increasing the level of conflict with local communities. From about 1906, resin collecting developed commercially, mostly extracted from chir pine plantations. In 1920, the UP Forest Department built India's largest yet resin and turpentine processing factory. However, plantation pines were not useful to hill communities; indeed, pine needles created treacherously slippery surfaces for their grazing animals. Further, much of the resin collection and timbering was done by wage laborers recruited from the plains. Hence, hill people objected, sometimes by burning plantations, with major outbreaks during the especially hot and dry summers of 1916 and 1921. Despite such resistance, Forest Departments extended reserve forests to cover 260,000 km^2 [100,400 mi^2] by 1947.

The Raj also used developing technology to build dams that produced hydroelectricity in a series of small projects (Darjeeling 1897, Kateri Falls [near Kurnool] 1904, Srinagar 1908, Mussoorie [Dehra Dun] 1909, Amritsar 1913, Shimla 1913, and Nainital 1922); some princely states did as well (Mysore 1902, Travancore 1906, Kashmir 1908); the private Tata company started supplying hydroelectric power to Bombay (1914). Many other projects, including the beginnings of rural electrification followed. During the 1930s, some provinces initiated large-scale projects of distributing tube-wells (individual waterproof metal casings bored into the earth to tap groundwater for irrigation or drinking).

Simultaneously, the Raj began multipurpose river development projects (made internationally famous by America's Tennessee Valley Authority [TVA], begun in 1933) that integrated electrical generation, flood control, and irrigation. "Modernizing" Indians also built such projects. Indeed, the princely state of Mysore constructed Krishnaraja Sagar Project on the Kaveri (begun 1916, filled 1924, and completed at 40 m [132 ft] high in 1931), which was among the earliest in India. The Raj also began planning similar multipurpose river development projects for the Damodar and Mahanadi rivers. Such massive hydraulic projects, which encompassed an entire basin and integrated multiple purposes, gained support from both Britons and some Indian nationalists (including Jawaharlal Nehru and Ambedkar, who would continue to push for such "modernizing" watershed-wide planning and harnessing after they achieved control over the central government, see Chapter 9).

As a central strategy, the Raj continued to try to divide India's land and people. The central government had occasionally split, reconfigured, or merged its Indian provinces for administrative or political reasons. In 1905, it partitioned Bengal Presidency by dividing predominantly Muslim areas in eastern Bengal from majority Hindu areas in the west. While the Raj claimed administrative justifications, this politically and economically weakened many Hindu landowners living in the imperial capital of Calcutta (in western Bengal) who were active in growing nationalist movements but who had their estates in what became East Bengal. Further, West Bengal was culturally diluted by incorporating Oriya speakers. This provincial partition also created more space for Muslim politicians who, the next year, founded the Muslim League (ML) movement to speak for their interests. Thereafter, viceroys repeatedly tried to use the ML and other minority-based political parties against the INC. While for decades M. A. Jinnah, as president of the ML and a leading member of the INC, tried to negotiate power sharing between them (most prominently in the 1916 Lucknow Pact), their agendas diverged (culminating in the 1947 partition of Pakistan and India).

In addition, this first partition of Bengal (the next would be in 1947) mobilized a range of widespread popular protests along nationalist, communal, class, ethnic, and other identities. Indian political demands were outpacing British efforts to diffuse them with inadequate concessions: the 1909 Indian Councils Act allowed very limited franchise election of a few Indians to provincial and central legislative councils but had a separate Muslim electorate and reserved seats. In 1911, however, the Raj rejoined Bengal's east and west. But at the same time, the Raj determined to weaken Calcutta as a center for political activism by shifting the imperial capital of India to a new, the purpose-built city of New Delhi, adjacent to the Mughal capital, Shahjahanabad (renamed Old Delhi). Designing and constructing this new capital city enabled the Raj to represent its imperial vision through architecture and modern technology (ironically just three decades before the end of the Raj). Scholars have contrasted the "public" services installed in New Delhi, primarily for government officials, with the inadequate investment in drinking water and sanitation in Old Delhi, where few Britons lived (Mann 2007; Sharan 2014).

The clash of empires and ethnicities in Europe that resulted in World War I shifted India's environmental history in several ways. Suddenly, Britain needed to accelerate its recruitment of Indian manpower and its extraction of India's other resources. Forest departments not only increased the rate of cutting, overriding established working plans, they also lost British personnel to the war effort. Indian grain producers and merchants saw prices rise significantly with export demand, enriching them but impoverishing many Indian consumers. Further, long-suppressed Indian factories now received government and economic encouragement to produce finished products, especially war materiel.

Additionally, WWI challenged the race-based cultural domination that had sustained the Raj. In all, about 1.5 million Indian soldiers and laborers served in British imperial armies, many of them on the

European Western Front, returning with military training and global perspectives. Indian officers gained promotions and status hitherto denied them. Further, in Britain and France, Indians of all ranks saw racial barriers fall, as they fought and died together with and fighting against white Europeans and occasionally associated with European women, despite official efforts to keep them separate. In India, Indians also rose in government departments, holding positions that had been previously held by only British men, many of whom never returned. For instance, until 1906, only two Indians had entered professional training as Imperial Forest Service officers, but this number increased rapidly during and after World War I.

The 1918–19 influenza epidemic that killed about 12–14 million Indians and the periodic regional outbreaks of the plague that killed roughly as many (1896–1921) brought much resented official interventions by the Indian Medical Service into Indian lives and homes, including body inspections and violating women's privacy. Elite Indians and some Britons questioned the long-standing but increasingly shaken claims by the Raj that it and imperial science had mastered India's environment. Nonetheless, global medical and public health advances and a post–World War I period of favorable monsoons resulted in declining infant and maternal mortality with little decline in birth rate and increases in adult longevity.

Many Indians expected recognition for their wartime contributions, encouraged by international promises of self-determination articulated by American President Woodrow Wilson and the League of Nations. Instead, British concessions were too scanty and came too late, like the Montague-Chelmsford reforms and the 1919 Government of India Act. These provided for direct elections but with very limited franchise (with separate Muslim electorates) for provincial legislative councils (dealing with public works and sanitation). But, key departments remained "reserved" in British hands (the "diarchy" system). Simultaneously, the 1919 Anarchical and Revolutionary Crimes Act ("Rowlatt Act") continued wartime restrictions on the press and authorized indefinite imprisonment without trial. Popular and elite-led peaceful and militant Indian protests both met brutal repression by the Raj, most notably in Amritsar (Punjab) in 1919, where hundreds of peacefully gathered Indians were massacred in Jallianwala Bagh park.

Natural resources were also heatedly contested. The 1927 Indian Forest Act attempted to increase government revenues from timber and non-timber forest products and to assert stronger state control over local community access. While it promised to protect legal rights by forest-dwellers, it did not recognize rights that had not been officially registered.

In some regions, including Kumaun, forest panchayats (local self-governing councils) arose from the 1920s. Yet, as would occur after independence, many foresters asserted power over local forest panchayats, even over nominally autonomous ones.

Indian wildlife also suffered from the effects of new military-developed technology in the form of higher-powered and more accurately sighted rifles. These enabled British trophy-hunters and Indian princes to increase their killing rates considerably. Cheetahs were finished off by trophy-hunters (Chavda 1995). Meanwhile, locally knowledgeable villagers and forest-dwellers continued to serve as trackers and usually unpaid luggage carriers, neither able to afford such expensive weapons nor get gun-licenses.

As the stock of desired game noticeably diminished, some of the most prominent hunters, like E. J. "Jim" Corbett (1875–1955), converted to conservation protection over selected species. British and elite Indian conservationists held an All India Conference for the Preservation of Wild Life in 1935, lobbying successfully for the creation of national parks, sometimes converted from hunting-oriented game reserves. The first of these (the 520 km^2 [200 mi^2] Hailey [later Corbett] National Park) was created in 1936 (this became the first site for Project Tiger in 1973). But in this process, some British and Indian elites also altered their portrayal of local communities from trackers and guides to poachers.

The post–World War I global boom had affected the Indian economy, now much more integrated with the world economic system. But India was also deeply affected by the global depression during the 1930s, as was weakening Britain. Elite and popular Indian nationalist movements gained momentum, celebrating disobedience and non-cooperation with the Raj, including its authority over the environment.

As a grudging British devolution of powers to property-owning Indians, the 1935 Government of India Act increased electoral franchise to about 30 million (15 percent of the population, including property-owning women). This Act also attempted to keep India divided by reinforcing provincial autonomy. In the subsequent 1937 election, eight of the eleven provinces elected INC governments while the ML won only a minority even of the seats reserved for Muslims. Many ambitious Indian industrialists backed the INC financially, while rich peasants led its rural support base. However, elected Indians could only to manage parts of the provincial government considered by the British to be less essential. Nonetheless, water and forests were provincial subjects, giving INC politicians experience in trying to manage these resources to meet popular expectations. Some politicians supported opening forestlands to their farmer-constituents, at the cost of nonvoting forest-dwellers and also Forest Department officials, who began to decry such "encroachments." Conversely, the new provincial governments were often frustrated by the entrenched bureaucrats in the irrigation, forest, and other departments.

These grudging incorporations of Indian elites into government were, however, belied by the viceroy's unilateral declaration in 1939 that India was at war with Germany, and then Japan. The beleaguered INC ministries resigned, unintentionally opening more space for the ML to work with the Raj. Economically, an increasingly desperate Britain extracted from India manpower, raw materials, manufactured products, and other resources, promising to repay in future – the "Sterling Balance" that Britain owed the Raj. In this war, some 2.5 million Indians served in British imperial armies. Many of those abandoned by their British officers when Singapore fell or in other British defeats joined the Indian National Army led by S. C. Bose that allied with the Germans and Japanese.

This war had major environmental consequences exceeding those of World War I. For instance, timbering in Reserved and Protected Forests increased considerably, even as many British foresters left to join the army, weakening enforcement of remaining limits. The Raj encouraged economic expansion, and some Indians prospered from the commercial drive for war profits from timbering, mining, and other resource-intense production. Further, the Japanese imperial army shattered the myth of white British military invincibility over Asians with triumphant conquests in Singapore, Burma, elsewhere in Southeast Asia, and Assam. Japanese warplanes repeatedly bombed almost undefended Calcutta. Battles in India's northeast, in particularly fragile ecologies, also destroyed native plants and animals, terminated wildlife protections, and left behind polluting chemicals and as yet unexploded munitions and mines.

The Raj was especially overwhelmed in vital Bengal province. A severe cyclone (October 1942) devastated rice-producing southwest Bengal, followed by massive flooding in the Damodar valley, compounding administrative chaos that had focused on rice extraction for the British war effort while destroying all boats to "deny" food and transportation to the expected Japanese invasion. The resulting massive famine with its attendant diseases, mainly in the Bengal countryside, killed 3–5 million people (reminiscent of the Bihar-Bengal famine that killed about 10 million in 1769–71, just after British rule there began). The massive human dislocation and cultural, economic, and environmental disruption continued through the Partition of Bengal between India and Pakistan in 1947.

The end of the war in Europe, and then the atomic-bomb culmination of the war in the Pacific, marked the final stage of the British Raj. With the rushed departure of the British, the new nations of India and Pakistan inherited many of the relationships between the environment and the state, as the next chapter considers.

9 West and East Pakistan and India following Independence (1947–71)

In August 1947, the departing British Raj inscribed man-made boundaries over South Asia's ecosystems and built-environments, including watersheds and canal, road, rail, communication, and other infrastructure networks. The new and hostile nations of Pakistan and India immediately each claimed the resources within their borders. Much of the severed subcontinent's Indus watershed went to West Pakistan, with some to India (and small parts in Afghanistan, Tibet, and China); the bulk of the Ganges basin went to India (with small parts in Nepal and Bhutan), but the eastern end of it became East Pakistan; India alone held the Deccan and southern Peninsula. West and East Pakistan and India, and provinces within them, thus each began with distinctive, unequal, and disrupted arrays of natural, human, and human-made resources.

Each new government retained most of the environmental legislation and administrative structure it inherited from the British Raj. Each subsequently passed dozens of laws addressing individual environmentally related problems (although, until the 1970s and 1980s, not the environment as a whole). Forests, mines, rivers, flora, and fauna became sources for raw materials to be developed rapidly: to construct a catch-up national industrializing economy during a period of accelerating global competition during the Cold War, to lessen the severe burden of widespread poverty, and to reward powerful urban and rural elites.

During the postindependence decades, each new government and emerging international bodies (e.g. the United Nations, Ford Foundation, International Union for Conservation of Nature [IUCN], and World Wildlife Fund for Nature [WWF]) generated vast amounts of information and numerous policies, programs, and reports. Additionally, within India and Pakistan, individuals, communities, popular and elite movements, NGOs, and lively public media spoke and wrote extensively about environment-related issues. Often multisided debates about events and policies developed at the international, national, provincial, and local levels. As the academic discipline of environmental history emerged during this period, scholars have used these diverse sources in different

Map 9.1 South Asia at Partition (1947)

combinations to create largely nation-based historiographies, although some (like this book) consider subcontinent-wide issues and interweave the environmental histories of independent Pakistan and India.

South Asia's 1947 Partition

The partition of South Asia that produced India and West and East Pakistan resulted from years of bitter negotiations and recriminations among British officials, the ML under M. A. Jinnah, the INC led by Jawaharlal Nehru, and diverse other elite and popular interests (see Map 9.1). Almost all parties accepted the European nation-state model with a federal structure based on British-style, bicameral parliamentary democracy. However, even as the British withdrew, many foundational issues remained unresolved, including where Pakistan would be created and for whom. But the post–World War II British government and especially its newly appointed last viceroy, Lord Louis Mountbatten (1900–79, viceroy March–August 1947; governor-general of India 1947–48), rushed into Partition.

Most Muslim-majority provinces went entirely to Pakistan, but Punjab and Bengal were to be divided by Boundary Commissions. While ML and INC Commissioners presented irreconcilable plans and demands, Chairman Cyril Radcliffe (1899–1977) inked these borders in just three hurried weeks. A British lawyer, he had no prior knowledge of the sub-continent or even up-to-date detailed maps.

Radcliffe largely followed the grudgingly agreed upon political formula that allotted contiguous Muslim majority districts to Pakistan. Although in a few places his demarcation protected major canal, rail, and road systems, overall his crude line cut through hitherto integrated ecosystems, infrastructures, and economies. Where Radcliffe drew the international boundary down the middle of rivers, for example, this created unantici-pated rival disputes over often-meandering waterways. Where he placed the boundary across a river or canal (sometimes his line crossed more than once), he created upper versus lower riparian conflicts. (The British also presumed that their imposed external borders with Afghanistan, Nepal, and China would stand, but these have periodically been challenged by those nations, especially in the 1962 India-China war and ongoing Pakistan-Afghanistan disputes.)

The departing British also decreed that the hundreds of princes, who ruled one-third of the subcontinent and a quarter of its population, became legally independent, their status to be settled later. Geographical location, personal and popular sentiment, and substantial pressure and incentives from the new governments led almost all princes eventually to merge their domains into either Pakistan or India. In Pakistan, some princes retained considerable autonomy for decades (and some continue to hold substantial political influence). In India, many princes negotiated special privileges and incomes (until the 26th Amendment to the Constitution ended them in 1971). Uncooperative princes faced force. Pakistan pressured the ruler of Kalat in Balochistan (population 150,000) into acceding. The Muslim government of Hindu-majority Junagadh (population 500,000) tried to join distant Pakistan, but India annexed it (which Pakistan still officially protests). The Muslim Nizam of Hindu-majority Hyderabad (population 14 million) claimed independence, but Indian troops seized it in 1949. The Hindu ruler of Muslim majority Jammu and Kashmir (population 3 million) initially claimed independence, but then suddenly opted for India, amid battles between the Pakistani and Indian armies, themselves recently partitioned out of the British Indian Army. Kashmir's identity remains hotly disputed with a UN-supervised "Line of Control" still separating Pakistani-held Azad ("Free") Kashmir from Indian-held Kashmir (where a half-million Indian troops are now trying to control ongoing popular resistance). Adding to its other strategic importance to each nation, Kashmir is the source of major tributaries in the Indus system – vital to West Pakistan and northwest India. (India's most recent annexation was Sikkim [population 250,000] in May 1975.)

Each new government asserted its exclusive sovereignty within its borders, realigning all territories, animals, plants, minerals, and all other natural and human-made resources as either Pakistani or Indian property, to be used for its national development. For instance, the Indus, Ganges, and Brahmaputra river systems now crossed international borders, with each rival claiming their vital waters. Wildlife walked, flew, or swam across these boundaries, but each new regime imposed its authority over all those on its side. Every human became a citizen, legally loyal to only India or Pakistan, on pain of treason. While statistics remain disputed even today, about 12 million people, finding themselves in the "wrong" country, either chose or were forced to emigrate – roughly half Hindus and Sikhs leaving Pakistan and half Muslims going there – with up to 2 million murdered and tens of thousands of women abducted and many more assaulted. Long-standing cross-border seasonal migrations by merchants, laborers, and pastoralists with their domesticated animals would legally cease (but sometimes illegally persist). Simultaneously, the central civil and military services and judiciary split roughly along religious "communal" lines, even as they divided movable government assets according to a negotiated formula: 22.7 percent for Pakistan and 77.3 percent for India.

Pakistan and India shared many colonial legacies – the institutions of the British Raj being substantially perpetuated but also disrupted in both nations. Their premier political leaders were British-trained Anglophone lawyers, committed in varying degrees to creating Western-style democratic nation-states comprised of individual citizens holding private property and electoral franchise rights, with a relatively free press. They also largely advocated "progress" and national development using Euro-American models of heavy industrialization and science-based management and use of natural resources.

Much of the actual structure of their respective administrations persisted from the British Raj, although the upper personnel were no longer British. Hence, civil officials, military officers, and judges in both new governments were professionally trained with strong intra-cadre bonds, but also with nationalist agendas. Below them, both governments continued to employ a multitude of lower-level administrators, guards, clerks, and other workers, trained in British bureaucratic procedures.

Both new governments also inherited the vast body of British Raj laws and administrative regulations, precedents, and practices. Indeed, many of these have continued in force until today, with no or only limited amendment. For instance, more than one-third of Pakistan's federal laws (and about as many of India's) affecting natural resources and their management were first framed by the British Raj, including the key Forest Act of 1878 (revised 1927) and the Canal and Drainage Act of 1873 (Ahmed and Kazi 2005; Divan and Rosencranz 2001). These and other resource-oriented laws and policies largely favored the state and its officials over users, sometimes even more after independence than in colonial times.

Further, in both new nations, escalating elite and popular resistance to the British Raj, followed by liberation, left continuing patterns of everyday struggle against all government controls, including state restrictions on resource use. Before independence, princes, British officers and officials, and their favored collaborators had, for instance, enjoyed privileged use of forests (for timbering and hunting), even while villagers and former forest-dwellers had often been barred from grazing, hunting, or collecting timber, fodder, and other forest products. At independence, many local communities took natural resources that they considered rightfully theirs and vitally needed, sometimes protecting them, occasionally using them unsustainably. Similarly, as the British Raj faded, some princes had heavily exploited resources within their states in preparation for their uncertain transition to citizen-entrepreneurs or politicians.

For many rural and urban people, the postindependence state remained a major source of threats to their local environment. For instance, government foresters, hydraulic engineers, and city-planners unilaterally exploited resources and displaced local communities in the name of national development. At the same time, however, municipal governments and urban planners were overwhelmed as refugees and rural immigrants joined urban populations, often constructing shelters, houses, and factories without official authorization or public services. Further, Indian and Pakistani elected politicians intervened in the use and distribution of resources like land, forests, and water, often to the dismay of "expert" officials charged with managing them.

On their part, South Asian district officials, foresters, canal engineers, and other professionals in the various branches of the British Raj's administration had long endured racial subordination by Britons ranked above them. As popular nationalist sentiment rose leading up to 1947, many felt they had to prove their own nationalism, if only to themselves.

After independence, overtly demonstrating commitment to their own new nation became both virtuous and advantageous for their careers. For instance, India's East Punjab Canal Department officials twice temporarily blocked the flow of key canals into Pakistan. Indeed, many national and provincial politicians and officials asserted their own "hydrologic" by proposing massive water diversion projects benefiting their nation rather than the "enemy" (Haines 2017).

Independent West and East Pakistan from Partition to the Indus River Treaty (1947–60)

Partition particularly crippled Pakistan. Most immediately, millions of incoming refugees and immigrants vitally needed water, food, clothing, housing, employment, and protection or recovery from violence. The western part of divided Punjab and the eastern part of divided Bengal comprised Pakistan's two largest resource centers, together containing over three-quarters of its population, but separated by 1,600 km [1,000 mi] of often hostile Indian territory.

Pakistan also began less developed economically. It contained only about 5 percent of the industries that had emerged under the British Raj; many of these had been owned and managed by Hindus who fled. Its raw materials had hitherto mostly supplied factories now within India. The railway lines inside Pakistan were not designed for its domestic economy (consequently, road transport has expanded postindependence while railway lines have languished). Overall, Pakistan started with few known natural resources except land and water.

Partition also left each wing of Pakistan a lower riparian state, vulnerable to upstream diversion. For instance, the Brahmaputra River flows from China through India into East Pakistan (now Bangladesh), but there is still no water-sharing agreement; nor does Pakistan have one with upper-riparian Afghanistan. Until the 1960 Treaty (discussed below) the divided Indus system caused antagonism between Pakistan and India (and disputes have welled up subsequently). The lower Ganges flowing from India into East Pakistan (now Bangladesh) also has long been contested (although a series of uneasy water-sharing agreements started in 1975).

The new Pakistan was also weaker and more divided than India in other ways. The British Raj's civil and military services contained relatively few Muslims, especially in senior positions. The premier ICS was only 9 percent Muslim. The new Pakistani Army continued to have a British commander-in-chief (until General Ayub Khan in 1951). Nonetheless, the professional training and institutional organization of Pakistan's administrative officials and military officers have meant that each has formed a powerful bloc, resilient to elected politicians and popular movements (including environmentalists) even today.

Pakistan's political leadership also proved less stable in the postindependence decades. Leading up to 1947, the ML had far more limited popular and organizational bases than the INC. ML leaders had mobilized the widest support for the creation of Pakistan by keeping their promises about its composition and future diffuse, on some issues even contradictory. Not only was the party's identification of the new nation's territorial bounds undefined, so was the nature of the new state. For instance, the ML convinced nascent Muslim-centered labor unions, pro-women's organizations, and other parts of civil society to subordinate their separate interests into the larger movement for Pakistan's creation. After independence, these institutions remained relatively weak compared to their counterparts in India, especially in West Pakistan, the part of the subcontinent most subject to security-state authoritarian rule during the British Raj.

Similarly, in the early 1940s, Jinnah had occasionally issued revolutionary appeals to the Muslim rural masses, attacking capitalism and elite oppression (Jinnah 1947). However, most ML funding came from large landholders and princes, who received assurances that they would retain power over resources in the new nation. Post-1947, this elite (especially in West Pakistan) has worked to perpetuate its own interests through avoiding land redistribution, capturing the local administration of water and other resources, and dominating political parties and the legislature (when it functioned). Generally, the locally most powerful users manipulated the system for their own benefit, for instance in accessing government subsidies and services like fertilizers and canal water in agricultural areas and drinking water, sanitation, and electricity in cities. Weaker individuals and groups often had to defer to powerful patrons for protection and access to resources and services.

In 1947, Pakistan was the world's largest Muslim nation, but whether it should be an Islamic state or a secular nation for Muslims has been disputed ever since. Some of Pakistan's most active and powerful NGOs and parties identify themselves as Islamic, often organized along sectarian lines. Most prominent have been the Jama'at-i Islami (founded 1941) and, more recently, an array of Islamist groups providing welfare or inflicting violence. Many politicians, judges, and official documents evoke Quranic justifications for their policies, including environmental regulations, some sincerely out of belief, others instrumentally to mobilize popular support.

Since Pakistan's inception, each ethnolinguistic and environmentally distinctive province has struggled to increase its own share of national

Map 9.2 East Pakistan

resources. Most major political parties are strongly based in one single province (or, in one key instance, Karachi city). Pakistan's eastern and western wings differed greatly, except that they both were territories with Muslim majorities.

In 1947, the eastern wing contained only 144,000 km² [55,600 mi²], 15 percent of Pakistan's land, but the majority of its citizens (see Map 9.2). The eastern wing also had a much more linguistically homogeneous population – over 98 percent Bangla speakers. Many landlords had been Hindu Bengalis who fled, although a much higher proportion of Hindus remained than in Pakistan's western wing (18 percent versus 1 percent of the population). In addition, some Urdu-speaking north Indian Muslims (popularly termed "Biharis") immigrated. Further, the mountainous Chittagong Hill Tracts in the southeast hold a dozen ethnic groups of forest-dwellers, each with its own language, many of them Christians, Buddhists, or followers of a local religion. The eastern wing also had a more uniform environment of low-lying rich alluvial soil suitable for wet-crops, especially rice and jute, although there are higher regions in the northwest and southeast. The Bengal delta has two primary water sources: inflowing rivers and the southwest monsoon (which overall averages over 2 m [6.6 ft] rainfall annually). The vast coastal Sundarbans is the world's largest continuous mangrove forest (shrinking but still roughly 10,000 km^2 [3,900 mi^2], 40 percent in India). But cyclones often devastate sections of this coast. For instance, in 1970, super-cyclone "Bhola," with winds up to 250 kph (150 mph), killed about 300,000 East Pakistanis, even more livestock and wildlife, and flooded 8,000 km^2 (3,000 mi^2); the ineffective Central Government response added to popular discontent less than a month before that year's decisive elections. While the ML was founded in Dhaka, from independence onward, East Pakistanis increasingly felt themselves and their Bengali culture marginalized, culminating in their violent 1971 secession.

While in 1947 West Pakistan contained less than half the nation's population, its politicians, army officers, and administrators dominated the whole nation (see Map 9.3). This wing has an area of 800,000 km^2 (310,000 mi^2), ranging from thousands of vast glaciers in the north (covering about 15,000 km^2 [5,800 mi^2]) to deserts and low-lying coasts (partly mangrove forest). Rainfall ranges from limited to scarce (averaging 250 mm/year [9.8 in/year] overall); 60–70 percent of the land is arid and unusable for agriculture, although some areas support grazing. Consequently, this wing's agricultural economy was almost entirely dependent on the largely glacial-runoff-fed Indus system, including its underlying groundwater. Further, each province within this western wing differs strongly in culture and environment, and each has long disputed the uneven distribution of the nation's resources.

Speakers of Punjabi (or Siraiki or another Punjabi dialect) totaled about a quarter of Pakistan's 1947 population with a fifth of its territory. Western Punjab had benefited greatly from the British Raj's extensive upper Indus canals. At independence, immigrating east Punjabi Muslims largely took over canal-irrigated farms from their fleeing Sikh owners; while Partition was initially traumatic for these immigrants, they soon integrated with culturally similar west Punjabis. Subsequently, Punjabis have predominated in Pakistan's national army, administration, agriculture, industry, and (often) politics, which many people in other provinces have resented.

Sindhi speakers comprised only about 6 percent of Pakistan's 1947 population and many of them worked as tenants on large agricultural

Map 9.3 West Pakistan

estates. Sindh is lower riparian to Punjab, having even more arid land. Many Sindhis feel subordinated and disrespected, and they are a minority even in their own province's cities, most notably Karachi. Yet, a Sindh-based political party (the Pakistan People's Party) rose repeatedly to power and remains a major force.

Pashto-speaking Pakhtuns totaled only about 6 percent of Pakistan's 1947 population (but a plurality of Afghanistan's) and includes 74,500 km^2 (28,800 mi^2). While the 1893 British-imposed Durand Line divided Pakhtuns in Afghanistan from those nominally under the British Raj, their mountainous terrain has always precluded outside control. Their long-standing ethnic nationalist demands resulted in the North-West Frontier Province (NWFP) being renamed Khyber

Pakhtunkhwa [KP] in 2010. Their province's forests are nearly half of West Pakistan's total, but have long been shrinking from uncontrolled commercial and local timbering, agricultural expansion, and reservoir construction for hydroelectricity and irrigation that largely benefits Punjab.

Baloch speakers totaled only 1–2 percent of Pakistan's 1947 population, but inhabit the largest province (347,000 km^2 [134,000 mi^2]). Most land is too dry for settled agriculture and supports only widely scattered pastoralists. While Balochistan has much of Pakistan's natural gas, coal, copper, and other mineral resources, these mostly benefit Punjab or Sindh, leaving most Baloch poor. Armed secessionist movements against Pakistan (and also against Iran, where a minority of Baloch live) have periodically recurred, as have violent suppressions by Pakistan's army.

During the independence period, many Urdu-speaking north Indian Muslim professionals, officials, officers, and ML leaders immigrated to Pakistan. They and their descendants are widely known as "Muhajirs," the name for early Muslims who emigrated with the Prophet Muhammad from Mecca to Medina in 1 Hijri/622 CE. But many communities already living in what became Pakistan regarded them as refugees. Totaling about 5 percent of Pakistan's 1947 population, Muhajirs often had more education and financial capital. They made their Urdu the national language, the core of Pakistan's Muslim identity, subordinating the native languages of the other West or East Pakistani communities. Muhajirs mostly migrated to West Pakistan and settled primarily in Karachi, its largest city, forming a plurality in this major center of industry and commerce and Pakistan's first national capital; their MQM political party has persistently dominated municipal government there. However, since many Muhajirs were Shi'ites, they are also a vulnerable minority religious community among Pakistan's predominantly Sunni Muslims.

Beyond these provinces, Pakistan has special status territories. The largest is Azad Jammu and Kashmir – the mountainous and thinly populated western third of that former kingdom. In addition, people living in the mountainous Northern Territories (Gilgit-Baltistan), FATA (Federally Administered Tribal Areas; now part of KP), and the current capital, Islamabad, have been semi-autonomous.

During Pakistan's first decade, its political center remained unstable. No head of state lasted long enough to resolve the new nation's fundamental issues, including Pakistan's constitutional structure (presidential or parliamentary, authoritarian or democratic), the role of Islam in politics, and the distribution of the nation's limited, constrained natural resources among the provinces and the center. Various political and military coups meant rapid, dramatic changes in government policies, although mitigated by continuity in the army, the established civil service, and entrenched landowners and businessmen. Further, the environment received little attention in the scramble to absorb voluntary and forced immigrants, construct the apparatus of government, and battle India.

M. A. Jinnah had been the premier figure in the Pakistan movement, the ML's "Sole Spokesman." At independence, he made himself governor-general, with popular acclaim as *Qaid-i Azam* ("Great Leader"). But he left a disputed legacy at his death from tuberculosis in 1948. Secularist Pakistanis still cite Jinnah's August 11, 1947, speech as president of Pakistan's Constituent Assembly, predicting the withering away of religious differences and declaring all citizens equal: "You may belong to any religion or caste or creed – that has nothing to do with the business of the State" (Jinnah 1947). In contrast, Islamists cite Jinnah's earlier declarations that Islam would be embodied in Pakistan's identity, laws, and policies.

On Jinnah's death, Prime Minister Liaquat Ali Khan (1895–1951, r. 1948–51) took over. A prominent ML leader and east Punjabi immigrant from a large landholding family, he envisioned an Islam-centered state. His government made tentative efforts to foster economic development and addressed a few isolated environmental issues (e.g. The Regulation of Mines and Oil Fields and Mineral Development Act of 1948) but implemented relatively little before his assassination in 1951. Then, a retired civil servant turned politician, Governor-General Ghulam Muhammad (1895–1956, r. 1951–55), declared martial law and dismissed the Constituent Assembly. However, the army and civil service forced his resignation and General Iskander Mirza (1899–1969, r. 1955–58) seized power, first as governor-general, then as president. He both presided over the signing of Pakistan's first Constitution in 1956 and then suspended it thirty months later by declaring martial law.

These relatively brief regimes all claimed natural resources for Pakistan's national development but with limited attention to enhancing or protecting them. Consequently, the British Raj's resource management policies, laws, and regulations largely continued, stressing state control over individual types of resources (not integrated environmental systems), punishment for locals who challenged that control, but few incentives for compliance or resource improvement. For instance, Pakistan's first National Forest Policy (1955) echoed the British Raj (and India's 1952 policy, see below) by declaring government ownership of all forest areas, classified by their utility to the nation. To increase forest cover, lands around canals were reserved for timber plantations. This policy did make some promises to protect habitat and wildlife from short-term commercial exploitation, to conserve soil quality, and to respect the intangible cultural value of forests. Other limited legislation addressed individual urban pollution problems, for instance industrial discharges and workplace safety (e.g. the 1956 Factories Act amending the 1934 Factories Act).

The central government created the Planning Board in 1953, which formulated Pakistan's First Five-Year Plan (1955–60) – a weak version of the Soviet centralized economic model for rapid development. This plan promised to build infrastructure that would enhance agriculture and small-scale production in rural areas, where 85 percent of the population lived. But this plan was only approved in mid-1956 and was never well implemented. Overall, agricultural production stagnated through the 1950s.

Further, each province largely controlled its own internal resources with its own policies and officials, who had considerable discretionary authority. For example, each province had its own forest department which was charged with maximizing timber supply using "scientific forestry" working plans (taught at the new Pakistan Forest Institute). Provincial forest department officials could choose to grant "reasonable" local uses. Such decentralization in theory brought decision-making closer to the local level, but at the cost of nationally coordinated policies and management. However, in practice, forests in neither wing of Pakistan received much protection.

Simultaneously, Pakistan claimed a prominent place in international conferences, negotiating treaties and agreements, seeking to match the status of much larger India. For instance, Pakistan (and India) agreed to the 1951 UN International Plant Protection Convention to protect sustainable agriculture, enhance global food security, and prevent plant pest spread. However, provincial, national, and international strictures have been relatively weakly implemented, due in part to local resistance, powerful commercial interests, and relatively underfunded government agencies.

After these brief central government regimes, with their diverse and not always consistent policies and agendas, the army made its first (of what would be four so far) military coups in October 1958 when Field Marshal Ayub Khan (1907–74, r. 1958–69) became chief martial law administrator, then president. His government created an indirect elective system ("Basic Democrats") that in 1960 confirmed his presidency. Thus, he and India's long-incumbent Prime Minister Jawaharlal Nehru were both strong enough to resolve the long-running dispute over the Indus River waters, so vital for West Pakistan's economy and northwest India's as well.

Independent India to the Indus River Treaty (1947–60)

Newly independent India shared much heritage with Pakistan, but there were major contrasts in their environmental histories. India was over twice as large (3.3 million km^2 [1.27 million mi^2]) and contained far more diverse ecosystems. For instance, rather than a single river basin (like the Indus for West Pakistan), India contained multiple major watersheds – those in the Deccan and South India flowing entirely within its borders. Hence, only about a third of India's river water entered from other countries (mostly from China, Nepal, and Bhutan). Droughts, floods, and earthquakes have deeply affected particular regions, but overall India has proven more resilient to natural disasters than either West or East Pakistan.

Further, although West Bengal and northwestern India suffered disruptions at Partition (as refugees fled or poured in and ecological and infrastructure networks were severed), these were much smaller proportionately than for Pakistan. Independent India contained almost all the subcontinent's nascent industry. While some railway lines had to be reconfigured and new ones built (particularly linking the isolated northeast with the rest of India), railways have proven vital to the nation's economy and sociocultural integration. At Independence, the most experienced non-British politicians, judiciary, civil servants, and military officers largely remained in place as successors to their British supervisors. The INC and civil society organizations (e.g. labor unions, women's groups, and other NGOs) had deeper roots and retained greater scope for legal protests and demands about distribution of resources, among other issues. From independence onward, news media, especially English and vernacular newspapers, have investigated government policies and actions and influenced public opinion.

For India's first decade, the relatively broad-based and entrenched INC governed at the center and in all provinces, under the dominating leadership of Prime Minister Jawaharlal Nehru (r. 1947–64). This enhanced nationally coordinated policies and programs. Thus, the new Indian nation started with less upheaval and more resources than Pakistan (and most other former colonies globally), although also a substantial proportion of the world's resource-deprived citizens (today about 20 percent of the globe's poor).

Since 1947, India's internal disputes over its national identity, while periodically bitter and occasionally punctuated by violence, have been largely managed with remarkable and sustained commitment to national unity and democracy. While many Muslims fled in 1947, as many decided to remain in India as lived in West or East Pakistan, forming a substantial but economically and political vulnerable minority (about 14 percent). Communal riots have killed thousands but not shattered the nation. So far, the Indian government has largely remained secular, meaning all religious communities can freely participate in politics, although there are still separate Muslim, Hindu, and Christian personal law codes and some political parties identify strongly with only one community.

The central government has largely tolerated sub-nationalist demands but not secession, which has been met by force (as is currently ongoing in Kashmir and the northeast). As we have seen, India's regions had historically each often been an independent kingdom. In population size and ethnolinguistic identity, many provinces are comparable to European nations (see Map 9.4). Starting in 1953 (extensively in 1956, and most recently in 2014), provinces have been divided or reorganized, defusing linguistically based popular movements, but creating additional interstate river disputes. However, particularly since the 1970s, economic disparities and differential access to national resources have produced both nonviolent environmental movements and also violent ethnic or "Naxalite" (Maoist revolutionary) militancy, especially among forest-dwellers.

As in Pakistan, provinces within India have considerable political autonomy and control over resources. (However, unlike Pakistan, India is not dominated by any one province, currently having 29 states and 7 union territories.) As demanded by provincially based INC leaders, the Indian Constitution allotted to the provinces independent authority over agriculture, coastal and intra-provincial fisheries, forests, land, mines, public health, sanitation, water-bodies, and wildlife. Consequently, the central ("Union") government's emerging national policies about these were dependent on ratification and implementation by provinces according to their own interests.

From the beginning, India has had much greater political continuity than Pakistan. India's original 1950 Constitution remains in place (although relatively easily amended by a supermajority in Parliament, more than 100 times so far), establishing a Westminster-style bicameral Parliamentary system. Except for the eighteen-month State of Internal Emergency (1975–77), the government's executive, legislative, and judicial branches have balanced and checked each other, as have the central and provincial governments, while the national civil services, army, and judiciary have remained largely apolitical.

Unlike Pakistan's relatively short-term leaders, Prime Minister Jawaharlal Nehru dominated the Indian central government for its first seventeen years (until his death in 1964). Even the strongest national

Map 9.4 Population equivalences, Indian provinces, Pakistan, and Bangladesh, 2018

political alternatives to Nehru had limited influence. M. K. Gandhi's abstention from official participation in the new Indian government and his assassination in January 1948 meant his ideals of localized hand-production in self-governing villages and of nonviolence in all actions received only nominal official recognition, although they have continued to inspire many politicians, activists, and grass-roots movements.

Nehru continued to push his vision for India's modernization in a range of areas. For instance, he recruited internationally famous town-planners and architects American Albert Mayer (1897–1981) and then Swiss-French Le Corbusier (1887–1965) to design the Modernist model city of Chandigarh (constructed 1949–60) as East Punjab's (and later also Haryana's) new capital. Nehru also remained strongly committed to nationwide centralized planning within a mixed socialist-capitalist economy, using the combined development models of the United States and USSR. Nehru personally chaired the INC's National Planning Committee from its founding in 1938 and then strongly backed his government's Planning Commission from Independence onward. His overall goal remained state-led advancement of India's economy based on science-guided maximum use of its natural and human resources for the national good and for all Indians equitably. The INC held support from many industrialists (seeking protection from international competition and access to raw materials), rich peasants (seeking subsidized water, seeds, fertilizer, and electricity), and bureaucrats (seeking control over national resources through selective issuing of quotas and licenses).

India's First Five-Year Plan (1951–55) focused on producing more food and electricity, particularly through stimulating farmers into higher levels of productivity and constructing major dam projects. Nehru wanted agricultural development to free India from dependence on massive grain imports and foreign aid (like the US Agricultural Trade and Development Assistance Act [PL 480]), which made India appear a helpless pauper internationally and partially constrained India's foreign policies during the Cold War. In 1947, electricity had reached only 0.3 percent of India's roughly half-million villages, so power production and distribution received priority. Nehru also supported India's nuclear program, with a research reactor opening in 1957 and a series of electricity-generating plants thereafter.

Much of this plan's infrastructure funding went into vast, expensive multipurpose river valley development projects: integrated networks of large-scale dams for water storage, flood control, and hydroelectricity, inspired by America's much celebrated TVA and comparably large-scale projects in the USSR (only later would the actual social and environmental costs and limited benefits of such American and Soviet megaprojects be understood). The Central Waterways, Irrigation and Navigation Commission (established 1945, becoming the Central Water and Power Commission in 1951) assessed hydraulic projects proposed or begun by the British and designed new ones. But these major dams also required sacrifices, especially by forest-dwellers who would be displaced by submergence, many without satisfactory resettlement or compensation.

In practice, benefits went largely to more politically powerful contractors, settled farmers, and city-dwellers.

The Damodar Valley Corporation was one of the largest early multipurpose projects, created in 1948 to construct (with World Bank loans) and manage a planned vast integrated network of dams and canals. This mostly autonomous corporation was only loosely under the Central Ministry of Irrigation and Power and only partly responsible to the provincial governments of the most affected states of Bihar and West Bengal. However, the corporation's overly ambitious plans outstripped its financial and political support and hydraulic and social engineering capacity. Only about half the proposed dams and canals were completed and those functioned well below predictions since sedimentation rapidly negated much promised hydroelectricity generation. Yet, nearly 100,000 people were displaced. Similarly, the Mahanadi River Project in Orissa/ Odisha completed only one (Hirakud) of its three projected large dams for hydroelectric and flood control – its construction taking a decade (1948–58) and officially displacing 110,000 people, but probably substantially more.

While such large dam projects[1] have largely gone out of fashion in the West, India has continued to construct them (as has Pakistan and China). Rarely have the promised benefits been realized environmentally or economically. When operating, hydroelectric generation is CO_2-free, but the inherent costs of construction and the methane released from submerged vegetation are usually not included in cost-benefit environmental analysis. Yet, today India has about 4,500 large dams (95 percent of them completed since 1950), with the Sardar Sarovar Dam the most controversial (see Chapter 10). The powerful postindependence vision of large-dam projects (as under the British Raj) took little notice of locally built and managed small dams and irrigation systems that have historically often proven more cost effective.

While "water" was subject to provincial authority, India's major rivers all crossed provincial borders, causing disputes. The 1955 Interstate Water Agreement (for the Indus system rivers on India's side of the border) and the 1956 Interstate Water Disputes Act (for rivers and canals within India) both created mediation procedures. Nonetheless, interprovincial clashes over these vital waters have often persisted for decades, with flare-ups during periodic droughts (e.g. between Karnataka and Tamil Nadu over the Kaveri, and the multistate conflict over the Ravi-

---

[1] "Big" (major) dams are conventionally defined as over 15 m (50 ft) high, or 5–15 m (15. 5–50 ft) high and impounding at least 3 million m^3 (108 million ft^3) of water.

Beas-Jumna system and the Indira Gandhi canal running 650 km [400 mi] into Rajasthan).

Nehru's administration also individually targeted other parts of the environment, mostly seeking to reorient raw material flows from imperial uses to India's resource-intensive national development. The accelerated, unsustainable timbering of World War II largely continued thereafter, without a period of forest recovery. This soon made clear to some the need for restoration of degraded forests and planting new ones for the sake of the nation's future timber and pulpwood supply. Hence, the 1952 National Forest Policy (amended 1988) ambitiously sought substantial extension of forest cover, thereby reducing land deterioration and pro-tecting wildlife while sustaining resource production, especially for the rapidly growing forest industries sector (e.g. paper, rayon, and resin). This policy, however, also perpetuated aspects of the British Raj's "scien-tific forestry" model and division into Protection Forests, National/ Production Forests, Village Forests for fuelwood and fodder, and private forests. This policy directed the reduction and regulation of grazing and swidden agriculture. Top foresters trained at the Dehra Dun Forestry School (today the Indira Gandhi National Forest Academy) and then served in provincial forest departments. Some provinces put privately owned forests under the authority of their forest departments. Many provincial forest departments fostered plantations using monoculture of tree species with high commercial value, although low usefulness to local communities. Due to political pressures and personal interests, however, some provincial foresters also granted timbering contracts, often at low, concessional rates to for-profit companies. So, aggregate deforestation accelerated.

Nehru had little personal commitment to wildlife, admitting "In no country life is valued in theory so much as in India, and many people would even hesitate to destroy the meanest or the most harmful of animals. But in practice we ignore the animal world" (Nehru 1956:158). Some provinces, however, developed nature sanctuaries. For instance, in 1949 Assam invited inspections and guidance from India's leading wildlife conservationist and ornithologist, Salim Ali, and American ornithologist S. Dillon Ripley (1913–2001, former wartime member of the US Office of Strategic Services intelligence agency, later head of the Smithsonian Institution). The next year, Assam renamed as "wildlife sanctuaries" what the British Raj had called "game sanctuaries," thus highlighting conservation rather than hunting for trophies or meat. In 1952, Nehru's government appointed an advisory Indian Board for Wildlife to try to coordinate provincial programs (although this board included some avid hunters). However, for their first decade, neither the national or provincial Wildlife Boards proved very effective.

Meanwhile, civil society organizations like the Bombay Natural History Society (BNHS) were active in pushing environmental research and advocacy. This society also worked to establish the India branch of the WWF, working in various ways toward the "wilderness ideal" of rolling back industrial exploitation of forests and other "natural habitats." Thus, the ongoing struggle over control of forests among the central and provincial governments, their foresters and revenue collectors, industrialists, and local communities was increasingly joined by international and domestic conservationists seeking to protect particular fauna and flora species.

The British Raj had characterized many forest-dwellers as "tribals." Although these people were now full citizens, Nehru's government tried to combine protection of their distinctive and supposedly isolated culture with their gradual development. His government continued the long official list ("schedule") of specific "tribes" whose members by birth were constitutionally entitled to separate "Scheduled Tribe (ST) Reservations": quotas in elections, education, and government employment. These policies echoed the British Raj in presupposing "tribal" communities were secluded, homogeneous in culture, economy, and society, and needing special protection from outsiders. However, as we have seen, the identities of forest-dwellers, pastoralists, and settled farmers were historically dynamic, as were their interactive relationships with each other, the environment around them, and the state.

Nehru's Second Five-Year Plan (1956–60) dedicated many of the nation's raw material resources to heavy industrialization within the public sector (i.e. government owned), especially the "commanding heights" of the economy like the steel and defense industries. A goal was national self-sufficiency, through "import-substitution" (i.e. any product that India could make should have its foreign competitors taxed out of competition). This policy (being successfully used by post–World War II Japan among others) would thus shelter domestic industries during their early phases from what Nehru called "the whirlpool of economic imperialism" (1947). The government also wanted the benefits of some competition but not the waste of over-production. So, the capitalist private sector was permitted to make consumer products; however, government regulated the most important ones (e.g. only two Indian automobile companies gained licenses and quotas for production).

Under this second plan, India's limited foreign exchange went to purchase needed fuels and primary machinery to maximize domestic

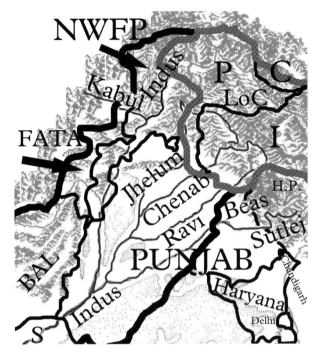

Map 9.5 Punjab

industrialization. But this meant reduction of spending on imported chemical fertilizers. Indeed, the pace of agricultural growth slowed, while population continued to rise, largely due to better health services. By 1960, Nehru sought expanded hydroelectric power and grain production by using his political strength to push to ratification the long-negotiated Indus River Treaty.

The Indus River Treaty 1960

In today's intensifying international debate over vital resource distribution between and within nations, many commentators have predicted "water wars." During the decade following Indian and Pakistani independence, conflicting nationalistic claims over the upper Indus River system proved particularly impassioned. The Indus and major tributaries (the Beas, Chenab, Jhelum, Ravi, and Sutlej) run partly within India especially within hotly contested Indian-held Kashmir (see Map 9.5).

Each nation forcefully advanced its own territorial claims as channels and riverbanks shifted and alluvial islands rose and subsided. Yet, neither nation alone could control the floods that inundated the Indus plain (1950, 1956, 1957).

The Sutlej was especially disputed, since Radcliffe's international border crossed it multiple times. The major canal headworks at Ferozpur stood on the Indian side, and its engineers unilaterally cut the flow into Pakistan in 1948 (and again in 1952). In retaliation, Pakistani engineers (and nationalist volunteers) dug a water-diverting cut upstream of Ferozpur. Then, high on the Sutlej and Beas, India constructed the massive Bhakra-Nangal dam-weir complex (1952–63). The 200 m (660 ft)-high Bhakra's reservoir displaced 36,000 people but irrigated 7 million hectares (17.3 million acres) and produced 2800MW of electricity for India. India also began further dams to distribute Indus system waters within India (e.g. the Harike barrage complex, constructed 1950–53).

Box 9.1

Jawaharlal Nehru celebrated the rising Bhakra-Nangal Dam complex:

"What a stupendous, magnificent work–a work which only that nation can take up which has faith and boldness! This is a … landmark not merely because the water will flow here and irrigate large portions of the Punjab … and fertilise the deserts of Rajasthan, or because enough electric power will be generated here to run thousands of factories and cottage industries which will provide work for the people and relieve unemployment. It is a landmark because it has become the symbol of a nation's will to march forward with strength, determination and courage … As I walked round the site I thought that these days the biggest temple and mosque and gurdwara is the place where man works for the good of mankind. Which place can be greater than this, this Bhakra-Nangal, where thousands and [hundreds of thousands] of men have worked, have shed their blood and sweat and laid down their lives as well? Where can be a greater and holier place than this … ? Then again it struck me that Bhakra-Nangal was like a big university where we can work and while working learn, so that we may do bigger things. The nation is marching forward and every day the pace becomes faster. As we learn the work and gain experience, we advance with greater speed … not only for our own times but for coming generations and future times." (Nehru 1954)

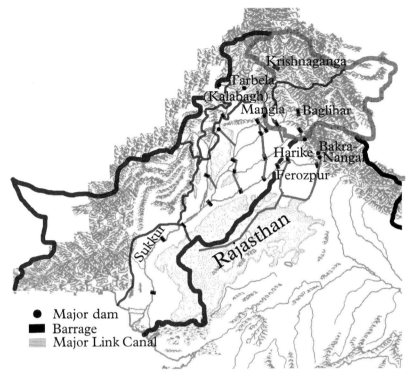

Map 9.6 Major dams, barrages, and major link canals in the Indus Basin, 2018

Starting in 1951, the World Bank and American advisors proposed apportioning the Indus watershed as an integrated system benefiting both India and Pakistan – a binational version of America's TVA (see Map 9.6). But these outsiders were frustrated in their appeals to the shared professionalism of Pakistani and Indian civil engineers, who instead had new, powerful national loyalties. Further, international law disputes about transnational rivers have produced a variety of incompatible principles for water allocation, including "chronology of use," "proportionate contribution" of each state's territory to the basin's waters, and the "obligation to cause no harm to downstream users" (Haines 2017). As the mainly upper-riparian state, India asserted the international convention of "absolute sovereignty": water flowing within a nation's boundaries are its property, fully usable. As the mainly lower riparian state, Pakistan countered with the "absolute territorial integrity" and "prior appropriation" principles: a downstream state has the legal right to continued customary uses and shares of naturally inflowing waters (including canals).

Negotiations about sharing stagnated, so in 1954 the World Bank and its multinational partners proposed division: each nation taking full but separate use of half the rivers. The Beas, Ravi, and Sutlej (until they crossed into Pakistan) went almost exclusively to India while the Chenab, Indus, and Jhelum went to Pakistan (with continued limited Indian uses of Chenab and Jhelum water in its part of Kashmir). A binational Permanent Indus Commission would address disputes as they arose, using established resolution mechanisms. To conclude this agreement, the World Bank offered the more affected Pakistan US$894 million ($6.8 billion in today's currency) as the Indus Basin Development Fund (much from the United States but almost 20 percent from India for its use of Chenab and Jhelum water).

While many commentators have lauded the Indus River Treaty as the most successful agreement between Pakistan and India and a model for international water-sharing, there are critics of its limitations. The treaty institutionalized partition of the rivers rather than optimizing overall use of the Indus system. The treaty also tacitly avoided the integrally related dispute over Kashmir.

Both Nehru and Ayub Khan proved politically strong enough to survive domestic accusations of national betrayal. Indeed, the treaty has remained in place despite two Indo-Pakistani wars and several near-wars. However, with the increasing hydroelectric and irrigation demands of both nations straining their capacity, and increasingly frequent flooding downstream (especially in Pakistan), bilateral tensions continued to arise (e.g. Pakistan's objections to India's hydroelectric projects, at Baglihar [built 1999–2008 on the Chenab] and at Kishnaganga [built 2007–17 on the Jhelum]). Nonetheless, post-treaty rapid growth of canal irrigation in both India and Pakistan vitally enabled their Green Revolutions.

India from the Indus Treaty into the Green Revolution (1960–71)

The Indus Treaty came after Nehru had continued in office for more than dozen years. His Third Five-Year Plan (1961–65) sought food-grain self-sufficiency ("food security") and more rapid national income growth. But India's politics were disrupted by international events (including two wars), domestic crises (including the deaths of two prime ministers), and challenging environmental and political forces.

In the Cold War context, Nehru had founded his Non-Aligned, Third World foreign policy on friendship with China, despite simmering disputes over their borders and Tibet (especially since Nehru gave refuge to the Dalai Lama and many supporters in 1959). Negotiating the apportioning of Brahmaputra water flowing from China into India (and then into East Pakistan) did not appear a concern to Nehru (although it has today become a looming issue). Then, in October 1962, China suddenly invaded the contested borderlands in India's northwest and northeast both. The unprepared Indian army suffered humiliating defeats, as did Nehru's prestige. Even after the Chinese voluntarily retreated, Nehru was politically and physically weakened. He died nineteen months later (May 1964).

Nehru's death shifted political power to strong INC provincial bosses ("The Syndicate"). None had much support beyond his province; none would defer to any of the others. Hence, they accepted as prime minister the respected but relatively politically weak Lal Bahadur Shastri (1904–66, r. 1964–66).

Within a year of Shastri's election, the 1965 India-Pakistan war broke out (each side claimed provocation by the other), India's second in three years. The southern battlefield was the long-disputed border in the ecologically fragile Rann of Kutch: during the monsoon, much is flooded; during the dry season, much is desert. Heavier fighting also erupted in Kashmir, along the contested ceasefire line. In Punjab, the Indian Army pushed toward Lahore, only 22 km (14 mi) from the border. Combat was halted with UK and UN intervention and then the USSR mediated a peace conference in Tashkent. Despite the human, financial, and environmental cost of the fighting, neither belligerent gained territory, and both lost much foreign aid. Shastri died suddenly the day after signing the declaration (January 10, 1966), having been in office just seventeen months.

The 1962 and 1965 wars along India's borders had more than the immediate effects of pollution by chemicals, exploded and unexploded munitions, and burned, rusting war materiel. Like Pakistan, India increased military expenditures. Further, with limited environmental consideration, armies drove new roads into borderlands, intended for moving troops but also opening conduits for timbering and other resource extraction, as well as tourism and other economic development.

The Syndicate next made Indira Gandhi (1917–84, r. 1966–77, 1980–84) prime minister. She was Nehru's only child (Gandhi was her late husband's name, no relation to "Mahatma" Gandhi). However, she had little experience in government, having served only as Minister of Information and Broadcasting in Shastri's brief cabinet. Instead of five-year plans, the government managed only annual ones (1966, 1967, 1968).

Municipalities, however, expanded their urban planning from the early 1960s, led by the Delhi Master Plan (1962). Yet, the pressures of rapid population rise, political and commercial interests, and administrative weaknesses often led to unregulated construction and overwhelmed public services, including water, sewage, and electricity (see Chapter 12). The cultural pattern of intermixing rich and poor residences with businesses and small-scale industries (often in the unregulated informal sector) clashed with Western-derived urban planning models.

A series of El Niño events caused weak monsoons (1963–66), coinciding with India's wars and political transitions, which decreased food production by 20 percent. This led to India's worst postindependence famine, with about 1.5 million deaths. For promised rapid, sustained grain production increases, the government turned to the "Green Revolution." Since agriculture is constitutionally a provincial subject, however, there were limits on national coordination and policy implementation, leading to regional variation due to politics and environment.

From the late 1950s, international plant scientists had hybridized varieties of wheat, rice, maize/corn, cotton, and other crops that, with heavy use of irrigation and chemical fertilizers and pesticides, could produce unprecedented high yields. Most famously American agronomist Norman Borlaug (1914–2009), the Rockefeller and Ford Foundations, Mexico's International Center for Maize and Wheat Improvement, and the Philippines' International Rice Research Institute had already shown considerable success with this Green Revolution model. Many of India's own domestic agricultural programs (like the All-India Coordinated Wheat Improvement Program of the Indian Council of Agricultural Research and the Consultative Group on International Agricultural Research) worked with these international advisors to concentrate on high-yield varieties and technologies tailored for already highly productive areas.

In the 1965–66 agricultural cycle, the government distributed 16,200 metric tonnes (17,860 US tons) of imported dwarf Mexican-variety hybrid wheat seeds. These plants concentrated rapid growth in their more abundant grain, while their shorter stalks kept them upright. Farmers need training in the necessary techniques but by 1969–70, 35 percent of India's 14 million hectares (34.6 million acres) of wheat were sown in these varieties (Borlaug 1970). Nitrogen fertilizer consumption doubled by 1969–70, an agricultural year when 50,000 tube-wells were bored for irrigation. This strategy, however, subordinated equitable rural wealth distribution below rising overall grain production by landowning farmers, who mobilized politically to demand ever more infrastructural investments and subsidies from national and provincial governments. In 1966, as the Green Revolution began, political tensions among Punjabi-speaking Sikh Jats, Hindi/Haryanvi-speaking Hindu Jats, and Pahari-speaking hill people meant that East Punjab was divided into three provinces, each dominated by one community: the northwestern plains (Punjab), the southeastern plains (the new province of Haryana), and the northeastern uplands (added to existing Himachal Pradesh [HP]). The Green Revolution was largely centered in the first two provinces, plus ecologically similar western sections of UP (and, with rice, parts of Tamil Nadu and Kerala).

Supporters and critics of the Green Revolution highlight different aspects, phases, and balance of benefits and costs. Borlaug's own 1970 Nobel laureate speech celebrates rapid Indian wheat production increases, from 11 million metric tonnes (12 million US tons) in the immediate pre-Green Revolution harvest (1964–65) to 18 million tonnes three years later. Indeed, total national grain increases of roughly 3 percent annually continued in subsequent decades.

Other commentators question these claims. Some attribute overall increases not solely to hybrid seeds but also to a coincident series of good monsoons in the late 1960s, high levels of subsidized inputs including fertilizer and electric tube-wells plus rural credit, agricultural extension education, expansion into hitherto unused or marginal lands, and heavy, unsustainable double- or even triple-cropping. There were also unplanned storage and distribution problems for the rapidly increased volume of grain and inefficient interventions by government in markets and interprovincial transfers. Further, agricultural labor employment initially increased, but then declined with mechanization. Long-term ecological stresses on land quality and water supply have meant either even more extensive agrochemical and irrigation inputs or reduced yield, even as the population continues to rise. Pesticide overuse (due to controlled prices and to weak regulation, education, and enforcement) has had accumulating detriments for human, insect, animal, and land health. In tube-well dependent areas, groundwater aquifers are being exhausted, with ever deeper shafts needed. In canal-fed areas, lands have become unproductive due to salinization and waterlogging.

Other areas of India's environment also went through parallel developments. Forest departments distributed exotic, fast-growing trees for maximum productivity. From 1965 onward, the National Planning Commission pressured provinces to improve their harbors and promote the use of motorized vessels and synthetic nets, thus substantially (but only temporarily) boosting the proportion of available fish harvested for domestic consumption and export (the "Blue Revolution"). Again, the extended environmental and social costs of such intensified forestry and mechanical fishing continue to emerge.

Meanwhile, Indira Gandhi's progressive political platform gained her popular backing and provisional support from leftist parties in Parliament. In November 1969, her faction split from the conservative Syndicate, creating the Congress (R) and Congress (O) respectively. She also raised India's stature internationally in 1969 by joining the IUCN (founded 1948 by governments and NGOs, currently the world's largest environmental information and guidance network) and hosting in New Delhi its General Assembly (predecessor to its World Conservation Congress). She nationalized fourteen major banks, tried to abolish the princes' privy purses (blocked temporarily by the Supreme Court), and pushed provinces for land redistribution from large landowners to the tiller. In the 1971 Parliamentary election, she won a sweeping victory based on her promise of *Garibi hatao* ("abolish poverty"). She then enhanced her strength by India's dramatic military victory in the December 1971 war that created Bangladesh out of East Pakistan.

West and East Pakistan from the Indus River Treaty into the Green Revolution and Division (1960–71)

While India was going through the uncertain political transition from Nehru to Indira Gandhi's eventual consolidation of power, General Ayub Khan ruled Pakistan for a decade (1958–69). He supervised the passage of the 1962 Constitution (Pakistan's second), stifled political opponents (banning them as corrupt), and his Presidential Secretariat formulated and directed Pakistan's Second Five-Year Plan (1960–65). With considerable military and development aid from the United States, its allies, and China (after the 1962 Sino-India war), Pakistan's agriculture and industry rapidly advanced, although with uneven benefits and environmental costs.

For West Pakistan, the Indus Treaty allowed widespread ecological transformations. Pakistan used its Indus Basin Development Fund to construct a network of water storage and hydroelectric dams, weirs, and interlink canals that diverted water from its allocated three western rivers to replace the lost irrigation from the three eastern rivers allotted to India. The Mangla Dam on the Jhelum (constructed 1961–67) initially displaced about 100,000 people to provide hydroelectric power, flood-control, and irrigation-water storage. Subsequently, Pakistan (with World Bank and other aid) has constructed numerous other Indus system projects providing substantial hydroelectricity and water control, including the Tarbela Dam (2,164MW, completed 1976, later raised to produce 3,478MW) on the Indus. Most of these have been planned, constructed, and operated by the Water and Power Development Authority (WAPDA), a massive parastatal organization established in 1958 on UN advice, while parts of the Indus system are still managed by provincial irrigation and drainage authorities. Overall, West Pakistan's Indus River integrated irrigation system became the world's largest, with over 58,000 km (36,000 mi) of canals that irrigated 16 million hectares (39.5 million acres), 90 percent of West Pakistan's agricultural lands. This vast hydraulic engineering was vital to Pakistan's Green Revolution, centered in Punjab and ecologically similar sections of Sindh.

As in India, repeated El Niño events in the early 1960s caused weak monsoons and some of Pakistan's worst famines. So Ayub's regime followed India in importing dwarf Mexican hybrid variety wheat: 37,800 metric tonnes (41,700 US tons) of seeds for the 1966–67 planting cycle. By 1969–70, high-yield varieties comprised 55 percent of Pakistan's wheat. Borlaug in his Nobel speech lauded Pakistan's rapid production increases from 4.6 million tonnes in the 1965 pre-Green Revolution harvest to 6, 6.5, and 7.6 million tonnes respectively in 1968, 1969, and 1970. This transformed West Pakistan into a substantial grain and cotton exporter to both East Pakistan and world markets.

While the broad Green Revolution process was similar in Pakistan and India, their specific environments, political and socioeconomic conditions, and types and levels of government intervention varied, as did some consequences. Pakistan's greater agricultural dependence on extensive canal irrigation caused delays and inequities in planting since glacial-melt water flows late in the agricultural season and also unequally benefits the usually richer canal head-enders above the poorer tail-enders. Uncertainties about when water will be available encourages overuse when it comes. Even more than in India, excessive canal irrigation has in some areas raised the groundwater level, causing waterlogging, increases in waterborne diseases, and salinization (hence, WAPDA from the early 1960s used deep tube-wells in massive Salinity Control and Reclamation Projects to flush down surface salts and lower groundwater levels). But in other areas, unsustainable private and state-managed tube-well extraction has increasingly dropped the water table unmanageably. Less rural electrification in Pakistan means more diesel-run tube-wells, with consequent dependence by farmers on fuel subsidies and by the nation on unstable world oil prices.

Further, in Pakistan, land reform was less extensive, and rural inequalities and poverty levels greater. Ayub sought to stimulate rapid rural economic development and reward supporters by allocating millions of newly irrigated hectares (mostly in Sindh) mainly to civil officials and military men. While his regime in 1959 proclaimed land ceilings of 200 hectares (500 acres) of irrigated and 400 hectares (1,000 acres) of unirrigated land in West Pakistan, entrenched landowning elites there largely retained their power, with high numbers of landless agricultural laborers. In East Pakistan, land-holdings tended to be more equally distributed; indeed, Ayub's administration raised the official land ceiling there from 33 to 48 hectares (82 to 120 acres). However, since hybrid high-yield IR8 rice suffered from East Pakistan's variable water conditions, the Green Revolution there had to await hybridization of new, more adapted varieties in the 1980s. Overall, compared to India, West Pakistan's Green Revolution developed a lower-input and lower-output model of agricultural production, with a much smaller domestic market (especially after 1971).

Nevertheless, during Pakistan's Third Five-Year Plan (1965–70) the Green Revolution combined with industrialization and expanding engagement with world trade to raise the national growth rate. For instance, Pakistan had no chemical industry in 1947, but has over the decades developed the foundation for one through creating lightly regulated chemical industrial estates and international collaboration. The first nuclear power plant was begun in Karachi (opened 1972). However, most gains were concentrated in the hands of a few favored West Pakistani families, so economic inequalities increased, both within West Pakistan and between it and the eastern wing.

Indeed, most of Ayub's political support and his developmental policies favored private and military economic interests centered in West Pakistan. For instance, he poured resources into a purpose-built new capital, Islamabad (built 1959–63, designed by Greek town-planner Constaninos Doxiadis [1914–75]), one of Pakistan's few examples of planned urban development. This project combined several goals: a Modernist architectural expression of Pakistan's modernity, secular leadership in the emerging community of Muslim nations, and a shift of political power from commercial Karachi to a site overshadowed by the Army's headquarters in neighboring Rawalpindi. To conciliate East Pakistanis, in 1961 Ayub commissioned American architect Louis Kahn (1901–74) to design a building in Dhaka, promised to be used for alternative legislative sessions with Islamabad (not completed until 1982, this building was never used by Pakistan, but today houses Bangladesh's legislature).

In 1962, Ayub's government revised the National Forest Policy, encouraging more intensive commercial use of forests – mostly located in the NWFP and in East Pakistan's Sundarbans and Chittagong Hill Tracts – as the source of raw materials for national development and revenues. Even the limited conservation provisions of the 1955 National Forest Policy were weakened. Farm forestry and state-owned wastelands grew fast-growing tree species with higher commercial value, using shortened rotation cycles that increased timber harvesting. Some private landholders were directed to plant at least a minimum number of such trees. State foresters had the power to expel forest-dwelling communities and ban their grazing and tree removal. Many foresters, however, found that implementing these policies created local resistance and disruptions reflecting badly on their careers, so they negotiated compromises, especially with influential locals. These policies, expanding industrialization, and growing numbers of immigrant farmers all increased the pace of deforestation and tensions between the state and forest-dwelling communities.

In particular, to integrate the Chittagong Hill Tracts into the rest of East Pakistan and to increase agricultural production there, the government encouraged immigration by lowland Bangla speakers. The tract's population surged from 26,000 in 1951 to 119,000 in 1961. One of the few dams built in East Pakistan was constructed on the Karnafuly River with little environmental impact assessment. Indeed, part of this hydropower dam's reservoir (completed in 1962) extended up into India, which accepted this submergence of its territory during a period of rapprochement following the Indus Treaty. The rest of this reservoir submerged about 22,000 hectares (54,400 acres), about 40 percent of the region's best arable land, and displaced about 100,000 people, mostly "tribals" (some emigrating to India's northeast adding to social and political tensions there). A new government agency, the Forest Industries Development Corporation, introduced mechanized logging using the reservoir for transport that facilitated timber extraction from previously inaccessible areas.

Until 1966, the Pakistan government had done little about its declining wildlife. But that year, following international trends, it invited the WWF to survey and recommend how to begin protecting select species using the IUCN model. In 1968, the waning Ayub Khan regime established a Wildlife Enquiry Committee to review this report. This led to the first Pakistani wildlife legislation, which attempted to provide for conservation of habitat for some non-game species (although limited to protected areas). Subsequently, national parks, wildlife sanctuaries, and game reserves were established as various provinces gradually legislated according to these recommendations. But these have had limited effectiveness in preventing hunting, especially by influential foreign and domestic dignitaries and by poachers for meat or export markets.

In January 1965, Ayub won a controversial and closer than expected reelection as president. Only months later, skirmishes and then open warfare erupted with India in the Rann of Kutch, Kashmir, and Punjab. In Tashkent, Ayub and Shastri signed the peace declaration, both accepting the stalemate.

Ayub had futilely promised Pakistan military victory and a "Decade of Progress." Instead, the army was discredited and demoralized, its weaponry and supplies exhausted. The economy suffered from foreign aid cuts. Further, Ayub was mired in family financial scandals, had long been ailing, and faced strong and coalescing popular and political opposition. To quell unrest, in 1969 he empowered the army chief, General Yahya Khan (1917–80, r. 1969–70), as chief martial law administrator. Yahya soon forced Ayub to resign, took over as president, and abrogated the Constitution. Overall, Ayub's regime showed little concern for equitable distribution of developmental benefits to the rising population, for resource efficiency, or for a degrading environment.

The main result of Yahya's brief regime was Pakistan's first ever free election (December 1970). The eastern wing united behind Sheikh Mujibur Rahman (1920–75), giving his Awami League the substantial majority of seats in the promised National Assembly (although none from West Pakistan). Yahya Khan indefinitely postponed the assembly, arrested Mujib, convicted him of treason, sentenced him to death, and banned the Awami League. In the eastern wing, popular resistance led to a bloody suppression by the Pakistani Army and its largely Islamist local allies, opposed by an Indian-supported revolt by east Bengali guerrilla forces. After the Indian army intervened in a short war (December 1971), the new nation of Bangladesh emerged. West Pakistan became the only Pakistan. The next chapter follows the subsequent environmental histories of all three nations.

10   India, Pakistan, and Bangladesh from Stockholm to Rio (1971–92)

Over the two decades from 1971 onward, South Asia's environmental history took new directions due to internal and global forces, with mixed results. Growing numbers of people began to recognize both the dangers of accelerating anthropogenic pollution and that the earth's environment must be considered as an integrated whole, an approach marked by the UN's first Conference on the Human Environment in Stockholm (June 1972). Of the more than 110 participating nations, India's Prime Minister Indira Gandhi was the only foreign head of state who took this conference and these issues seriously enough to attend. She spoke passionately for the world's poor, rhetorically asking "Are not poverty and need the greatest polluters?" (Indira Gandhi 1972). Some successive international reports, conferences (including at Rio in 1992), and funding would develop her argument that equitable and sustainable human development was vital to environmentalism and that richer nations had special responsibilities for their historic pollution while poorer nations needed special scope to catch up economically. However, the UN (and Stockholm's Principle 21) reiterated that every nation has the right to regulate its own use of all resources within its borders (without harming other nations). Thus, national interests prevented a unified or fully effective program at Stockholm and subsequently. For instance, the two recently divided nations that had been Pakistan also sent delegations to Stockholm, but both China and Pakistan challenged Bangladesh's credentials, so it did not vote.

Nationalism also intensified within South Asia. The third war between India and (West) Pakistan produced the new nation of Bangladesh in 1971. Yet, the environmental policies and practices of India, Pakistan, and Bangladesh have parallels as they reflected international principles and the sometimes contradictory agendas of foreign aid donors, internal elites, and local communities. All three nations had periods of authoritarian rule, which produced much of their foundational environmental legislation. The judiciary in all three took leadership in formulating and imposing environmental protections. Working through the courts and on their own, key parts of each nation's civil society, including popular movements and NGOs, asserted their rights to natural resources and protections for other living species and the environment generally.

By the 1992 Rio Conference, India, Pakistan, and Bangladesh had accomplished much but still faced challenging environmental issues. Similar environmental legislation by their respective governments had uneven levels of implementation. Popular and elite environmental movements rose up in each nation; however, differing conditions affected their effectiveness in varying ways. Overall, intranational, subcontinental, and global developments made all three more vulnerable to ever larger environmental dangers, including overexploited and increasingly polluted natural resources, fauna and flora species extinction, and climate change.

Due to growing international and national awareness of the environment, the quantity and range of primary and secondary sources for its history in India, Pakistan, Bangladesh have also increased. Many of the laws, policy statements, and reports used in this chapter (and the following ones) have been issued by the Indian and Pakistani governments and are available in English and online (although the Bangladesh government tends to issue many of its documentation only in Bangla, largely for nationalist reasons). Scientists, administrators, NGOs, and others have created new means for measuring current and historic trends for land, atmosphere, water, and many species, and much scholarship reflects this work. Along with intensity and extent of environmental challenges, both scholarly and popular secondary literature has also vastly increased although heated debates continue about the causes, goals, and means. These conflicts were often presented in oppositional terms, including, for example, overpopulation versus inequalities of access to resources at the international and national levels, human development versus conservation of endangered animal and plant species, and state versus private versus community ownership of natural resources (see Map 10.1).

India from Stockholm to Rio (1971–92)

Over the early 1970s, Prime Minister Indira Gandhi established her dominance nationally and prominence internationally. Her Congress (R) party had won a strong parliamentary majority in 1971, followed by India's rapid victory over Pakistan in the war liberating Bangladesh. Her party also governed in most provinces. In 1970–71, India was the first presiding country in the G-77, a coalition of developing nations. Following the 1972 Stockholm conference, she was a strong voice for the Third World movement and the concept of differentiated

Map 10.1 South Asia in the late twentieth century

responsibilities between developed and developing nations (where the former need to do more to reduce pollution than the latter).

Prime Minister Gandhi also tried to impose her own agendas on India, including about the environment. While encouraging economic development, she also incorporated some conservationist goals that were being advocated by both Indian and international NGOs (especially for protecting charismatic megafauna she favored). In 1967, she had welcomed a US Smithsonian Institution project to survey and assess India's wildlife and its habitats. This report highlighted how much damage had already been done and the pressing need for more protections. Reflecting the growing global awareness that the environment needed to be considered as a whole, her administration established India's National Committee on Environmental Planning and Coordination (1972) as the apex policy-setting body. However, the committee became dominated by government bureaucrats who increasingly encumbered its efficacy. Further, this committee's actions were constrained since each province constitution-ally had authority over many aspects of its own environment. Additionally, despite her concern for aspects of the environment, Gandhi also favored economic development. Hence, for instance, in 1972 she approved the state-owned Indian Oil Corporation's Mathura petroleum refinery despite its air pollution damage to the neighboring Bharatpur (Keoladeo Ghana) bird sanctuary and the Taj Mahal in Agra.

Nonetheless, in 1972 her regime also passed the breakthrough Wildlife (Protection) Act, which established the model for government control over both all species within designated protected areas and endangered wildlife species everywhere. Although some customary uses of non-timber forest products were allowed for communities living in or near wildlife sanctuaries, this legislation was based on the IUCN protectionist model for national parks and sanctuaries that minimizes domesticated animal and human activity (except scientific study and tourism). Despite this Union Act and the guidance of the National Board for Wildlife (established 1972), there was wide variation across India. Each state legislature individually had to pass a "consent resolution" and establish its own Wildlife Advisory Board, with members from that province's government, forest department, and citizens. Further, provincial Forest Departments needed the cooperation, manual labor, and local knowledge of forest-dwellers to keep peace, extract valuable timber, and deal with dangerous animals, so they "tolerated" local uses and violations. In some provinces (e.g. UP and HP), state-run Forest Development Corporations took over the entire process of timber extraction, replacing commercial contractors. (This 1972 Act remains authoritative today, although amended in 2003 to strengthen its penalties against commercial and local violators.)

Commitment by international and national environmentalists and Indira Gandhi's personal concerns led to internationally funded Project Tiger, launched in 1973. Hunting and habitat loss had diminished the wild tiger population to fewer than 2,000. Under this project, specific areas, often already within national parks, received special status as tiger reserves (the tiger population has since risen, although how much remains disputed). Other charismatic, endangered wildlife species with powerful cultural and/or ecological significance also had their own "projects" (e.g. Project Elephant, started 1992). Critics assert that such megafauna con-servation projects reflect combinations of increased Union government interventions, international agendas and funding, and shifting middle-class attitudes, often overriding the predatory effects of these protected animals on nearby rural human communities and limiting vital national economic development. Overall, the number Indian of natural parks and sanctuaries doubled in the 1970s to over 100 (and would nearly double again during the 1980s).

Likewise, her government passed the 1974 Water (Prevention and Control of Pollution) Act (amended in 1988 but still the prevailing legislation). But "water" was also constitutionally a provincial subject. Hence, each state legislature had to consent and create its own administrative agency to set licensing standards for its own bureaucracy to begin to implement, with varying degrees of commitment and success.

Her Fifth Five-Year Plan (1974–78) and subsequent ones included Integrated Tribal Development Projects. These sought coordinated programs for roadbuilding, housing, and other infrastructure, education, and health. But relations among forest-dwelling communities, nearby villagers, and provincial government foresters often remained contested. Indira Gandhi's 1970 election promise to "abolish poverty" had raised many expectations, mobilizing long-subordinated communities into violent and nonviolent movements.

Forest-dwellers had historically arisen against government-sponsored interventions. An uprising in Naxalbari village (West Bengal) in 1967 had sparked revolutionary Maoism, producing various armed factions loosely under the Communist Party of India (Marxist-Leninist). During the 1971 war, the Indian army had distributed many weapons to *Mukhti Bahini* (Bangladeshi "Freedom Force") guerrillas, and some flowed back into India, further escalating levels of violence. These armed insurrections gradually spread, especially in heavily forested districts in central India, and were met with heavy police suppression campaigns (which continue today).

After years of resistance by villagers in the Tehri-Garhwal region of the Himalayan foothills, where heavy floods and deforestation had increasingly caused deep erosion and landslides, a landmark nonviolent confrontation occurred in 1973. Peaceful protestors interposed themselves between loggers working for the Indian-owned Symonds sporting goods company and the trees it had purchased from the government. But villagers also needed this wood for their agricultural implements. This Chipko (literally "stick to" or "hug," hence more broadly "tree-hugger") movement became globally famous. Socialists, Gandhians, members of forest-products cooperatives, and women's groups (*Mahila Sabhas*) were all active in this movement, but in different proportions at different times and places. Later commentators passionately but divergently attribute primacy to each of these actors. Subsequently, many Indian and international environmental movements have taken inspiration from and imitated this initial Chipko movement. However, popular mobilization in this region gradually shifted to the successful demand for creation of its own new province, Uttarakhand (split off from UP in 2000).

Meanwhile, Indira Gandhi faced a range of challenges beyond even her control. A series of weak monsoons in the early 1970s brought droughts to various regions and forced India to import grain again, as population rise outstripped slowing Green Revolution production growth. The Organization of the Petroleum Exporting Countries (OPEC) caused the international oil price to quadruple in 1973–74, draining foreign currency reserves. Nonetheless, she continued to push forcefully against international and provincial limits on her power. In May 1974, her government openly tested a "peaceful nuclear explosive," proving that India stood among the world's nuclear-armed nations. But the test also reduced foreign aid and weakened India's moral position globally.

Accusations of campaign misdeeds in Indira Gandhi's own 1971 parliamentary election had been rising through the courts, with each verdict against her. Finally, the UP Provincial High Court ordered her to resign and remain out of politics for six years. Emboldened, opposition politicians led massive strikes and proclaimed "total revolution," calling on the army not to obey government orders.

In June 1975, Gandhi suddenly declared a state of internal "emergency" (which India's president endorsed, making it constitutional). Her government eventually jailed without trial more than 100,000 politicians and other citizens who opposed her, banned strikes, imposed censorship on the press, and postponed the scheduled parliamentary elections. With virtually no remaining checks on her political authority, she could now assert her personal vision for the nation. Her government amended the Constitution both to elevate the prime minister and president above judicial authority and also to bring the environment under Union control by shifting it to the "concurrent list" (i.e. provincial legislatures could continue to pass laws dealing with their own resources, but now the central government asserted overarching authority over environmental issues).

Specifically, the 42nd Amendment (1976) required the government to "endeavour to protect and improve the environment and safeguard the forests and wildlife of the country." Additionally, it became a fundamental "duty of every citizen of India ... to protect and improve the natural environment including forests, lakes, rivers and wildlife, and have compassion for living creatures." These provisions provided the basis for national engagement with the environment, broadly envisioned.

Her government also created the National Commission on Social Forestry in 1976, charged with increasing tree supplies massively for national advancement plus local community uses. Reserve Forests and Sanctuaries were to continue their long-term Uniform System Working Plans for timber, sustaining both government revenues and intensified industrial needs. Owners of private lands were encouraged to plant fast-growing, profitable tree species for maximum productivity. Under "Social Forestry," wastelands, degraded government forests, and community commons were all dedicated to growing trees for local use like fuel and fodder, as well as timber for sale.

While provinces varied, most distributed seedlings of eucalyptus (*Eucalyptus obliqua*) native to Australia, pine, or poplar, all suitable for fast-growing monoculture plantations. The long-term environmental and social costs of this social forestry policy were either unknown or disregarded. For example, eucalyptus is especially water-demanding, while monoculture plantations diminish biodiversity, exclude pastoralists and grazing animals, and reduce rural employment (growing trees needs less labor than other crops). India's move toward social forestry would be followed in subsequent decades by Pakistan and then Bangladesh.

During "the Emergency," Gandhi came to rely heavily on her second son, Sanjay (1946–80). While not holding any government office, he strongly pushed provincial, municipal, and village officials and the police to meet quotas for vasectomies – what he considered the most cost-effective way to slow India's population rise, which was dissipating its economic development gains. Under his heavy pressure, the rate of sterilizations tripled to 8.3 million during the Emergency. Sanjay also personally led police to "beautify" cities – through forced of slum clearances, most notably in heavily Muslim Old Delhi, with inadequate provision for the displaced.

These authoritarian assertions raised international protests but suppressed domestic ones. To prove her popularity, after eighteen months, Gandhi released her jailed political opponents and held the postponed parliamentary elections (March 1977). A wide array of opposition politicians united in their hostility to her regime as the Janata coalition. Even some members of her cabinet joined, leaving her with only the rump Congress (I [for Indira]). Unexpectedly, the Janata won, selected octogenarian Syndicate leader Morarji Desai (1896–1995) as prime minister and ordered the arrest of Gandhi and Sanjay.

The diverse factions within Janata, however, disagreed on most issues other than reversing Gandhi's policies. On the one hand, Janata nationalistically expelled US multinationals, most prominently Coca-Cola and IBM. On the other hand, Desai's regime supported massive dam projects. In 1978, construction began Tehri Dam on the Bhagirathi (upper Ganges) River in Garhwal, which would create a 42 km^2 (16 mi^2)

reservoir to irrigate 270,000 hectares (667,000 acres) and to supply drinking water and 2,400MW of electricity (mostly to New Delhi), but at the cost of submerging the Hindu pilgrimage town of Tehri and 100 villages, containing about 85,000 people. Delaying (but not successfully halting) this project was an array of local groups being displaced, Gandhians against big dams, Hindus defending a holy site, geologists predicting disaster from earthquakes in this seismically active region, and hydraulic engineers calculating rapid siltation that would reduce the dam's benefits. (In 1992, the Supreme Court rejected the final legal appeal against the Tehri Dam, and, with funding from Russia, it was operational by 2003.)

Similarly, Prime Minister Desai supported the Kerala provincial government's project in the Silent Valley of its Nilgiri Mountains in the Western Ghats. This dam promised to irrigate 10,000 hectares (24,710 acres), generate 240MW of electricity, and provide 2,000 jobs. But its reservoir would submerge a biodiversity hot spot, although it would displace few humans. Opposition mounted from international and national environmentalists (including the WWF) and local groups headed by a science teachers' association (Kerala Sastra Sahitya Parishad). Various factors (including the 1978 disastrous north Indian floods in that hurt the economy) led to the shattering of Desai's coalition after two years (1977–79). His brief Janata Party successor, Prime Minister Charan Singh (1902–87, r. 1979–80), was convinced to delay the Silent Valley dam.

Gandhi led her Congress (I) party to electoral victory (January 1980), promising a return to development through law and order. Distrustful of everyone except Sanjay (now her deputy prime minister and heir apparent), she pushed to centralize in her own hands authority over the Union government, provincial governments, and her own political party. She also used her power to advance her own interests in environmental issues. She pressured the Kerala government to withdraw Silent Valley project in 1983 and then made it a national park. This and later battles over big dams suggest that defending biodiversity might succeed politically with the right connections but defending local people's rights against displacement by submergence was more difficult.

Her Sixth Five-Year Plan (1980–84) highlighted increases in rural employment, poverty reduction, and also had a chapter on the environment. Yet, this listed "shifting cultivation" as a major environmental "problem." Further, her regime also created the Department of Environment (1980), which began to identify major problems and propose appropriate policies to ameliorate them. Her major 1980 Forest Conservation Act (still in place today) prevented provinces from regularizing encroachments by immigrant farmers and from reclassifying or leasing out Reserved Forests for commercial logging without Union government approval. This Act also pushed provinces for accelerated social forestry. Forest Departments thereby expanded their authority not only over forest-dwellers but additionally over newly tree-planted community and private lands, requiring official Union government clearance for any tree cutting or infrastructure construction in these areas. Similarly, her 1981 Air (Prevention and Control of Pollution) Act also both addressed a growing problem and asserted greater Union government powers over that part of the environment. (This Act, amended 1987, remains the prevailing legislation today.) In addition, Gandhi personally intervened in any issue that caught her attention. Her political dominance over many provincial regimes also enabled her to accelerate the expansion of national parks and sanctuaries.

Meanwhile, Indian activists and NGOs increasingly investigated environmental issues and publicized both problems and solutions; among the most influential from the late 1970s has been Anil Agarwal (1947–2002) and his Centre for Science and Environment in New Delhi. Leading Indian and international environmentalists were advocating "eco-development," which called for buffer zones surrounding core environmentally protected areas as villagers are weaned away (or alienated) from their use of forests by creating alternative "green" income sources. Indeed, Indira Gandhi's regime in 1980 appointed a team led by environmentalist and scholar Dr. Madhav Gadgil (1942–) to plan the Nilgiri Biosphere reserve for preserving the ecosystem within a matrix of human settlement and use, based on UNESCO's Man and the Biosphere program. When finally "notified" (implemented) in 1986, this covered 5,560 km^2

Box 10.1

Prime Minister Indira Gandhi's directive to provincial chief ministers:

> "I have received a number of reports about the degradation and mis-utilization of beaches in our coastal states by building and other activity ... the beaches have aesthetic and environmental value as well as other uses. They have to be kept clear of all activities at least up to 500 metres from the water at the maximum high tide. If the area is vulnerable to erosion, suitable trees and plants have to be planted on the beach sands without marring their beauty. Beaches must be kept free from all kinds of artificial development. Pollution from industrial and town wastes must be also avoided totally." (Indira Gandhi 1981)

(2,150 mi^2) in three provinces (Kerala, Karnataka, Tamil Nadu), with five national parks and wildlife sanctuaries as cores, connected by buffers. Similarly, in 1982, the Task Force of the National Committee on Environmental Planning and Coordination (which Indira Gandhi had appointed during the Emergency, headed by prominent environmentalist Zafar Futehally [1920–2013] of the BNHS and WWF) recommended ecodevelopment. To conduct research and to train the necessary staff, her government created the Wildlife Institute of India in 1982 (made autonomous 1986).

From the early 1980s as well, India's Supreme Court began innovatively to extend its interventions into environmental issues, especially through Public Interest Litigation (PIL). In many British-based judicial systems, and hitherto in India, a plaintiff had "locus standi" only if personally suffering a legal injury. But in a series of rulings, the Supreme Court broadened "standing" for environmental issues by citing the 1976 Constitutional Amendment making it obligatory for both the state and every citizen to "protect and improve the environment." Hence, even without any basis in specific legislation, any citizen could bring a PIL appeal on the environment's behalf against any government agency or private business. Eventually, the Court accepted even an individual's letter as a legal PIL appeal.

Further, the Court began to act *suo moto* (on its own initiative), for instance based on a newspaper article a judge happened to read. Various judges kept themselves and their colleagues informed about new concepts and trends in international environmental law, attending conferences and publishing articles. Delegating research the justices had no time or expertise to conduct, the Court appointed panels of experts and institutions (e.g. the National Environmental Engineering Research Institute, Nagpur) to investigate and recommend actions for the Court to order. In all this, the Indian Supreme Court pioneered its activist role by interpreting the Constitution and legislation broadly, acting as a legislative body creating new rules and policies, and functioning executively by ordering government agencies to implement often detailed actions. (Supreme Courts in Pakistan and Bangladesh later followed these Indian precedents.)

This South Asian "green" judicial activism has been praised and critiqued. Many politicians and bureaucrats seem willing to have judges (who had largely apolitical appointments based on seniority and secure tenure until retirement) take responsibility for actions disliked by powerful commercial and other special interests. The fear of being ruled in contempt of court also motivates officials to act, thus cutting through red-tape barriers to accomplish major projects. But this deference also allows politicians and bureaucrats to await judicial initiative. Further, judges are not necessarily environmental experts, and are often unconstrained by the complexities, financial costs, or the full implications of their orders. Cases often arise ad hoc, as do the delegating appointments by courts of investigative institutions or individuals, including activist lawyers and recently retired judges. Overall, judges often frame environmental issues and "public interest" from their own personal perspective as mostly male, middle-class, Westernized, urban professionals.

After 1980, Prime Minister Indira Gandhi, having returned to office with widespread public support, was determined to secure her legacy and weaken political opposition. When Sanjay fatally crashed his high-performance airplane just six months after the 1980 election, Gandhi pressed her reluctant elder son, Rajiv (1944–91, a professional pilot in a government-owned airline) to take over as deputy prime minister and heir apparent. Simultaneously, Gandhi maneuvered to fragment her political opponents in various provinces. In Punjab, she had tolerated violent Sikh separatists demanding secession as "Khalistan," but when the violence exceeded her limits, she ordered the army in May 1984 to seize Amritsar's "Golden Temple" – both the holiest Sikh shrine and a base for Khalistan militants. Two of her personal bodyguards, who were Sikh, assassinated her in October. While Rajiv took over as prime minister, many Sikh homes and shops were burned, with about 2,000 Sikhs killed by her infuriated supporters. (The Khalistan separatist movement would devastate Punjab until the early 1990s, when it faded due to police suppression, Punjab's economic development, and reduced Pakistani covert support).

In December 1984, only months into Rajiv Gandhi's regime, a runaway chemical reaction in a Union Carbide India factory released into Bhopal city's air approximately 24–35 metric tonnes (26–38 US tons) of deadly methyl isocyanate (CH_3NCO), causing at least 3,000 immediate human deaths, 20,000 long-term fatalities, and much other environmental damage. This largest industrial accident in world history resulted from multiple acts of negligence in safety equipment and operation. The owner and operator was a subsidiary of the US multinational corporation, Union Carbide, but had substantial Indian private and government ownership. As liability cases accumulated, in March 1985 Rajiv's government passed a law taking exclusive authority to represent the victims legally. While American executives heading Union Carbide successfully resisted extradition, the Indian Supreme Court negotiated (February 1989) a $470 million settlement, which the government would administer. Many victims and their advocates have found this settlement and government remediation inadequate.

Reelected in 1985 with a large majority, Rajiv created the Ministry of Environment and Forests and also appointed a National Wastelands Development Board. He brought technocrats into his circle of advisors, trying to override legislative and administrative weaknesses in environmental protections. He created and chaired the National Water Resource Council (1985), which included provincial chief ministers, since "water" was on the state list. This council set about devising projects and policies that would coordinate improvement in national fresh water stocks. One result was India's first-ever National Water Policy (1987). But, concentrating on water supply, this policy did little for improving water conservation, reducing waste, or pollution.

His Central Pollution Control Board set standards for harmful chemicals and particles and created a national monitoring network. This formed the basis for the extensive 1985 Ganges Action Plan under the Ganges Authority, which the prime minister heads. This authority used massive Union government funds to build a series of treatment plants for waste discharges all along this most economically and environmentally vital and, to most Hindus, sacred river. But provincial and municipal resistance to funding the operation and maintenance of these treatment plants slowed and weakened implementation. Indeed, during three years of hearings, the Supreme Court extensively intervened, ordering in 1988 hundreds of factories closed and a series of specific directives trying to force a range of municipalities and agencies into action. But this plan has still largely fallen short of its ambitious goals.

In 1986, Rajiv's government passed the umbrella Environmental Protection Act. This landmark legislation defined the environment widely to include "water, air and land and the interrelationship which exists among and between water, air and land and human beings and other living creatures, plants, microorganisms and property." Further, this Act provided the central government with extensive powers to frame rules, regulations, and enabling legislation. It also included the concept of Environmental Impact Assessment (EIA) as a prerequisite for government approval of a project (although EIAs were not widely implemented for nearly a decade, and even then often not effectively).

Rajiv's "modernizing" government engaged in international conferences, speaking for the developing world. The 1987 Montreal Protocol on Substances that Deplete the Ozone Layer recognized that richer countries bore greater historical and moral responsibility for this problem. So poorer countries should receive technological and financial support and more flexibility in the transition to chemicals less harmful for the vital ozone layer of the stratosphere than chlorofluorocarbons (CFCs).

Rajiv's administration also supported other large-scale infrastructure projects, in particular the massive Narmada Valley Development Plan: a proposed hydroelectric and irrigation network of 30 big dams, 135 medium dams, and 3,000 small dams, with lengthy canals (mostly moving water from forested Madhya Pradesh into arid southern Gujarat). This project had been originally suggested in 1946, but only moved forward after 1985 when the World Bank loaned US$450 million (of the budgeted $3 billion cost) and the Japanese government loaned $200 million for turbines for the first big dam, the Sardar Sarovar. The scale and international involvement in this dam drew national and international public attention to the displaced (who are often overlooked in smaller dam projects). Eventually the World Bank and the Japanese government withdrew, although the Sardar Sarovar project continued with Indian government funding. (From 1995–99, India's Supreme Court issued a series of stay orders and then permissions as this dam rose to 163 m [540 ft] high; it is now functioning.)

But Rajiv Gandhi's technocratically oriented government proved unable to manage the vast and entrenched bureaucracy at the Union and provincial levels, resistant political interests within the Congress (I) and outside it, or the scale of the nation's problems, including environmental ones. For instance, his regime decided in 1988 to stop provinces from profiting from timber contracts by amending the Forest Conservation Act and asserting a National Forest Policy that required prior Union government approval of any leasing of government forest land to anyone (individuals, corporations, or communities) and for any clear-cutting of any natural forest anywhere. The goal was preserving biodiversity, erosion control, and ambitious afforestation to produce forest cover of 66 percent in the hills and 33 percent nationally (levels that have never been achieved). However, many provincial politicians, contractors, private owners, and local communities protested this sweeping government intervention, which had unforeseen consequences in empowering foresters, hobbling various activities not particularly harmful to the environment, and leaving small and middle farmers as the only legal producers of wood for industry. Nonetheless, this policy also recognized that local communities needed biomass fuel, so it allowed foresters to permit locals to use of fodder, minor forest produce, construction timber, and fuelwood. Further, to solve the impending "fuelwood crisis," the policy advocated planting imported mesquite (*Prosopis julifora*) in wastelands and commons. This native North American bush survives arid conditions and has thorns, so it resists grazing animals. Gradually, village women (who were the primary users) adjusted their gathering and cooking practices but mesquite has invaded endangered desert ecosystems (e.g. the Indian Wild Ass [*Equus hemionus khur*] Sanctuary in Gujarat).

Rajiv's government also instituted technology-forcing deadlines for environmental improvement. For instance, the 1989 Motor Vehicles Rules required higher automobile emission standards, which necessitated manufacturing upgrades. However, while government action improved air and water quality in some areas, these continued to deteriorate overall. India's major cities stand among the most dangerously air-polluted in the world. Finally, after the Congress (I) lost a series of provincial elections and, as a major corruption scandal in the army's purchase of Swedish howitzers from the Bofors corporation implicated Rajiv, the December 1989 parliamentary election ended his regime.

The diverse Janata Dal coalition won a small majority, electing as prime minister Rajiv's former defense minister and leading accuser, V. P. Singh (1931–2008). During his less than a year in office (1989–90), his populist measures included Joint Forest Management (JFM). This concept of participatory collaboration between local communities and forest departments was being advocated globally by the World Bank and major NGOs like the Ford Foundation. Variations on this model had already been initiated in some provinces, for instance in West Bengal's Forest Protection Committees from 1972. JFM's goal was to restore local communities as stakeholders through a return to "authentic" grassroots participatory democratic traditions and (in theory) reduction of state control, which had not proven effective in either preventing deforestation or helping vulnerable social groups. Provincial government foresters negotiated increasing numbers of JFM "memorandums of understanding" (MOUs) with village-level user committees in which the latter would protect nearby forests but also share in the timbering profits; some 20,000 MOUs nationally were signed in the first decade and over 120,000 in the following decade. But many foresters found working with local communities, instead of excluding them from forests, a difficult readjustment. In some villages, forest protection bodies already existed. More often, however, foresters created of new committees, used standardized MOU forms, and directed the planting and felling schemes, which anyway only covered degraded forests (until 2000). Further, many existing and new committees empowered elder, high-status males who already ran the villages. Villages and pastoralists without an agreement lost their customary usage rights. But supporters of these JFMs have found some provide access by women and other historically subordinated villagers, especially in provinces that required quotas for these groups (Agarwal 2010).

Overall, JFM has continued to expand in India (and in Bangladesh and Pakistan), paralleled by Participatory Irrigation Management of canals.

Meanwhile, the judiciary independently advanced various environmental protection initiatives. For example, the Supreme Court began in 1990 to incorporate the emerging international concept of intergenerational equity. This principle holds that PIL advocates for people yet unborn have standing to demand judicial protections for their future environment.

The Janata Dal coalition proved even more fragile than the earlier Janata. V. P. Singh's Janata Dal successor, Chandra Shekhar (1927–2007), lasted only six months (falling May 1991). In the subsequent election, Rajiv seemed to be leading the Congress (I) back; however, he was assassinated. The Congress (I) won a plurality in Parliament, hurriedly selecting as prime minister P.V. Narasimha Rao (1921–2004), who governed through an unstable coalition (1991–96).

During this extended period of political uncertainty at the center, no Five-Year Plans were formulated (1989–91). Government finances depended on foreign borrowing, thus constraining investment in sustainable development just as the Rio Conference was advocating it. Subsequently, international and domestic economic pressures finally forced the Indian government to shift away from Nehru's socialist model toward "neoliberalization," with powerful effects on the environment, as the next chapter discusses.

The United Nations Conference on Environment and Development (Rio de Janeiro, June 1992)

Held on the twentieth anniversary of the Stockholm conference and reaffirming its Declaration, Rio's "Earth Summit" highlighted the connection between environmental protections and human development, especially for the poor, including women. As the Cold War was withering away, the Rio Conference reflected shifting national interests, including among the diverse nations of the "global South." But, to achieve sufficient consensus, the nonbinding "Rio Declaration" largely only consolidated many of the anthropocentric, nation-based, but international environmental policy developments over the intervening two decades. In particular, it built on the 1987 World Commission on Environment and Development (Brundtland Report) "Our Common Future" model of sustainable development while conserving natural resources. It also highlighted intergenerational equity, the precautionary principle that precluded rather than just punished pollution, the polluter-pays principle (full financial responsibility for all environmental damage from a project), and the need for EIAs. Rio thus focused on the financial and technical issues around global international cooperation for biodiversity, reforestation, ecosystem integrity, and resource conservation. The conference also led to the Statement of Forest Principles, the Convention on Biological Diversity, and the UN Framework Convention on Climate Change (see Chapter 12).

Governments in most developing nations welcomed Rio's "common but differentiated responsibilities" principle that recognized the historic accountability of developed economies for global environmental degradation and the need for them to transfer technologies and financial resources for sustainable development to poorer ones. Hence, for example, the internationally funded Global Environment Facility, managed by the World Bank, to support ecodevelopment projects. But the key questions remained disputed: who would pay, how much, and who or what was to be sustained and developed. Indeed, India, Pakistan, Bangladesh, and many other nations of the global South questioned the World Bank's governance structure, which wealthy Western countries largely control. In addition, the Rio Conference also issued Agenda 21, a 700-page action plan, with initial estimated costs of $1.36 trillion.

Pakistan from Division to Rio (1971–92)

Pakistan, since its traumatic 1971 loss of its eastern half, continued its alternation between democratic and authoritarian regimes. After more than a dozen years of military rule, the Pakistan People's Party (PPP) of Zulfikar Ali Bhutto (1928–79) had won the 1970 election in West Pakistan (81 of the 138 National Assembly seats in West Pakistan) by promising Islamic socialism, people's power, and restoration of national pride. During Bhutto's dynamic years in office (1971–77), first as civilian chief martial law administrator and president, then as prime minister, he asserted himself over any who opposed his vision for Pakistan's people and environment.

While Bhutto had initially mobilized Pakistan's nascent labor unions, he increasingly suppressed their strikes and other demands. He created the Federal Security Force and the People's Guards, militias personally loyal to him that further weakened the already discredited army. He nationalized major banks, industries (particularly those owned by his political opponents, most notably the Punjab-based Sharif family), and the ghi, cotton, and rice-husking trades (which Muhajirs dominated). To reduce the power of large landowners, he promised land redistribution (enforced only selectively against his opponents). He diluted the elite

Civil Service of Pakistan – heir to the British Raj's ICS – by merging it with other civil services.

Bhutto also raised Pakistan's national pride and position internationally. From 1972, he poured funds into two rival nuclear weapons labs (one using enriched uranium, the other plutonium), spurred on by India's more advanced nuclear program and substantial conventional military superiority. He invited the other leaders of Muslim majority nations to Islamabad for an Islamic Summit under his leadership. Bhutto also cultivated diplomatic and military links with China, countering the growing India-Soviet alliance.

While newly installed Bhutto did not attend the 1972 Stockholm Conference (as had Indira Gandhi), he began to institute measures that made environmental issues part of his international and domestic programs. Bhutto sustained Pakistan's leadership among developing nations by ratifying international agreements, including the Convention on Protection of the World Cultural and Natural Heritage (1972) and the Convention on International Trade in Endangered Species of Wild Fauna and Flora (signed 1973, ratified 1976).

Pakistan also designated protected areas for endangered species, using the IUCN model. However, planning national parks and sanctuaries, surveying and assessing their ecologies, and respecting the needs of their local human communities all proved controversial. For instance, Bhutto's administration proposed (1973) and then proclaimed (1975) the 2,300 km^2 (890 mi^2) Khunjerab National Park in Gilgit to protect endangered Marco Polo sheep (*Ovis ammon polii*), legally banning all human activity there. This park, like many others in South Asia, would remain disputed. On the one hand, Pakistan's National Council for Conservation of Wildlife (appointed 1974 to guide provincial wildlife departments for better management of Protected Areas) and the WWF advocated and funded the wilderness model which excluded humans (except researchers and tourists) to protect this endangered sheep species. Opposing them, local communities resisted expulsion, supported by international advocates of a multipurpose park model that permitted regulated domestic grazing and hunting. Meanwhile, the local economy remained disrupted and the sheep population shrank.

Pakistan's new 1973 Constitution (its third in seventeen years) largely reflected Bhutto's vision and agenda. This Constitution preceded India's 1976 constitutional amendment by shifting environmental issues onto the concurrent list, thus giving the central government overarching authority over provinces. This Constitution, however, had no formal statement about the environmental rights or duties of the state or its citizens. Nonetheless, it provided legal grounds for PIL against polluters (although

Pakistan's judiciary waited a decade to accept PIL cases, until after India's Supreme Court set that precedent).

Bhutto used his new constitutional power to assert his control over Pakistan's environment. He first created the Environment and Urban Affairs Division (1974), which soon became a distinct Ministry of Environment (1975). Its staff began drafting a consolidated Federal Environmental Law (not completed until 1983, during the next regime). Bhutto's National Forestry Committee (appointed in 1972) produced a revised National Forest Policy (1975). This put private tree plantations less directly under the authority of provincial foresters but strengthened even further foresters' power to exclude local people from their customary use of state forests, justified as halting deforestation. He had Pakistan join the IUCN in 1975.

To validate Bhutto's mandate, he held a parliamentary election in January 1977. Despite slowed annual economic growth (partly due to major Indus floods in 1973 and 1976), his PPP triumphed, winning 435 of the 460 National Assembly seats. However, his opponents accused him and his party of widespread intimidation, including murder. In July 1977, the army chief whom Bhutto had selected, General Zia ul-Huq (1924–88), suddenly seized power in a military coup (Pakistan's third successful one so far). Zia suspended the 1973 Constitution and eventually tried and executed Bhutto (while imprisoning his eldest child, Benazir Bhutto [1953–2007], among others).

During General Zia ul-Huq's decade in power (1977–88) as chief martial law administrator then president, he repeatedly promised restoration of democracy, even as he worked to extend his powerbase within and beyond the army. Military officers (both serving and retired) headed ever more government and quasi-government corporations. Military welfare and retirement funds expanded their ownership of key parts of the economy. From 1984 onward, Zia stoked nationalist sentiment by clashing against Indian troops in the environmentally hostile Siachen Glacier. To mobilize popular backing, his regime's Fifth and Sixth Five-Year Plans (1978–83, 1983–88) promised services, loans, and other inputs for rural and small-scale industrial development.

Further, Zia made Islamization one of his main domestic agendas, evidently both from his personal piety and to solicit support from Islamists. Hitherto, various regimes had proclaimed their commitment to Islam, but Zia instituted the Federal Shariah Court (1979), making Islamic law the test of all legislation. This Court, for instance, declared all interest as anti-Quranic *riba* (usury/interest) and directed Pakistan to shun capitalism. Zia also instituted "*Hudood* laws" which, most notably, devalued women's legal testimony and made them dependent on male guardians and also made "blasphemy" against Islam a capital offense (these largely remain in effect today). Overall, a range of Islamist parties and movements gained influence during his administration.

Some advocates of Islam assert its essentially environmentalist theology. They argue that Allah revealed His divinity by creating the world and all living beings, so all creatures should have the same relationship toward Him of "submission" (the Arabic root meaning of "Islam"). Human Muslims have the conscious capacity to act, and therefore bear special responsibilities toward all other beings; pollution disrespects God. Such advocates assert that secular environmentalism lacks moral commitment. However, Pakistan and other Islam-based states have not actually implemented much Islamic environmentalism.

Internationally, Zia's position strengthened substantially with the Soviet invasion of Afghanistan (December 1979). This made Pakistan a "frontline state" for the West, which largely accepted his regime's legitimacy and poured in military aid, both directly and also unofficially during its transit across Pakistan to the Islamist Mujahidin in Afghanistan. Eventually, 3–5 million mostly Pakhtun refugees (a third of Afghanistan's population) would flee to Pakistan's NWFP and Balochistan, putting major burdens on fragile ecosystems there. Further, refugee camps became recruiting grounds for the Islamist Mujahidin and later Taliban. Pakistan's military Inter-Services Intelligence (ISI), which often operated outside the government's effective control, fostered and tried to direct these militant Islamist groups.

To help stimulate the economy, Zia revised Pakistan's National Forest Policy (1980). Like India's earlier social forestry policy, this encouraged afforestation on privately owned lands of fast-growing tree species as raw material for industries and for fuelwood. However, like many central government initiatives, this lacked effective implementation by provinces.

In 1983, Zia overrode political and commercial opposition to decree the Pakistan Environment Protection Ordinance, applicable to all provinces. This was the nation's first comprehensive environmental law, gratifying international aid agencies including the World Bank, the Asian Development Bank (ADB), and various NGOs (and preceding Indian's comparable umbrella legislation by two years). This ordinance authorized federal and provincial legislation and Environmental Protection Agencies to regulate pollution and other environmentally harmful actions. It established the Pakistan Environmental Protection Council as the apex policy-making body, chaired ex-officio by President Zia (although he never convened it). Following international models, it required all projects likely to affect the environment adversely to file an EIA, documented with detailed scientific studies.

Zia's ordinance has remained the basis for Pakistan's subsequent environmental legislation, but its implementation and enforcement have remained largely ineffective. This ordinance did not specify the assessment process, and EIAs applied only to new industrial construction. Further, few Pakistanis had the training to undertake them. So, for a decade, EIAs were rarely conducted unless international funding agencies insisted and directed them.

In 1984, Zia held a national referendum equating his presidency with "progress" toward democracy, "the preservation of the ideology of Pakistan," and bringing the nation into "conformity with the injunction of Islam as laid down in the Holy Quran and Sunnah of the Holy Prophet [Mohammad] (Peace be upon him)." Officially, 97.7 percent of voters approved. President Zia used this to legitimate his fundamental revisions of the long-suspended Constitution; crucially, the 8th Constitutional Amendment gave the president power to dismiss any elected prime minister and dissolve the national legislature.

Meanwhile, Zia's government continued to ratify international agreements about aspects of the environment. These included the Convention on Wetlands (ratified 1978), the UN Convention on the Law of the Sea (1982), the Vienna Convention on the Protection of the Ozone Layer (1985), the Montreal Protocol (1987), and the Convention on the Conservation of Migratory Species of Wild Animals (adopted 1979, ratified 1987). His regime also passed legislation authorizing the creation of formal Water Users Associations (aka Participatory Irrigation Management), which expanded by the 1990s into as many as 14,000 associations.

By the mid-1980s, however, opposition to Zia's regime had increased, both within Pakistan and internationally. The global petroleum price surge (1979–81) meant high remittances from millions of Pakistanis working in the Persian Gulf, but also rising fuel import costs. Severe droughts (1986–87) constrained development and enhanced discontent. Russian withdrawal from Afghanistan (completed February 1989) dried up Western military, financial, and diplomatic support for Zia. Yet, the consequences of the war persisted in Pakistan, including millions of Afghan refugees, dozens of well-armed Islamist groups, and widespread opium and heroin smuggling and addiction.

Further, diverse opposition parties allied as the Movement for the Restoration of Democracy, led by Benazir Bhutto (exiled heir to PPP leadership). Despite personal danger, she returned to Pakistan (April 1986), receiving widespread acclaim for campaigning against Zia. In August 1988, Zia's military transport plane crashed, killing him, top army commanders, and the American ambassador. This suddenly left

Benazir the leading candidate in the long-postponed national election (December 1988).

Prime Minister Benazir Bhutto's first regime (1988–90) resumed civilian rule but also began a decade of political instability at the center. Many within Pakistan and internationally expected much from her as the face of restored democracy in Pakistan, as Western-educated (Harvard and Oxford universities), as the first woman heading a predominantly Muslim nation, and as Pakistan's youngest-ever premier. However, her regime was dependent on the unruly PPP and the reluctant army, while the anti-Zia political alliance fragmented.

Her relatively weak government passed few measures, but many of her supporters pushed through programs benefiting them personally. For instance, her government in 1989 shifted to the private sector the profitable sale and distribution of pesticides, vastly increasing their use, but with little agricultural benefit and much chemical pollution. Despite annual GDP growth increases, criticism of her regime grew, with expanding allegations of corruption, especially against her husband, Asaf Ali Zardari (1955–). Within two years, President Ghulam Ishaq Khan (1915–2006, r. 1988–93), with the support of the army and much of the political establishment, dismissed her government under the 8th Amendment.

The subsequent election (November 1990) was won by Nawaz Sharif (1949–) and his Punjab-based Pakistan Muslim League (PML) at the head of a nine-party coalition which included Sunni Islamist parties. His family had suffered nationalization of its steel and other industries under Zulfikar Bhutto, but during the Zia regime had recovered much of its wealth and its political power in their Punjab province. Sharif's administration tried to accelerate GDP growth through economic liberalization, especially privatization of the public sector, including power-generation. Such measures subordinated environmental protections to rapid development. But the economy suffered during the Persian Gulf War (1990–91), which created rising imported petroleum costs and declining remittances from Pakistanis there.

Sharif also recognized that provinces had legal powers over their resources. His 1991 interprovincial Indus Water Accord established a surface water entitlement for every province, which it could allocate at its discretion (this accord was possible since his PML governed every province). A new Indus River System Authority officially regulated and monitored water distribution, but the actual use of the water remained highly politicized, particularly during droughts when upper-riparian Punjab took more than Sindh felt justified.

Sharif's 1991 National Forest Policy, which was heavily influenced by international donor agencies, promised to integrate all stakeholders and improve the environment. But these goals remained broadly stated and not well implemented. Years of uncontrolled logging (especially in NWFP) resulted in destructive floods (1991–92). Consequently, in 1993, the central government ordered a moratorium on commercial timber harvesting (this order was repeatedly renewed until 2001, when it was lifted). Nonetheless, provincial foresters often restricted local users, alienating them, while powerful commercial interests ("timber mafia") continued deforestation.

Resonating with international movement toward JFM, Pakistan's twenty-five-year Forestry Sector Master Plan (1992–2017) promised to engage local people in the protection and management of local environment, including forests and rangelands. However, local communities were still largely marginalized by Forest Departments, negating the benefits of this collaboration. Indeed, while the population rose, Pakistan's natural forests continued to shrink (they now cover less than 3 percent of the nation, giving it one of the world's lowest ratios of forest cover, about 0.05 ha/capita, while the world average is 1.1 ha/capita).

Pakistan issued its own ambitious National Conservation Strategy (1992). Sharif's coalition depended on Islamist political parties, so this Strategy evoked Quranic concepts and moral values, especially *haquq al-abad* ("community spirit and responsibility") and self-restraint in *qanaat* ("worldly consumption"). Further, at the 1992 Rio conference, Pakistan took a major role as current chair of G-77. There, heavily indebted Pakistan argued for debt-for-nature swaps through which poorer nations paid-off their international loans by promising to preserve their forests and other natural resources.

Domestically, however, Sharif's regime ended in 1993 when President Gulam Ishaq Khan dismissed it for corruption under the Constitution's 8th Amendment. Sharif appealed in the Supreme Court. To resolve this crisis, the Court and Army negotiated the dissolution of the legislature, resignations of the prime minister and president, and a new election in October. Thus, Pakistan's government remained fragile, undermining its capacity to enforce environmental protections. The next chapter shows the nation's continued alternation between weak civilian and military regimes, while domestic and international pressures on its environment intensified.

Bangladesh from Independence to Rio (1971–92)

Bangladesh's violent origin in 1971 and its overall social political, and physical conditions made it a particularly fragile new nation, with many resources but also many challenges. During the quarter-century that it was East Pakistan, it had been economically, culturally, and politically subordinated to the western wing, with little industry and heavy foreign-exchange dependence on exporting raw jute (a commodity being replaced internationally by synthetic materials for rope and sacking). Many West Pakistani leaders, from Jinnah onward, had regarded Bengali language and culture as too associated with Hinduism to be truly Islamic. Indeed, much East Pakistani popular mobilization had been associated with its Bangla-language movement. During its Independence war, Mukhti Bahini, pro-Pakistan Islamist militias, and the Pakistani and Indian armies all devastated the society and land. Up to 10 million refugees (disproportionately Hindu) had fled for shelter in India during the war (nearly as many refugees as the total for the 1947 Partition). Further, Bangladesh's location at the head of the funnel-shaped Bay of Bengal and its low-lying contour make it particularly subject to floods and cyclones and especially vulnerable to accelerating climate changes. Thus, after liberation, the new nation faced daunting recovery on all fronts.

Most newly independent Bangladeshis entrusted their nation's hopes to Sheikh Mujibur Rahman (r. 1972–75), whose Awami League had won almost every East Pakistani constituency in 1970. After his release from imprisonment in West Pakistan (January 1972), he immediately took over as Bangladesh's president and then prime minister. Advocating socialism, his regime seized property and businesses abandoned by fleeing West Pakistanis and nationalized many other nonagricultural parts of the economy. He rapidly asserted his national vision, presiding over writing the Constitution (adopted November 1972, heavily amended, occasionally suspended, but still in place). His party swept the March 1973 national legislative elections.

Notably, although the Constitution did not mention "environment," Mujib acted on environmental issues from early in his relatively brief regime, following his own inclinations, domestic interests, and pressures from international donors of vitally needed foreign aid. While still president, he issued the Water Pollution Control Ordinance and the Bangladesh Wildlife (Preservation) Order. The latter provided a broad framework for national parks, wildlife sanctuaries, and state and private game reserves, largely following IUCN guidelines (Bangladesh joined the IUCN in 1973). After the National Assembly convened, it expanded his orders. For example, the 1974 Bangladesh Wildlife (Preservation) (Amendment) Act listed many specific species, each with a particular level of protection. These detailed lists seemed extensive then, but their specificity meant that only listed species were legally protected. Further, budgetary and personnel constraints have severely limited actual enforcement.

His government and the economy received substantial support from international agencies and foreign governments, whose own agendas thus strongly guided the management and reengineering of Bangladesh's environment (and its development generally). For example, in 1972 the World Bank directed a Land and Water Resources Sector Study which recommended small- and medium-scale flood control, drainage, and irrigation projects, later funded as the Irrigation Management Programme by the ADB and the Canadian and Dutch governments, among others. In 1974, the World Bank organized the Bangladesh Aid Group, with more than two dozen governments and institutions participating and designing programs. The ADB, the United Nations Development Program (UNDP), and many individual foreign governments also funded their own extensive projects. The Bangladesh government had only nominal control over many of these.

Nevertheless, committed members of civil society created numerous and extensive domestic NGOs. Most notably BRAC (founded 1972, now entitled the "Bangladesh Rural Advance Committee") and the Grameen Bank (founded 1983) became global leaders for their extensive and innovative integrated development projects centered on microcredit loans to poor rural women to escape from their cycle of debt to traditional moneylenders and wholesalers. These NGOs organized women borrowers into support groups, with training programs. Nobel laureate and Grameen Bank founder Muhammad Yunus (1940–) powerfully articulated for both domestic and international audiences the benefits of this model. Supporters and critics both highlight the extremely high loan-payback rates, the former as proof of success, the latter as evidence of severe social and institutional pressure on impoverished women-borrowers. Expanding into many sectors of society, these international and domestic NGOs have set agendas and accomplished much in terms of social services and infrastructure building, which both fostered and reflected the Bangladesh government's instability and weak administrative capacity.

Mujib's regime soon faced rising tensions among many competing Bangladeshi interests. Many on the left expected radical social and economic change and believed his policies too limited; many on the right, who valued stability, found them extreme. Further, Mukhti Bahini veterans expected war service rewards, while regular army officers, who had been subordinated to West Pakistanis, now wanted to command.

Mujib tried to gain control over Bangladesh's unstable economy and politics. He asserted centralized planning with his First Five-Year Plan (1973–78). In January 1975, he deeply amended the young Constitution, abolished all political parties except his own, and became president again.

Then in August, a coup led by army majors assassinated Mujib and almost all his family. A welter of counter-coups followed.

This period of volatility only subsided in November 1976 when Army Chief General Ziaur Rahman (1936–81) asserted martial law. He tried to bridge conflicts between the regular army and Mukhti Bahini veterans, having been one of the only 5 percent of officers in the regular Pakistani Army who were Bengali, had broadcast the declaration of Bangladesh's independence, and then had fought prominently in the liberation war. Declaring himself president (April 1977), Zia asserted his own vision for Bangladesh, including continued attention on the environment. Among other early decrees, he issued an umbrella Environmental Pollution Control Ordinance (1977), extending the powers of a reconstituted Environmental Pollution Control Board over the entire environment and all forms of pollution harmful to all forms of life. While not enforceable in practice, the comprehensiveness of this environmental order placed Bangladesh legally in advance of both Pakistan and India (whose comparable legislation came later, in 1977 and in 1986 respectively, the former also by military decree).

Official policies, however, sometimes compounded commercial interests and socioeconomic and political pressures that harmed the environment. For instance, following a major drought in half the nation that destroyed much of the rice harvest, in 1978 Zia's regime implemented a major resettlement program for about 25,000 Bangla-speaking farmers into the Chittagong Hill Tracts, one of Bangladesh's two major forested areas. This resulted in major deforestation as these farmers cleared land for fields and illegal logging spread. This process was accelerated by government dam, highway, and other infrastructure construction. A sometimes-violent guerrilla movement by the non-Bangla-speaking forest-dwelling communities arose that would last decades. Similarly, Bangladesh's other major forested area, the Sundarbans, also suffered logging, wildlife killing, and tensions among the state, local communities, and domestic immigrants. Further, Zia's government issued a Forest Policy (1979) reasserting state control over forests under a restructured Forest Department that would use scientific management to optimize raw material production for the nation. This two-page policy manifesto largely presupposed that forests had to be protected from local communities.

While Zia gained much popularity for himself and his newly created Bangladesh National Party (BNP), army mutinies and coup attempts punctuated his regime. Centralized planning and environmental programs were disrupted and could not effectively resume. Then, in May 1981, yet another army coup assassinated him, which, along with a super-cyclone, initiated further instability.

Families forced off their agricultural land expanded the labor supply for growing export-oriented industries: "Ready Made Garments" and farmed prawns/shrimp. These new industries, however, had cumulatively detrimental environmental impacts. Bangladesh's urban-based clothing industry depends on largely unregulated housing, factories, and labor while rural prawn ponds often replace mangroves, can increase salinization, used trapped wild larvae, and are subject to devastating disease outbreaks.

Following Zia's assassination, his widow, Begum Khalida Zia (1945–), took charge of his BNP, blaming the Awami League for her husband's problems. The BNP highlighted the nation's Islamic identity and allied politically with Islamist parties. Her major opponent was Begum Sheikh Hasina Wazed (1947–), Mujibur Rahman's daughter, who inherited his Awami League and blamed BNP supporters for her father's assassination. The Awami League stressed the nation's Bengali identity (shared with India's West Bengal province) and was often more favorably inclined toward India.

Promising to bring order, in 1982, General H. M. Ershad (1930–) seized power as chief martial law administrator, then proclaimed himself president. He eventually created his own political party, Jatiya, with a strong base in rural Bangladesh, strengthened by his 1984 Land Reforms Ordinance granting rights to tenant farmers and authorizing elected village councils. But most development funding came from foreign aid, whose donors had their own goals. So Ershad's Third Five-Year Plan (1985–90) and New Industrial Policy resumed the effort by the central government to liberalize much of the economy, partially privatizing many state-owned corporations and encouraging domestic and international commercial investment. Bangladesh also profitably exported labor, particularly servants and construction workers into the Arab world and soldiers into UN peacekeeping missions (from 1988 onward).

Ershad's regime also reasserted government control over Reserved Forests and other natural resources. He decreed a Department of Environmental Pollution Control (1985), restructured into the Ministry of Environment and Forest (1989). Guided by the UNDP and World Bank, his regime produced a National Water Plan (1987). The UN recognized Ershad's efforts with its 1988 Environment Award.

Nonetheless, a series of devastating floods (1985, 1987, 1988) covered much of the nation, killing thousands of people, hundreds of thousands of livestock, and most of the rice crop. For instance, in 1988, summer river torrents (which Ershad blamed on India) combined with monsoon rains to severely affect 70 percent of the land and people (killing over 2,000 by drowning or subsequent diseases) and then that year's massive fall cyclone compounded destruction along the coast, making sea-inundated land infertile for years. These led the World Bank to coordinate a multi-donor Flood Action Plan (1989–94) to design and construct of a vast series of small dams, barrages, and embankments. Although Bangladeshi activist lawyers argued that this construction would displace more than a million people and damage wetlands and other fragile ecosystems, the Supreme Court declined to intervene in this prestigious internationally funded project.

Meanwhile, lawyers (including the Bangladesh Environmental Lawyers Association) and justices brought a series of environmental cases into the Supreme Court, especially using PIL. Following India's pioneering judiciary (but usually not going as far), Bangladeshi courts broadly interpreted both the legal standing of appellants and the definition of environmental rights. Thus, the courts more effectively than the government pushed the bureaucracy into action.

Rising popular dissatisfaction with Ershad's regime and often violent protests were led by both the BNP and the Awami League. He resigned in 1990. But he has continued to lead his still-popular Jatiya party and has retained influence through political arrangements with successive governments.

To neutrally supervise the national election, Chief Justice of the Supreme Court Shahabuddin Ahmed (1930–) stood in as caretaker president (1990–91). During his eleven months in office, he established a high-level task force to set development strategies and prepare for the Rio Conference. The resulting report included the first comprehensive study of Bangladesh's environment; this became the foundation for many subsequent policies and programs. But government environmental actions continued to be deeply affected by events (like 1991 super-cyclone Gorki which killed almost 140,000 Bangladeshis) and the agendas of foreign aid donors and international and domestic NGOs. In the 1991 election, Begum Khalida Zia's victorious BNP-led multiparty coalition elected her Prime Minister. At Rio, Bangladesh articulated the needs of Third World nations for sustainable development and the responsibility of rich nations to compensate for their decades of air pollution. Yet, South Asia's natural resources have suffered from pressures that would intensify into the twenty-first century, as the next chapter considers.

11   India, Pakistan, and Bangladesh into the Twenty-First Century

Over the last quarter century, human effects on the world's environment, as well as governmental, popular, and scientific awareness and understanding of those effects, have been accelerating significantly. Yet, policies and funding for mitigation remain sources of disagreement. India, Pakistan, and Bangladesh stand at the center of many of these developments and disputes. Governments, NGOs, the UN, and other bodies have advocated treaties, conventions, and policies to address the causes and consequences of environmental degradations. Since 1988, the experts of the Intergovernmental Panel on Climate Change have been assembling and assessing the latest information and issuing periodic reports. Some commentators point to vital problems of widely unsustainable resource exploitation producing unhealthy levels of air, land, and other pollution, absolute shortages of clean drinking and irrigation water, and shrinking animal habitats; all these they attribute to rapidly rising human populations and consumption (see Figure 11.1). Other commentators highlight the inequitable distribution and inefficient use of the earth's resources, internationally and within nations, as the real challenges facing humanity. The growing extent and complexity of all this, and the uncertain outcomes of the range of past and current human actions, mean that this chapter (even more than earlier ones) must be selective and suggestive in its approach.

India, Late Twentieth into the Twenty-First Century

Since the late twentieth century, pressures on India's natural resources have intensified along with conflicts over unequal access to them. The nation's human population of 1.3 billion is growing and will soon exceed China's. The levels of per-capita human resource consumption and degradation have risen as well, both from the aspirations of elite and expanding middle classes and the survival needs of the 150 million Indians living without adequate nutrition. Changes in the globe's climate

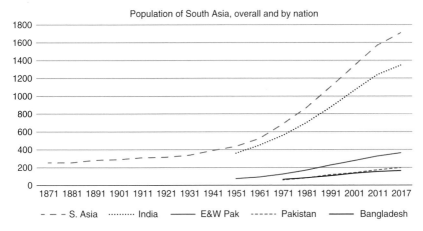

Figure 11.1 Population in South Asia, overall and by nation

are increasingly affecting India, which is particularly vulnerable (like Pakistan and Bangladesh). Many fauna and flora species are facing extinction and the distribution of surviving species is shifting. Even as government laws and policies and elite and popular movements seek to shape the environment, the full consequences for ecosystems of all these factors are only partially understood.

Simultaneously, India has been emerging as a rising global economy, political force, and nuclear-armed power, with consequent growing environmental impacts on the world. Over this period, the nation haltingly shifted away from Jawaharlal Nehru's foundational socialist and secularist policies. Instead, India has increasingly engaged with the capitalist-centered world economy and Hindu nationalism has unevenly risen. Some central and provincial government policies are advancing environmental protections, but others are accelerating its deterioration.

In June 1991, newly elected Congress Party Prime Minister Narasimha Rao faced shrinking foreign currency reserves and massive international debts. These forced his regime to accept liberalization of the economy, with partial opening to multinational corporations. Many leading Indian economists, most prominently Finance Minister Dr. Manmohan Singh (1932–), already advocated structural reform that would end the constraining license and quota production system and the import-substitution model that dated from Nehru's administration. These new policies were incorporated in the Eighth Five-Year Plan (1992–96), which also had the explicit provision that all development projects must incorporate environmental protections.

Indeed, India's growing international and national commitments to environmental protections resulted in a series of measures that accorded with the Rio Convention and its Agenda 21. Rao's government's Policy Statement for Abatement of Pollution (1992) had the guiding principles of: preventing pollution at its source, using the best available technology, the polluter pays for all damage, and disseminating education and information for the public to encourage its participation in decision-making. Similarly, the National Conservation Strategy and Policy Statement on Environment and Development (1992) called for sustainable development "in unison with the environmental perspective." Parliament also passed the 73rd Constitutional Amendment that devolved some authority and budgets to village, block, and district level panchayats (elected councils) with responsibility for natural resource management. (Later, the 1996 Panchayat (Extension to Scheduled Areas) Act officially gave forest-dwelling village councils more authority over the lands and natural resources around them.) These accorded with the international trend for incorporating local stakeholders.

Similarly, with World Bank and other international funding and guidance, in 1992 Rao's administration also initiated a pilot program using the "integrated conservation and development project" approach of eco-development in national parks and sanctuaries. In practice, however, these programs often meant relocating forest-dwellers while only promising alternative "green" sources of income. Indeed, the World Bank revoked funding for the Simlipal Tiger Reserve and National Park in Odisha for poor treatment of the displaced (although now classed as a UNESCO biosphere, Simlipal still has about 10,000 forest-dwellers within it). Overall, while involvement of local communities in sustainable development has made some progress, administrative deficiencies and the external pressures of commerce and politics have continued.

Engaging with other international movements, in 1994 Rao's administration ratified the Convention on Biodiversity, the UN Framework Convention on Climate Change, and established the Ministry of New and Renewable Energy to advance alternative sources of much needed electricity. Indeed, India's domestic manufacture of solar panels and wind turbines has increased, which is a long-term investment strategy of Rao's and subsequent administrations. Renewables are still small but growing sources of India's energy needs that promise to slow India's increasing use of expensively imported petroleum and natural gas and highly polluting but domestically abundant soft lignite coal.

Simultaneously, India's Supreme and provincial High Courts have continued to issue sweeping and very specific directives about the environment. Even before the Rio Declaration, the Supreme Court had begun to apply the anticipatory precautionary and the polluter pays principles. Further, courts also began to incorporate the internationally emerging (but controversial) concept of "carrying capacity": the scientifically calculated amount of pollution an ecosystem could assimilate considering all pollution sources, not just the single proposed project's input, and still remain within official pollution limits. This both sought to cap pollution amounts at a site but also permitted increases up to that cap.

Court orders cut through barriers to administrative action, but often had unanticipated consequences. In 1996, for instance, the Supreme Court responded to PIL about deforestation by suspending all tree felling in all forests in many provinces (except when part of a Union government Forest Working Plan) and halting all wood-based industrial activity. While officially reducing the deforestation rate, this sweeping order had considerable untoward economic and social costs to legal businesses and local users, while black-market timber felling and processing continued.

Similarly, responding to a suit by the WWF for enforcement of the Wildlife Act to protect endangered species, in 1997 the Supreme Court ruled that forest departments must either expel all the approximately 3–4 million forest-dwellers in India's more than 600 protected areas, or else legally "settle" their resource rights. Such a sudden vast expulsion would be impractical and highly disruptive, so implementation stagnated. (This conflict continued until partially mitigated by the 2006 Scheduled Tribes and Other Traditional Forest Dwellers [Recognition of Forest Rights] Act, implemented in 2008, which limited such expulsions.)

Likewise, in response to New Delhi's visibly unhealthy vehicular air pollution, the Court directed the government to constitute an Environment Pollution (Prevention and Control) Authority for the National Capital Region. In 1998, the Court ordered the banning there of all busses, taxicabs, and motor-rikshaws unless powered by compressed natural gas. The Court thereby unilaterally selected the sole permitted fuel, one whose distribution system was not yet in place. Nonetheless, this order slowed the rise in Delhi's toxic air pollution.

Such detailed directives show both the power of the Court's leadership in implementing vital environmental measures but also the ad hoc nature of such judicial activism. To assist the judiciary in the rapidly growing number of environmental cases, the government created the National Environmental Tribunal (1995) and the National Environmental Appellate Authority (1997). These bodies were part-judicial, part-technical appointed panels empowered to considered civil cases about hazardous chemicals using the polluter pays principle of liability for all damage.

The end of Rao's regime in 1996 began nearly two decades of political instability at the center. Opening the economy to international competition benefitted some Indian corporations, but this and tentative dismantling of state-owned industries also meant many voters felt economically insecure. Neither the center-left Congress nor the center-right Bharatiya Janata Party (BJP) proved able to win a parliamentary majority, instead alternately patching together coalitions to govern. Since regionally based parties held the parliamentary balance, the resulting regimes lacked uniform platforms on many issues, including the environment. Each party in each coalition negotiated for cabinet ministries with the most patronage for its leaders, regardless of the minister's competence; protection of the environment often proved uninteresting to powerful politicians.

Over these decades, however, electoral support for the BJP's platform of Hindu nationalism rose unevenly. The BJP's populist campaigns against the Congress combined attacks on its entrenched corruption and its supposed privileging of Muslims (based on Nehruvian secularism). After the May 1996 election, the BJP's A. B. Vajpayee (1924–) advanced his claim to be prime minister, but, after just thirteen days in office, failed to gain a parliamentary majority. Instead, a weak "United Front" governed as minority, with the BJP and Congress providing just enough votes from the outside to prevent its collapse. This flimsy administration lasted only two years, first under Prime Minister H. D. Deve Gowda (1933–, r. 1996–97) and then, when he fell to factionalism, under Prime Minister I. K. Gujral (1919–2012, r. 1997–98).

Gujral had an interest in international politics about the environment, having attended the 1972 Stockholm conference. In international meetings on climate change, India argued that the flow of greenhouse gases (GHG) that developing countries emitted must be permitted to rise to the level of developed nations, which had historically created almost all the current stock of atmospheric pollution. The Kyoto Protocol (1997, ratified by India in 2002) reflected this argument.

After the March 1998 election, the BJP-led National Democratic Alliance in Parliament elected Prime Minister Vajpayee. While Vajpayee's government largely continued India's engagement with the global economy and environmental movements, it also asserted Indian nationalism. In May, his regime exploded five nuclear weapons at a test site only 230 km (143 mi) from the Pakistan border; Pakistan responded with its own nuclear weapon tests. However, after just thirteen months, Vajpayee's coalition shattered. Nonetheless, as caretaker prime minister, Vajpayee ordered the costly repulse of Pakistan's military incursion into

Indian-held Kashmir at Kargil (May–July 1999). Neither side fired its nuclear weapons and this brief, localized war ended with Pakistan's embarrassing forced withdrawal. This strengthened the BJP's nationalist reputation; in the October 1999 election, Vajpayee led a reconstituted coalition back into office, which it retained for the full five-year term (until 2004).

This regime survived various environmental and political challenges. There were successive drought years (1998–2001). In January 2001, a massive 7.7 magnitude earthquake shocked western Gujarat, killing up to 20,000 people. The December 13, 2001 attack by Pakistan-based Islamist terrorists on India's Parliament nearly provoked another war.

Another international issue concerned knowledge about and owner-ship of biomes, including newly created transgenic ones. Seed banks, for instance, collect from around the world and preserve these for future use, preventing species extinction. However, multinational corporations (mostly in the West and Japan) have been "bioprospecting": taking dis-tinctive plant species and other natural products from lesser developed countries and analyzing their medical and other valuable properties for commercial gain. The US Patent and Trademark Office, European Patent Office, and International Patent Classification systems grant exclusive rights of intellectual ownership about the processing and use of natural and synthesized substances. Some controversial patents (e.g. medical uses of turmeric and neem) seem to some commentators to be "biopiracy": stealing traditional knowledge from indigenous people by outsiders for profit (Shiva 1997). Legally, under the WTO and Trade-Related Aspects of Intellectual Property Rights, patent holders can pro-hibit or charge even traditional users. In response, the Indian government in 2001 initiated the Traditional Knowledge Digital Library into which researchers codified all possible written evidence of Indian medical "prior art." The People's Biodiversity Register similarly collects from oral tradi-tions. These online databases provide legal evidence of Indian national "ownership," precluding patents by others (including Indian citizens). They also make accessible for commercial use the richness of Indian knowledge, controlled by nondisclosure agreements and licensing fees. These goals were also included in India's Biological Diversity Act (2002) and Action Plan (2003).

As a related issue, multinational corporations are creating geneti-cally modified (GM) plants, which they license to users. Advocates claim increases in productivity and pest-resistance, and thus decreased pesticide use. Many opponents of GM decry the consequences – moral, biological, and economic. Despite protests, after six years of field-testing, in 2002 the BJP government approved commercial cultivation of transgenic Bt (*Bacillus thuringiensis*)-cotton in six provinces, licensed from the Indian-owned Maharashtra Hybrid Seeds Company (Mahyco) and the US-based multinational Monsanto. But unregulated Bt-cotton was already being spread by Indian seed companies and farmers. By 2004, varieties of Bt-cotton were legally sold widely. In 2009, the government gave provisional approval to Mahyco to sell Bt-brinjal (eggplant/aubergine) seeds, but public protests caused suspension of that approval in 2010. Evidently, GM food is more controversial than cotton. (However, commercial release of Bt-brinjal was approved by Bangladesh in 2013 and Indian farmers have been gaining unregulated access.)

The Supreme Court, followed by provincial High Courts, continued to accept a broadening range of cases relating to the environment. By 2000, some courts were reserving part of the week exclusively for environmental issues: panels of judges sitting as "Forest Benches" or "Green Benches." However, courts still had overwhelmingly busy schedules (in 2006, for example, the Supreme Court already had 40,000 pending cases of all types while Indian courts in total had about 25 million). In 2002, the Supreme Court established the Central Empowered Committee (composed of government officials and NGO representatives) to oversee implementation of its environment-related orders and, from 2010, the National Green Tribunal to hear and rule on environmental cases.

Vajpayee's regime also advanced many liberalizing economic policies. For instance, inadequate electrical generation and inefficiencies and deficits by provincial electricity corporations have been both severely constraining India's industrialization and frustrating rural and urban households. The Electricity Act (2003) tried to increase the nation's power supply through allowing more private, de-licensed generation investment including by renewable projects, commercial competition, and interprovincial power-trading. However, once again, India's strong provincial authority and implementation problems meant considerable inefficiencies and variety of practices.

Factionalism within the BJP-led coalition led in 2004 to the election of the Congress-led United Progressive Alliance [UPA]. Real power within the Congress was, however, with Sonia Gandhi (1946–), the Italian-born widow of assassinated Rajiv. Declining the premiership, she instead selected economist Manmohan Singh as prime minister.

During this ten-year administration, liberalization continued along with many environmental-related acts and policies in the face of political and environmental challenges. Regionally based parties limited the UPA's coherence. The Pacific Tsunami that devastated much of India's southeast coast (2004) and Mumbai's unprecedented flash-flooding (2005) made clear the pressing need for coordinated national, state, and local-level disaster planning and damage remediation. The National Disaster Management Authority (2005) became the apex policy-making body for all types of disasters (excluding droughts). This authority provides guidelines for its counterpart in each province. The Eleventh Five-Year Plan (2007–2012) included disaster preparation, not just response. Yet, the 2008 floods from the Kosi River as it entered India from Nepal, the 2013 floods in Uttarakhand that killed up to 30,000 people and destroyed ten big and nineteen small hydropower projects, and the widespread 2017 monsoon flooding, among other human-exacerbated natural disasters, showed the limits of such government policies.

Singh's regime issued India's National Environment Policy (2006), which comprehensively addressed a range of issues. It combined the goals of sustainable and equitable development using EIAs for inland and coastal projects as well as plans to reduce the hazards of climate change. The National Action Plan on Climate Change (2008) and India's position at the UN climate summit at Copenhagen (2009), reflected the government's revised position that India could not continue on the path of unfettered economic growth, ignoring environmental concerns. Rather it should use climate change mitigation as a source for green development. As part of the National Action Plan on Climate Change, the Green India Mission promises substantial carbon sequestration (50–60 million tonnes [55–66 US tons] of CO_2 equivalent annually by 2020) through afforestation and improved forest and tree quality. The Twelfth Five-Year Plan (2012–17) also pushed for rapid but also inclusive, sustainable, low-carbon growth. Corporations legally must invest in social responsibility programs (from 2013). In some instances, local and national protests prevented environmental degradation and displacement of forest-dwellers, and also respect for their religious beliefs (for example, the suspension in 2010 of the bauxite mining licenses granted to British-based, Indian-owned Vedanta Resources at a forest-dweller's sacred mountain in a Reserved Forest in Odisha).

After a decade, however, accumulated public frustrations with the Singh administration and appeals to Indian (especially Hindu) nationalism led in 2014 to a massive BJP electoral victory under Prime Minister Narendra Modi (1950–). As long-time chief minister of Gujarat, Modi had developed reputations for achieving economic progress but also for anti-Muslim rhetoric and actions (particularly leading to and after the 2002 riots that killed thousands of Gujarati Muslims). For the first time in thirty years, a single party held a Parliamentary majority, giving Modi scope to impose his policies.

Modi's Prime Minister's Office has taken over from the Planning Commission and has launched array of programs. For instance, the Swachh Bharat Abhiyan (Clean India Movement) promises to improve public health, especially though eliminating open defecation by subsidizing the construction of 12 million home or public toilets. However, these toilets mostly discharge into pits, not sewers, so the disposal of dry carriage human waste remains a continuing source of social stigma and disease for the hundreds of thousands of people who clean these toilets, buckets, and pits by hand (Bhasha Singh 2014). Simultaneously, his government has loosened environmental protections to encourage industrial development and foreign investment. Some limits on GM crops have been lifted. While Modi added "Climate Change" to the responsibilities of the Minister of Environment and Forests, its budget was slashed. Articulating Modi's vision for India's energy and environmental future is its Intended Nationally Determined Contribution to climate change declaration (see Chapter 12).

Pakistan, Late Twentieth into the Twenty-First Century

As international and national challenges have risen for Pakistan's people and environment, its government has gone through three phases, thus continuing patterns that have persisted since independence. Over the last decade of the twentieth century, the series of relatively weak civilian administrations issued environmental laws and policies but simultaneously encouraged economic development unbound by them. Then, a military dictator took over, bringing a period of political stability amidst rising domestic and international pressures, many of them environmentally based. Since 2008, Pakistan has again had frail civilian regimes, while environmental pressures have intensified.

After the Army and Supreme Court brokered the ouster of Prime Minister Nawaz Sharif and President Gulam Ishaq Khan, parliamentary elections were held in October 1993. For the second time, Benazir Bhutto's PPP won. Nonetheless, her regime remained insecure and divided between proclaiming environment protections and encouraging unchecked economic development. She continued to engage Pakistan in prominent international environmental treaties, ratifying in 1994 the UN Convention on Biological Diversity and the UN Framework Convention on Climate Change. She also created a Cabinet Committee on Climate Change.

Yet, she simultaneously sought to reinvigorate Pakistan's sagging economy by continuing liberalization, including encouraging foreign investment that overrode environmental restrictions. Her 1994 Independent

Power Policy, for example, promised investors exemptions from EIAs and other checks on their construction, use of any type of fuel and technology, and choice of site. Several international for-profit companies negotiated lucrative guarantees and high electric prices, and constructed oil- or coal-fired plants. Benazir herself performed the groundbreaking ceremony for the Chinese Dongfang Electric Company–built Lakhra Coal-Fired Thermal Power Station in Sindh for which no EIA had been conducted. Journalists (especially Pakistan's investigative English-language media) raised public outcry against this and several other potentially polluting power projects. But Pakistan badly needed increased electrical generation, so many projects got "No Objection Certificates" from understaffed provincial environmental protection agencies.

Both the Supreme and provincial High Courts, however, were asserting more active roles in punishing environmental pollution of air, noise, land, or water (as the Indian Supreme Court had been doing for a decade). For instance, in 1992, the Supreme Court ordered the Karachi municipal government to repair leaking drinking-water pipes being contaminated by nearby open storm drains being used for sewage disposal. The Supreme Court's most cited precedent concerning the environment came in *Shehla Zia* v. *Water and Power Development Authority* (SC 693 of 1994) when it ruled that

The word 'life' has not been defined in the Constitution but it does not mean nor can be restricted only to the vegetative or animal life or mere existence from conception to death. Life includes all such amenities and facilities which a person born in a free country is entitled to enjoy with dignity, legally and constitutionally. A person is entitled to protection of law from being exposed to hazards . . . [in this case electromagnetic fields emanating from a high-voltage grid station in a residential neighborhood].

The Court also supported the precautionary principle but did not require conservation or ecologically beneficial use of natural resources.

Leading international and domestic NGO's also advanced environmental causes. For instance, the Agha Khan Foundation established environmental resource centers (1993) while Leadership for Environment and Development [LEAD] Pakistan (supported by Rockefeller Foundation) registered in 1995 to train professionals and managers about sustainable development. In 1996, the Federation of Pakistan Chambers of Commerce and Industry and the Netherlands Government co-launched the Environmental Technology Program for Industry to promote ecological and environmentally friendly technologies and products. Subsequently, several Chambers of Commerce of the Industries created Standing Committees on the Environment.

Meanwhile, Benazir Bhutto's capacity to sustain political support weakened further. Renewed accusations of corruption, particularly against her husband, Asaf Ali Zardari, heightened tensions. She had appointed him chairman of Pakistan's new Environmental Protection Council, among other positions. In November 1996, the president she had selected, Farooq Leghari (1940–2010, r. 1993–97), used the Constitution's 8th Amendment to dismiss her government; Zardari was tried and imprisoned for murder and corruption.

In the subsequent election (February 1997), Nawaz Sharif and his PML-led coalition won a large majority of seats in the National Assembly, enabling him to consolidate power. To prevent yet another presidential dismissal, his government rapidly repealed the 8th Amendment. Further, his followers intimidated Supreme Court judges, necessitating their protection by the Army. Hence, each branch of the state continued to vie for power over the nation's resources.

Sharif's government in 1997 passed the umbrella Pakistan Environmental Protection Act, superseding and expanding President Zia's 1983 Ordinance. This Act defined "environment" to include: "all land, air, and water, all living things, all ecosystem and ecological relationships, socio-economic conditions, and all kinds of pollution, including chemical, biological, thermal, radiological, noise, and aesthetic." It required the Union and provincial administrations to implement the many international treaties and protocols that Pakistan had ratified over the decades. The Pakistan Environmental Protection Council was empowered to establish National Environmental Quality Standards and grew to include more provincial government, industry, and NGO representatives. Aggrieved citizens could file complaints about pollution damage to newly authorized Environmental Tribunals for serious violations or to Environmental Magistrates for lesser offenses.

While this 1997 Act remained the basis for subsequent environmental regulation, it had severe limitations. For instance, the Act did not fully incorporate the polluter-pays principle, which was part of Rio's Agenda 21 that Pakistan had accepted five years earlier. Few tribunals were established, and those were usually part-time. Many of the Act's provisions remained unimplemented, with insufficient government funding, weak administrative expertise, and unclear standards. It concentrated on reducing pollution from new industrial construction, since nonindustrial and ongoing activities would not initiate an EIA. In the face of political pressures from developers and industrialists, even these EIAs often came after construction had begun, with limited public participation, mitigation provisions, or monitoring of compliance. For instance, multinational

Shell Oil's Pakistan subsidiary conducted an EIA even as it explored for oil and natural gas within the Kirthar National Park in Sindh.

In addition to this Union Act, various provinces established their own policies, including authorizing participatory resource user groups and elected village management committees for forests (NWFP) and water (Punjab and Sindh) with stated goals of increased participation by women and other customarily unrepresented sectors. These policies, however, also met with mixed results due to lack of local involvement, continued control by professional foresters and canal officials, and the political and economic power of vested interests. Nonetheless, in some instances, village bodies have challenged such outside pressures.

Adding to the stresses on Pakistan's environment and economy were international ambitions, particularly matching much larger India. After India tested its nuclear weapons (May 1998), Pakistan soon did the same. International condemnation and aid sanctions followed, hurting Pakistan's smaller and more internationally dependent economy more than India's. This came at a time of successive drought years (1998–2001).

Pakistan's military incursion at Kargil on the Line of Control in Kashmir and its embarrassing forced withdrawal (July 1999) divided Sharif from the army chief he had selected, General Pervez Musharraf (1943–). In October, Sharif suddenly ordered Musharraf dismissed and replaced, refusing to allow his airborne plane to land on Pakistani soil. Safely on the ground, Musharraf suspended the Constitution, arrested Sharif for air-hijacking, kidnapping, and terrorism, but then permitted his exile and withdrawal from politics. Thus, Pakistan began the twenty-first century yet again under military rule, as it had been for well over half its existence.

Musharraf immediately proclaimed his determination to order and modernize Pakistan, taking the businesslike title "Chief Executive." He declared (October 17, 1999):

We are not a poor nation as generally perceived. In fact we are rich. We have fertile land that can produce three crops a year. We have abundant water to irrigate these lands and generate surplus power. We have gas, coal and vast untapped mineral resources – and above all a dynamic and industrious people. All these await mobilization.

He also announced his seven-point program for progress.

His *Khushhal* [Welfare] Pakistan Program intended comprehensive public-sector development, creating employment through microcredit and infrastructure construction and improvement. This included building roads and water supply and sewer systems, and desilting canals and lining them against seepage. Local communities would propose and carry out projects, making them stakeholders. After three years, this entire program was to be devolved to provincial control. Evoking the Islamic principle of *zakat* ("charity"), he created a rehabilitation and vocational training program for *Mustahiqeen* ("deserving people," using morality- and means-test bases). Further, he promised to distribute a million hectares (2.4 million acres) to landless agricultural laborers.

In June 2001, Musharraf declared himself president (while remaining army chief). His position internationally was greatly strengthened following the September 11, 2001, al-Qaeda terrorist attacks in the United States. Much Western criticism of his military dictatorship ceased when he made Pakistan the frontline state against the Afghan Taliban, largely sponsored by Pakistan's ISI. His official policy reversal then brought to Pakistan massive US military and non-military aid (which had been suspended in 1998 because Pakistan's nuclear weapons tests, conducted under him as army chief).

Musharraf's ambitious agenda produced an array of programs and plans. He sought to stimulate industry by ending the decade-long official ban on all commercial timber harvesting (which had been widely evaded anyway). He also took over as chair of the Pakistan Environment Protection Council; his new National Forest Policy (1999, revised draft 2001) promised JFM, social forestry, and sustainable development (echoed in provincial forest policies, e.g. NWFP in 2001). Nonetheless, the government continued to stress punishment for violations rather than incentives for compliance or reforestation. This promise of community participation was extended to other damaged ecosystems through Pakistan's National Environmental Action Plan (2001) and Perspective Plan (2001–11), with some of the same problems about implementation. Also in 2001, Musharraf's regime issued new National Environmental Quality Standards Rules, Sustainable Development Fund Rules, and Pollution Charge for Industry Rules, among others. His government's other programs and actions plans addressed other environmental topics, including Biodiversity (2000), Desertification (2002), Water (2002), Energy Security (2005), Sanitation (2006), Renewable Energy (2006), Disaster Management (2006), Hazardous Waste (2007), and Wetlands (2007). Curricula about the environment and environmental law continued modestly to expand in both M.Sc. and law programs.

In 2005, his regime's new National Environmental Policy provided broad guidelines that intended comprehensively to coordinate and advance the work of government agencies, civil society, the private sector, and all other stakeholders for conserving, protecting, and improving all aspects of Pakistan's environment. Musharraf recommenced the long-disrupted Five-Year Planning process. Further, his

government participated in ongoing international conferences, protocols, and treaties about the environment, including acceding to the
Kyoto Protocol (2005).

The actual implementation of all his regime's directives, action plans,
programs, and policies, however, remained challenging. He ordered
a renewal of the hitherto largely ineffective EIA processes. However,
this fostered the "business" of for-profit consulting companies that maneuvered projects through EIA screening. His target of enhancing protected areas to 12 percent of the country has officially been achieved, with
over 350 protected areas, including about 30 national parks (most provincially managed, but some privately). Yet, well over half these protected
areas are provincial, local, or private game reserves. Even among the
national parks, only few have effective (or any) management plans or
means of enforcement.

Seeking to legitimate his regime in Pakistan's and the world's eyes,
in June 2002 Musharraf had staged a carefully worded referendum on his
presidency (officially 98 percent of voters supported him). He restored
the Constitution (much modified by his Legal Framework Order) and
followed this in October with a parliamentary election in which his
favored PML(Q) party and its allies formed the government. However,
a major terrorist attack on India's Parliament in December 2002 and
renewed militancy in Kashmir (both widely seen as having Pakistani
backing) made India and other governments question Musharraf's
motives, or else his control over his military.

There were also other limits to Musharraf's power and his administration's effectiveness. From 1998–2002, repeated severe droughts (especially in Sindh and Balochistan) reduced agricultural production and
increased rural poverty. In 2003, the Greek tanker *Tasman Spirit* wrecked
and spilled oil over 14 km (8.7 mi) of the Karachi coast, with impact over
2,000 km^2 (775 mi^2) of seabed. The massive October 2005 earthquake in
Azad Kashmir revealed the government's unpreparedness.

Further, popular protests proved able to block some of Musharraf's
major projects. In December 2005, he ordered construction of the long-
delayed Kalabagh Dam on the Indus in NWFP. This immense dam
promised to deliver 2,000MW of electricity, flood control, and irrigation,
mostly benefiting Punjab. However, powerful resistance arose among
communities in the NWFP, who would be displaced by the vast reservoir
and feared waterlogging and salinization, and in Sindh, who anticipated
reduced Indus irrigation water and seawater penetration even further
upriver. Eventually, Musharraf had to abandon construction of this dam.

In impoverished Balochistan, the project to develop a deep-water port
at Gwadar on the strategic Arabian Sea (on the land ceded to Pakistan

from Oman in 1958) advanced with Chinese financing and technicians. Yet, this sparked often violent opposition by Baloch nationalists who saw few gains and further intrusion by outsiders. Similarly, natural gas extraction inland provoked other Baloch into armed insurrection. Meanwhile, Pakistan-based Taliban compounded disruption of society and the economy. Hence, government programs for development, public health (like polio inoculation), and environmental protections broadly faltered in several regions.

Simultaneously, Pakistan's judiciary continued to assert its authority over a range of environmental and other issues. The Supreme and provincial High Courts appointed commissions and ordered various Union and provincial government agencies to enforce their directives. These court interventions were based on PIL, national and provincial laws, Pakistan's international treaty obligations, and the personal interests of judges.

But in March 2007, Musharraf sought to curb an increasingly assertive Supreme Court by suspending Chief Justice I. M. Chaudhury (1948–) and promoting more compliant judges. Mass protests by lawyers, his legally questionable reelection as President by the legislature, and the return from exile of Benazir Bhutto all further threatened Musharraf's position. In November 2007, he declared a national state of emergency, suspending the Constitution and sixty judges (two-thirds of the upper judiciary). Benazir's assassination in December, court-forced restoration of the Constitution, reappointment of the fired judges, the return from exile of Nawaz Sharif, and losses by Musharraf's supporters in the February 2008 elections, followed by a legislative coalition between Nawaz Sharif and Asaf Ali Zardari (widower heir to the PPP), all eventually combined to compel Musharraf's resignation in August and then exile.

Zardari's presidency (2008–13) survived its full term but remained weak in the face of shallow public and legislative support and challenges from a range of forces. Reflecting his regime's incapacity to control Pakistani-based Islamist terrorists, some attacked India's Mumbai (November 26–29, 2008), murdering over 160 and wounding hundreds. India's restrained response avoided yet another threatening war. Meanwhile, petroleum and food prices rose in 2008, followed by the global financial recession, which shocked Pakistan's internationalized economy, reducing GDP growth to 1.7 percent (2008–09). In summer 2010, rainfall of 3.4 m (11.2 ft) in 72 hours across the north caused massive Indus floods inundating a fifth of the country, displacing 20 million people, killing some 1.6 million livestock, and ruining much of the standing crop. Powerful cyclones and other major floods followed.

Zardari's government's inadequate response highlighted its ineffectiveness, in contrast with relief efforts by the Army and Islamist charities. Violating Pakistani sovereignty were the US assassination of Osama bin-Laden (May 2011) and the many US drone strikes (despite official Pakistani denial of permission for them), which revealed both the complicity of competing elements in the Army and the lack of central government control. The Supreme Court under restored Chief Justice Chaudhury in 2012 dismissed Prime Minister Gillani (1952–) for not resuming the investigation into Zardari's corruption.

Zardari's fading regime relinquished much authority to provincial governments, increasing their share of the national income and control over their natural resources. Subnationalist demands from Pakhtuns forced renaming of their province as Khyber Pakhtunkhwa (2010). In April 2010, his regime passed the 18th Constitutional Amendment, weakening the power of the president in favor of the prime minister, and abolishing the "concurrent list," thus devolving "environment and ecology" (among many other subjects) to the provinces. This increased regional responsibility for resource management and protection and brought decision-making closer to local stakeholders. However, without a Union Ministry of Environment, nationwide coordination and policies weakened. The Pakistan Environmental Protection Agency's jurisdiction became limited to international treaties and federally administered territories, like the national capital and the Exclusive Economic Zone between the 19 km (12 mi) coastal provincial limit and the 322 km (200 mi) national limit. Further, many provincial agencies lacked sufficient administrators trained and experienced in environmental assessment, monitoring, and enforcement. For instance, in 2012, Punjab had only four administrators reviewing projects even part time, and the approval rate of EIAs was over 99 percent (Fischer 2014). The National Power Policy (2013) includes developing coal-fired thermal power plants using massive (estimated 175-billion-tonne reserve) coalfields in the Thar Desert, Sindh, to shift coal-fired electricity production from its current 1 percent to 40 percent in the near future.

Simultaneously, Pakistan opened to over $62 billion of Chinese investment as the China-Pakistan Economic Corridor across the middle of Pakistan into western China. This vast project envisions further development of Gwadar port and China-Pakistan collaboration in many military, communications, and energy projects (see Map 11.1). The full environmental impacts of all these projects remain uncertain.

Nawaz Sharif returned as Prime Minister for the third time (June 2013) with a parliamentary majority for his PML-Nawaz party. Zardari's term as president ended in September. For the first time in Pakistan's history,

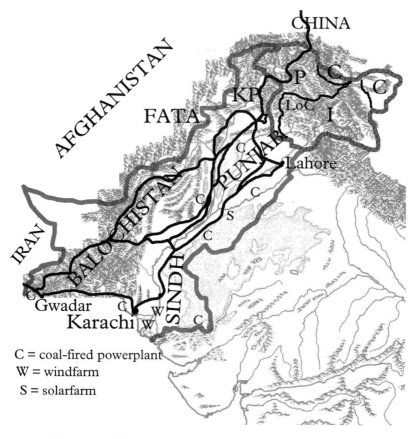

Map 11.1 China–Pakistan Economic Corridor: New highways and energy plants

one elected regime completed its full term and gave way (generally peace-fully) to another.

The Ministry of Climate Change, having been recreated in 2012, demoted in 2013, was restored in 2015 (but occasionally left without a minister). Ministry staff began revising existing policies and programs, including the National Forest Policy and Green Pakistan Programme of tree plantations, but these only provided guidelines, since forests are a provincial subject. Sharif's Pakistan 2025 (2014) plan optimistically proposed a somewhat broad roadmap for the nation. Showing instability in environmental policy-making, however, Pakistan delayed submitting for the Paris conference its "Intended Nationally Determined Contributions" (see Chapter 12).

While Pakistan's economy picked up with the help of massive IMF loans, Sharif's regime struggled to retain control. Extensive flooding continued annually, and Karachi suffered a record heat wave (2015) that killed over 1,200 people. Although the Army officially stayed out of politics, it exerted considerable control. Violent Islamist movements, particularly in the forested northwest, and Baloch nationalist movements both challenged government authority at all levels. Then, in July 2017, the Supreme Court ordered Sharif to resign and leave politics for corruption (the third time he had been dismissed as prime minister). A transitional prime minister, Shahid Abbasi (1958–, r. 2017–18), supervised the 2018 election, held while Sharif was imprisoned. The Pakistan Tehreek-e Insaf party of Imran Khan (1952–) won a National Assembly plurality and has promised corruption-free expansion in power production. But this new and largely untested coalition government will need to formulate comprehensive policies that protect Pakistan's overburdened environment.

Bangladesh, Late Twentieth into the Twenty-First Century

Over the last twenty-five years, Bangladesh has developed economically, is improving the conditions of its people, and put in place some environmental legislation and policy formation. Building on Acting President Ahmed's transitional government (1990–91), Prime Minister Begum Khalida Zia's BNP-led coalition government (1991–96) ratified Rio's Convention on Biological Diversity (1994). Her National Environment Policy (1992), Environment Conservation Act (1995, amended 2000, 2002, 2010), and National Environment Management Action Plan (1995–2005) used broad definitions of the environment and of the role of government agencies in controlling it. Her government also addressed specific sectors of the environment where there were major problems.

Yet, much of this attention on protecting aspects of the environment has been due to pressure from international donors, domestic NGOs, and the courts. For instance, guided by the ADB and the UNDP, Bangladesh's twenty-year Forestry Master Plan (1993) and the National Forest Policy (1994) officially moved away from encouraging commercial industrial supply and instead called for long-term collaborative community, private, and governmental reforestation. These reflected international trends and followed India's lead toward social forestry and co-management (JFM) – although in practice, many Bangladeshi forest-dwellers lost their customary access to forest products. The stated Plan and Policy goals were raising forest cover to 20 percent of the nation, 10 percent of national forests made protected areas, and the designation of additional national parks and wildlife sanctuaries, especially enhancing ecotourism. These sought to curb the extensive illegal logging in both the Chittagong Hill Tracts and the Sundarbans, including in Reserved Forests, despite the established moratorium on the industrial and commercial harvest of timber from all forests. However, the quality of reforestation has suffered from the selection of commercially valuable but locally unsuitable species and underfunding of site preparation and postplanting maintenance and protection. Nor has development of wildlife sanctuaries been all environmental advocates expected in terms of total area or contiguous habitats.

The Green Revolution came later in Bangladesh than in India and Pakistan. International and Bangladeshi agricultural scientists had to develop special varieties of high-yield hybrid rice that flourished in its distinctive ecology of wide water-level fluctuation. Political instability also limited programs for seed, fertilizer, pesticide, and small-scale irrigation equipment distribution. But during the 1990s, these programs spread more rapidly, along with importation of diesel pump and tubewell sets for the dry winter season crop in the north and northwest. While yields rose significantly, however, so have problems of soil exhaustion, salinization, and dropping freshwater aquifers experienced elsewhere. Nonetheless, saline-tolerant hybrid rice (BR40 and BR41) extended production further downriver in coastal areas.

As the end of Begum Khalida Zia's parliamentary term approached, the opposition increasingly organized street protests, particularly in Dhaka, the capital and largest city. Her government held an election in February 1996 that the opposition boycotted. This forced another election in June supervised by a neutral caretaker government, which Begum Hasina's Awami League won.

Begum Hasina's administration moved forward in several key environmental issues. Better relations with India enabled her to negotiate improved water-sharing agreements, in particular a thirty-year treaty about India's long-disputed Farakka Barrage (built 1961–75). This weir is just 16 km (10 mi) upstream from the border, diverting Ganges water away from Bangladesh and down the Hooghly River toward Kolkata. But this water-sharing agreement had provisions only about the quantity, not the quality (in terms of pollution and salinity), of the water India releases into Bangladesh.

Various disasters brought the need for environmental protections to the fore, albeit often briefly. For example, the US-based Occidental corporation obtained permission to explore for natural gas at Magurchara (near

Sylhet) in June 1997, but its test-well exploded and the consequent fire spread through the Lawachara National Park for two weeks (two further blowouts nearby at Canadian Niko corporation wells occurred in June 2005). Nonetheless, in the name of national energy needs, international exploration of gas fields and power plant construction has continued to be permitted, even in environmentally vital and fragile areas like the Sundarbans.

In 1997, Begum Hasina's government concluded the Chittagong Hill Tract Peace Accord. This recognized some landownership rights and local governance for these forest-dwelling groups and devolved some authority to a new Hill District Council. While the pressures of immigration by Bangla-speaking farmers and commercial and agricultural deforestation continued, this accord reduced (but did not end) resentment and violence there. Similarly, the UNDP-guided Sustainable Environment Management Project (1997) had various governmental and civil society bodies create policies for community-based participatory ecosystem management.

Begum Hasina's 1997 Environmental Conservation Rules required all existing, as well as proposed, industrial projects to obtain from the Department of Environment an "Environmental Clearance Certificate" (EIA) with the level of screening determined by the potential harm of its type of activity. In 1998–99, the National Fisheries Policy, the National Water Policy, the National Industry Policy, and the National Agriculture Policy all promised to ensure equitable as well as efficient management of all the nation's resources. The amended National Forest Act (2000) officially included participatory social forestry but, in practice, retained the dominance of government foresters. But in all these areas, administrative underfunding, particularly lack of monitoring and enforcing mechanisms, and statutory loopholes, led to numerous official clarifying circulars, notifications, and emendations. Indeed, due to irregularities in spending and procedures, some projects were terminated by their international sponsors. For example, the ADB closed the Sundarban Biodiversity Conservation Project (initiated in 1998) after just three years.

Following the earlier actions of India and Pakistan, Bangladesh created judicial bodies dedicated to environmental issues through the 2000 Environment Court Act. The repeated amendment of this Act (2002, 2010) and the Environmental Conservation Rules (amended 2000, 2002) suggest how much more needs to be done to produce long-term beneficial effects. For instance, the steep decline in hilsa (*Tenualosa ilisha*) fisheries is particularly important since this fish species is culturally vital to Bangladeshi cuisine.

When Begum Hasina's term ended, a brief caretaker government supervised the 2001 elections. A victorious four party BNP-led coalition, which included the Jama'at-i Islami, reelected Begum Khalida Zia as prime minister. Bangladesh ratified the Kyoto Protocol (2001). Her government advanced some initiatives, for instance issuing the Brick Burning (Control) (Amendment) Act (2001), the Ozone Layer Depleting Substances (Control) Rules (2004), the National Biodiversity Strategy and Action Plan (2004), the National Adaptation Programme of Action (2005, revised 2009), and the Noise Pollution (Control) Rules (2006). Responding to pressure from international and domestic environmentalists, her regime banned polythene bags (2002) and wild prawn larva collection (2006).

Supported by international donors (particularly the ADB and USAID and guided by the IUCN), her regime revived social forestry and co-management of forests through its National Environmental Policy (2003–08) and Social Forestry Rules (2004). The Ministry of Environment and Forest created a social forestry wing. One goal was conflict resolution in protected areas, both between humans and animals and also between local communities and government foresters. For instance, the 2002 Nishorgo Support Project (initiated by the Forest Department with USAID funding) created pilot integrated co-management committees in five protected areas and their buffer zones including at Satchari and Lawachara (both near Sylhet). The Forest Department was supposed to create culturally appropriate "green" alternative income generating activities, including ecotourism, for members of Forest Users Groups. But only limited improvements resulted, among them illegal felling was reduced somewhat as local people joined forest protection patrols. Yet, since decision-making power remained with the Forest Department, these policies remained largely symbolic. For example, foresters authorized a private contract for palm oil seed harvesting in Satchari National Park without even consulting with the local co-management committee. Further, local resistance to government meant that the critical Chittagong Hill Tracts remained outside of this social forestry initiative. Overall, these measures did little to reduce the rate of deforestation.

Another major environmental health issue remains arsenic poisoning in rural drinking water. Over the late twentieth century, about 11 million tubes wells had been bored across Bangladesh's countryside, mostly funded by international donors. These replaced often waste-polluted water sources and provided almost 90 percent of villagers with microbiologically safe water. These new wells also usually meant less time and labor for women who customarily fetched water. However, there were untoward consequences. Influential villagers arranged to have wells bored conveniently close for their households or fields, often making poorer villagers dependent. Further, by the 1990s, scientists discovered naturally occurring arsenic in the aquifers tapped by many of these tube-wells, exposing tens of millions to harmful drinking and irrigation water. Since even closely spaced tube-wells showed widely variable arsenic levels, new programs were needed to test, paint dangerous tube-wells red, and reeducate people to avoid them, however inconvenient. Women who complied often had to fetch water from much further away. However, this distancing from supervision by males and mothers-in-law sometimes also gave them more freedom of movement; to prevent that freedom, sometimes men took over the water-carrying burden (Sultana 2009).

Bangladesh's 2004 National Policy for Arsenic Mitigation and Implementation Plan provided funds to villages where more than 80 percent of wells were dangerous. Chemists devised mechanisms to precipitate arsenic out of stored water, but so far these add cost and are cumbersome. Then, a 2004 Bangladesh Health Service survey questioned the extent of the crisis, finding that nearly half of the tested households had access to water meeting official national arsenic standards of 50 parts per billion (ppb) (international limits are only 10 ppb). This report suggested that wells had been misdiagnosed, that naturally occurring iron may have precipitated the arsenic during storage, or that arsenic levels in aquifers vary over time. Nonetheless, such issues reinforce public lack of confidence in the government's expertise and programs.

Two branches of government also questioned the competency of Begum Khalida's regime. The judiciary continued to take the lead in specific environmental issues. For instance, in responses to PIL, the courts ordered the government to: ban two-stroke rickshaw engines in Dhaka; institute regular inspections for all cars; cancel licenses of vehicles nine or more years old; ban hydraulic/air-horns on buses and trucks; and convert government-owned vehicles from petrol or diesel to compressed natural gas.

Even more powerfully, the army acted to end government corruption and ineffectiveness. Over the decades, Bangladesh has provided over 80,000 personnel to UN peacekeeping forces around the world, more than any other nation. The UN pays hundreds of millions of dollars annually for these soldiers and they receive better training, pay, and equipment than their own government provides. Having been posted to over forty-five separate conflict zones, officers saw personally how they could mediate political crises. After Begum Khalida's term ended in October 2006, and after months of public unrest, the army took over as a transitional government, with a civilian economist and retired civil-servant Fakhruddin Ahmad (1940–, r. 2007–09) as chief advisor. The stated goal was to clean up the electoral rolls and end the "two Begum" political alternation between the BNP and Awami League. Both Begums and their family members were arrested or allowed to leave the country. This government invited Nobel laureate Muhammad Yunus of the Grameen Bank to form a new, clean political party; he finally declined rather then get involved in politics.

Despite some progress, this transitional regime faced challenges. In November 2007, super-cyclone Sidr struck with unprecedented force, causing massive coastal damage, affecting half the country's people, animals, and crops. Better preparation and response kept the human death toll to about 4,200, still substantial but only a fraction of the fatalities from the 1970 cyclone. In December, the Forest Department banned all timber harvesting from the Sundarbans to assist recovery. The Emergency Cyclone Recovery and Restoration Project (2007) through the World Bank not only provided immediate assistance, it also developed evacuation plans, rehabilitated existing embankments and cyclone shelters, and built hundreds of new, better-equipped ones. Thus, Bangladesh's disaster management policies stress preparation for cyclones and floods, rather than just paying the larger costs of recovery. (These measures proved valuable when super-cyclone Aila hit in May 2009, causing much damage but even fewer fatalities.)

Nonetheless, when the transitional government held parliamentary elections in December 2008, the BNP boycotted, claiming improper constraints. Instead, the Awami League-led "Grand Alliance" of fourteen parties won over 80 percent of the seats, reelecting Begum Hasina as prime minister (January 2009). Her regime responded to international and domestic initiatives about the particularly fragile parts of the environment. For instance, her government prepared the Bangladesh Tiger Action Plan (2009–17) for planned, integrated conservation in the Sundarbans. In 2009, Bangladesh was one of the first countries to introduce a Climate Change Strategy and Action Plan for low-carbon and sustainable growth with preparation for natural disaster recovery and with attention to improving gender equity. Her government prepared an Integrated Resources Management Plan (2010–20) for the Sundarbans. Nonetheless, deforestation continues as timber demand outstrips production, reducing forest cover to about 1.4 percent of the country and to 0.016 ha/capita (the lowest in South Asia).

International donors established the Bangladesh Climate Change Resilience Fund (2010), under the World Bank administration. Indeed, without international donors, many government agencies would have almost no income. For instance, about 80 percent the understaffed Forest Department's budget comes from international funding of specific projects. However, the World Bank and other international funding agencies have occasionally reduced their support for major infrastructure projects where they discovered ineffectiveness and substantial corruption.

Begum Hasina's regime amended the Constitution in 2012. Among other provisions, section 18A promises that "The state shall endeavour to protect and improve the environment and preserve and safeguard the natural resources, biodiversity, wetlands, forests and wildlife for the present and future citizens." This echoed Indira Gandhi's 1976 constitutional amendments (during her authoritarian Emergency), which also reinforced wide-ranging judicial interventions into environmental issues.

Begum Hasina's government also asserted an array of environmental actions. These included the National Disaster Management Act (2012). Her Wildlife Act (2012) highlighted ecotourism and allowed official declaration of more "Ecologically Critical Areas." The National Aquaculture Development Strategy and Action Plan (2013) promised to "improve the welfare of the resource-poor people depending on the aquatic resources for livelihood, reduce poverty by stimulating employment and improving income, conserve if not enhance the natural resources on which livelihoods are based, promote the sustainable development of rural communities, increase export earnings, and contribute to the creation of wealth for the nation and improvement in the welfare of the people." Indeed, inland fish farming has in the last decade vastly increased (harvesting some 2.2 million metric tonnes [2.4 million US tons] by 2016, almost all for domestic markets), exceeding the wild-catch fish industry. The Brick Making and Kiln Establishment (Control) Act (2013) promised to facilitate units toward less air polluting technology. The Water Act (2013) promised integrated development, management, and conservation of water resources. But, often these policies and plans have had weak implementation and inadequate planning and protection that have limited their efficacy.

Simultaneously, to crush the weakened BNP and Islamic party opposition, Begum Hasina's government arrested, tried, and (in some cases) executed its leaders, some for supporting Pakistan in 1971, others for terrorism or for corruption. The January 2014 parliamentary election, which the BNP boycotted, renewed Begum Hasina's mandate. Her government intensified its prosecution of political opponents, devastating the BNP, but also moved somewhat from the secular platform her party had advocated from its inception, thereby coopting religious support from her opponents.

The 2014 settlement of a forty-year-old maritime boundary dispute among India, Myanmar, and Bangladesh enabled the creation of Bangladesh's first marine protected area: "The Swatch of No Ground" covering 1,738 km^2 (671 mi^2), a steep undersea depression of the Bay of Bengal that is a nursery for dolphins, porpoises, sharks, turtles, and whales. This international settlement also enabled Bangladesh to extract petroleum and natural gas from its allocated seabed.

Electricity shortages are constraining Bangladeshi development. India is funding a coal-fired power generation plant in Bangladesh's Sundarbans. Further, late in 2017, Begum Hasina's government borrowed US$19 billion from Russia to construct a huge 2,400MW nuclear power plant only 50 km (31 mi) from the Indian border, with a proposed completion date of 2025. This plant alone promises to increase the national electricity supply by 15 percent, with CO_2-free generation. However, since all three South Asian nations will have substantial nuclear- and coal-production, they all face the long-term environmental costs of these technologies.

From September 2017, her administration has been sheltering some 650,000 more Muslim Rohingya fleeing into Bangladesh's southern borderlands to escape ethnic cleansing by the Myanmar army (almost as many Rohingya had earlier immigrated to Bangladesh, as well as substantial numbers to India and Pakistan). The Rohingya language is close to the Bangla dialects of that region and these Muslim refugees have so far been sheltered. But that border region is also already overpopulated and environmentally fragile, so the long-term consequences are incalculable.

Overall, Bangladesh has recently made impressive progress, particularly in the health of its people, with a persistent annual rise of GDP of over 6 percent. Population growth has slowed from 2.7 percent to about 1.4 percent per annum. There is near-universal access to primary education, with gender equity. Women's participation in the public labor force has risen considerably, particularly in the urban-based ready-made garment industry. While working and living conditions for such laborers remain unhealthy (e.g. the April 2013 collapse of the Rana Plaza factory alone killed some 1,100 workers, and there have been numerous fatal factory fires), international pressure from governments, NGOs, and clothing retailer associations has helped improve safety and working conditions. Nonetheless, rapid deforestation, air, water, and land pollution, fauna and flora species extinction continue. With denser population and agriculture, higher rate of urbanization, and greater vulnerability to sea-level rise, Bangladesh has also tended to lag behind India and

Pakistan in setting and enforcing environmental standards and sanctions. Using illustrative examples, this book's final chapter briefly brings together current environmental conditions in South Asia and its component nations through case studies at the national, subcontinental, and international levels.

12   National, Subcontinental, and Global Issues in South Asia

The environmental history of the Indian subcontinent shows constant change along the distinctive patterns, but also much regional diversity. Beginning with its transoceanic migration into its current location as South Asia, this history shows how global forces have shaped its geology and, interacting with solar, atmospheric, and oceanic forces, its tropical but regionally diverse climate. Indeed, the geographic and climatic features often associated with South Asia today, including the Himalayan mountains and two seasonal monsoons, resulted from extensive interactions among these forces. Similarly, the current array of flora, fauna, and human cultures living in South Asia resulted from hundreds of centuries of immigrations, adaptations, and interrelations. While internal and foreign empires have occasionally bound together South Asia's regions, most have retained their specific ecologies and some degree of autonomy, reiterating the historic tensions between them and the subcontinent as a whole. Over time, humans long settled in South Asia and also more recent immigrants, including Muslims and British colonizers, developed technologies to extract and transform natural resources on ever more extensive scales until, during the last century especially, resource stocks are being exhausted. The independent nations of India and Pakistan have just turned seventy-one (Bangladesh only forty-seven) – an age comparable with a single human lifetime.

With the independence of the nation-states of India, Pakistan, and (later) Bangladesh, much of the available primary source material and secondary analysis highlight each nation individually. Yet, as the last three chapters have shown, they share much, but are also distinctive due to their disparate human and natural compositions and political and economic trajectories. To suggest and illustrate these national parallels, and also their differences, we can turn to three indicative issues that are respectively primarily intranational, competitive among the three South Asian nations, and international (See Map 12.1).

Map 12.1 South Asia in the twenty-first century

Urbanization and Its Waste

All three South Asian nations are rapidly urbanizing, shifting significantly the historic distribution of resources. Agriculture remains vital to each of their economies and ecologies, so current climatic changes of concentrated rainfall and CO_2 and temperature rise have major consequences. Simultaneously, urban growth rates are rising (3 percent annually for Bangladesh, slightly less for Pakistan and India), mostly due to immigration from rural areas. This is producing growing proportions of the population living in urban areas (Pakistan, 39 percent; Bangladesh, 36 percent; and India, 33 percent) and also megacities of scale unprecedented in South Asian (or global) history: Delhi (18–24 million, depending on the definition of metropolitan area), Dhaka (15–22 million), Karachi (14–18 million), and Mumbai

(12–21 million). Many of South Asia's cities are also among the world's most polluted.

Concentrated urban populations can be more energy efficient, but they also make concentrated demands on water, air, power, and other resources. Much of the growth in South Asia's cities is unplanned, largely unregulated, and inadequately served by infrastructure. For instance, in economically thriving Delhi, the municipal government has designated 1,200 "approved colonies" but over 1,600 "unauthorized colonies" (plus another 600 "unauthorized but regularized colonies"). Even in authorized housing areas, drinking water, air pollution, electricity supply, and sanitation are unsatisfactory. Most municipal waste, including hazardous waste, is dumped in landfills that already far exceed their carrying capacity. There, 300,000–400,000 unregulated, unsalaried "waste pickers" do most of the city's recycling by hand, selling what they sort to private wholesalers. Based on documentation by the NGO Centre for Science and the Environment and the National Green Tribunal, the Delhi High Court (June 2017) constituted the Delhi State Legal Services Authority "to formulate and implement [a] long term action plan regarding collection, removal and disposal of all waste" (Delhi State Legal Services Authority 2017). This authority optimistically (and punitively) recommended that all urban-dwellers must practice compulsory waste-sorting at the source, with heavy fines for offenders, and improved collection, processing, and disposal by adequate numbers of well-paid municipal workers. Each of South Asia's other megacities has comparable issues. Indeed, this pattern of civil society initiatives backed by court orders to the bureaucracy about vast environmental problems, including urban pollution, has become characteristic for all three South Asian nations.

Ship-breaking or Ship-recycling

The vast increase in global trade of the past half-century caused, and became possible due to, the proliferation of transoceanic shipping on ever-larger and more numerous vessels with technological shifts, including the containerization of cargoes and the widening of the Panama Canal (the Suez Canal was also recently expensively upgraded). Roughly 700–1,000 large, oceangoing ships are annually sold off for scrap due to deterioration after about a twenty- to thirty-year sea-life. Often brokers pay cash, rename, re-document, and reflag the worn-out vessel in low-regulation ("Black Flag" or "flag of convenience") nations like Panama, Liberia, Belize, or Comoros (sometimes multiple times). They thus seek to obscure the ownership history and legal liability and to evade the Basel

Convention on the Control of Transboundary Movements of Hazardous Wastes and their Disposal (adopted 1989, in force from 1992, amended 1995) and also the policies of the International Maritime Organization and the International Labor Organization. The Hong Kong International Convention for the Safe and Environmentally Sound Recycling of Ships (adopted 2009, not yet in force) provides potential guidelines that address some aspects of vessel dismantling (but not disposal of the waste, for instance).

Bangladesh, India, and Pakistan compete against each other (and with China, Turkey, and elsewhere) for recyclable materials and the many jobs that ship-breaking requires. Suitable, gently sloping shorelines with high-tidal ranges, low Bangladeshi, Indian, and Pakistan labor costs, and relatively lax pollution regulation enforcement, mean that about 70 percent of these scrapped ships are dismantled and recycled in South Asia. These ship-breaking sites are clustered for network economies along short beachfronts or mudflats (in Sitakunda near Chittagong, Alang-Sosiya in Gujarat and secondarily near Mumbai, and Gadani near Karachi). Each vessel's tonnage is 80–90 percent metal, becoming relatively inexpensive feedstock for the nation's iron and steel mills; indeed, almost everything aboard that has recycling value ends up being used. The supply of obsolete ships varies considerably over time, so recycling rewards low capital investment and labor pool flexibility. Direct employment varies seasonally and annually: between 10,000 and 60,000 workers each in Bangladesh and India (fewer in Pakistan), with many more dealing with the resulting valuable recyclable materials. However, each vessel also contains unusable and hazardous waste including oils, electronics, paints, and heavy metals; older vessels also contain polychlorinated biphenyls (PCBs) and other persistent organic pollutants, and asbestos. The ship-breaking industry in each nation regards any costs from the enforcement of environmental pollution or worker safely protections as reducing its competitiveness (see Figures 12.1 and 12.2).

The broad historical trajectories of ship-breaking in Bangladesh, Pakistan, and India are parallel, but also distinctive. Since the 1970s, domestic entrepreneurs in each nation raised cash from largely unregulated financial networks to purchase relatively inexpensive, obscurely owned, and decaying ships; recruited low-wage manual laborers to disassemble these ships (largely by hand); purchased the minimal equipment they needed (mostly gas handheld torches, with heavy equipment of winches and cranes often taken from the ships); and assembled networks of purchasers for the steel, cables, wires, and other usable components. Unusable waste is often dangerously dumped in the ocean.

Figure 12.1 Graveyard of ships, Chittagong, Bangladesh. Photograph: Rez Click / Moment / Getty Images

Frequent worker injuries and deaths, oil spills and other major accidents, and domestic and international news media and activists, however, all eventually drew the attention of NGOs like Greenpeace and then official government notice. Environmental- and human rights-oriented judiciaries intervened to halt the industry (e.g. in India in 2006, 2007, 2012; Bangladesh in 2009 and 2010–11; but less in Pakistan) but then have often bowed to industry pressure by only ordering minimal worker and environmental safety precautions. Likewise, governments drew up regulations (e.g. India's 2003 Hazardous Waste Rules and Gujarat's 2006 Ship Recycling Regulations and Bangladesh's 2011 Hazardous Waste and Ship Breaking Waste Management Rules and 2018 Ship Recycling Act). The somewhat better-financed, organized, and regulated Indian ship-breaking industry operates under the Gujarat Maritime Board (a semipublic institution) while Bangladesh and Pakistan have private industry associations and less effective government control. Until the nations of South Asia (and their global rivals) coordinate their regulations with each other and with developed nations, however, market forces will continue their competition at the cost of their respective environments and workers. The international e-waste, used clothing, and other recycling industries have many parallels to ship-breaking in that rich nations export their pollution to developing nations.

Figure 12.2 Ship-breaking yards of Bangladesh through the foggy and toxic atmosphere. Photograph: SUC / E+ / Getty Images

Nationally Determined Contributions to Climate Change

As part of the UN Framework Convention on Climate Change leading up to the 2015 Paris Conference of Parties, individual nations offered their Intended Nationally Determined Contribution (INDC) for greenhouse gas reductions. This approach sought to avoid the bargaining among nations with competing interests that had frustrated the Copenhagen conference and other attempts at a single, mandatory global plan. India, Pakistan, and Bangladesh have much in common, being among the world's very most vulnerable nations to climate change effects. These effects include: sea-rise submergence of heavily populated areas; intensified cyclones; instability in vital monsoon rainfall; rising temperatures reducing crop yields, increasing glacial melt rates, and causing hazardous heat episodes; low resilience among their millions of impoverished citizens; and vast costs for remediation and disaster relief.

Consequently, India, Bangladesh, and Pakistan each prepared its own INDC, hedged with qualifications about commitment and need for international funding. These three had some parallels but also distinctive features reflective of their particular political and environmental conditions. Narendra Modi's BJP and Begum Hasina's Awami League-led governments both had particularly strong political positions domestically, with major electoral victories in 2014; Pakistan missed the deadline due to political infighting (which left the Ministry of Climate Change leaderless), but finally submitted its imprecise INDC a month late. Since the Paris Agreement came into force (November 2016), these INDCs are now officially Nationally Determined Contributions [NDCs].

As developing nations, India, Pakistan, and Bangladesh all independently asserted that they have very low per-capita emissions and historically had not been a major contributor to the current problem of climate change due to atmospheric greenhouse gases. Nonetheless, in absolute terms, India is the world's third largest current GHG emitter (after China and the United States).

In their stated reasons for their commitments, Pakistan and Bangladesh took more secular, scientific positions about their relatively energy-light economies, while India additionally cited the Vedas and Mahatma Gandhi to claim India's eternal harmony with and respect for nature. They concurred, however, that "Nations that are now striving to fulfill this 'right to grow' of their teeming millions cannot be made to feel guilty of their development agenda as they attempt to fulfill this legitimate aspiration" (as India put it). Simultaneously, however, each offered ambitious proposals to bring down its additions to the current GHG flow (from "business as usual" levels) while sustaining economic growth based on domestic and international actions.

Their proposed domestic reductions all relied heavily on "maximizing coal output and managing coal fired power stations in a carbon-neutral way" (Bangladesh) using claimed "supercritical technologies" (India, Bangladesh), although this technology has yet to be proven. India did not mention its own exporting of GHG from its massive new but conventional coal-fired electricity-generating project in Bangladesh's part of the fragile Sundarbans.

In addition, each nation presented programs for intensified renewable solar- and wind-energy sources, with India and Pakistan also starting biofuel projects using oily seeds from a hardy Central American–native semi-evergreen, *Jatropha curcas*. India also has twenty nuclear power plants, with more planned; Pakistan has several; Bangladesh is planning one. Despite the historical limitations of dam projects, India lauded its "vast hydro potential," as did Pakistan (although also highlighting "micro and small-scale hydro plants"). Overall, India pledged 40 percent cumulative electric installed capacity from non-fossil fuel sources by 2030. Further, the NDCs all promised domestic, industrial, and agricultural energy efficiencies and reforestation for carbon-storage. India and Bangladesh specified REDD+ (Reducing Emissions from Deforestation and Forest Degradation) that fosters the conservation, sustainable management of forests, and enhancement of forest carbon stocks in developing countries.

No nation can address climate change issues alone. Bangladesh's NDC only considered the power, transport, and industry sectors, because the government lacks sufficient data for quantified assessment of other sectors. Its NDC promised 5 percent reduction of increase in GHG based on its own resources, but 15 percent reduction with internationally financed mitigation, adaptation, capacity building, and technology transfer. Overall, Bangladesh's estimated total cost for mitigation is $27 billion plus for adaptation $42 billion. India promised to reduce emission intensity by 33–35 percent from current trends but estimated needed domestic and international investments for its proposed climate change actions totaling $2.5 trillion. Subject to ongoing consultations with its provinces, Pakistan projected needed investments of $5.5–40 billion (depending on GHG reductions of 10–20 percent) "which only can be realized through international support." The World Bank, ADB, and other international bodies advanced different cost estimates for each nation. However, even making some adaptation and mitigation progress and building the resilience of communities will be extremely expensive. Yet, not making the greatest progress possible will be even more costly in terms of recovery from disasters and overall degradation of the environment.

Understanding from South Asia's Long Environmental History

The history of the Indian subcontinent's environment shows continual but uneven change due to an array of human and nonhuman causes, with a range of powerful effects. Many of these effects are apparent only by taking a long-term perspective and comparing and contrasting various regional ecologies. Living conditions for humans and for specific species of fauna and flora populations have varied over time, regionally, and for the subcontinent as a whole. As communities developed technologies, particularly as states and religious movements emerged, their cultural valuations of the world around them, and their power to affect that world, shifted. Many of these communities, kingdoms, and empires emerged within South Asia, but always as part of larger, global processes. Over the last two centuries, human environmental effects have intensified, as have South Asia's interactions with the rest of the earth. Post-

1947, the new nations of India, Pakistan (and then Bangladesh) have tried independently to control the environments within their borders. Only by understanding South Asia's environmental history as a whole and as part of the world, however, can we engage effectively with current and future conditions.

Bibliographical Essay

Chapter 1

The formal study of South Asia's environmental history has expanded rapidly in recent decades, with many methodologies and often conflicting analyses. These disciplines have developed powerfully through path-breaking work by scholars (Arnold 1988; Baviskar 1995; Eaton 1993; Gadgil and Guha 1992, 1995; Gadgil and Vartak 1975; Grove 1995; Sumit Guha 1999; Sivaramakrishnan 1999; Skaria 1999) and NGOs, especially the Centre for Science and the Environment (its work is available through its *Citizens Reports* [1982–] and other published and online materials [www.cse.org]).

This chapter's disciplinary model develops from McNeill (2003), who uses the model of a circus with three rings but all under one tent. The chapter's three wave or generation model develops from Agrawal and Sivaramakrishnan (2000:8–12). An effective means for surveying this field is through recent insightful scholarly review articles that focus on books grouped around a theme (Beattie 2012; Uday Chandra 2015; Cole 2016; Mann 2013; Mawdsley 2004; Rangarajan 1996; Rashkow 2014; Alpa Shah 2007; Sivaramakrishnan 2008, 2015). Another means of access to a variety of studies is edited volumes containing recent articles on a theme or topic (Agrawal and Sivaramakrishnan 2000; Cederlof and Sivaramakrishnan 2006; Ranjan Chakrabarti 2009; Deepak Kumar et al. 2011; McNeill et al. 2010; Moor and Gowda 2014; Rangarajan 2007; Saberwal and Rangarajan 2005; Rangarajan and Sivaramakrishnan 2014; Shahabuddin and Rangarajan 2007; Sivaramakrishnan and Agrawal 2003) or foundational articles (Arnold and Guha 1995; Gadgil and Thapar 1990; Grove et al. 1998; Kapur 2011; Madsen 1999; Rangarajan and Sivaramakrishnan 2012). Valuable surveys place South Asia in larger contexts (Beinart and Hughes 2007; Greenough 2001; Ramachandra Guha 1995, 2000a, 2006; Habib 2010; Richards 2003; Sutter 2003). Economic history deeply affects environmental history (Dharma Kumar et al. 1982–83). Some articles of the Subaltern

Studies school of historiography from the perspective of revolutionaries have environmental implications (Ranajit Guha et al. 1982–2012). Actor Network Theory attempts to show the agency of flora and fauna as nonhuman actants (Vinita Damodaran et al. 2015; Hughes 2013; Pawson 2008; Rangarajan 2013).

Chapter 2

The best overall compilation of South Asia's historical geography remains Schwartzberg (1978; also available at dsal.uchicago.edu/refer ence/schwartzberg) but there are more recent studies of the evolving geology (Jason Ali and Aitchison 2008; Briggs 2003) or climate (Owen et al. 2002).

There is limited physical source material on the early peopling of the subcontinent (Allchin and Petraglia 2007; Gangal et al. 2014; Ganjoo and Ota 2012; Hawkey 2002) or the earliest established human communities (Dennell and Petraglia 2012; Morrison 2014; Petraglia et al. 2012). Scholars have tried to reconstruct ancient Indian human history using biological markers (Vishwanathan et al. 2004), oral traditions (R. C. and S. C. Roy 1937), or comparative evidence of other forest-dwellers (Bailey and Headland 1991). While one should not assume continuity between today's forest-dwellers and those first humans in South Asia, scholars have also used anthropological methodologies to study current forest-dwellers (Baviskar 1995; Karlsson and Subba 2006; Alpa Shah 2010; Skariya 1999). Some work particularly concentrates on women and the environment (Agarwal 2010; Banerjee and Bell 2007; Jewitt 2000; Shiva 1988).

Chapter 3

Scientists have recovered evidence about the physical environment for the Indus and Vedic periods (Bryson and Schuldenrein 2008; Donges 2015; Giosan et al. 2012; Mayewski et al. 2004; Wanner 2008; Xu et al. 2015). Current archaeological evidence for the Indus Civilization is available at www.Harappa.com and in surveys (Abraham et al. 2013; Kenoyer 2000, 2012; Petraglia and Allchin 2007; Possehl 2002; Wright 2010) and in specific articles on its origins (Dilip Chakrabarti 2014; Gangal et al. 2014; Hawkey 2002; Kingwell-Banham et al. 2015; Misra 2001), social order (Kenoyer 2000; Sinopoli 2015; Valentine et al. 2015), or final stages (Robbins Shug et al. 2013; Varma 1991). Due to current security and nationalist concerns, excavation of Indus sites (and even preservation of exposed ones) have greatly reduced, although analysis of already recovered materials and evidence continues.

The Rig Veda is available in several English translations (Jamison and Brereton 2014; O'Flaherty 1981). The introductions to those translations and other scholars provide insights about environmental attitudes (Patton 2000; Zimmermann 1987). The issue of Hinduism and environmentalism remains particularly contentious (Alley 2002; Feldhaus 2003; Govindrajan 2018; Haberman 2006; Mawdsley 2006; Nelson 1998; Rashkow 2015; Snodgrass et al. 2008; Tomalin 2009).

Chapter 4

Scholars have analyzed environmental ideas in Buddhist, Hindu, Islamic, or Jain religious texts (Ali and Flatt 2012; Chapple 2002; Chapple and Tucker 2000; Duara 2014; Pandian and Ali 2010; Julia Shah et al. 2007). Some works concentrate on forests (Falk 1973; Haberman 2013; Menzies 2010; Parkhill 1995; Rawat 1991; Thapar 2001) or on elephants (Olivelle 2016; Trautmann 2015). The epics *Ramayana* and *Mahabharata* are available in several English translations (Valmiki 1984–2017; Vyasa 1973–2003). Scholars have also analyzed various environmental aspects of these epics (Pollock 1991) and the ideology and practice of "caste" or varna and jati (Bayly 1999; Sumit Guha 1999; Gurukkal 2015).

The Mauryan Empire extended state control over the environment (Thapar 1997). The post-Mauryan decline has received attention (R. S. Sharma 1987; Ashish Sinha et al. 2007). Sanskrit culture and the Shastras address much about the environment (Dilip Chakrabarti 2014; Kaul 2010; Kautilya 2013; Manu 2004; Pollock 2006).

Scholars have studied the Dravidian south and its socioeconomy (Ludden 1999; Zvelebil 1975), relations to forest-dwellers (Nugteren 2008), water (Mollinga 2003; Mosse 2003), or Tamil poetry and its landscape model (Ramanujan 1967).

Chapter 5

Primary sources provide evidence about the environment and the rise of sultanates (Elliot 1873–77 [which should be read with corrections by Hodiwala 1939–57]; Ibn Battuta 1976). Scholars have analyzed the interaction between the environment and Muslims (Digby 1971; Eaton 1993; Foltz et al. 2003; Sumit Guha 1999; Sunil Kumar 2007; Wink 1990–2004). Scholars have also studied the Vijayanagara empire and Deccan (Eaton and Wagoner 2014; Ganeshaiah et al. 2007; Murali

1995; Sinopoli and Morrison 1995; Stein 1989; Stoker 2016), or provided primary sources (Sarasvati 1925; Nilakanta Shastri and Venkataramayayya 1946).

The Portuguese and other early Europeans engaged India with the world system (Subrahmanyam 2005) or through the "Columbian Exchange" (Crosby 1972).

Chapter 6

The Mughal Empire and its contemporaries produced extensive primary sources (Abu al-Fazl 1873–94; 'Alamgir 1908; Babur 2002; Jahangir 1914; Khan 1947). Scholars have surveyed all or parts of its history (Farooqi 1988; Fisher 2015; Habib 1982; Moin 2012; Richards 1993), administration (Athar Ali 1985), built environment (Asher 1992; Blake 1993), or specific environmental issues (Dale 2004; Habib 1999; Pandian 2001; Chetan Singh 1995).

Chapter 7

The Marathas were the most extensive Indian successor to the Mughal Empire (Gordon 1993). A growing number of arriving Europeans wrote about India and its environment (Johnson 1822; Fisher 2007). The environment effects and policies of the EIC have received much scholarly attention overall (Arnold 1996; Arnold and Guha 1995; Vinita Damodaran et al. 2015; Harrison 1999), in particular regions (Cederlof 2014; Ranajit Guha 1996; Karlsson 2011; Saikia 2011; Sengupta 1980), or with respect to forests (Grove 1995). The role of South Asia within the emerging Eurocentric world system has also been analyzed extensively (Vinita Damodaran et al. 2015; Dharma Kumar et al. 1982–83).

Chapter 8

The British Raj created numerous source materials about the extensive environmental changes it caused and tried to regulate. The British Library (London) and the National Archives of India (New Delhi), of Pakistan (Islamabad), and of Bangladesh (Dhaka), plus provincial and district libraries and record rooms all hold vast number of rich primary source materials for researchers, including selective printed collections of their records. Various European officials (Ribbentrop 1900; Stebbing 1926) and Indians (Nehru 1947; Tandon 1968) described their experiences and advocated particular policies or valuations of the colonial state's relationship to the environment. This "high colonial" period has also much generated much (and often contending) secondary source material. Key issues include the respective roles Europeans and Indians held in the creation (and awareness) of environmental degradation (Grove 1995; Deepak Kumar et al. 2011). Many works focus on particular components of the environment including: canals and dams (Agnihotri 1996; Imran Ali 2003; D'Souza 2006a, 2006b; Gilmartin 1994, 2015; Hardiman 1995; Iftekhar Iqbal 2010; Islam 1997; Lewis 2007; Mosse 2003; Mustafa 2013; Stone 1984; Stoddard 2009; Whitcombe 1972), cities (Arnold 2013; Mann 2007; Metcalf 2002; Prashad 2001; Sharan 2014; Wilhelm 2016), "natural sciences" (Arnold 2000, 2008; Drayton 2000), pollution (Arnold 2016; Pratik Chakrabarti 2015), railways (Das 2015; Kerr 2007; MacGeorge 1894), or cartography (Edney 1987). Specific environmental features and events have received scholarly attention including agriculture (Krishna 2012; Richards et al. 1985; Satya 1997), cyclones (Kingsbury 2018), diseases (Klein 1988; Zeheter 2015), famines (Arnold 1988; Davis 2002; Greenough 1982; Klein 1984; Mukherjee 2017), forests and forest-dwellers (Barton 2002; Barton and Bennett 2008; Dangwal 2009; Patak 2002; Rajan 2006; Rangarajan 1996b; Rao 2008; Saravanan 2016; Sivaramakrishnan 1999, 2000, 2008; Strahorn 2009; Tucker 2012), pastoralists (Saberwal 1999), or wildlife (Chavda 1995; Divyabhanusinh 2005; MacKenzie 1988; Rangarajan 2013). Books and articles also study princely India (Cohen 2011; Hughes 2013, 2015; Thaha 2009). Alternative models to the British, particularly those of M. K. Gandhi include his own works (1909, 1948), Nehru (1947), or studies by others (Ramachandra Guha 1997; Vinay Lal 2000a, 2000b).

Chapters 9–11

The partition of South Asia's environment into West and East Pakistan and India caused major disruptions (Chatterji 2007; Chester 2009). Some studies consider transnational issues like rivers and water (Biswas et al. 2009; Chellaney 2011; Gunawardena et al. 2015; Haines 2017; Lahiri-Dutt and Samanta 2013; Narain and Prakash 2016; Prakash et al. 2013; Roth and Vincent 2013), the Green Revolution (Borlaug 1970; Erenstein 2010; Rinku 2001), or the effects and cultural meanings of climate change (Chakrabarty 2009; A. Damodaran 2010; Dubash 2012; Rashid and Paul 2014; Ray 2011; Anushree Sinha et al. 2015). However, the effects of partition varied by nation and region, which has also meant divided, nation-based historiographies, despite the shared continuities from the colonial period and subsequent developments.

International lenders have published individual national environmental assessments (Asian Development Bank 2004; World Bank 2006a, 2006b). Each of the three governments also issues extensive reports, for instance on endangered animals or forest-dwellers. A former maker of Indian government environmental policy explained the political process (Ramesh 2015).

A large number of scholarly studies focus specifically on India, including agriculture (Baker and Jewitt 2007; Baranski 2015; Kolady and Lesser 2012; Minsky 2015; Mollinga 2015; Patel 2013), cities (Ahmad 2018; Nagendra 2016; Nair 2005; Rademacher and Sivaramakrishnan 2013), dams and water (Asthana 2009; Baghel 2014; Hardiman 1995; Klingensmith 2007; Nilsen 2012; Ray 2008; Werner 2015), environmental law and politics (Agrawal 2005; Cullet and Koonan 2011; Divan and Rosencranz 2001; Nandimath 2009; Jain 2011; Khanna and Naveen 2005; Panigrahi and Amirapun 2012; Rajagopalan 2011; Mukul Sharma 2012; Sivaramakrishnan 2011), forests (Kent 2013; Lele and Menon 2014; Malhotra et al. 2001; Menon et al. 2013; Nugteren 2005; Saikia 2011; Satyajit Singh 2016; Sundar et al. 2001), forest-dwellers (Chandra 2015; Corbridge 1988; Ramachandra Guha 1999; Prasad 2003; Alpa Shah 2010), villagers (Gold and Gujar 2002), or wildlife (Divyabhanusinh 2005; Government of India 2005, 2010; Jhala et al. 2015; Lewis 2005; Locke and Buckingham 2016; Rangarajan and Shahabuddin 2006; Rastogi et al. 2012; Sekhar 2013; Shahabuddin 2010; Valmik Thapar 2001). Especially controversial are discussions of Chipko (Ramachandra Guha 2000b; Shiva and Bandyopadhyay 1986; Weber 1989), biopiracy (Kidd 2012; Mathur 2003; Shiva 1997, 2007), or e-waste (Wath et al. 2011).

Some scholars concentrate on Pakistan's administration (Nadeem and Hameed 2008), agriculture (Niazi 2004), e-waste (Mehreen Iqbal et al. 2015), forests (Tanvir Ali 2007), laws and politics (Ahmed and Kazi 2005; Ahsan and Khawaja 2013; Fischer 2014; Jawad Hassan 2001; Parvez Hassan 2007; Talbot 2015), national parks (Aftab and Hickey 2010), pollution (Colbeck et al. 2010a, 2010b; Coutinho and Butt 2014), or water (Azizullah et al. 2011; Mustafa 2013).

While Bangladesh has a relatively short history, there are already numerous studies on its agriculture (Habiba et al. 2015; Huq et al. 2013), laws and policies (Clemett 2002; Momtaz 2002), forests (Chowdhury 2014; Muzaffar et al. 2011), urbanization (Dewan and Corner 2014), or water (Dasgupta et al. 2015; Ramanathan et al. 2015; Sultana 2009).

Chapter 12

There are numerous studies of today's environmental conditions in South Asia (World Bank 2006a, 2006b). Scholars have analyzed ship-breaking (Galley 2014; Rahman et al. 2016) and organizations provide current evidence (www.gmbports.org, www.imo.org, and www.shipbreakingplatform .org). Each nation's INDC/NDC is available on its official website and at www4.unfccc.int/Submissions/INDC/Submission%20Pages/submissions .aspx. International bodies have assessed these (Amponin and Evans 2016).

References

Abraham, Shinu Anna, Praveena Gullapalli, and Teresa Raczek (2013). *Connections and Complexity: New Approaches to the Archaeology of South Asia* (Left Coast Press).

Abu al-Fazl (1873–94). *Ain-i Akbari*, trans. H. Blochmann, H. S. Jarrett, 3 vols. (Asiatic Society of Bengal).

Aftab, E. and G. M. Hickey (2010). "Forest Administration Challenges in Pakistan: The Case of the Patriata Reserved Forest and the 'New Murree' Development," *International Forestry Review*, 12/1:97–105.

Agarwal, Bina (2010). *Gender and Green Governance: The Political Economy of Women's Presence Within and Beyond Community Forestry* (Oxford University Press).

Agnihotri, Indu (1996). "Ecology, Land Use and Colonisation: The Canal Colonies of Punjab," *Indian Economic and Social History Review*, 33/1:37–58.

Agrawal, Arun (2005). *Environmentality: Technologies of Government and the Making of Subjects* (Duke University Press).

Agrawal, Arun, and K. Sivaramakrishnan, eds. (2000). *Agrarian Environments: Resources, Representations, and Rule in India* (Duke University Press).

Ahmad, Zarin (2018). *Delhi's Meatscapes* (Oxford University Press).

Ahmed, Ijaz, and Muneeza Kazi (2005). *Environmental Law in Pakistan: Governing Natural Resources and the Processes and Institutions that Affect Them*, 5 Parts (IUCN).

Ahsan, Irum, and Saima Amin Khawaja (2013). *Development of Environmental Laws and Jurisprudence in Pakistan* (Asian Development Bank).

'Alamgir (1908). *Rukaat-i-'Alamgiri*, trans. Jamshid H. Bilimoria (Luzac).

Ali, Daud, and Emma J. Flatt, eds. (2012). *Garden and Landscape Practices in Pre-Colonial India: Histories from the Deccan* (Routledge).

Ali, Imran (2003). *The Punjab Under Imperialism, 1885–1947* (Oxford University Press).

Ali, Jason, and Jonathan Aitchison (2008). "Gondwana to Asia: Plate Tectonics, Paleogeography and the Biological Connectivity of the Indian Sub-Continent from the Middle Jurassic through Latest Eocene (166–35 Ma)," *Earth-Science Reviews* 88:145–66.

Ali, Tanvir (2007). "Impact of Participatory Forest Management on Financial Assets of Rural Communities in Northwest Pakistan" *Ecological Economics* 6/3: 588–93.

Allchin, Bridget, and Michael Petraglia, eds. (2007). *The Evolution and History of Human Populations in South Asia* (Springer).

Alley, Kelly (2002). *On the Banks of the Ganga: When Wastewater Meets a Sacred River* (University of Michigan Press).

Amponin, Janet, and James Evans (2016). *Assessing the Intended Nationally Determined Contributions of ADB Developing Members* (Asian Development Bank).

Appell, Virginia, and M. Saleem Baluch (2003). "Mitigating the Effects of Drought through Traditional and Modern Water Supply Systems in Balochistan," in Waqar A. Jehangir and Intizar Hussain, eds., *Poverty Reduction through Improved Agricultural Water Management* (International Water Management Institute, Islamabad), pp. 241–59.

Arnold, David (1988). *Famine: Social Crisis and Historical Change* (Basil Blackwell).

Arnold, David (1996). *The Problem of Nature: Environment, Culture and European Expansion* (Blackwell).

Arnold, David (2000). *Science, Technology and Medicine in Colonial India* (Cambridge University Press).

Arnold, David (2008). "Plant Capitalism and Company Science," *Modern Asian Studies* 42/5:899–928.

Arnold, David (2013). "Pollution, Toxicity and Public Health in Metropolitan India, 1850–1939," *Journal of Historical Geography* 42:124–33.

Arnold, David (2016). *Toxic Histories: Poison and Pollution in Modern India* (Cambridge University Press).

Arnold, David, and Ramachandra Guha, eds. (1995). *Nature, Culture and Imperialism: Essays on the Environmental History of South Asia* (Oxford University Press).

Asian Development Bank (2004). *Country Environmental Analysis: Bangladesh* (Asian Development Bank).

Asher, Catherine (1992). *Architecture of Mughal India* (Cambridge University Press).

Asthana, Vandana (2009). *Water Policy Processes in India: Discourses of Power and Resistance* (Routledge).

Athar Ali, M. (1985). *Apparatus of Empire* (Oxford University Press).

Azizullah, Azizullah, Muhammad Nasir Khan Khattak, Peter Richter, and Donat-Peter Hader (2011). "Water Pollution in Pakistan and Its Impact on Public Health: A Review," *Environment International* 37:479–97.

Babur (2002). *Baburnama*, trans. W. M. Thackston (Modern Library).

Baghel, Ravi (2014). *River Control in India: Spatial, Governmental and Subjective Dimensions* (Springer).

Bailey, R. C., and T. N. Headland (1991). "The Tropical Rain Forest: Is It a Productive Environment for Human Foragers?" *Human Ecology* 19/2:115–22

Baker, Kathleen, and Sarah Jewitt (2007). "Evaluating 35 Years of Green Revolution Technology in Villages of Bulandshahr District, Western UP, North India," *Journal of Development Studies* 43/2:312–39.

Bamshad, Michael, T. Kivisild, W. S. Watkins, et al. (2001). "Genetic Evidence on the Origins of Indian Caste Populations," *Genome Research* 11:994–1004.

Banerjee, Damayanti, and Michael Mayerfeld Bell (2007). "Ecogender: Locating Gender in Environmental Social Science," *Science and Natural Resources* 20:3–19.

Baranski, Marci R. (2015). "Wide Adaptation of Green Revolution Wheat: International Roots and the Indian Context of a New Plant Breeding Ideal, 1960–1970," *Studies in History and Philosophy of Biological and Biomedical Sciences* 50:41–50.

Barton, Gregory (2002). *Empire Forestry and the Origins of Environmentalism* (Cambridge University Press).

Barton, G. A., and B. M. Bennett (2008). "Environmental Conservation and Deforestation in British India 1855–1947: A Reinterpretation," *Itinerario* 32: 83–104.

Baviskar, Amita (1995). *In the Belly of the River: Tribal Conflicts over Development in the Narmada Valley* (Oxford University Press).

Bayly, Susan (1999). *Caste, Society and Politics in India from the Eighteenth Century to the Modern Age* (Cambridge University Press).

Beattie, James (2012). "Recent Themes in the Environmental History of the British Empire," *History Compass* 10/2:129–39.

Beinart, William, and Lotte Hughes (2007). *Environment and Empire* (Oxford University Press).

Bhimsen (1972). *Tarikh-i-Dilkasha*, trans. Jadunath Sarkar (Department of Archives, Bombay).

Biswas, Asit K., R. Rangachari, and Cecelia Tortajada, eds. (2009). *Water Resources of the Indian Subcontinent* (Oxford University Press).

Blake, Stephen (1993). *Shahjahanabad* (Cambridge University Press).

Borlaug, Norman (1970). "Nobel Lecture: The Green Revolution, Peace, and Humanity," www.nobelprize.org/nobel_prizes/peace/laureates/1970/borlaug-lecture.html (accessed 11/11/2017).

Briggs, John (2003). "The Biogeographic and Tectonic History of India," *Journal of Biogeography* 30:381–88.

Bryson, Reid, and Joseph Schuldenrein (2008). "Water Supply and History: Harappa and the Beas Regional Survey," *Antiquity* 82:37–48.

Cederlof, Gunnel (2014). *Founding an Empire on India's North-eastern Frontiers, 1790–1840: Climate, Commerce, Polity* (Oxford University Press).

Cederlof, Gunnel, and K. Sivaramakrishnan, eds. (2006). *Ecological Nationalisms: Nature, Livelihoods, and Identities in South Asia* (University of Washington Press).

Centre for Science and the Environment (1982-). *Citizens Reports 1-* (Centre for Science and the Environment). www.cseindia.org (accessed 11/11/2017).

Chakrabarti, Dilip (2014). "India beyond the Indus Civilisation," in Colin Renfrew and Paul Bahn, eds., *Cambridge World Prehistory* (Cambridge University Press) vol. 1, pp. 433–46.

Chakrabarti, Pratik (2015). "Purifying the River: Pollution and Purity of Water in Colonial Calcutta," *Studies in History* 31/2:178–205.

Chakrabarti, Ranjan, ed. (2009). *Situating Environmental History* (Manohar).

Chakrabarty, Dipesh (2009). "The Climate of History: Four Theses," *Critical Inquiry* 35:197–222.

Chakravorty, Ranes (1993). "Diseases of Antiquity in South Asia," in Kenneth F. Kiple, ed., *Cambridge World History of Human Disease* (Cambridge University Press), pp. 408–12.

Chandra, Uday (2015). "Towards Adivasi Studies: New Perspectives on 'Tribal' Margins of Modern India," *Studies in History* 31/1:122–27.

Chapple, Christopher Key, ed. (2002). *Jainism and Ecology: Nonviolence in the Web of Life* (Harvard University Press).

Chapple, Christopher Key, and Mary Evelyn Tucker, eds. (2000). *Hinduism and Ecology: The Intersection of Earth, Sky, and Water* (Harvard University Press).

Chatterji, Joya (2007). *The Spoils of Partition: Bengal and India 1947–1967* (Cambridge University Press).

Chavda, Divyabhanush (1995). *The End of the Trail: The Cheetah in India* (Banyan).

Chellaney, Brahma (2011). *Water: Asia's New Battleground* (Georgetown University Press).

Chester, Lucy (2009). *Borders and Conflict in South Asia* (Manchester University Press).

Chowdhury, Mohammad, ed. (2014). *Forest Conservation in Protected Areas of Bangladesh: Policy and Community Development Perspectives* (Springer).

Clemett, Alexandra (2002). *Review of Environmental Policy and Legislation in Bangladesh* (BEEL).

Cohen, Benjamin (2011). "Modernising the Urban Environment: The Musi River Flood of 1908 in Hyderabad, India," *Environment and History* 17: 409–32.

Colbeck, Ian, Zaheer Ahmad Nasir, and Zulfiqar Ali (2010a). "State of Ambient Air Quality in Pakistan: A Review," *Environmental Science and Pollution Research* 17:49–63.

Colbeck, Ian, Zaheer Ahmad Nasir, and Zulfiqar Ali (2010b). "State of Indoor Air Quality in Pakistan: A Review," *Environmental Science and Pollution Research* 17:1187–96.

Cole, Camille (2016). "From Forest to Delta: Recent Themes in South Asian Environmental History," *South Asian History and Culture* 7/2:208–19.

Corbridge, Stuart (1988). "The Ideology of Tribal Economy and Society: Politics in the Jharkhand, 1950–1980," *Modern Asian Studies* 22:1–42.

Coutinho, Miguel, and Hamza Butt (2014). "*Environmental Impact Assessment Guidance for Coal Fired Power Plants in Pakistan* (IUCN).

Crosby, Alfred (1972). *The Columbian Exchange: Biological and Cultural Consequences of 1492* (Greenwood).

Cullet, Philippe, and Sujith Koonan (2011). *Water Law in India: An Introduction to Legal Instruments* (Oxford University Press).

Dale, Stephen (2004). *Garden of the Eight Paradises* (Brill).

Dalrymple, William, and Anita Anand (2017). *Koh-i-Noor: The History of the World's Most Infamous Diamond* (Bloomsbury).

Damodaran, A. (2010). *Encircling the Seamless: India, Climate Change, and the Global Commons* (Oxford University Press).

Damodaran, Vinita, V. Winterbottom, and A. Lester, eds. (2015). *The East India Company and the Natural World* (Palgrave).

Dangwal, Dhirendra (2009). *Himalayan Degradation: Colonial Forestry and Environmental Change in India* (Cambridge University Press).

Daniel, E. Valentine (1987). *Fluid Signs* (University of California Press).

Das, Pallavi (2015). *Colonialism, Development, and the Environment: Railways and Deforestation in British India, 1860–1884* (Palgrave).

Dasgupta, Susmita, Mainul Huq, Asif Zaman, et al. (2015). *Urban Flooding of Greater Dhaka in a Changing Climate: Building Local Resilience to Disaster Risk* (World Bank).

Davis, Mike (2002). *Late Victorian Holocausts* (Verso).

Delhi State Legal Services Authority (2017). *Recommendations for Long Term Action Plan for Solid Waste Management in Delhi* (Delhi State Legal Services Authority).

Dennell, Robin, and Michael Petraglia (2012). "The Dispersal of *Homo Sapiens* across Southern Asia: How Early, How Often, How Complex," *Quaternary Science Reviews* 47:15–22.

Dewan, Ashraf, and Robert Corner, eds. (2014). *Dhaka Megacity: Geospacial Perspectives on Urbanisation, Environment and Health* (Springer).

Digby, Simon (1971). *Warhorse and Elephant in the Delhi Sultanate: A Study of Military Supplies* (Orient Monographs).

Divan, Shyam, and Armin Rosencranz (2001). *Environmental Law and Polity in India: Cases, Materials and Statutes* (Oxford University Press).

Divyabhanusinh (2005). *The Story of Asia's Lions* (Marg).

Donges, J. F., R. V. Donner, N. Marwan, et al. (2015). "Non-linear Regime Shifts in Holocene Asian Monsoon Variability: Potential Impacts on Cultural Change and Migratory Patterns," *Climate of the Past* 11:709–41.

Doron, Assa, and Robin Jeffrey (2018). *Waste of Nation: Garbage and Growth in India* (Harvard University Press).

Drayton, Richard (2000). *Nature's Government: Science, Imperial Britain and the "Improvement" of the World* (Yale University Press).

D'Souza, Rohan (2006a). *Drowned and Dammed: Colonial Capitalism and Flood Control in Eastern India* (Oxford University Press).

D'Souza, Rohan (2006b). "Water in British India: The Making of a 'Colonial Hydrology'," *History Compass* 4/4:621–28.

Duara, Prasenjit (2014). *The Crisis of Global Modernity: Asian Traditions and a Sustainable Future* (Cambridge University Press).

Dubash, Navroz, ed. (2012). *Handbook of Climate Change in India: Development, Politics, and Governance* (Routledge).

Eaton, Richard (1993). *Rise of Islam and the Bengal Frontier, 1204–1760* (University of California Press).

Eaton, Richard, and Philip Wagoner (2014). *Power, Memory, Architecture: Contested Sites on India's Deccan Plateau, 1300–1600* (Oxford University Press).

Edney, Matthew (1987). *Mapping an Empire: The Geographical Construction of British India, 1765–1843* (University of Chicago Press).

Elliot, H.M. (1873–77). *History of India as Told by Its Own Historians*, ed. John Dowson, 8 vols. (Trubner).

Erenstein, Olaf (2010). "Comparative Analysis of Rice–Wheat Systems in Indian Haryana and Pakistan Punjab," *Land Use Policy* 27:869–91.

Falk, Nancy E. (1973). "Wilderness and Kingship in Ancient South Asia," *History of Religions* 13/1:1–15.

Farooqi, Naim (1988). "Moguls, Ottomans, and Pilgrims," *International History Review*, 10/2:198–220.

Feldhaus, Anne (2003). *Region, Pilgrimage, and Geographical Imagination in India* (Palgrave MacMillan).

Fischer, Thomas (2014). *Environmental Impact Assessment Handbook for Pakistan* (IUCN).

Fisher, Michael H. (2007). *Visions of Mughal India* (I.B. Tauris).

Fisher, Michael H. (2015). *A Short History of the Mughal Empire* (I.B. Tauris).

Foltz, Richard, Frederick Denny, and Azizan Baharuddin (2003). *Islam and Ecology: A Bestowed Trust* (Harvard University Press).

Gadgil, Madhav, and Ramachandra Guha (1992). *This Fissured Land: An Ecological History of India* (Oxford University Press).

Gadgil, Madhav, and Ramachandra Guha (1995). *Ecology and Equity: The Use and Abuse of Nature in Contemporary India* (Routledge).

Gadgil, Madhav, and Romila Thapar (1990). "Human Ecology in India: Some Historical Perspectives," *Interdisciplinary Science Reviews* 15/3:209–23.

Gadgil, Madhav, and V.D. Vartak (1975). "Sacred Groves of India: A Plea for Continued Conservation." *Journal of the Bombay Natural History Society* 72/2: 313–20.

Galley, Michael (2014). *Shipbreaking: Hazards and Liabilities* (Springer).

Gandhi, Indira (1972). "*Speech*" (Conference on the Human Environment).

Gandhi, Indira (1981). "Directive to Chief Ministers," quoted in Divan and Rozencranz, p. 477.

Gandhi, Mohandas K. (1909). *Indian Home Rule/Hind Swaraj* (International Printing Press) [also available at www.mkgandhi.org (accessed 11/11/2017)].

Gandhi, Mohandas K. (1948). *The Story of My Experiments with Truth* (Public Affairs Press).

Ganeshaiah, K. N., R. Uma Shaanker, and R. Vasudeva (2007). "Bio-resources and Empire Building: What Favored the Growth of Vijayanagar Empire," *Current Science* 933/2:140–46.

Gangal, K., Graeme R. Sarson, and Anwar Shukurov (2014). "Near-Eastern Roots of the Neolithic in South Asia," *PLoS ONE* 9 (5)journals.plos.org/plosone/article?id=10.1371/journal.pone.0095714.pone.0095714 (accessed 11/11/2017).

Ganjoo, R. K., and S. B. Ota (2012). "Mountain Environment and Early Human Adaptation in NW Himalaya, India: A Case Study of Siwalik Hill Range and Leh Valley," *Quaternary International* 269:31–7.

Gilmartin, David (1994). "Scientific Empire and Imperial Science: Colonialism and Irrigation Technology in the Indus Basin," *Journal of Asian Studies* 53/4: 1127–49.

Gilmartin, David (2015). *Blood and Water: The Indus River Basin in Modern History* (University of California Press).

Giosan, Liviu, Peter D. Clift, Mark G. Macklin, et al. (2012). "Fluvial landscapes of the Harappan Civilization," *Proceedings of the National Academy of Sciences of the United States of America* 109/26:10138–39.

Gold, Ann, and Bhoja Ram Gujar (2002). *In the Time of Trees and Sorrows: Nature, Power, and Memory in Rajasthan* (Oxford University Press).

Gordon, Stewart (1993). *Marathas, 1600–1818* (Cambridge University Press).

Government of India (2005). *Report of the Tiger Task Force: Joining the Dots* (Ministry of Environment and Forests).

Government of India (2010). *Report of the Elephant Task Force: Gajah: Securing the Future for Elephants in India*, ed. Mahesh Rangarajan et al. (Ministry of Environment and Forests).

Government of India (2013). *Statistical Profile of Scheduled Tribes in India*, 2nd ed. (Ministry of Tribal Affairs).

Government of Pakistan (2014). *Vision Pakistan 2025: One Nation—One Vision* (Ministry of Planning).

Govindrajan, Radhika (2018). *Animal Intimacies: Interspecies Relations in India's Central Himalayas* (University of Chicago Press).

The Graphic, London (June 1882).

Greenough, Paul (1982). *Prosperity and Misery in Modern Bengal: The Famine of 1943–44* (Oxford University Press).

Greenough, Paul (2001). "*Naturae Ferae*: Wild Animals in South Asia and the Standard Ecological Narrative," in James C. Scott, and Nina Bhatt, eds., *Agrarian Studies: Synthetic Work at the Cutting Edge* (Yale University Press), pp. 141–85.

Grove, Richard (1993). "Conserving Eden: The (European) East India Companies and their Environmental Policies on St. Helena, Mauritius and in Western India, 1660 to 1854," *Comparative Studies in Society and History* 35/2: 318–51.

Grove, Richard (1995). *Green Imperialism: Colonial Expansion, Tropical Island Edens and the Origins of Environmentalism, 1600–1860* (Cambridge University Press).

Grove, Richard, Vinita Damodaran, and Satpal Sangwan, eds. (1998). *Nature and the Orient: The Environmental History of South and Southeast Asia* (Oxford University Press).

Guha, Ramachandra (1995). "Radical American Environmentalism and Wilderness Preservation: A Third World Critique" in J. Baird Callicot and Michael P. Nelson, eds., *The Great New Wilderness Debate* (University of Georgia Press), pp. 271–79.

Guha, Ramachandra (1997). "Mahatma Gandhi and the Environmental Movement" in Ramachandra Guha and Juan Martinez-Alier, eds., *Varieties of Environmentalism: Essays North and South* (Earthscan), pp. 153–68.

Guha, Ramachandra (1999). *Savaging the Civilized: Verrier Elwin, His Tribals, and India* (University of Chicago Press).

Guha, Ramachandra (2000a). *Environmentalism: A Global History* (Oxford University Press).

Guha, Ramachandra (2000b). *The Unquiet Woods: Ecological Change and Peasant Resistance in the Himalayas*, 2nd ed. (Oxford University Press).

Guha, Ramachandra (2006). *How Much Should a Person Consume? Environmentalism in India and the United States* (University of California Press).

Guha, Ranajit (1996). *Rule of Property for Bengal*, reprint (Duke University Press).

Guha, Ranajit, et al., eds. (1982–2012). *Subaltern Studies*, 12 vols. (Oxford University Press and Permanent Black).

Guha, Sumit (1999). *Environment and Ethnicity in India, 1200–1991* (Cambridge University Press).

Gujarat Marine Board, http://www.gmbports.org/ship-recycling-yards (accessed 11/11/2017).

Gunawardena, E.R.N., Brij Gopal, and Hemesiri Kotagama, eds. (2015). *Ecosystems and Integrated Water Resources Management in South Asia* (Routledge).

Gurukkal, Rajan (2015). "The Making and Proliferation of Jati: A Historical Inquiry," *Studies in History* 31/1:30–50.

Haberman, David (2006). *River of Love in an Age of Pollution* (University of California Press).

Haberman, David (2013). *People Trees: Worship of Trees in Northern India* (Oxford University Press).

Habib, Irfan (1982). *Atlas of the Mughal Empire* (Oxford University Press).

Habib, Irfan (1999). *Agrarian System of Mughal India* (Oxford University Press).

Habib, Irfan (2010). *Man and Environment: The Ecological History of India, A People's History of India* (Aligarh Historians Society).

Habiba, Umma, Md. Anwarul Abedin, Abu Wali Raghib Hassan, and Rajib Shaw (2015). *Food Security and Risk Reduction in Bangladesh* (Springer).

Haines, Daniel (2017). *Rivers Divided: Indus Basin Waters in the Making of India and Pakistan* (Hurst).

Hardiman, David (1995). "Small-Dam Systems of the Sahyadris," in David Arnold and Ramachandra Guha, eds., *Nature, Culture and Imperialism* (Oxford University Press), pp. 185–209.

Harappa.Com www.harappa.com (accessed 11/11/2017).

Harrison, Mark (1999). *Climates and Constitutions: Health, Race, Environment and British Imperialism in India, 1600–1850* (Oxford University Press).

Hassan, Jawad (2001). "Country Report Pakistan Environmental Law," *Asia Pacific Journal of Environmental Law*, 6/3&4:319–32.

Hassan, Parvez (2007). "Environmental Protection, Rule of Law and the Judicial Crisis in Pakistan," *Asia Pacific Journal of Environmental Law* 10/3&4:167–81.

Hawkey, D.E. (2002). "The Peopling of South Asia: Evidence for Affinities and Microevolution of Prehistoric Populations from India/Sri Lanka," *Spolia Zeylanica* 39:1–300.

Hodiwala, Shahpurshah (1939–57). *Studies in Indo-Muslim History; A Critical Commentary* (S.H. Hodivala).

Hughes, Julie (2013). *Animal Kingdoms: Hunting, the Environment, and Power in Indian Princely States* (Harvard University Press).

Hughes, Julie (2015). "Royal Tigers and Ruling Princes: Wilderness and Wildlife Management in the Indian Princely States," *Modern Asian Studies* 49/4: 1210–60.

Huq, S.M. Immamul, Shoaib, and Jalal Uddin Muhammad (2013). *Soils of Bangladesh* (Springer).

Ibn Battuta, Muhammad (1976). *Rehla*, trans. Mahdi Husain (Oriental Institute); excerpted in Ross Dunn (1986). *Adventures of Ibn Battuta* (University of California Press).

Indian Genome Variation Consortium (2005). "The Indian Genome Variation Database (IGVdb): A Project Overview," *Human Genetics* 118:1–11.

International Maritime Organization, www.imo.org/en/OurWork/Environment/ShipRecycling (accessed 11/11/2017).

Iqbal, Iftekhar (2010). *The Bengal Delta: Ecology, State and Social Change, 1840–1943* (Palgrave-MacMillan).

Iqbal, Mehreen, Knut Brivik, Jabir Hussain Syed, et al. (2015). "Emerging Issue of E-waste in Pakistan: A Review of Status, Research Needs and Data Gaps," *Environmental Pollution* 207:308–18.

Islam, M. Mufakharul (1997). *Irrigation, Agriculture and the Raj: Punjab, 1887–1947* (Manohar).

Jahangir (1914). *Tuzuk-i-Jahangiri*, trans. Alexander Rogers, ed. Henry Beveridge, 2 vols. (Royal Asiatic Society).

Jain, Pankaj (2011). *Dharma and Ecology of Hindu Communities: Sustenance to Sustainability* (Ashgate).

Jamison, Stephanie, and Joel Brereton (2014). *Rigveda: The Earliest Religious Poetry of India* (Oxford University Press).

Jalais, Annu (2010). *Forest of Tigers: People, Politics, and Environment in the Sundarbans* (Routledge).

Jewitt, Sarah (2000). "Mothering Earth? Gender and Environmental Protection in the Jharkhand, India," *Journal of Peasant Studies* 27/2:94–131.

Jhala, Y. V., Q. Qureshi, and R. Gopal, eds. (2015). *The Status of Tigers in India* (National Tiger Conservation Authority).

Jinnah, Muhammad Ali (1947). *Speeches and Writings*, ed. Jamil-ud-Din Ahmad, 2 vols. (Shaikh Muhammad Ashraf).

Johnson, Daniel (1822). *Sketches of the Field Sports as Followed by the Natives of India* (Longman, Hurst, Rees, Orme, and Browne).

Kapur, Nandini Sinha (2011). *Environmental History of Early India: A Reader* (Oxford University Press)

Karlsson, Bengt (2011). *Unruly Hills: A Political Ecology of India's Northeast* (Berghahn).

Karlsson, Bengt, and Tanka B. Subba (2006). *Indigeneity in India* (Kegan Paul).

Kaul, Shonaleeka (2010). *Imagining the Urban: Sanskrit and the City in Early India* (Permanent Black).

Kautilya (2013). *Arthashastra*, trans. Patrick Olivelle as *King, Governance, and Law in Ancient India: Kautilya's* Arthasastra (Oxford University Press).

Kenoyer, Jonathan Mark (2000). "Wealth and Socioeconomic Hierarchies of the Indus Valley Civilization," in Janet Richards and Mary Van Buren, eds., *Order, Legitimacy, and Wealth in Ancient States* (Cambridge University Press), pp. 88–109.

Kenoyer, Jonathan Mark (2012). "The Indus Civilisation," in Colin Renfrew and Paul Bahn, eds., *Cambridge World Prehistory* (Cambridge University Press), vol. 1, pp. 407–32.

Kent, Eliza (2013). *Sacred Groves and Local Gods: Religion and Environmentalism in South India* (Oxford University Press).

Kerr, Ian (2007). *Engines of Change: The Railroads that Made India* (Praeger).

Khan, Saqi Mustaid (1947). *Maasir-i 'Alamgiri*, trans. Jadunath Sarkar (Royal Asiatic Society of Bengal).

Khanna, Shomona, and T. K. Naveen (2005). *Contested Terrain: Forest Cases in the Supreme Court of India* (Society for Rural Urban and Tribal Initiative).

Kidd, Ian (2012). "Biopiracy and the Ethics of Medical Heritage: The Case of India's Traditional Knowledge Digital Library," *Journal of Medical Humanities* 33/3:175–83.

Kingsbury, Benjamin (2018). *An Imperial Disaster: The Bengal Cyclone of 1876* (Oxford University Press).

Kingwell-Banham, Eleanor, Cameron A. Petrie, and Dorian Q. Fuller (2015). "Early Agriculture in South Asia" in Graeme Barker and Candice Goucher, eds., *Cambridge World History* (Cambridge University Press), pp. 261–88.

Kiple, Kenneth (2006). "The History of Diseases," in Roy Porter, ed., *The Cambridge History of Medicine* (Cambridge University Press).

Klein, Ira (1984). "When the Rains Failed," *Indian Economic and Social History Review* 21/2:185–214.

Klein, Ira (1988). "Plague, Policy and Popular Unrest in British India," *Modern Asian Studies* 22/4:723–55.

Klingensmith, Daniel (2007). *"One Valley and a Thousand": Dams, Nationalism, and Development* (Oxford University Press).

Kolady, Deepthi, and William Lesser (2012). "Genetically-engineered Crops and Their Effects on Varietal Diversity: A Case of Bt Eggplant in India," *Agriculture and Human Values* 29:3–15.

Krishna, Sumi (2012). *Agriculture and a Changing Environment in North-eastern India* (Routledge).

Kumar, Deepak, Vinita Damodaran, and Rohan D'Souza, eds. (2011). *The British Empire and the Natural World: Environmental Encounters in South Asia* (Oxford University Press).

Kumar, Dharma, et al., eds. (1982–83). *Cambridge Economic History of India*, 2 vols. (Cambridge University Press).

Kumar, Sunil (2007). *The Emergence of the Delhi Sultanate, 1192–1286* (Permanent Black).

Lahiri-Dutt, Kuntala, and Gopa Samanta (2013). *Dancing with the River: People and Life on the Chars of South Asia* (Yale University Press).

Lal, B. B., and K. N. Dikshit (1985). "A 2000-Year-Old Feat of Hydraulic Engineering in India," *Archaeology* 38/1:48–53.

Lal, Vinay (2000a). "Gandhi and the Ecological Vision of Life: Thinking beyond Deep Ecology," *Environmental Ethics* 72:149–68.

Lal, Vinay (2000b). "Too Deep for Deep Ecology: Gandhi and the Ecological Vision of Life" in Christopher Key Chapple and Mary Evelyn Tucker, eds., *Hinduism and Ecology* (Harvard University Press), pp. 183–212.

Lele, Sharachchandra, and Ajit Menon, eds. (2014). *Democratizing Forest Governance in India* (Oxford University Press).

Lewis, Michael (2005). "Indian Science for India's Tigers?: Conservation Biology and the Question of Cultural Values," *Journal of the History of Biology* 38:185–207.

Lewis, Michael (2007). "The Personal Equation: Political Economy and Social Technology on India's Canals, 1850–1930," *Modern Asian Studies* 41/5: 967–94.

Locke, Piers, and Jane Buckingham, eds. (2016). *Rethinking Human-Elephant Relations in South Asia: Conflict, Negotiation and Coexistence* (Oxford University Press).

Ludden, David (1999). *An Agrarian History of South Asia* (Cambridge University Press).

MacGeorge, G.W. (1894). *Ways and Works in India: Being an Account of the Public Works in that Country from the Earliest Times up to the Present Day* (Archibald Constable).

MacKenzie, John M. (1988). *The Empire of Nature: Hunting, Conservation and British Imperialism* (Manchester University Press).

McNeill, J.R. (2003). "Observations on the Nature and Culture of Environmental History," *History and Theory* 42:5–43.

McNeill, John, Jose Augusto Padua, and Mahesh Rangarajan, eds. (2010). *Environmental History: As If Nature Existed* (Oxford University Press).

Madsen, Stig Toft, ed. (1999). *State, Society and the Environment in South Asia* (Curzon).

Malhotra, Kailash C., Yogesh Gokhale, and Ketaki Das (2001). *Sacred Groves of India: An Annotated Bibliography* (Development Alliance).

Mann, Michael (2007). "Delhi's Belly: On the Management of Water, Sewage and Excreta in a Changing Urban Environment during the Nineteenth Century," *Studies in History* 23/1 n.s.:1–31.

Mann, Michael (2013). "Environmental History and Historiography on South Asia: Context and Some Recent Publications," *Südasien-Chronik-South Asia Chronicle* 3:324–57.

Manu (2004). *The Law Code of Manu*, trans. Patrick Olivelle (Oxford University Press).

Marx, Karl (1853). "The Future Results of British Rule in India," in *New York Daily Tribune* (8 August).

Mathur, Ajeet (2003). "Who Owns Traditional Knowledge?," *Economic and Political Weekly* 2003:4471–81.

Mawdsley, Emma (2004). "India's Middle Classes and the Environment," *Development and Change* 35/1:79–103.

Mawdsley, Emma (2006). "Hindu Nationalism, Neo-traditionalism and Environmental Discourses in India," *Geoforum* 37:380–90.

Mayewski, Paul, Eelco E. Rohling, J. Curt Stager, et al. (2004). "Holocene Climate Variability," *Quaternary Research* 62:243–55.

Menon, Ajit, Christelle Hinnewinkel, and Sylvie Guillerme (2013). "Denuded Forests, Wooded Estates: Statemaking in a Janmam Area of Gudalur, Tamil Nadu," *Indian Economic and Social History Review* 50/4:449–71.

Menzies, Robert (2010). "Forest Paradigms in Vrat Kathas," *Journal for the Study of Religion, Nature and Culture* 4/2:140–49.

Metcalf, Thomas (2002). *An Imperial Vision: Indian Architecture and Britain's Raj* (Oxford University Press).

Minsky, Lauren (2015). "Of Health and Harvests: Seasonal Mortality and Commercial Rice Cultivation in the Punjab and Bengal Regions of South Asia," in Francesca Bray, Peter A. Coclanis, Edda L. Fields-Black, and Dagmar Schafer, eds., *Rice: Global Networks and New Histories* (Cambridge University Press), pp. 245–74.

Misra, V.N. (2001). "Prehistoric Human Colonization of India," *Journal of Bioscience* 26/4:491–531.

Moin, Ahmed Azfar (2012). *Millennial Sovereign* (Columbia University Press).

Mollinga, Peter (2003). *On the Waterfront: Water Distribution, Technology and Agrarian Change in a South Indian Canal Irrigation System* (Orient Blackswan).

Mollinga, Peter (2015). "Farmers' Suicides as Public Death: Politics, Agency and Statistics in a Suicide-Prone District (South India)," *Modern Asian Studies* 40/5: 1580–605.

Momtaz, S. (2002). "Environmental Assessment in Bangladesh: A Critical Review," *Environmental Impact Assessment Review* 22:163–79.

Moor, Raphaelle, and M.V. Rajeev Gowda, eds. (2014). *India's Risks: Democratizing the Management of Threats to Environment, Health, and Values* (Oxford University Press).

Morrison, Kathleen (2014). "Conceiving Ecology and Stopping the Clock: Narratives of Balance, Loss, and Degradation" in Mahesh Rangarajan and K. Sivaramakrishnan, eds., *Shifting Ground* (Oxford University Press), pp. 39–64.

Mosse, David (2003). *The Rule of Water: Statecraft, Ecology, and Collective Action in South India* (Oxford University Press).

Mukherjee, Janam (2017). *Hungry Bengal: War, Famine and the End of Empire* (Hurst).

Murali, Atluri (1995). "Whose Trees? Forest Practices and Local Communities in Andhra, 1600–1922," in David Arnold and Ramachandra Guha, eds., *Nature, Culture, Imperialism* (Oxford University Press), pp. 86–122.

Mustafa, Daanish (2013). *Water Resource Management in a Vulnerable World: The Hydro-hazardscapes of Climate Change* (I.B. Tauris).

Muzaffar, Sabir Bin, M. Anwarul Islam, Dihider Shahriar Kabir, et al. (2011). "The Endangered Forests of Bangladesh: Why the Process of Implementation of the Convention on Biological Diversity Is Not Working," *Biodiversity and Conservation* 20:1587–601.

Nadeem, Obaidullah, and Rizwan Hameed (2008). "A Critical Review of the Adequacy of EIA Reports—Evidence from Pakistan," *International Journal of Environmental, Chemical, Ecological, Geological and Geophysical Engineering* 2/ 11:146–53.

Nagendra, Harini (2016). *Nature in the City: Bengaluru in the Past, Present, and Future* (Oxford University Press).

Nair, Janaki (2005). *The Promise of the Metropolis: Bangalore's Twentieth Century* (Oxford University Press).

Nandimath, O.V. (2009). *Oxford Handbook of Environmental Decision Making in India: An EIA Model* (Oxford University Press).

Narain, Vishal, and Anjal Prakash, eds. (2016). *Water Security in Peri-Urban South Asia: Adapting to Climate Change and Urbanization* (Oxford University Press).

Nehru, Jawaharlal (1947). *Discovery of India* (Meridian).

Nehru, Jawaharlal (1954). "Speech Inaugurating the Bhakra-Nangal Dam" (8 July) http://celebratingnehru.org/english/nehru_speech4.aspx (accessed 11/11/2017).

Nehru, Jawaharlal (1956). "Forward," in E.P. Gee, *Why Preserve Wildlife?* (Indian Board of Wildlife).

Nelson, Lance, ed. (1998). *Purifying the Earthly Body of God: Religion and Ecology in India* (State University of New York Press).

Niazi, Tarique (2004). "Rural Poverty and the Green Revolution: The Lessons from Pakistan," *Journal of Peasant Studies* 31/2:242–60.

Nilakanta Shastri, K.A., and N. Venkataramayayya, eds. (1946). *Further Sources of Vijayanagara History*, 3 vols. (University of Madras).

Nilsen, Alf (2012). *Dispossession and Resistance in India: The River and the Rage* (Routledge).

Nugteren, Albertina (2005). *Belief, Bounty, and Beauty: Rituals around Sacred Trees in India* (Brill).

Nugteren, Albertina (2008). "Darubrahma: The Continuing Story of Wood, Trees, and Forests in the Ritual Fabric of Jagannath," *Journal for the Study of Religion, Nature, and Culture* 2/1:4–9.

O'Flaherty, Wendy Doniger, trans. (1981). *Selected Hymns from the Vedas* (Penguin).

Olivelle, Patrick (2016). "Science of Elephants in Kautilya's *Arthasastra*," in Piers Locke and Jane Buckingham, eds., *Conflict, Negotiation, and Coexistence* (Oxford University Press), pp. 74–91.

Owen, Lewis A., Robert C. Finkel, and Marc W. Caffee (2002). "Note on the Extent of Glaciation throughout the Himalaya during the Global Last Glacial Maximum," *Quaternary Science Reviews* 21:147–57.

Pandian, Anand (2001). "Predatory Care: The Imperial Hunt in Mughal and British India," *Journal of Historical Sociology* 14/1:79–107.

Pandian, Anand, and Doud Ali, eds. (2010). *Ethical Life in South Asia* (Indiana University Press).

Panigrahi, Jitendra K., and Susruta Amirapun (2012). "Assessment of EIA System in India," *Environmental Impact Assessment Review* 35:23–36.

Parkhill, Thomas (1995). *The Forest Setting in Hindu Epics: Princes, Sages, Demons* (Mellen University Press).

Patak, A. (2002). *Law, Strategies, Ideologies: Legislating Forests in Colonial India* (Oxford University Press).

Patel, Raj (2013). "The Long Green Revolution," *Journal of Peasant Studies* 40/1:1–63.

Patton, Laurie (2000). "Nature Romanticism and Sacrifice in Rigvedic Interpretation," in Christopher Key Chapple and Mary Evelyn Tucker, eds., *Hinduism and Ecology* (Harvard University Press), pp. 39–58.

Pawson, Eric (2008). "Plants, Mobilities and Landscapes: Environmental Histories of Botanical Exchange," *Geography Compass* 2:1464–77.

Petraglia, M.D., and B. Allchin, eds. (2007). *Evolution and History of Human Populations in South Asia* (Springer).

Petraglia, Michael, Peter Ditchfield, Sacha Jones, et al. (2012). "The Toba Volcanic Super-Eruption, Environmental Change, and Hominin Occupation History in India over the Last 140,000 Years," *Quaternary International* 258: 119–34.

Pollock, Sheldon (1991). "The *Ramayana*: Myth and Romance?," in Robert Goldman, trans., *The Ramayana of Valmiki, Volume III: Aranyakanda* (Princeton University Press).

Pollock, Sheldon (2006). *The Language of the Gods in the World of Men: Sanskrit, Culture, and Power in Premodern India* (University of California Press).

Possehl, Gregory (2002). *The Indus Civilization: A contemporary perspective* (Altamira).

Prakash, Anjal, Sreoshi Singh, C. G. Goodrich, and S. Janakarajan, eds. (2013). *Water Resources Policies in South Asia* (Routledge).

Prasad, Archana (2003). *Against Ecological Romanticism: Verrier Elwin and the Making of an Anti-Modern Tribal Identity* (Oxford University Press).

Prashad, Vijay (2001). "Technology of Sanitation in Colonial Delhi," *Modern Asian Studies* 35/1:113–55.

Rademacher, Anne, and K. Sivaramakrishnan, eds. (2013). *Ecologies of Urbanism in India: Metropolitan Civility and Sustainability* (Hong Kong University Press).

Rahman, S. M. Mizanur, Robert M. Handler, and Audrey L. Mayer (2016). "Life Cycle Assessment of Steel in the Ship Recycling Industry in Bangladesh," *Journal of Cleaner Production* 135:963–71.

Rajagopalan, R. (2011). *Environmental Studies: From Crisis to Cure*, 2nd ed. (Oxford University Press).

Rajan, Ravi (2006). *Modernizing Nature: Forestry and Imperial Eco-Development, 1800–1950* (Oxford University Press).

Ramanathan, A. L., Scott Johnston, Abhijit Mukherjee, and Bibhash Nath, eds. (2015). *Safe and Sustainable Use of Arsenic-Contaminated Aquifers in the Gangetic Plain: A Multidisciplinary Approach* (Springer).

Ramanujan, A. K. (1967). *Interior Landscape: Love Poems from a Classical Tamil Anthology* (Indiana University Press).

Ramesh, Jairam (2015). *Green Signals: Ecology, Growth, and Democracy in India* (Oxford University Press).

Rangarajan, Mahesh (1996a). "Environmental Histories of South Asia: A Review Essay," *Environment and History* 2/2:129–43.

Rangarajan, Mahesh (1996b). *Fencing the Forests: Conservation and Ecological Change in India's Central Provinces, 1860–1914* (Oxford University Press).

Rangarajan, Mahesh (2013). "Animals with Rich Histories: The Case of the Lions of the Gir Forest, Gujarat, India," *History and Theory* 52:109–27.

Rangarajan, Mahesh, ed. (2007). *Environmental Issues in India* (Pearson).

Rangarajan, Mahesh, and G. Shahabuddin (2006). "Debate: Displacement and Relocation from Protected Areas: Towards Biological and Historical Synthesis," *Conservation and Society*, 4/3:359–78.

Rangarajan, Mahesh, and K. Sivaramakrishnan, eds. (2012). *India's Environmental History*, 2 vols. (Permanent Black).

Rangarajan, Mahesh, and K. Sivaramakrishnan, eds. (2014). *Shifting Ground: People, Animals, and Mobility in India's Environmental History* (Oxford University Press).

Rao, Neema A. (2008). *Forest Ecology in India: Colonial Maharashtra 1850–1950* (Foundation).

Rashid, Harun, and Bimal Paul (2014). *Climate Change in Bangladesh: Confronting Impending Disasters* (Lexington).

Rashkow, Ezra (2014). "Idealizing Inhabited Wilderness: A Revision to the History of Indigenous Peoples and National Parks," *History Compass* 12/10: 818–32.

Rashkow, Ezra (2015). "Resistance to Hunting in Pre-independence India: Religious Environmentalism, Ecological Nationalism or Cultural Conservation?," *Modern Asian Studies* 49/2:270–301.

Rastogi, Archi, Gordon M. Hickey, Ruchi Badola, and Syed Ainul Hussain (2012). "Saving the Superstar: A Review of the Social Factors Affecting Tiger Conservation in India," *Journal of Environmental Management* 113:328–40.

Rawat, Ajay, ed. (1991). *History of Forestry in India* (Indus).

Ray, Binayak (2008). *Water: The Looming Crisis in India* (Lexington).

Ray, Binayak (2011). *Climate Change: IPCC, Water Crisis, and Policy: Riddles with Reference to India and Her Surroundings* (Lexington).

Ribbentrop, B. (1900). *Forestry in British India* (Government of India).

Richards, John (1993). *Mughal Empire* (Cambridge University Press).

Richards, John (2003). *The Unending Frontier: Environmental History in the Early Modern Centuries* (University of California Press).

Richards, John, James R. Hagen, and Edward Haynes (1985). "Changing Land Use in Bihar, Punjab and Haryana, 1850–1970," *Modern Asian Studies* 19/3: 699–732.

Rinku, Murgai (2001). "Post-Green Revolution in Indian and Pakistani Punjabs," *World Bank Research Observer* 16/2:199–218.

Robbins Schug, Gwen, Rinku Murgai, Mubarik Ali, and Derek Byerlee (2013). "Infection, Disease, and Biosocial Processes at the End of the Indus Civilization," *PLoS ONE* 8 (12) journals.plos.org/plosone/article?id=10 .1371/journal.pone.0084814 (accessed 11/11/2017).

Roth, Dik, and Linden Vincent, eds. (2013). *Controlling Water: Matching Technology and Institutions in Irrigation Management in India and Nepal* (Oxford University Press).

Roy, R.C., and S.C. Roy (1937). *The Kharias*, 2 vols. (Catholic Press).

Saberwal, Vasant (1999). *Pastoral Politics: Shepherds, Bureaucrats, and Conservation in the Western Himalaya* (Oxford University Press).

Saberwal, Vasant, and Mahesh Rangarajan (2005). *Battles Over Nature: Science and the Politics of Conservation* (Orient Blackswan).

Saikia, Arupjyoti (2011). *Forests and Ecological History of Assam* (Oxford University Press).

Sarasvati, Rangasvami (1925). "Political Maxims of the Emperor-Poet Krishnadeva Raya," *Journal of Indian History* 4/3:61–88.

Saravanan, Velayutham (2016). *Colonialism, Environment and Tribals in South India, 1792–1947* (Routledge).

Satya, Laxman (1997). *Cotton and Famine in Berar, 1850–1900* (Manohar).

Schwartzberg, Joseph, ed. (1978). *Historical Atlas of South Asia* (University of Chicago Press). [also available at dsal.uchicago.edu/reference/schwartzberg" (accessed 11/11/2017)].

Sekhar, Nagothu (2013). "Local People's Attitudes toward Conservation and Wildlife Tourism around Sariska Tiger Reserve, India," *Journal of Environmental Management* 689:339–47.

Sengupta, Nirmal (1980). "Indigenous Irrigation Organisation in South Bihar," *Indian Economic and Social History Review* 37/2:157–87.

Shah, Alpa (2007). "The Dark Side of Indigeneity?: Indigenous People, Rights and Development in India," *History Compass* 5/6:1806–32.

Shah, Alpa (2010). *In the Shadows of the State: Indigenous Politics, Environmentalism and Insurgency in Jharkhand, India* (Duke University Press).

Shah, Julia, John Sutcliffe, Lindsay Lloyd-Smith, et al. (2007). "Ancient Irrigation and Buddhist History in Central India: Optically Stimulated Luminescence Dates and Pollen Sequences from the Sanchi Dams," *Asian Perspectives* 46/1:166–201.

Shahabuddin, Ghazala (2010). *Conservation at the Crossroads: Science, Society and the Future of India's Wildlife* (Permanent Black).

Shahabuddin, Ghazala, and Mahesh Rangarajan, eds. (2007). *Making Conservation Work: Securing Biodiversity in This New Century* (Permanent Black).

Sharan, Awadhendra (2014). *In the City, Out of Place: Nuisance, Pollution, and Dwelling in Delhi, c.1850–2000* (Oxford University Press).

Sharma, Mukul (2012). *Green and Saffron: Hindu Nationalism and Indian Environmental Politics* (Permanent Black).

Sharma, R.S. (1987). *Urban Decay in India (c.300–c.1000)* (Munshiram Manoharlal).

Shipbreaking Platform, www.shipbreakingplatform.org (accessed 11/11/2017).

Shiva, Vandana (1988). *Staying Alive: Women, Ecology, and Survival in India* (Kali for Women).

Shiva, Vandana (1997). *Biopiracy: The Plunder of Nature and Knowledge* (South End Press).

Shiva, Vandana (2007). "Bioprospecting as Sophisticated Biopiracy," *Signs* 32/2: 307–13.

Shiva, Vandana, and J. Bandyopadhyay (1986). "The Evolution, Structure, and Impact of the Chipko Movement," *Mountain Research and Development* 6/2: 133–42.

Singh, Bhasha (2014). *Unseen: The Truth about India's Manual Scavengers*, trans. Reenu Talwar (Penguin).

Singh, Chetan (1995). "Forests, Pastoralist and Agrarian Society in Mughal India," in David Arnold and Ramachandra Guha, eds., *Nature, Culture, Imperialism* (Oxford University Press), pp. 21–48.

Singh, Satyajit (2016). *The Local in Governance: Politics, Decentralization, and Environment* (Oxford University Press).

Sinha, Anushree, Armin Bauer, and Paul Bullen, eds. (2015). *The Environments of the Poor in South Asia: Simultaneously Reducing Poverty, Protecting the Environment, and Adapting to Climate Change* (Oxford University Press).

Sinha, Ashish, Kevin G. Cannariato, Lowell D. Stott, et al. (2007). "A 900-Year (600 to 1500 A.D.) Record of the Indian Summer Monsoon Precipitation from the Core Monsoon Zone of India," *Geophysical Research Letters* 34:1–5.

Sinopoli, Carla (2015). "Ancient South Asian Cities in Their Regions," in Norman Yoffe, ed. *Cambridge World History* (Cambridge University Press), vol. 3, pp. 319–42.

Sinopoli, Carla, and Kathleen Morrison (1995). "Dimensions of Imperial Control: The Vijayanagara Capital," *American Anthropologist* 97/1 n.s.:83–96.

Sivaramakrishnan, K. (1999). *Modern Forests: Statemaking and Environmental Change in Colonial Eastern India* (Stanford University Press).

Sivaramakrishnan, K. (2000). "State Sciences and Development Histories: Encoding Local Forestry Knowledge in Bengal," in Martin Doornbos, Ashwani Saith, and Ben White, eds., *Forests: Nature, People, Power* (Blackwell), pp. 61–88.

Sivaramakrishnan, K. (2008). "Science, Environment and Empire History: Comparative Perspectives from Forests in Colonial India," *Environment and History* 14/1:41–65.

Sivaramakrishnan, K. (2011). "Environment, Law and Democracy in India," *Journal of Asian Studies* 70/4:905–28.

Sivaramakrishnan, K. (2015). "Ethics of Nature in Indian Environmental History," *Modern Asian Studies* 49/4:1261–310.

Sivaramakrishnan, K., and Arun Agrawal, eds. (2003). *Regional Modernities: The Cultural Politics of Development in India* (Oxford University Press).

Skaria, Ajay (1999). *Hybrid Histories: Forests, Frontiers, and Wildness in Western India* (Oxford University Press).

Snodgrass, Jeffrey G., Satish Kumar Sharma, Yuvraj Singh Jhala, et al. (2008). "Lovely Leopards, Frightful Forests: The Environmental Ethics of Indigenous Rajasthani Shamans," *Journal for the Study of Religion, Nature, and Culture* 2/1:30–54.

Srinivas, M.N. (1952). *Religion and Society among the Coorgs of South India* (Oxford University Press).

Stebbing, E. P. (1926). *The Forests of India*, 3 vols. (John Lane).

Stein, Burton (1989). *Vijayanagara* (Cambridge University Press).

Stoddard, Brian (2009). *Land, Water, Language and Politics in Andhra: Regional Evolution in India since 1850* (Routledge).

Stoker, Valerie (2016). *Polemics and Patronage in the City of Victory: Vyasathirta, Hindu Sectarianism, and the Sixteenth-Century Vijayanagara Court* (University of California Press).

Stone, Ian (1984). *Canal Irrigation in British India* (Cambridge University Press).

Strahorn, Eric (2009). *An Environmental History of Postcolonial North India: The Himalayan Tarai in Uttar Pradesh and Uttaranchal* (Peter Lang).

Subrahmanyam, Sanjay (2005). *Explorations in Connected History*, 2 vols. (Oxford University Press).

Sultana, Farhana (2009). "Fluid Lives: Subjectivities, Gender and Water in Rural Bangladesh," *Gender, Place and Culture* 16/4:427–44.

Sundar, Nandini, Roger Jeffery, and Neil Thin (2001). *Branching Out, Joint Forest Management in Four Indian States* (Oxford University Press).

Sutter, Paul (2003). "Reflections: What Can US Environmental Historians Learn from Non-US Environmental Historiography?," *Environmental History* 8/1: 109–29.

Talbot, Ian (2015). *Pakistan: A New History*, 2nd ed. (Hurst).

Tandon, Prakash (1968). *Punjabi Century* (University of California Press).

Thaha, S. Abdul (2009). *Forest Policy and Ecological Change: Hyderabad State in Colonial India* (Cambridge University Press).

Thapar, Romila (1997). *Asoka and the Decline of the Mauryas* (Oxford University Press).

Thapar, Romila (2001). "Perceiving the Forest: Early India," *Studies in History* 17/1 n.s.:1–16.

Thapar, Valmik, ed. (2001). *Saving Wild Tigers, 1900–2000* (Permanent Black).

Tomalin, Emma (2009). *Biodivinity and Biodiversity: The Limits to Religious Environmentalism* (Ashgate).

Trautmann, Thomas (2015). *Elephants and Kings: An Environmental History* (University of Chicago Press).

Tucker, Richard (2012). *A Forest History of India* (Sage).

United Nations Framework Convention on Climate Change, "Nationally Determined Contributions," www4.unfccc.int/Submissions/INDC/Submissio n%20Pages/submissions.aspx (accessed 11/11/2017).

Valentine, Benjamin, George D. Kamenov, Jonathan Mark Kenoyer, et al. (2015). "Evidence for Patterns of Selective Urban Migration in the Greater Indus Valley (2600–1900 BC): A Lead and Strontium Isotope Mortuary Analysis," *PLoS ONE* 10 (4) journals.plos.org/plosone/article?id=10.1371/jour nal.pone.0123103 (accessed 11/11/2017).

Valmiki (1984–2017). *Ramayana*, trans. Robert Goldman et al., 7 vols. (Princeton University Press).

Varma, Supriya (1991). "Villages Abandoned: The Case for Mobile Pastoralism in Post-Harappan Gujarat," *Studies in History* 7/2 n.s.:279–300.

Vishwanathan, H., E. Deepa, R. Cordaux, et al. (2004). "Genetic Structure and Affinities among Tribal Populations of Southern India," *Annals of Human Genetics* 68:128–38.

Vyasa (1973–2003). *Mahabharata*, trans. J. A. B. van Buitenen and James L. Fitzgerald, 4 vols. (University of Chicago Press).

Wanner, Heinz, Jurg Beer, Jonathan Butikofer, et al. (2008). "Mid- to Late Holocene Climate Change: An Overview," *Quaternary Science Reviews* 30:1–38.

Wath, Sushant, P. S. Dutt, and T. Chakrabarti (2011). "E-waste Scenario in India, Its Management and Implications," *Environmental Monitoring and Assessment* 172:249–62.

Weber, Thomas (1989). *Hugging the Trees: The Story of the Chipko Movement* (Penguin).

Werner, Hanna (2015). *The Politics of Dams: Developmental Perspective and Social Critique in Modern India* (Oxford University Press).

Whitcombe, Elizabeth (1972). *Agrarian Conditions in Northern India: The United Provinces under British Rule, 1860–1900* (University of California Press).

Wilhelm, Janine (2016). *Environment and Pollution in Colonial India: Sewerage Technologies Along the Sacred Ganges* (Routledge).

Wink, Andre (1990–2004). *Al Hind: The Making of the Indo-Islamic World*, 3 vols. (Brill).

World Bank (2006a). *Dhaka, Bangladesh Country Analysis*, Bangladesh Development Series, Paper No. 12.

World Bank (2006b). *Pakistan, Strategic Country Environmental Assessment*, 2 vols. Report 36946-PK.

World Bank (2016). *Pakistan: (Intended) Nationally Determined Contribution* (World Bank).

Wright, Rita (2010). *The Ancient Indus: Urbanism, Economy, Society* (Cambridge University Press).

Xu, Hai, Kevin M. Yeager, Jainghu Lan, et al. (2015). "Abrupt Holocene Indian Summer Monsoon Failures: A Primary Response to Solar Activity?," *The Holocene* 25(4):677–85.

Zeheter, Michael (2015). *Epidemics, Empire and Environments: Cholera in Madras and Quebec City, 1818–1910* (University of Pittsburgh Press).

Zimmermann, Francis (1987). *The Jungle and the Aroma of Meats: An Ecological Theme in Hindu Medicine* (University of California Press).

Zvelebil, Kamil (1975). *Tamil Literature* (Brill).

Index